Cinema under National Reconstruction

Cinema under National Reconstruction

State Censorship and South Korea's Cold War Film Culture

HYE SEUNG CHUNG

Rutgers University Press
New Brunswick, Camden, and Newark, New Jersey
London and Oxford

Rutgers University Press is a department of Rutgers, The State University of New Jersey, one of the leading public research universities in the nation. By publishing worldwide, it furthers the University's mission of dedication to excellence in teaching, scholarship, research, and clinical care.

Library of Congress Cataloging-in-Publication Data

Names: Chung, Hye Seung, 1971– author.
Title: Cinema under national reconstruction : state censorship and South Korea's Cold War film culture / Hye Seung Chung.
Description: New Brunswick : Rutgers University Press, 2024. | Includes bibliographical references and index.
Identifiers: LCCN 2024005177 | ISBN 9781978838710 (paperback) | ISBN 9781978838727 (hardcover) | ISBN 9781978838734 (epub) | ISBN 9781978838741 (pdf)
Subjects: LCSH: Motion pictures—Korea (South)—History—20th century. | Cold War in motion pictures.
Classification: LCC PN1993.5.K6 C543 2024 | DDC 791.43095195—dc23/eng/20240403
LC record available at https://lccn.loc.gov/2024005177

A British Cataloging-in-Publication record for this book is available from the British Library.

Copyright © 2025 by Hye Seung Chung
All rights reserved

No part of this book may be reproduced or utilized in any form or by any means, electronic or mechanical, or by any information storage and retrieval system, without written permission from the publisher. Please contact Rutgers University Press, 106 Somerset Street, New Brunswick, NJ 08901. The only exception to this prohibition is "fair use" as defined by U.S. copyright law.

References to internet websites (URLs) were accurate at the time of writing. Neither the author nor Rutgers University Press is responsible for URLs that may have expired or changed since the manuscript was prepared.

∞ The paper used in this publication meets the requirements of the American National Standard for Information Sciences—Permanence of Paper for Printed Library Materials, ANSI Z39.48-1992.

rutgersuniversitypress.org

To my father Chung Sang Ho (1932–2022)

Contents

Note on Text	ix
Chronology	xi
A List of Agencies and Acronyms	xv
Introduction: Archival Revisionism and New Korean Film Historiography	1
1 Fending off Darkness, Uplifting National Cinema: Korean Film Censorship and *The Stray Bullet*	16
2 From *Blackboard Jungle* to *The Teahouse of the August Moon*: Censoring Hollywood in Postcolonial Korea	45
3 Myths of Martyrs and Heroes in a Godless Land: Interagency Regulation of 1960s Anticommunist Films	82
4 Cinematic Censorship as Sentimental Education: Indoctrinating Gaiety as National Emotion in Yushin-Era Youth Comedies	116
5 Censors as Audiences and Vice Versa: Sex, Politics, and Labor in 1981	139
6 Beyond Oral Histories and Trade Legends: A Bourdieusian-Foucauldian Deconstruction of Anti-Censorship Myths	166
Epilogue: Media Ratings, the End of Censorship?	184
Acknowledgments	191
Notes	193
Index	221

Note on Text

The romanization of Korean names in this book follows the McCune-Reischauer system, which is the academic standard endorsed by the Library of Congress. Exceptions to this rule are names of filmmakers and political leaders whose spellings are known to English-speaking readers, such as Bong Joon-ho, Chun Doo Hwan, Jang Sun-woo, Syngman Rhee, and Park Chung Hee. Whenever Korean authors' works that have been published in English are cited, their names are presented the way that they are printed in source materials. Korean and other East Asian names appear in their native standard, with surname first (except for names printed otherwise in English-language publications). Local currency (Korean won and Japanese yen) was converted to U.S. dollars applying historical foreign exchange rates, not those of today. These figures are approximations based on available data and historical conversion accuracy cannot be guaranteed. Finally, all quotations from Korean-language sources have been translated by Hye Seung Chung.

Chronology

This brief chronology lists major events in Korean film censorship along with key historical and political events.

1910 Japan annexes Korea.
1926 The Motion Picture Film Censorship Regulations mandate that producers and importers submit censorship prints and explanatory scripts to the Government General of Korea (GGK).
1945 The United States Army Military Government in Korea (USAMGK) starts occupation of the southern half of the Korean Peninsula after the Japanese surrender.
1946 USAMGK's Act 115 stipulates that the public screening of motion pictures to fifteen or more persons, with or without charging for admission, requires permission from U.S. occupation authorities.
1948 The Republic of Korea (ROK) is founded and inherits the exhibition permit system principle of Act 115.
1955 Jurisdiction of motion picture censorship is transferred from the Ministry of Public Information (MPI) to the Ministry of Education (MoE).
1960 The April 19 Revolution topples Syngman Rhee's regime and state film censorship is abolished. The National Motion Picture Ethics Committee (NMPEC), Korea's first civil regulatory body, is founded.
1961 Park Chung Hee's May 16 military coup halts democratic reforms and film censorship is transferred back to the MPI's jurisdiction. Yu Hyŏn-mok's *The Stray Bullet* (a.k.a. *Aimless Bullet*) is banned.

1962 The nation's first Motion Picture Law is proclaimed. Regulatory rules for unacceptable motion picture content are legalized. The production registration system is introduced, enabling the state to intervene in the preproduction stage of filmmaking.

1966 An amendment to the Motion Picture Law formalizes preproduction review of screenplays as official part of the censorship process.

1968 The MPI is renamed and reorganized as the Ministry of Culture and Public Information (MCPI).

1969 Regulators from three state agencies—the MCPI, the Ministry of the Interior (MoI), and the Korean Central Intelligence Agency (KCIA)—start to participate in joint censorship meetings on a regular basis.

1970 The MCPI commissions a civil board, the Art and Culture Ethics Committee (ACEC), to review screenplays.

1972 The Yushin Constitution is proclaimed and Park Chung Hee removes all limits to his tenure and executive power.

1976 The ACEC is succeeded by the Public Performance Ethics Committee (PPEC), a semiautonomous regulatory entity for stage plays, musical recordings, and motion picture scripts.

1979 The PPEC is handed the authority to review finished prints, in addition to screenplays, on behalf of the MCPI. Park Chung Hee is assassinated.

1980 The Kwangju Uprising is brutally suppressed by General Chun Doo Hwan. Preproduction screenplay review is nominally abolished, although the MCPI/PPEC continues to give "feedback" to scripts submitted with production registration applications.

1981 Chun Doo Hwan is inaugurated as ROK president and announces the "New Culture" policy to support the artistic programs and creativity of culture industry personnel.

1984 The Motion Picture Law is amended to accommodate a shift from "censorship" to "regulation" systems. The chairman of the PPEC, not the minister of the MCPI, is now recognized as the chief administrator of motion picture regulation.

1987 Noh Tae-woo is elected by direct presidential elections following the June Uprising.

1993 ROK returns to civil rule, ending more than three decades of military rule.

1996 The Constitutional Court rules the PPEC's mandatory regulatory review of motion pictures prior to public exhibition unconstitutional.

1997 The Korean Performance Art Promotion Association (KPAPA) is launched to implement the rating system based on the new Motion Picture Promotion Law.

1998 Longtime opposition leader and ex–political prisoner Kim Dae-jung is elected as ROK president.

1999 The KPAPA is replaced by the Korea Media Rating Board (KMRB). Kim Dae-jung appoints Kim Su-yong, a Golden Age auteur and vocal opponent of censorship, as inaugural KMRB chairman.

A List of Agencies and Acronyms

This list consists of key film censorship or regulation agencies or organizations in Hollywood and the Republic of Korea frequently referenced in acronyms throughout the book.

Hollywood

    Motion Picture Producers and Distributors of America (MPAA: 1922–1945) [trade]
    Motion Picture Association of America (MPAA: 1945–2019) [trade]
    Motion Picture Association (MPA: 2019–present) [trade]
    Production Code Administration (PCA: 1934–1968) [trade]
    Classification and Rating Administration (CARA: 1968–present) [trade]

Republic of Korea

    First Republic (1948–1960)
        Ministry of Public Information (MPI: 1948–1968) [state]
        Ministry of Education (MoE: 1948–1990) [state]
    Second Republic (1960–1961)
        National Motion Picture Ethics Committee (NMPEC: 1960–1961) [private/civil]
    Supreme Council for National Reconstruction (1961–1963)
        Ministry of Public Information (MPI) [state]
    Third Republic (1963–1972)
        Korean Central Intelligence Agency (KCIA: 1961–1981) [state]
        Ministry of Public Information (MPI) [state]

　　　　Ministry of Culture and Public Information (MCPI: 1968–1989) [state]
　　　　Ministry of the Interior (MoI: 1948–1988) [state]
　　　　Art and Culture Ethics Committee (ACEC: 1967–1976) [private/civil]
　Fourth Republic (1972–1979)
　　　　Korean Central Intelligence Agency (KCIA) [state]
　　　　Ministry of Culture and Public Information (MCPI) [state]
　　　　Ministry of the Interior (MoI) [state]
　　　　Art and Culture Ethics Committee (ACEC) [private/civil]
　　　　Public Performance Ethics Committee (PPEC: 1976–1997)
　　　　　　[private/civil]
　Fifth Republic (1980–1987)
　　　　Ministry of Culture and Public Information (MCPI) [state]
　　　　Public Performance Ethics Committee (PPEC) [private/civil]
　Sixth Republic (1988–present)
　　　　Public Performance Ethics Committee (PPEC) [private/civil]
　　　　Korean Performance Art Promotion Association (KPAPA: 1997–1999)
　　　　　　[private/civil]
　　　　Korea Media Rating Board (KMRB: 1999–present) [private/civil]

**Cinema under National
Reconstruction**

Introduction

Archival Revisionism and New Korean Film Historiography

In describing the emergence of New Korean Cinema from the late 1980s to the mid-2000s, a period of commercial and artistic revival that coincided with South Korea's much-delayed and hard-fought democratization and transition to civil society, Darcy Paquet states, "Korean cinema did not win its freedom in a day, and the process of undoing the damage wrought by decades of bad policies took years."[1] Paquet's implicit equation between the authoritarian state, widely known for its bad public policies (including censorship), and the arrested growth of national cinema is a rhetorical maneuver that has been adopted frequently in both scholarly and journalistic accounts of South Korean film historiography. Surprisingly, such associative moves on the part of critics (who are indeed critical of the state) can be even found in government-funded publications such as *Korean Cinema: from Origins to Renaissance* (2006), an open access anthology of English language essays that the Korean Film Council (KOFIC: Yŏnghwa chinhŭngwiwŏnhoe) has made available on its state agency website. The volume includes, among other topics, a short thematic essay on Korean film censorship. Interestingly, the KOFIC commissioned that topic not to a scholar but to an attorney, Im Sang-hyŏk, whose free-speech advocacy is apparent in the essay's concluding paragraph: "For a long time, the public was deprived of any opportunity to even discuss freedom of expression . . . under colonial rule and military governments. Films were reduced to a means for the government's promotion of ideology and preservation of order."[2] Free-speech advocates are not only naysayers of film censorship. Drawing upon Jacques Derrida's philosophy of ethics,

Chŏng Su-jin goes as far as condemning Korean film censorship, including the motion picture industry's post-1997 shift to a media rating system, as an extension of state "violence" (*p'ongnyŏk*) in both authoritarian and postauthoritarian eras. For Chŏng, cultural control serving the political interests of state elites is an immoral, not simply undemocratic, barrier to the creation of a "peaceful and just society" for all.[3]

As might be expected, among the harshest critics of government censorship are the many cultural producers whose freedom of expression had been infringed or trampled upon by the military regimes of Park Chung Hee (Pak Chŏng-hŭi: 1961–1979) and Chun Doo Hwan (Chŏn Tu-hwan: 1980–1988). Since the arrival of democratic civil society in 1993, their critical view of authoritarian censorship under Cold War military dictatorships has been widely publicized in memoirs, newspaper columns, media interviews, and oral history recordings. Writer-director Yi Chang-ho (Lee Jang-ho), the son of a state film censor and a New Wave maverick best known for making popular youth films such as *Heavenly Homecoming to Stars* (*Pyŏldŭrŭi kohyang*, 1974) and *A Fine Windy Day* (*Paramburŏ choŭn nal*, 1980),[4] has been one of the most vocal opponents of government film censorship over the years. In a 2019 press conference for the Korean Film Archive (KOFA: Hang'ukyŏngsang charyowŏn)'s public exhibition of film censorship documents (titled "Forbidden Imagination, Scars of Repression"), Yi called censorship "nonsense," citing his own personally meaningful example of being barred from using the First Lady's given name (Sun-ja) in the lyrics of a song sung by marines in *A Fine Windy Day*. As the legend goes, Yi simply dropped the "S" and changed the name to "Un-ja," but his film's audience was still savvy enough to decipher the censored syllable and was purported to have laughed during screenings. The veteran director went on to declare, "In its one hundred-year history, Korean cinema grew up while being beaten (by censors) constantly. . . . Persevering through such hardship made today's prosperity possible."[5] When Yi made this speech, Bong Joon-ho (Pong Chun-ho)'s *Parasite* (*Kisaengch'ung*, 2019) had just received the prestigious Palme d'Or at the seventy-second Cannes International Film Festival and was rumored to be a front-runner among Oscar contenders. With the unprecedented international success of *Parasite* lifting national spirits, the all-too-familiar master narrative of a suffering nation/cinema and its eventual triumph in the global arena against all odds could not have been more appealing or pride boosting to Korean people.

Golden Age auteur Kim Su-yong, celebrated for his Antonioni-like masterpieces from the 1960s and 1970s such as *Mist* (*Angae*, 1967) and *Night Journey* (*Yahaeng*, 1977), accompanied Yi at the press conference. During the event, Kim likewise denounced state censorship, musing, "Had it not been for censorship . . . Bong Joon-ho would have arrived in Korean cinema fifty years earlier."[6] Kim's anticensorship stance is well documented in his memoir *My Love Cinema*. Reminiscing about the Park regime's motion picture policies in the 1960s, Kim writes, "At that time, film censorship destroyed Korean directors' creative urges most viciously and cruelly. 'Ideology' and 'obscenity' were go-to menus for censors in the Ministry of Public Information [MPI: Kongbobu] and screenings were not allowed without consent of the Korean Central Intelligence Agency [KCIA: Chungangjŏngbobu]'s staff."[7] The director then provides an account of his direct confrontation with state censors at a Christian Academy–sponsored seminar titled "Limitations of Film Censorship," which took place on May 23, 1968. "When it was my turn to present," Kim recollects, "I yelled at MPI censors, 'You committed the cruelty of cutting my fingers. Be aware that directors' consciousness and blood are flowing in our films.'"[8] In the latter pages of his memoir, Kim cites *Night Journey*—a racy art film about two bank employees who pursue nonmarital sexual enticements in their shared apartment after treating each other with a modicum of professional distance as a manager and a teller at work—as Exhibit A of "vicious and cruel censorship." The director explains, "Indiscriminate scissoring was waiting at the site of censorship and ultimately 53 cuts were made." Kim further claims that those 53 changes to the film necessitated editing 106 linked scenes, resulting in a total of "159 instances of destructive montage" against his directorial intention or vision as an artist.[9]

The Korean Film Archive's Opening of Censorship Documents and Its Impact

When Kim's memoir was published in 2005, there was no way to verify if the director's version of the story was factual. The situation drastically changed after the KOFA's 2016 opening of digitized censorship documents for 4,193 Korean films (and two foreign films, Jean-Luc Godard's *Breathless* [*A bout de souffle*, 1960] and Sato Hajime's *The Golden Bat* [*Ogon batto*, 1966]) for onsite public research in the national archive's film reference library. One year after the full transition to the new media rating system in 1997, the KOFA inherited state censorship documents of 10,021 film properties submitted for approval between 1954 and 1997 (3,946 domestic feature films, 3,938 foreign feature films, 1,537 domestic "cultural" films such as documentaries and government films, 431 foreign "cultural" films, etc.). Most of those documents originated from the government agency that administered film censorship between the 1960s and the 1980s: the MPI, or the Ministry of Culture and Public Information (MCPI: Munhwagongbobu), as it was called between 1968 and 1989.[10] As such, in this book, I classify the unnamed collection as MPI or MCPI film censorship files for convenience. Digitized censorship files can be accessed via the archive's library computers by searching individual film titles (not special collection names) in the central database and by clicking the tab labeled as Simŭisŏryu, or Regulatory Documents. The public can also request access to the original paper files (such as foreign film regulation documents unavailable in the digital database) in the archive's Paju preservation center. This rare collection, which represents the largest of its kind (government censorship documents of a single national film industry) in the world, had been off-limits to the public until 2010, when the KOFA started to open it to selected researchers before transitioning to full onsite digital access in 2016. As of this writing, the KOFA has further released 507 censorship files (related to the anticommunist film genre and auteur films directed by major Golden Age filmmakers, Kim Ki-yŏng, Kim Su-yong, Shin Sang-ok, Yi Man-hŭi [Lee Man-hee], and Yu Hyŏn-mok) for distance-learning–style open access on their website for any registered users. The *Night Journey* censorship file in particular (available for online open access) discredits Kim's aforementioned story from his memoir. On April 1, 1977, the MCPI sent a short memo to the film's production company, T'aech'ang Entertainment, informing them that their censorship application for *Night Journey* had been rejected due to excessive sex scenes and its overall decadent tone.[11] Three days later, T'aech'ang resubmitted a voluntarily censored cut along with a memo detailing the differences between the earlier print and the new one (which cleaned up the sexual content and foul language in twenty-three scenes).[12] The MCPI's exhibition permit issued on April 9, 1977, records the precise number of cuts and edits that state censors requested (in addition to voluntary editing that had been already made): cuts of nine scenes, the shortening of one scene, and the deletion of one dialogue passage. To quote Detective Sŏ T'ae-yun (Kim Sang-kyŏng) in Bong Joon-ho's *Memories of Murder* (*Salinŭi ch'uŏk*, 2003), "The documents never lie." While the MCPI's initial rejection did result in substantial amounts of self-censorship, with the goal of toning down the perceived obscene content of nearly two dozen scenes, archival evidence debunks the claim that "vicious and cruel censorship" ruined 159 moments of chained montage in Kim's film.

The postauthoritarian era empowered the 386 Generation (the student movement generation who were born in the 1960s, went to college in the 1980s, and pursued careers as thirty-something professionals when civil rule returned), which emerged as a formidable political and cultural force when the two successive liberal administrations of Kim Dae-jung (Kim Tae-jung: 1998–2003) and Roh Moo-hyun (No Mu-hyŏn: 2003–2008) made conscious efforts to redress state-sponsored atrocities of the past. In that relatively liberalized political climate, motion picture censorship became a powerful synecdoche for the authoritarian government, and aging "victimized" artists and their younger advocates felt compelled to talk back to that political apparatus of state control with a performative air of wrathful denunciation and playful mocking of past regimes' draconian stupidity. Even trained psychiatrists would likely find it difficult to understand the collective state of mind that relished trade legends and myths—like the ones put forth by Yi and Kim (cited above)—and unironically accepted them as authoritative accounts of film history without seeking corroborating evidence from multiple parties involved in film censorship. To some readers' minds, pursuing "objective" evidence rather than validating victims' testimonies without second-guessing is itself an insult to the sacred memory of martyrs (protestors and activists who were tortured, maimed, or even killed while fighting

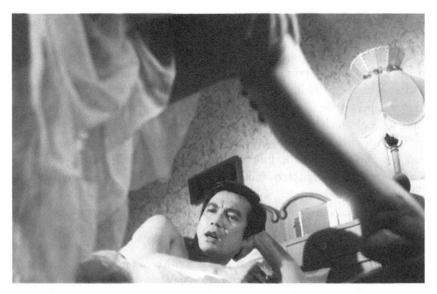

FIGURE I.1 The censorship file reveals that only nine scenes, not 159 as director Kim Su-yong claims, were ordered to be cut from *Night Journey* (1977), a racy art film about two bank employees who pursue nonmarital sexual enticements.

for democracy against U.S.-backed military dictatorships) from the not-so-distant authoritarian past that continues to haunt far too many.

As a researcher who was trained in the evidence-based material history of censorship during my doctoral years, and who was encouraged by my film professors at the University of California, Los Angeles (UCLA) to not make any claims without investigating archival files and verified facts first, I have long harbored doubts about the remarkably consistent master narrative (both journalistic and academic) of Korean film censorship as described above. It was not until the summer of 2016 that my suspicion was confirmed by a presentation titled "Toward a Study on History of Korean Film Censorship," delivered by KOFA head researcher Cho Jun-hyoung (Cho Chun-hyŏng) at the Korean Film Workshop that was held at the University of California (UC), Berkeley on July 15–16, 2016. Listening to Cho's presentation in the audience, I was thrilled to witness the long-awaited shattering of a master narrative that had been firmly entrenched in both popular and academic discourses. Drawing upon the archival files related to Yi Tu-yong's mystery thriller *The Last Witness* (*Ch'oehuŭi chŭngin*, 1980), a case study to be spotlighted in chapter 6 of this book, Cho disputed the director's oral history claim of state censors' cutting fifty minutes of footage for political reasons. According to primary documents in the MCPI file, it was market conditions, not political censorship, that motivated the production company's voluntary shortening of the director's cut (from 158 minutes to 120 minutes) for easier theater bookings.

One cannot overemphasize the crucial role that the KOFA's opening of censorship archival materials is playing in reshaping Korean film censorship studies and providing access to much-needed empirical evidence for historical research. Prior to that point, researchers tended to base their arguments on secondary evidence, including oral histories of filmmakers (particularly directors) or newspaper articles, contributing to the circulation of rumors, myths, and legends, some of which have been debunked by recent Korean-language revisionist studies. Although its impact is not yet widely felt in English-speaking academia,[13] a small group of Seoul-based film historians spearheaded this effort, publishing journal articles, book chapters, and KOFA blogs based on newly discovered archival evidence. The same year Cho gave his presentation at UC Berkeley, the KOFA published an edited collection titled *The Censorship System inside Korean Film History* (*Han'gukyŏnghwa sok kŏmyŏl chedo*), with scholarly essays by Cho Jun-hyoung, Pak Sŏn-yŏng, Pak Yu-hŭi, Song A-rŭm, and Yi Sun-jin that cite excerpts of censorship documents from the archive. Several of the book's contributors (Cho, Pak Yu-hŭi, and Song) along with three U.S.-based scholars (Jinsoo An of UC Berkeley, Namhee Han of Queens College, and myself) met in August 2021 (via Zoom), January 2022 (via Zoom), and August 2022 (in person) for a series of Berkeley Korean Film Workshops to discuss our latest archival scholarship under the theme of "Authoritarian Modalities and Film Censorship." Two of this book's chapters (1 and 4) were presented in that workshop and benefited from peer feedback from fellow presenters and esteemed respondents from both sides of the Pacific Ocean, including Thomas Doherty, a leading scholar in American film censorship studies, and Kyeong-Hee Choi, an expert on the censorship of colonial literature.

This significant archival turn in Korean film censorship studies following the KOFA's release of MPI/MCPI files can be compared to similar trends in Hollywood historiography after the Motion Picture Association of America (MPAA)'s 1983 opening of Hollywood's self-regulatory censorship documents (Production Code Administration [PCA] files for 19,500 film properties submitted for approval between 1927 and 1967) for public research at the Margaret Herrick Library in Los Angeles. Subsequent research and scholarship drawn from the archive, as Daniel Biltereyst and Roel Vande Winkel argue, enabled a "more sophisticated view on film censorship [as a] key mediating factor in discourses that govern American film industry and film culture."[14] Lea Jacobs's *The Wages of Sin: Censorship and the Fallen Woman Film, 1928–1942* (1991), Ruth Vasey's *The World According to Hollywood, 1918–1939* (1997), Thomas Doherty's *Pre-Code Hollywood: Sex, Immorality, and Insurrection in American Cinema, 1930–1934* (1999) and *Hollywood's Censor: Joseph I. Breen and the Production Code Administration* (2007), Stephen Prince's *Classical Film Violence: Designing and Regulating Brutality in Hollywood Cinema, 1930–1968* (2003), and Ellen C. Scott's *Cinema Civil Rights: Regulation, Repression, and Race in the Classical Hollywood Era* (2015) are among the major studies that have extensively consulted and cited

PCA files. These and other studies prove that the U.S. film industry's self-regulation was not simply prohibitive but also productive in generating more nuanced representations of sex, violence, race, ethnicity, and nationality prior to the Production Code's gradual dismantling in the 1960s.

The availability of censorship documents was instrumental in reevaluating the role of the Production Code and its enforcement agency, the PCA (which was replaced by the MPAA rating board in 1968). In his 1981 book *A History of Narrative Film* (printed prior to the opening of PCA files to researchers), David A. Cook grumbled, "The Code as a whole was obviously restrictive and repressive ... and in a very real sense, kept [American films] from becoming as serious as they might have been, and perhaps should have been."[15] After public access to the PCA archive enabled empirical research on censorship documents of individual films (detailing the internal censor's day-to-day operations and extensive communications with studio personnel, external censors, foreign diplomats, civic pressure groups, and other concerned parties), academic discourse began to shift and become more nuanced, highlighting how censorship might contribute to *greater*, rather than less, productivity and ingenuity. This revisionist recalibration of critical discourse is epitomized by Doherty's archive-based evaluation: "Far from being an impediment, the in-house censorship regime facilitated the artistic creativity and industrial efficiency of the vaunted Golden Age of Hollywood. [The PCA] maintained the gold standard by helping the major studios refine the substance, polish the surface, and corner the market."[16]

On August 9, 2021, as a respondent to the Berkeley Korean Film Workshop held on Zoom, Doherty observed some of the conspicuous parallels between Hollywood's PCA and South Korea's MPI/MCPI regulations despite the key difference between the former's self-regulatory measures and the latter's state-based form of censorship. The American historian commented, "Whether it is Park Chung Hee's censorship or the [Hollywood] Production Code or the commercial conditions of Disney Studios, every filmmaker works within fairly strict guidelines. Think of the metaphor of the sonnet in which there are formal rules, but unlimited possibilities as to what you can create within those parameters." Furthermore, Doherty compared "a revolution in censorship studies in America" in the mid-1980s with the opening of PCA files to "a similar phenomenon in Korea where Korean scholars are tackling such files for the first time" and benefiting from "the new possibility of having definitive answers to questions of procedure and regulation that could not exist without such new archival materials."[17] Having spent several years researching PCA files (along with other studio and U.S. government files) and then extensively citing them in my previous publications—*Hollywood Asian: Philip Ahn and the Politics of Cross-Ethnic Performance* (2006) and *Hollywood Diplomacy: Film Regulation, Foreign Relations, and East Asian Representations* (2020)—I was drawn to this project for the unique opportunity to apply my expertise in Hollywood censorship and develop new Korean film historiography from transnational, comparative perspectives. I conducted preliminary research of KOFA censorship archive materials during research trips to Seoul in 2017 and 2019. After the hiatus of international travel for over a year due to COVID-19, I resided in Seoul between August 2021 and July 2022 as a Fulbright scholar and was able to delve deeper into the KOFA collection along with other Korean-language sources (books, periodicals, magazines, newspapers, etc.) contained in public and university libraries.

Needless to say, MPI/MCPI censorship files are treasured primary sources for film historians with both Korean-language proficiency (many documents of the 1950s and 1960s also require knowledge of classical Chinese) and skills in analyzing regulation documents in the broader context of the film industry's relationship with the state, the public, and various social institutions. Even though my transnational background as a Korean-born, UCLA-trained film scholar meets the double criteria of language proficiency and area knowledge, my ambition to reconstruct a comprehensive history of Korean film censorship was thwarted by lack of access to supplementary archives such as industry production files and other government agencies' documents on motion pictures. Unfortunately, most film companies from the 1950s to the 1980s went out of business years ago and even the few surviving ones, such as Hapdong Film (producer of *The Martyred* [*Sungyoja*, 1965], a case study in chapter 3) and Hwachŏn Trading (producer of *The March of Fools* [*Pabodŭlŭi haengjin*, 1975] and *Declaration of Fools* [*Pabosŏnŏn*, 1983], analyzed in chapters 4 and 6, respectively), do not maintain public archives open to research. Access to other state archives is severely limited because the National Archives of Korea (NAOK: Kukkagirogwŏn) only accepts duplication requests for *individual* documents that must be made sight unseen based solely on titles and bare descriptions (such as dates, ministry names, and length) in their catalog. Unlike in the U.S. National Archives and Records Administration (NARA where multiple boxes of entire record groups can be pulled in carts for open public viewing), researchers are only allowed to access specific documents, not grouped files or folders, searched by the catalog and called in advance, even if they visit the NAOK's Sŏngnam branch on the outskirts of Seoul. I requested copies of almost all documents searchable by relevant keywords such as film censorship or regulation in their catalog but was disappointed at the content of the packet delivered to the archive's downtown Seoul office after weeks of delay.

In the early months of Fulbright research in Seoul, I was dispirited by the inability to freely cross-reference multiple archives (of both the industry and the government) and put them in dialogue as I did for my Hollywood history books. Devoted to a comparative analysis of Hollywood and Korean censorship of two MGM films, *Blackboard Jungle* (1955) and *The Teahouse of the August Moon* (1956), chapter 2 is the only part of this book that benefited from unrestricted access to a variety of archival collections housed at the Margaret Herrick Library, including PCA files, the Richard Brooks Papers, the Daniel Mann

Papers, and the Jack Cummings Papers. Ultimately, I learned to accept the reality of limited primary sources and was forced to creatively fill gaps through secondary sources such as KOFA scenario collections, KOFA oral history transcriptions, state and trade publications, and Naver News Library (the largest Korean search engine's database of historical newspapers). To reiterate Doherty's analogy cited above, strict PCA guidelines were to Hollywood filmmakers what the fourteen-line (stanza, quatrain, and couplet) rule was to Shakespearean sonnet poets. They were both inspirational, rather than limiting, structural forms for imaginative, resourceful creators. My experience of writing this book oddly resembles this lesson from historical censorship: a paradoxical process that fostered creativity and productivity within the restrictive boundaries of the possible.

Chapter Overview: A Brief History of Korean Film Censorship

As I will describe in greater detail in chapter 1, the origins of Korean film censorship can be traced back to the 1926 Motion Picture Film Censorship Regulations (Hwaltongsajin kŏmyŏlguch'ik). That law mandated that producers and importers submit censorship prints and explanatory scripts to the Government General of Korea (GGK: Chosŏn ch'ongdokpu) for centralized regulatory review, which prioritized such concerns as security, morals, and public health. However, it was the United States Army Military Government in Korea (USAMGK), the GGK's successor, that—with its exhibition permit system—established the prototype of South Korea's motion picture censorship. In October 1946, the USAMGK proclaimed Act 115, which stipulated that the public screening of motion pictures to fifteen or more persons, with or without admissions, required permission from U.S. occupation authorities. When the Republic of Korea (ROK) was founded in August 1948, its inaugural administration under Syngman Rhee (Yi Sŭng-man) inherited Act 115 as their principle of motion picture regulation. As exemplified by Hollywood's self-regulatory history, the conditional release system is instrumental in bolstering the enforcing power of regulators. Although the Production Code was proclaimed in 1930, uniform enforcement was delayed until 1934, when members of the Motion Picture Producers and Distributors of America (MPAA after 1945) made a pact among themselves not to distribute or exhibit any films lacking the in-house regulatory agency (PCA)'s seal of approval.[18] What distinguishes Korean film censorship from Hollywood's preemptive self-regulation (which morally cleansed Hollywood products in preparation for external censorship board review in the United States and abroad) is that different state agencies were involved in vetting both Korean and foreign motion pictures for their suitability for national exhibition. The first agency that took over censorship responsibilities from its USAMGK counterpart was the MPI, but the jurisdiction for motion picture regulation was transferred to the Ministry of Education (MoE: Mungyobu) in

1955. For a brief period of democratization following the April 19 Revolution of 1960 (which toppled Rhee's autocratic regime), the National Motion Picture Ethics Committee (Yŏnghwayulli chŏn'gukwiwŏnhoe), Korea's first civil regulatory body, reviewed motion pictures until Park's May 1961 military coup. After the 1962 proclamation of the nation's first Motion Picture Law (Yŏnghwabŏp), the MPI consolidated the previously divided regulatory activities under its single administrative control.

However, it would be a mistake to assume that the MPI/MCPI was an all-powerful state apparatus that oppressed filmmakers throughout Cold War military regimes from the 1960s to the 1980s. In fact, the ministry never acted alone. Several other government branches representing different social and political concerns were involved in motion picture regulation. For example, the Ministry of the Interior (MoI: Naemubu) was concerned with policing and child protection while the KCIA prioritized national security matters. The Ministry of National Defense (MND: Kukpangbu) was consulted for military representations related to warfare and troops. Between 1969 and 1979, staff from the MCPI, the MoI, and the KCIA regularly participated in joint censorship meetings and negotiated their diverse regulatory agendas. In addition to state agencies, the MCPI also collaborated with civil boards to review and approve screenplays during the preproduction stage of filmmaking (a requirement that was officially legalized with the 1966 amendment of the Motion Picture Law). Between 1970 and 1976, the Art and Culture Ethics Committee (ACEC: Yesulmunha yulliwiwŏnhoe) was in charge of reviewing screenplays while the MCPI approved finished prints. In 1976, the ACEC was succeeded by the Public Performance Ethics Committee (PPEC: Kongyŏn yulliwiwŏnhoe), a legalized regulatory entity for stage plays, musical recordings, and motion picture scripts. In 1979, the semiautonomous committee (consisting of civil elites such as journalists, professors, writers, filmmakers, film critics, etc.) was handed the authority to review finished prints, in addition to screenplays, on behalf of the MCPI. It is notable that on their institutional website, the Korea Media Rating Board (KMRB: Yŏngsangmul tŭnggŭpwiwŏnhoe) identifies 1966 (when the ACEC was founded) as the starting year of their operations. In other words, civil participation in motion picture regulation predates South Korea's return to civil rule (in 1993) and the ruling of state censorship as unconstitutional (in 1996). This chronology stresses the operational continuity between a hybridized form of state-private (*kwan-min*) regulation under Park's and Chun's military regimes and the postauthoritarian rating system, which thus far has not received much academic attention.

While the conundrum of enforcing socially mandated ethical guidelines of motion picture production without mangling works of art has been a universal challenge of film regulation around the world, the emphasis on "national views" (*kukkagwan*) in the history of Korean motion picture regulation is worth discussing. Unlike Hollywood's self-regulation guidelines, the Production Code, which was coauthored by a Jesuit priest (Father Daniel A. Lord) and was grounded in religious ideals of upright morality, South Korea's state-administered film censorship privileged national or political interests from the outset. In his oral history interview with the KOFA research team in 2009, Yi Sŏng-ch'ŏl, the manager of the MPI's Motion Picture Division from 1953 to 1955, singled out "ideology" (*sasang*), followed by sexual morality, as the primary censorship concern during the Korean War since the government did not want to steer its people toward "antiwar" (*panjŏn*) sentiments through negative media influence.[19] In May 1955, the MoE, the ministry in charge of recommending imports of foreign motion pictures, announced that they would prohibit screenings of films that (1) undermined national prestige and insulted the dignity of a head of state; (2) indoctrinated ideology conducive to constitutional disorder; (3) dealt with antistate activities, mutiny, or mass prison escape; (4) harmed the public good politically, diplomatically, economically, and educationally; (5) damaged national customs and public morals; (6) depicted lawbreaking and destruction; (7) had extremely low production value; and (8) hindered the advancement of national culture.[20] It is also notable that the first four of the fifteen clauses comprising the 1962 Motion Picture Law's enforcement regulations can be broadly categorized under the rubric of ideological control. The law mandated that exhibition permits might be denied for motion pictures that (1) undermined the Constitution and damaged national prestige; (2) did not portray the nation and its flag in a respectful way; (3) harmed international relations by disrespecting the customs of Free World allies and their national feelings; and (4) distributed favorable propaganda profiting foreign countries in conflict with the ROK.[21] While the "usual suspects" such as explicit expressions of sexuality, foul language, gruesome violence, and mockery of social institutions (law, education, religion, etc.) were key regulatory items for South Korean motion pictures as elsewhere, historical specificities of the divided Cold War nation under perpetual security crises also determined the unique directions that film policy would take under military rule.

Despite such propagandistic rules on paper, archival evidence points to strong correlations between state and industry interests and habitual collusion between representatives of the two parties in administering film regulation. It was the MPI's responsibility to accommodate a wide range of public opinion from different political, religious, and social groups (including varying agendas of other ministries) in their observance of motion picture content to serve the nation's collective good. However, the ministry's other important mission was to protect and foster the ROK's film industry; the last thing that they wanted was to cause financial losses to production or distribution companies by prohibiting sales of their products on the basis of abstract, ideological reasons. The case studies of chapters 2 and 3 point to the fact that the MPI's responses to religious lobbying against blasphemy on the screen and public outrage against "pro-Japanese" Hollywood imports were no more than half-hearted, self-protective public relations gestures. Far from being impartial guardians of public morality or ideologically committed propagandists, state regulators could be likened to double agents whose main role was to mediate industrial and public interests. As chapter 1 demonstrates, the MPI often acted in a mediating capacity, lifting suspensions of exhibition (pressured by national security concerns of other government branches such as the MoI and the KCIA), guiding content revisions, and advocating for trade interests over political orthodoxy.

The book consists of six chapters in addition to the introduction and the epilogue. Titled "Fending off Darkness, Uplifting National Cinema: Korean Film Censorship and *The Stray Bullet*," chapter 1 defines censorship as a dialogical process of cultural negotiations wherein the state, the film industry, and the public wage a rhetorical battle over the definitions and functions of national cinema. After charting the origins and early history of Korean film censorship, I challenge the established historical narrative that construes Yu Hyŏn-mok's *The Stray Bullet* (*Obalt'an*, 1961) as a victim of anticommunist paranoia under Park Chung Hee's military dictatorship. Archival evidence suggests that the film's two-year ban (1961–1963) occurred primarily because of its tonal incompatibility with the new government's cultural policy of cheerful national uplift. In the Park era, the nation-state aimed to foster a particular mode of affirmative emotions while discouraging negative feelings through the affective monitoring of national cinema. By comparing the contrasting overseas reception of Yu's uncompromisingly dark social-problem film and Kang Tae-jin's more hopeful family drama *The Coachman* (*Mabu*, 1961), the chapter demonstrates the universal appeal of uplift cinema advocated by the Korean state.

Under the title "From *Blackboard Jungle* to *The Teahouse of the August Moon*: Censoring Hollywood in Postcolonial Korea," chapter 2 examines the controversies surrounding two Glenn Ford star vehicles that received theatrical releases in South Korea in the early 1960s. Written and directed by Richard Brooks, who was himself no stranger to censorship in his home country of the United States, *Blackboard Jungle* (1955) disturbed various sectors of Korean society (from public educators to government officials) for its sensational depiction of an inner-city vocational high school in which teachers are routinely attacked by juvenile delinquents and teen gangs. In this chapter, I offer a comparative analysis of the KOFA's MPI censorship file with the MPAA's PCA file. While Korean state censors and Hollywood's internal censors shared similar concerns about sexuality and violence, the former applied a distinctive local interpretation of MGM's production as a "purification" (*chŏnghwa*) story that echoes the stated aims of Park's new military government. The second case study, director Daniel Mann's *The Teahouse of the August Noon* (1956), likewise demonstrates how postcolonial censorship debates generated new meanings for an Orientalist tale of U.S. military occupation in Okinawa. The unique category of *waesaek* (Japanese color) was deemed taboo in postcolonial Korean culture as part of ongoing decolonializing efforts. For nationalist producers and critics, *The Teahouse of the August Moon* functioned as a significant political symbol to test the state's commitment to protect the Korean film industry under the perceived threat of the Japanese cultural invasion ahead of diplomatic normalization with Japan.

Chapter 3, titled "Myths of Martyrs and Heroes in a Godless Land: Interagency Regulation of 1960s Anticommunist Films," introduces readers to the various censorship discourses surrounding two 1960s anticommunist films set in North Korea: Yu Hyŏn-mok's *The Martyred* (*Sungyoja*, 1965) and Kim Su-yong's *Accusation* (*Kobal*, 1967). The MPI's permissive regulation allowed the former's producers to freely explore polemical ideas about religion expressed in Richard E. Kim's original novel (including the pastor-hero's open admission of his disbelief in God's existence), which drew the ire of Korean Protestants upon the film's release. None of the three government branches involved in film regulation (including the KCIA and the MND) made any heavy-handed interventions to control the images of North Koreans despite the state's anticommunist film policy. I challenge my own thesis of reasonable, if bureaucratic, film censorship under Park's dictatorship in the case study of *Accusation*. This KCIA-sponsored biopic depicts the life of Yi Su-gŭn, who was vice president of North Korea's Central News Agency when he defected to South Korea in 1967. As an overt anticommunist propaganda project, the film passed the MPI's censorship review with minor revisions. Its exhibition permit was invalidated two years later, however, after the KCIA announced that Yi had been identified as an infiltrated North Korean spy. The KCIA was the mastermind of this political scandal, fabricated to cover up its mishandling of its most valuable defector (who unlawfully expatriated from South Korea in a failed attempt to seek asylum in a third country). In this case, the KCIA had absolute power to make and unmake a hero out of Yi, killing both the subject (who was hurriedly executed after a rushed trial) and the film about him.

Titled "Cinematic Censorship as Sentimental Education: Indoctrinating Gaiety as National Emotion in Yusin-Era Youth Comedies," chapter 4 explores the role of state film censorship in shaping the tone of screen comedy during the Yushin period (1972–1979), sometimes referred to as the "Dark Age" of South Korea's film industry. After the 1945 liberation, the authoritarian regimes of Syngman Rhee and Park Chung Hee promoted *myŏngnang* ("gaiety") as a wholesome, productive national sentiment in their cultural campaigns and media regulation policies. Focusing on the case study of Ha Kil-jong's *The March of Fools* and drawing upon censorship documents, this chapter examines the subversive power of Yushin-era youth comedy in providing social critiques of authoritarian military culture while complying with the *myŏngnanghwa* ("becoming or making cheerful") policy.

Under the title "Censors as Audiences and Vice Versa: Sex, Politics, and Labor in 1981," chapter 5 investigates two social-problem films—Yi Wŏn-se's *A Little Ball Launched by a Dwarf* (*Nanjangiga ssoaollin chakŭn kong*, 1981) and Kim Su-yong's *The Maiden Who Went to the City* (*Tosiro kan chŏnyŏ*, 1981)—with particular attention to censorship as a form of audience feedback and agential participation. Both texts were mutated significantly from their original forms (Cho Se-hŭi's eponymous novel for the former and the PPEC/MCPI–approved initial release for the latter) due to censorial interventions and calls for more respectful and positive representations of marginal social identities: the disabled, evictees, and underclass working girls. It is tempting to read these films as evidence of nefarious cultural control by Chun Doo Hwan's new military regime built upon the blood and slain bodies of hundreds of innocent protesters or bystanders of Kwangju massacred by government paratroopers in May 1980. Evidence from the KOFA censorship archive challenges the previous critical consensus that Chun's so-called 3S (sport, screen, sex) policy encouraged mindless sex on screen in the 1980s as an intentional political strategy. On the contrary, PPEC regulators (who saw themselves as "the first objective audiences") of the Chun era made concerted efforts to curtail gratuitous sex scenes and encourage producers to uplift their films.

Titled "Beyond Oral Histories and Trade Legends: A Bourdieusian-Foucauldian Deconstruction of Anti-Censorship Myths," chapter 6 aims to unpack the famous censorship myths surrounding *The Last Witness* and *Declaration of Fools* through the lens of New Censorship Theory. As a French philosopher-theorist who influenced New Censorship scholars considerably, Pierre Bourdieu saw censorship as a self-regulatory system of euphemizing for potentially offensive materials in anticipation of negative market reception. As such, controversial double rape scenes were self-censored in the regulatory review process of *The Last Witness* (which, as described above, was voluntarily cut due to market conditions inhospitable to feature films longer than the industry-standard two-hour running time). Another French theorist who is frequently cited in censorship studies is Michel Foucault, who deemed what on the surface seems like a top-down level of authoritarian control as an example of discursive power relationships, which are ultimately productive and enabling rather than simply repressive and inhibitive. Moreover, Foucauldian scholars of censorship emphasize creators' pleasure of battling, fooling, and outwitting censors (Yi Chang-ho, for example, intended *Declaration of Fools* as an absurd nonsense film to dupe and mock state censors). Drawing upon archival evidence, this chapter demonstrates such a dynamic of power manifest in state censorship of the South Korean film industry under Chun's military dictatorship. In the process, I call for a more nuanced understanding of regulating divisive content (related to sex, law, and crimes) in a comparative context by evaluating Korean case studies in relation to the PCA regulatory standards for Hollywood cinema.

Korean film historians and researchers had to wait another three decades from the point of the MPPA's opening of its PCA files to access the censorship archive of their national cinema and initiate a reevaluation of the state's industrial oversight as a productive contributor to filmmaking. For artistically ambitious directors such as Kim Su-yong and Yi Chang-ho whose testimonies are cited earlier, the state-directed control (both content and tone) of national cinema was a mere extension of repressive political censorship by undemocratic military regimes. However, in order for Korean film censorship studies to mature and develop a more subtle, accurate perspective on the past, it is imperative to avoid the various pitfalls of auteurism (including the intentional fallacy) and to broaden our critical view of the complex role played by government censors during a tumultuous time of national reconstruction under perpetual security crises stemming from regional and global Cold War conflicts. I eagerly await future studies that might likewise take advantage of the KOFA collection and illuminate other deserving case studies, including motion pictures that—owing to limitations of space and time—I was not able to spotlight in this volume.

1

Fending Off Darkness, Uplifting National Cinema

Korean Film Censorship
and *The Stray Bullet*

In his seminal essay "The Concept of National Cinema," Andrew Higson notes, "Very often national cinema is used prescriptively rather than descriptively, citing what *ought* to be the national cinema, rather than describing the actual cinematic experiences of popular audiences."[1] These authoritative interpellators of national cinema often operate independently from the spheres of industry/production and box-office/popular consumption. They include critics and intellectuals who are inclined to "reduce national cinema to the terms of a quality art cinema, a culturally worthy cinema steeped in high cultural and/or modernist heritage of a particular nation state, rather than one which appeals to the desires and fantasies of the popular audiences."[2] Equally relevant players are national censors who are simultaneously prohibitive and productive in regulating the perimeters of permissible images and sounds on the silver screen according to sociocultural norms of a given historical period. In the Park Chung Hee (Pak Chŏng-hŭi) era (1961–1979), the nation-state aimed to foster a particular mode of affirmative emotions while discouraging negative feelings through the affective monitoring of national cinema. Borrowing the United States Department of State's label of Republic-era Chinese cinema in the 1930s, I define the Park administration's film policy as that of "national uplift" consistent with the state goals of nation building, reconstruction, and modernization.

Marshaling archival evidence and centering on the troubled exhibition history of Yu Hyŏn-mok's social-problem film *The Stray Bullet* (a.k.a. *Aimless Bullet, Obalt'an*, 1961), I here chart the origins and early history of Korean film censorship. In the process, as stated in the introduction, I define censorship as a dialogical process of cultural negotiations wherein the state, the film industry, and the public fight out a battle over the definitions and functions of national cinema. Challenging the established historical narrative that construes this masterpiece of South Korean cinema as a victim of anticommunist paranoia under Park's military dictatorship, I demonstrate that the film's controversial ban was caused primarily by its tonal incompatibility with the new government's regulatory policy of encouraging cheerful cinematic affect to uplift national spirits. Beyond particular dialogue passages or singular images, the nation-state suppressed what Christopher Faulkner calls "the affective identities which characterize the heterogenous or marginal elements of society [and] provoke *consternation,* because they are themselves excessive or violent in some ways, presenting themselves with the force of a charge or a shock."[3] Despite the retrospective critical canonization of Yu's blatant portrayal of postwar social ills in the 1980s—a radical era of united student-labor or *minjung* (people's) activism— the repeated cries of desperation that fill the soundtrack, voiced by members of a North Korean refugee family, were largely rejected by both domestic theatergoers and stateside film festival attendees two decades earlier. In contrast with the miserable ending of *The Stray Bullet*, Kang Tae-jin's *The Coachman* (*Mabu*, 1961) features a happy, uplifting ending in which a poverty-stricken family celebrates the good news of the eldest son's success in the bar exam. Unlike Yu's depressing film, Kang's feel-good family drama was warmly embraced by Western audiences when it competed at the 1961 Berlin International Film Festival. This contrasting overseas reception indicates the universal appeal of uplift cinema, advocated by the Korean state, which prescribed what national cinema *should* be through film regulation.

Twin Cinemas: National Uplift in 1930s China and 1960s South Korea

The Production Code—Hollywood's set of moral guidelines that shaped industry self-regulation from 1930 to 1968—acknowledges motion picture producers' responsibility to the public, who has placed "high trust and confidence" in them to provide "a universal form of entertainment." Nevertheless, with respect to framing films as "entertainment without any explicit purpose of teaching or propaganda," the Code goes on to elaborate that producers "know that the motion picture within its own field of entertainment may be directly responsible for spiritual or moral progress, for higher types of social life, and for much correct thinking."[4] In response to a series of censorship crises in the pre-Code era (1930–1934), a period inundated with violent or salacious material in the form of gangster films, horror pictures, and sex comedies, the American film industry formed the Production Code Administration (PCA) in order to enforce strict self-regulation prior to external censorship review by seven state boards, thirty-one municipal boards, and 200–250 ad hoc local boards, not to mention mostly government-controlled foreign censorship boards.[5] As described in the introduction, members of the Motion Picture Producers and Distributors of America (MPPDA, now MPA [Motion Picture Association]) had made an internal trade agreement among themselves not to distribute or exhibit any films lacking the PCA's seal of approval. This conditional release practice gave enforcing power to the in-house regulator, who was entrusted with the task of interpreting and implementing the Production Code, a detailed self-regulatory treatise catering to various external censorship demands, from suppression of sex, violence, and profanity to respectful representations of religion, law enforcement, and foreign nationals.

Unlike in the United States, where it was institutionalized as self-regulation *within* the industry that protected the financial investments of the studios and safeguarded trade respectability, both in China in the 1930s and in South Korea in the 1960s, film censorship was developed as a part of a conscious nation-building project. Under the leadership of Generalissimo Chiang Kai-shek (who united the country in 1927), the Republic of China proclaimed the Chinese Motion Picture Law of 1930 and established the first national censorship board, under the auspices of the Ministries of Education and the Interior in 1931. In South Korea, under the emergency junta of another general, Park Chung Hee, the nation's first Motion Picture Law (Yŏnghwabŏp) was enacted in 1962. The Ministry of Public Information (MPI: Kongbobu) consolidated divided regulatory activities under the single administrative control of the state. One can detect certain key parallels between the nation-building agendas and cultural principles of Chiang's and Park's military regimes. Both governments saw cinema as a medium of national "uplift" to project the ideals of nation building, modernization, and cultural enlightenment.

The term "uplift" concerning film censorship was first used by Willys R. Peck, the U.S. consul general in Nanjing who mediated many disputes between the Republic-era Chinese government and the Hollywood studios in the 1930s. Several diplomatic crises stemmed from Orientalist studio productions with Chinese settings and controversial ethnic images such as *Shanghai Express* (1932) and *The General Died at Dawn* (1936) that angered local censors and citizens. In a letter to the MPPDA's foreign manager, Frederick H. Herron, dated November 4, 1933, Consul Peck wrote, "Filmmaking in China has certain definite 'uplift' objects and it is clearly intimated that foreign films which pursue the same subjects will be favored, and those which do not will be censored. I have explained to the Chinese that American films are designed to amuse their audiences and have no avowed educational purpose. Nevertheless, the Chinese authorities seem determined to regard motion pictures as a means for improving the Chinese public and advancing the interests of the nation."[6] This perception of filmmaking and issues of censorship as matters of public education is a view that has been shared by East Asian countries across different time periods. It is easy to detect a similar understanding of national cinema as a tool for cultural uplift in Park's film policies throughout the 1960s and 1970s.

For example, in both the 1930 law and the 1962 law, national interests are prominently foregrounded, unlike in Hollywood's Production Code, which was governed primarily by universal moral principles based on religious doctrines. Article 10 of the Production Code was the only provision on nationality, but it called for fair representations for "the history, institutions, prominent people, and citizenry of *other* nations,"[7] not those of the United States, as a means of discouraging offensive images of foreign countries that might be detrimental to international sales. Article 2 of the Chinese Motion Picture Law, in contrast, mandated that films could be barred from exhibition if they were (1) injurious to the dignity of Chinese people; (2) contrary to the Three Principles of the People (democracy, nationalism, people's welfare/livelihood); (3) detrimental to good morality and public order; and (4) promoting superstition or heterodoxy.[8] The Republic-era Nationalist government took the role of cinema seriously and sought to suppress undesirable subjects that might prove harmful to public morals, national unity, and international prestige. These included the expression of explicit sexuality, the invocation of superstition, the use of local dialects, and the portrayal of Japanese and Western imperialism, banditry, civil war, natural disasters, epidemics, and poverty.

Article 5 of the enforcement regulations (*sihaenggyuch'ik*) of the Korean Motion Picture Law stipulated that the minister of the MPI might not approve exhibition of films that (1) undermined the Constitution and damaged national prestige; (2) did not portray the nation and its flag in a respectful way; (3) harmed international relations by disrespecting the customs of Free World allies and their national feelings; (4) distributed propaganda profiting foreign countries in conflict with the Republic of Korea (ROK); (5) depicted religion as an object of sarcasm, mockery, or hatred; (6) deliberately mocked or vilified clergy; (7) legitimized superstition; (8) mocked or insulted educators under the democratic system; (9) damaged the dignity and justice of courts; (10) provoked audience impulses to imitate crimes by justifying or glorifying criminals or portraying cunning criminal methods; (11) portrayed murders committed by kinfolk or depicted excessively cruel murder scenes; (12) justified revenge except for films that were set in an era or area where revenge was lawful; (13) damaged normative feelings of shame by stimulating the sexual urges of audience members and violated wholesome sexual morality with portrayals of exposed genitals or breasts, sexual acts, and obscene contacts; (14) portrayed naked bodies and men and women taking baths together; and (15) harmed public order and morals.[9] While most items on this list governing issues of religion, crime, sexuality, and public morality had equivalent provisions in the Production Code (which appears to have served as the model for Korean legislators), the first four clauses explicitly called attention to issues of national prestige and security, even more so than the Chinese counterpart enacted more than thirty years earlier.

Prior to discussing how motion picture regulation rules affected the outcome of so-called impure (*pulsun*) films produced or imported during the brief transitional period when state censorship was suspended (1960–1961), it might be helpful to draw a rough sketch of the man who rose to power through a coup d'état on May 16, 1961 (known as *o-il-uk* or 5.16). The surprise coup was met with little resistance, terminating a short-lived Second Republic under Prime Minister Chang Myŏn's parliamentary government, which succeeded the First Republic of Syngman Rhee's authoritarian rule (1948–1960). Called the Supreme Council for National Reconstruction (SCNR: Kukkajaegŏn ch'oegohoeŭi), Park Chung Hee's emergency junta declared its having taken control of the legislative, executive, and judicial branches of the government. The council pledged that the new government would (1) be first and foremost anticommunist; (2) observe the United Nations Charter and all international agreements and cooperation with the United States and all other free nations; (3) terminate corruption and social ills; (4) end despair and hunger by stabilizing the national economy, (5) unify Korea as an anticommunist nation, and (6) turn over the reins of government to fresh and conscientious political leaders once their tasks are achieved.[10] The SCNR was replaced by the Third Republic on December 17, 1963, following presidential elections that Park narrowly won. Hyug Bae Im distinguishes "much of Park's directly elected presidential terms (1963–1971) as a case of 'soft authoritarianism,' and his subsequent period of rule as a 'garrison state.'"[11] Born to a poor peasant family in North Kyŏngsang Province in 1917 during the colonial period, Park was trained to be an officer in Japan and joined the Imperial Army in Manchuria. Before 1948, he was a member of the Workers' Party of South Korea (Namchosŏn Rodongdang) and was arrested in a security crackdown on leftist elements in the army during the Yŏsu-Sunch'ŏn rebellion. After dodging a death sentence by collaborating with authorities in identifying communist cells in the South Korean army, Park served as an intelligence officer during the Korean War. As Byung-Kook Kim puts it, "Park was a populist with a deep contempt for South Korea's traditional elites, whom he held responsible for the *Chosŏn* dynasty's colonial subjugation in 1910, but he was also an elitist with a dirigiste vision of modernization, critical of his people's alleged passivity, opportunism, indolence, and defeatism."[12] In his 1971 book *To Build a Nation*, Park compares his military committee to "the doctors attempting to save a desperately ill patient [whose] future health cannot be maintained unless steps are taken to protect him from the virus that caused his illness."[13] In another part of the book, Park calls himself a manager of "a pilfered household or a bankrupt firm." Although his vision was bleak, the self-congratulatory leader reminiscences, he had to "rise beyond this pessimism to rehabilitate the household...and break, once and for all, the vicious cycle of poverty and economic stagnation."[14]

Park's philosophy of messianic political missions might explain why state film censorship under his developmental regime waged a cultural war against negative or defeatist emotions on-screen such as pessimism, nihilism, despair, and melancholia. For state bureaucrats, such emotions were deemed contrary to the affirmative, "can-do" national spirit that the military government was set on cultivating. What is more, the "revolutionary" regime saw such emotions as the root of the social ills and emblems of a corrupt bygone era, "the virus" that they sought to eradicate in order to protect a healthy body politic. According to Mabel Berezin, the nation-state is a "mobilizer of political emotion" that creates "communities of feeling" through public rituals.[15] For Park's antiliberal regime, movie theaters were what Roman Catholic churches were to fascist Italy: privileged cultural sites where new national identities were constructed through collective emotional participation in shared screen fiction. As Berezin points out, after the collapse of long-established regimes, nation-states are forced to "rewrite the rules of national belonging" and marshal "the symbolic and emotional practices" as affective tools for the polity.[16] In particular, a cathartic Aristotelian story arc was conducive to nurturing a compliant citizenry through affective screen therapy. In this respect, fending off unproductive darkness and negativity was an important mission of film regulation under the Park regime, which sought to propagandize the invented narrative of national salvation and progress.

Censorship Before 1962: From Colonial Regulations to the Motion Picture Ethics Committee

Enacted on January 20, 1962, South Korea's first motion picture law mandated that producers notify the MPI before producing films and that they should receive the MPI's exhibition permits before releasing them into theaters for public consumption (installing a double censorship system with both screenplay review in preproduction and print review in postproduction). Similarly, imports of foreign films or exports of Korean films required the MPI's "recommendations." Additionally, the law stipulated that the exhibition of any motion picture could be stopped if it was shown without a permit or aroused concerns about "harming public security [*kongan*] or morals [*p'ungsok*]."[17] On July 24 of the same year, the MPI proclaimed "enactment regulations" for production registration, import/export recommendations, and exhibition approval. Article 5 of these rules specified permission standards for unacceptable content as quoted previously. These content rules were periodically revised and updated by the MPI according to trends and controversies of recent productions (the same way Hollywood's Production Code was revised several times to accommodate industrial and cultural changes). Although 1962 was the first year when South Korean film censorship was formally legalized and streamlined, various forms of state regulation existed prior to that point.

The origins of Korean film censorship date back to the Japanese colonial period. On July 5, 1926, the Motion Picture Film Censorship Regulations (Hwaltongsajin kŏmyŏlguch'ik) were enforced, requiring producers and importers to submit censorship prints and explanatory scripts to the Government General of Korea (GGK: Chosŏn ch'ongdokpu) for centralized regulatory review prior to public exhibition. Article 3 of the law mandated that the seal of censorship approval be granted only to films deemed unharmful to "security, morals, or public health." There are no surviving archival records that might shed light on precisely how colonial authorities defined these concepts and applied them to their day-to-day review process. As Kim Tong-ho argues, "These standards were too broad and could be arbitrarily interpreted by individual censors. Later they were coopted as the basis for suppressing leftist or nationalist tendencies of Chosŏn films."[18] Yi Hwa-jin, on the other hand, has identified "kisses and embraces" in foreign films as the most frequent targets of censorship cuts, comprising 70 percent of all deleted scenes (6,160) between 1926 and 1936.[19] Yi further observes that the GGK demonstrated a "cinephobic" outlook on the potentially negative effects of motion pictures relative to the rise of imitative crimes and delinquency among adolescents and children in the colony.[20] By the time the GGK enacted the Chosŏn Film Law (Chosŏn yonghwaryŏng) on January 4, 1940, the situation had changed dramatically. Film censorship transitioned from a normative regulatory system of eliminating objectionable elements to safeguard the public interest to a more encompassing form of control over production, distribution, and exhibition, with a view to incorporating filmmaking as a part of the wartime propaganda machinery. Enforcement regulations of the law, enacted on July 7, 1941, made imperial political aims explicit by listing insults to the imperial family, damage to the Japanese empire's prestige, and impediments to control of Chosŏn (Korea) among the reasons for failing censorship.[21]

After Korea was liberated from Japanese colonial rule on August 15, 1945, the United States Army Military Government in Korea (USAMGK) formally occupied the southern half of the peninsula with its Soviet counterpart controlling the area north of the thirty-eighth parallel division line. On October 8, 1946, the military government proclaimed Act 115 on permission of motion pictures, declaring an abolition of the Chosŏn Film Law and its propaganda-oriented film policy. The USAMGK replacement law, however, stipulated that the public exhibition of motion pictures to fifteen or more persons, with or without admissions, required permission from its office of public information (entrusted with the authority to demand eliminations or revisions of parts or reject entire films). The new system not only deliberately targeted small-group screenings of socialist film collectives but also was discriminatorily protective of Hollywood's interests by exempting USAMGK-sponsored films from censorship requirements.[22] The American occupation government's law was a shock to Korean filmmakers who anticipated a liberation from colonial censorship. It appeared to them that the USAMGK had inherited not only the Japanese

Empire's GGK building but also their cultural policy. The culturally insensitive requirement that all screenplays must be fully translated into English for censorship review added an insult to an injury. The Federation of Chosŏn Filmmakers (Chosŏn yŏnghwadongmaeng) and seven other cultural organizations issued a joint statement, denouncing Act 115 as "colonial film policy" detrimental to the "democratic reconstruction" of Korean films.[23]

After the ROK was launched on August 15, 1948, Syngman Rhee's administration based their motion picture censorship on USAMGK Act 115 in the absence of motion picture legislation, maintaining the military government's exhibition permit (sangyŏnghŏga) system. The main point of contention in 1950s film regulation was the question of administrative jurisdiction. As was the case during the Nanjing decade (1927–1937) when Chinese national film censorship was first established, different state authorities vied for control over motion pictures, a powerful medium for national entertainment, public education, and government propaganda. Initially, the MPI took over the task from its counterpart in the USAMGK, but soon territorial conflicts developed between the MPI and the Ministry of Education (MoE: Mungyobu) due to contradicting administrative laws dividing duty of communications (the former's domain) and arts (the latter's sphere). After years of debate and confusion, the jurisdiction for motion picture censorship was transferred to the MoE in 1955. Other than these two branches, the Ministry of National Defense (MND: Kukpangbu) and the Ministry of the Interior (MoI: Naemubu) were major players that intervened in film regulation whenever military or security issues were at stake. Differing views on the same films across competing government branches led to the controversial action of retracting censorship approval given by one ministry and demanding additional cuts or revisions to appease another.

One such case is the 1944 British screen adaptation of Shakespeare's play *Henry V*, imported to South Korea during the Korean War. After passing the MPI's censorship review and receiving the MoE's recommendation for school viewing, *Henry V* was shown to preview audiences in November 1952, while the Korean War was taking place. The MND stepped in when the period drama—notable for actor, producer, and director Laurence Olivier's masterful work in front of and behind the camera—caused controversy over its alleged antiwar sentiment. The military branch confiscated the film's screenplay and recensored it, claiming that the interagency agreement to be consulted in censorship review for military-related films was violated. The MPI expressed its support for the MND's decision, handing down responsibility for failed censorship to the MoE.[24] Similarly, in August 1955, the exhibition permit issued by the MoE for *Piagol* (1955), a locally produced film about North Korean guerilllas continuing their fight in the Chiri Mountains after the cease-fire, was suspended on the scheduled release date due to the MND's and MoI's national security alarm. Poet Kim Chong-mun, director of MND's Division of Troop Information and Education, criticized the film for "heroizing Red partisans" who remain committed to communist ideology until their demise, which is brought about by internal strife and betrayals.[25] The production company had to reapply for a new permit, which was issued one month later after interagency joint review of a recut version, one that had to accommodate changes to make the film's anticommunist message clearer.

The emergence of the Second Republic, South Korea's first democratic government, on June 15, 1960, was a direct result of the April 19 Revolution (*sa-il-gu* or 4.19), which forced the resignation of autocratic leader Syngman Rhee following fraudulent March elections. The new parliamentary government added an amendment to the ROK Constitution's Article 28, Section 2, indicating that "restrictions on citizens' freedom and rights [for maintenance of order and public welfare] cannot include permission or censorship of press or publications." When pressed by journalists asking whether the MoE's film censorship was constitutional under the amendment, the new Ministry of Justice (MoJ: Pŏpmubu) opined that motion pictures should be protected under Article 28 since it invalidated USAMGK Act 115.[26] On August 5, 1960, in accordance with the revised Constitution, the National Motion Picture Ethics Committee (NMPEC: Yŏnghwayulli chŏn'gukwiwŏnhoe) was founded as South Korea's first autonomous regulation (*chayulkyŏmyŏl*) agency free from state intervention. Its twenty-eight founding members represented various sectors of society, including film, art, literature, education, law, religion, and the press. The NMPEC is often cited as the primary reason why several of the most socially conscious masterpieces of South Korean cinema, such as *The Housemaid* (*Hanyŏ*, 1960), *The Coachman*, and *The Stray Bullet*, all arrived between August 1960 and May 1961, a short period when the committee was existent.

There is some truth to this critical consensus. Unfortunately, no surviving NMPEC documents are available on which to base an objective assessment of the first Korean attempt at consensus-based civil censorship of motion pictures without mediation of state power. Nevertheless, judging from the many controversies surrounding the NMPEC, reported by daily newspapers between 1960 and 1961, it can be inferred that this experiment failed to live up to the industry's and the public's high expectations. Detailing the NMPEC's "motion picture ethics rules," an August 7, 1960, report in *Han'guk Ilbo* perceptively predicted, "Although the committee is expected to contribute to maintaining autonomy of motion picture ethics by replacing state censorship, one can imagine that its operations will face considerable challenges as they have no legal power to enforce regulation to dissenting filmmakers."[27] The NMPEC rules were divided among five umbrella headings (nation/society, law, public morals, sex, and education/religion) with two to five subsections under each category. Its general principles were "preventing motion pictures that trample humanity and lower civic morality" and "preempting antistate activities, sympathy for crimes, and damage to good morals."[28] While a democratic provision of "respecting civil rights and denying bureaucracy-centered ideology" stands out, NMPEC principles of regulation were not any more permissive than the enforcement regulations of the 1962 Motion Picture Law. If anything, more prohibitive items were missing in the latter, such as "cruelty against women, children, or animals," "surgical operations on the disabled and the wounded," "justified prostitution," "perversion or aberrant sexuality," and "childbirth scene."[29]

If the NMPEC's regulations were laxer than what preceded or succeeded them, the cause might have rested not in more democratic principles but in weaker authority. As an independent civil organization jointly operated and financed by the Korean Film Producers Association (KFPA: Hang'ukyŏnghwa chejakjahyŏp'oe), the Korean Foreign Film Distributors Association (KFFDA: Hang'ukoegukyŏnghwa paegŭphyŏp'oe), and the National Association of Theater Owners (NATO: Chŏn'gukgŭkjangju yŏnhap), the committee had difficulty establishing its authority and enforcing concrete rules of regulation to parties that paid their bills—the same kinds of difficulty experienced by the MPPDA in the early 1930s before the formation of the more effective PCA in 1934. The NMPEC's professed goal of educating and "edifying" filmmakers to voluntarily avoid antisocial materials, such as imitative murders, obscenity, mistreatment of women and children, glorified adultery, and mockery of educators, was overly idealistic and impractical. The NMPEC came under fire on September 10, 1960, merely one month after its opening, after daily newspapers reported their sight-unseen issuance of the regulatory seal for a film that was still in the final stage of editing. The agency made a flimsy excuse that the mistake occurred due to the production company's rush to get the release print of its noir-infused melodrama *Have I Come to Cry?* (*Ullyŏgo naega wattŏnga*, 1960) ready for exhibition. To impartial observers, the incident belied the NMPEC's disempowerment to stand up for the public and for ethical issues against the industry and commercial interests. This became even clearer in March 1961, when all twenty-eight founding members of the committee were replaced by thirteen new members nominated by the KFPA and the KFFDA who flaunted their entitlement to select who should regulate motion pictures to advance trade interests.

A bigger controversy about NMPEC operations concerned foreign imports thematizing adultery and juvenile delinquency. Louis Malle's scandalous *The Lovers* (*Les amants*, 1958), a film that explores the sexual awakening of a bourgeois woman, Jeanne (Jeanne Moreau), who cheats on both her husband and her lover with a young anthropology student, caused uproar within the National Parent Teacher Association (NPTA: Chŏn'guk sachi'nhoe), which threatened the MoE to take a legal action unless the obscene work—deemed harmful to impressionable children—was taken out of public circulation. Newspaper editorials deplored the new government's "erotic film policy" allowing importations of such controversial films as *The Red and the Black* (*Le rouge et le noir*, 1954), *Lady Chatterley's Lover* (*L'Amant de lady Chatterley*, 1955), and *The Lovers*, which had even come under scrutiny and been restricted in countries where more liberal sexual morals were prevalent. For example, the British Board of Film Censors (BBFC) considered an erotic bedroom scene in Malle's film (in which "the 'act of love' is shown visibly and audibly" against the sonic background of a Brahms sextet) something that "goes far beyond anything we accept for public exhibition in the cinema."[30] The board had difficulty enforcing a few cuts of this and another (bathroom) sex scenes to the film's U.K. distributor, Mondial Films Inter-Distribution. The company appealed to the London County Council for permission to show the uncut print in England's capital city. After several rounds of negotiations with the distributor following the local council's rejection of the request, the BBFC gave a restricted X certificate to the cut version of *The Lovers*. Across the Atlantic, *Lady Chatterley's Lover* was denied an import license by the New York Education Department for "expressly or impliedly [portraying] acts of sexual immorality... as desirable, acceptable or proper patterns of behavior."[31] Kingsley International Pictures, the distributor of the D. H. Lawrence adaptation, appealed, but the New York Court of Appeals upheld the denial, arguing that "the picture as a whole 'alluringly portrays adultery as proper behavior.'" The case went to the United States Supreme Court, which ruled in June 1959 that New York state's film licensing statute violated the First Amendment guarantee of freedom to express ideas.[32] Similarly, Ohio theater owner Nico Jacobellis was charged with obscenity for showing *The Lovers* in a Cleveland suburb. The police confiscated the print and the exhibitor was fined $2,500. The state court upheld the conviction, but the U.S. Supreme Court reversed it in 1964. In his opinion, Justice Potter Stewart argued that only hardcore pornography should qualify for obscenity. "I know it when I see it," famously declared the judge, quickly adding, "the motion picture involved in this case is not that."[33]

Although NMPEC regulators passed *The Lovers* after careful, lengthy deliberation over the course of three meetings (where conservative voices within the committee, such as a Catholic priest and a Protestant minister, likely expressed dissenting opinions to their more liberal peers who advocated for artistic freedom), the public backlash against Malle's film was greater than what the regulatory board had anticipated. In fact, negative reactions were strong enough to sanction the MoE's prerogative to revive censorship for foreign films. Despite the unconstitutionality of motion picture censorship during the Second Republic, the MoE proclaimed its zero-tolerance policy for "adultery films" (*pullyunyŏnghwa*) from abroad in October 1960, invoking Customs Law Article 126, which prohibited importation of publications, paintings, sculptures, and other artifacts detrimental to public security and morals.[34] The ministry strengthened import recommendation criteria for foreign films by replacing screenplay review with print review in order to prevent salacious visual materials (not described on paper) from getting a blind pass. This move made the NMPEC appear toothless and obsolete in the eyes of foreign film distributors.

The NMPEC's authority was further undermined by another controversary surrounding British filmmaker Edmond T. Grévill's exploitation teenpic *Beat Girl* (1960). On January 27, 1961, the NMPEC decided to suspend the film's release (scheduled in February), citing harmful effects on adolescent and youth audiences. Not only did the civil board find the premise of a sixteen-year-old protagonist from a wealthy family performing striptease and aspiring to be a professional stripper unacceptable, but it also looked harshly at the film's portrayal of Beat-generation rebellion and destructive activity (such as a reckless car race and a game of "chicken" on railroad tracks with an approaching train). The NMPEC's evaluation of "Beat" images cross-culturally mirrors that of the BBFC, which advised Willoughby Film Productions on April 7, 1959, after reviewing the revised script of *Beat Girl*: "The youngers seem to us to be too 'beat,' too irredeemably nasty. It would be better if there were more high spirits and less viciousness. It takes the dramatic conflict out of the picture if these teenagers appear to be past praying for or not worth saving.... It certainly does not justify their offensive rudeness to older people. [We] would like to see them as real people, looking for fun and excitement, but not nasty or depraved."[35] Echoing the sentiment of their British counterpart, the NMPEC furthermore articulated a culturally specific concern that the irrational delinquency of the British gang would be embraced by Korean youth audiences, fresh from the April 19 Revolution, as justified rebellion against the social status quo.[36] The NMPEC's unprecedented decision was initially ignored by the MoE, which sided with the film's distributor (claiming that the NMPEC had no legal authority to make a demand that would incur heavy financial losses to Segi Corporation [Segi-sangsa or Century Trading Company], the importer of *Beat Girl*).[37]

The state censorship file on *Beat Girl* (available for on-site research at the Korean Film Archive [KOFA: Han'gukyŏngsang charyŏwŏn]) contains an exhibition registration certificate, one that was issued by the MoE on the same day when the NMPEC voted to suspend the film in an all-member meeting. Later, the ministry explained it as a mistake (the certificate was granted without reviewing the print according to the practice established in the wake of the aforementioned controversy surrounding *The Lovers*). Moreover, that "mistake" occurred during an interim period when the section chief seat of their culture division was vacant. The internal MoE memo summarizes the film as a reform story of a teenaged runway girl who returns home and reconciles with her stepmother after rebelling against her parents and associating with a Beat gang. There is also an appendix that lists six dialogue passages and six scenes (including controversial strip shows) to be removed or shortened with the distributor's consent.[38] After the NMPEC filed a complaint to the MoE, threatening to disband themselves in protest, the ministry revoked the certificate, suspended the upcoming release, and invited seventeen dignitaries (including chief editors of major daily newspapers, writers, college deans, delegates from the MoE, the MoJ, and the MPI, a representative of the KFPA, etc.) to a public preview screening. The ministry also instructed Segi Corporation to avoid using the controversial title *Chŏlmŭn yuch'edŭl* (*Young Flesh*), which had drawn negative media attention, and to advertise their forthcoming release under the original English title (*Beat Girl*) instead.³⁹ The low-budget teenpic was finally allowed to be released on February 15, 1960, after it had agitated different sectors of society, from concerned parents and teachers of the NPTA to public prosecutors who vowed to investigate customs officers for neglecting their duty by admitting the print from Great Britain.

Although the MoE handed an olive branch to the NMPEC by confirming its commitment to collaborating with them in foreign film regulation and restricting the showings of *Beat Girl* in second- or third-run theaters, the incident was a visible reminder to film producers and distributors that the civil committee had no administrative or judicial power over their trade activities. The NMPEC's advisory role was precarious without an enforcing bargaining chip (comparable to the MPPDA's conditional release system with a five-figure fine leviable to violators) and destined to fail when conflicts of interest arose with more powerful entities such as trade associations and government branches. Imperfect and dysfunctional, the NMPEC nevertheless represented a democratic ideal of the April 19 Revolution. Although it was forced to retire prematurely when the May 16 coup put an abrupt halt to various political and cultural reforms of the Second Republic, its principle of civil regulation was inherited by other nongovernmental boards (the Art and Culture Ethics Committee [Yesulmunha yulliwiwŏnhoe] and its successor, the Public Performance Ethics Committee [Kongyŏn yulliwiwŏnhoe]) that partnered with the MPI in reviewing and regulating screenplays in the 1970s.

Reasons for *The Stray Bullet*'s Ban

In his 1995 memoir *Film Life*, Yu Hyŏn-mok reminiscences about the censorship history of his neorealist masterpiece *The Stray Bullet*:

> During my career as a film director, there were many cuts made by censorship's scissors. Each time, it felt like a part of me was being cut.... The most unique case was *The Stray Bullet* of 1961. I began shooting in the late period of [Syngman Rhee's] Liberal Party. With the arrival of April 19 and the ensuing "freedom of expression," I was able to change the scenario more bravely. At the time of the original release, only one scene in which a disabled veteran angrily urinates in front of the Bank of Korea building was cut. But after the May 16 coup, the military government suspended the film's exhibition on the grounds that its content was too dark and [actress] No Chae-sin's line "*Kaja! Kaja!*" [Let's go! Let's go!] meant returning to North Korea. This was not even an act of scissoring but a wholesale condemnation to rotting in the shadows.⁴⁰

An almost identical account of the film's banning was reported by *Variety* on November 13, 1963: "[*The Stray Bullet*] was made in 1960 under great difficulties and sparse capital. It was then banned by the government because of its dark picture of unemployment and because of a phrase spoken over and over by the war-crazed grandmother: 'Let's get out of here!' which could be interpreted as meaning 'back to our home in North Korea' (Director Yu [at the San Francisco Film Festival] insisted, through Korean government interpreters, that it was meant just as a cry to leave a miserable situation)."[41] Subsequently, the account of *The Stray Bullet* being banned by Park's new regime due to the repeated line "*Kaja! Kaja!*" has been retold by several historians and scholars on both sides of the Pacific. Kelly Y. Jeong, for example, writes, "*The Stray Bullet* was banned for what the censors considered its suspicious ideological content, as revealed (they argued) in the insane mother's repeated cry, which the censors believed showed her wish to go back to the communist North."[42] The author further condemns the era's strict state censorship for not only infringing "the freedom of the press and artistic expression to suppress the voices that were critical of the government" but also being too "opaque" and "never made clear, which often led to artists preemptively censoring their own work and even their imagination to continue to work."[43] Drawing upon Ho Hyŏn-ch'an, my own coauthored work in the past made a similar claim prior to the KOFA's opening of censorship documents: "The anti-communist government banned the film, suspecting a pro-North subtext couched in recurring scenes where the North Korean refugee family's demented matriarch... yells, 'Let's get out of here!'"[44] According to Ho, the film's director defended his work against the charge of pro-North sympathy, arguing that the line expressed a desire for a utopian society.[45]

Regardless of Yu's creative license as an adaptative screen artist, Yi Pyŏm-sŏn's short story on which the film was based makes it clear that the destination of the crazed matriarch's mantra is her hometown north of the thirty-eighth parallel, which the family had left seven years earlier to escape a communist purge of landowner families. In the original story, an underpaid accounting clerk called Song Ch'ol-ho (played by Kim Chin-gyu in the film) repeatedly attempts to explain to his mother (No Chae-sin in the film) that they are unable to go back home because of the division. The homesick mother is confused: "I don't understand it. I never will. Thirty-eighth parallel. Are you trying to tell me they built a wall there that goes right up to the sky? Who on earth do you think would stop me from going home?" The son tries to persuade his mother in vain that South Korea is a "free country" where they can "at least live and endure life," unlike in the North where they will almost surely meet an immediate and untimely demise. The son's pleading is useless. The woman who led "a peaceful and abundant life" in the past is unable to believe that her wretched existence in Seoul's Liberation Village (Haebangch'on) shantytown, with "its crate-like shacks tacked one upon the other, perched in cavities that had been scaped out of the mountainside," is really a "liberation" (as the misleading name of the northern settler area suggests).[46] That feeling of entrapment in poverty extends to the rest of the characters, especially to Ch'ol-ho, who is overburdened with his duty as the extended family's patriarch. He has too many mouths to feed (those of

FIGURE 1.1 Yu Hyŏn-mok's *The Stray Bullet* (1961) is set in Seoul's Liberation Village, a shantytown for northern settlers freed from communism, but not urban poverty.

his mother, two brothers, sister, pregnant wife, and young daughter) but only meager wages to do so. Although suffering from a terrible toothache for an extended period, he cannot afford a visit to the dental clinic. His sister Myŏng-suk (Sŏ Ae-ja) turns to military prostitution, servicing American GIs for economic survival. His unemployed war veteran brother Yŏng-ho (Ch'oe Mu-ryong) is taken into police custody after a botched bank heist. His malnourished wife (Mun Chŏng-suk) dies during the delivery of their baby. At the end of this hopeless narrative, Ch'ol-ho aimlessly shouts *"Kaja!"* to a baffled taxi driver and his helper after naming one destination after another: home where his mother and daughter await, the university hospital where his dead wife and newborn son are located, and the police station where his brother is detained.

When General Park Chung Hee rose to power through the May 16 coup in 1961, one of the first things that his military junta SCNR did was to stop the public screenings of thirty-five domestic and twenty-two foreign films deemed "impure" (*pulsun*) prior to those motion pictures' recensoring. Among those titles were realist social-problem films *Money* (*Ton*, 1958) and *The Stray Bullet*; crime dramas *Hell's Flower* (*Chiokhwa*, 1958) and *Prisoner No. 72* (*72ho ŭi choesu*, 1959); family dramas *The Coachman* and *Third-Rate Manager* (*Samdŭng kwajang*, 1961); and cross-cultural literary adaptations *Katusha* (1960), and *Jean Valjean* (1961). After a six-month review, the new military government banned one Korean film (*The Stray Bullet*) along with six foreign ones. While foreign films—such as *The Red and the Black*, *Lady Chatterley's Lover*, *Young Sinners* (*Les tricheurs*, 1958), *Tempest* (*La Tempesta*, 1958), *I Spit on Your Grave* (*J'irai cracher sur vos tombres*, 1959), and *Beat Girl*—were barred on moral grounds, Yu's film was singled out for political reasons due to its realistic portrayal of postwar poverty and social malaise.[47]

Archival evidence from *The Stray Bullet*'s censorship file, accessible digitally at the KOFA, debunks several political myths surrounding the film's ban during Park's military junta rule. It was during the final days of the *democratic* Second Republic when Yu's film first got into trouble. After passing the NMPEC's regulatory review with an instruction to cut a cruel shot of a mother hanging with a crying child on her back in a sewer passage of Ch'onggaech'ŏn Canal (where Yŏng-ho with a stolen cash bag is chased by police),[48] *The Stray Bullet* was released in Kukje Theater on April 13, 1961, to lukewarm reviews. Given its uncompromisingly depressing storyline, the film's commercial prospects were dismal from the onset and Yu had difficulty finding producers who were willing to take a risk and invest in his pet project. Rescue came from his lighting director, Kim Sŏng-ch'un, who financed the project using his personal savings, with other cast and crew members (including the industry's biggest stars such as Kim Chin-gyu and Ch'oe Mu-ryong) donating their labor pro bono or for nominal fees.[49] Due to funding shortages, the film took thirteen months to complete. By one estimate, the film cost only 40 percent, or 8 million Korean hwan (U.S.$12,300), of the average production budget of most postwar Korean films.[50] The profound despair that ran through the screenplay and captivated Yu's auteur vision was understandably not welcomed by a general moviegoing public seeking entertainment and comfort. The film's creative blending of different film traditions (the documentary aesthetics of Italian neorealism, depth-of-field staging in deep focus reminiscent of Orson Welles and Gregg Toland's collaborations, German expressionistic lighting and mise-en-scène, Hollywood genre conventions associated with melodrama and film noir) might have been overwrought to lay audiences as much as it was awe inspiring to cinephiles. Although Yu remembered that bars near Kukje Theater boomed with intellectuals who wanted to discuss the film over drinks at the time of its original release, the early critical reviews were mixed.

Im Yŏng-ung wrote, for example, "*The Stray Bullet* is too sentimental and conventional to depict modern Korea's desperate situation.... Overall, the excess of episodes made the film too scattered. In particular, the direction in the second half loses focus.... In the end, overzealous directing of a poorly organized script led to a failed representation of today's Korea without taming its own drive."[51] Im complained about the digressive plotline revolving around Yŏng-ho's accidental romantic reencounter with a former army nurse [Mun Hye-ran] who is unexpectedly murdered by a stalking neighbor in the midway. For the critic, the romantic plot (absent in the original story) is excessive and gratuitous, as the nurse character's primary role is to leave a revolver that Yŏng-ho uses for the attempted bank robbery, the film's dramatic focus in the latter part.[52] Writing for the daily newspaper *Kyŏnghyang Sinmun*, another reviewer was kinder: "Yu Hyŏn-mok portrayed 'reality' with his patient direction. There are many subtle efforts in camera work and sound recordings. In one sentence, this work was made with an overpowering will and the mere fact that it became the standard for Korean art cinema and explored selfhood seriously is more than enough to compensate for its weaknesses."[53]

The MoI's Security Bureau head had more pressing problems with the film than unbalanced storytelling or directorial digressions. On April 19, 1961, one month prior to the May 16 coup, the MoI sent an interagency memo to the MoE, referring to *The Stray Bullet* as "potential material for communist propaganda" against South Korea. The Security Bureau head opined that the film was socially and morally irresponsible by "denying any hope for Korea's past and future" and "inciting irresolute masochism and despair among audience members."[54] The short memo indicated that the MoI's review of the recently released film was conducted at the request of the MoE. The Security Bureau head closed the report by stating that it would be difficult to recommend the film for public exhibition. On May 28, 1961, ten days after Park's military coup, the MoI, now working under a different regime, sent a second report to the MoE discussing "public opinion" that *The Stray Bullet* was loaded with procommunist propaganda and thus in violation of the state's anticommunist policy. The report consisted of two parts. Under the "overall impression" category, the Security Bureau concluded that Yu's film "denies any hope for Korean society, provokes rebellions and desperation of the unemployed and proletariats, and gives an impression that a communist revolution might be necessary." Under the category of "impure scenes and parts," the MoI cited several specific textual elements as incriminating evidence: (1) The film is based on the negative view of Korea as exemplified by such dialogue as "It doesn't matter whether the setting is before or after the April 19 Revolution"; (2) the theme song "A Lonely Life in the Wasteland" is ideologically subversive; (3) the film propagandizes a hatred for capitalist society through its extreme expressions of wealth differentials between the rich and the poor; (4) the film aggravates anti-American sentiment by exaggerating the debauchery of American soldiers; and (5) the film ends miserably without implying any solution to collective despair of veterans, the unemployed, or underpaid, underclass citizens.[55]

To contemporary readers, the MoI's labeling of the film as procommunist, anticapitalist propaganda might sound paranoid (recalling, to a certain extent, the Red Scare in McCarthy-era America). This is especially ironic considering the fact that Yu's characters are ordinary citizens or apolitical subjects who simply struggle to survive in conditions of economic adversity rather than consciously revolting against the social status quo. Even Yŏng-ho, the black sheep of the family, repents near the ending of the narrative and expresses remorse for his failed crime to his elder brother in the police station (unlike his literary counterpart, who regrets not having killed a guard to ensure a safe escape). However, archival evidence contradicts the established scholarly and journalist narrative that the film's ban was brought about by government bureaucrats' anticommunist paranoia over a North Korean refugee's refrain, "*Kaja! Kaja!*" The MoI's second report, which prompted interagency censorship re-review, does not even reference this line. It is also notable that regulatory restrictions on the film for security reasons were first discussed *prior to* the May 16 coup. This fact contradicts the narrative that Park's military regime took away the artistic freedom allowed under the Second Republic policy of no official state censorship.

The MPI censorship file on *The Stray Bullet* documents two censorship review meetings. Arranged by the MoE and involving representatives of the MoI, the MoJ, the MoE, and the Korean Central Intelligence Agency (KCIA: Chungangjŏngbobu), the first meeting took place on July 20, 1961. Immediately afterward, the MoE notified Kim Sŏng-ch'un of Taehan Production that, in consideration of public opinion, the exhibition of *The Stray Bullet* was suspended until further notice. The second meeting took place sometime between January 26 and 29, 1962. In this meeting, arranged by the MPI, representatives of the MoI, the MoE, the MPI, and the KCIA unanimously voted for a ban on the film's exhibition. The MPI file contains the KCIA regulator Paek Yŏng-sŏk's short report, which sheds light on what state agencies might have discussed. The report states, "The film is an outstanding work of art that sharply portrays the honest protagonist's miserable life as he struggles with poverty. However, because it exposes social ills and the misery of people before the May 16 coup, it contradicts the new government's ideal of national reconstruction and may have adverse effects should screenings be allowed in the current political environment. Therefore, suspension of its exhibition is warranted."[56] While the MoI's policing of what it deemed procommunist, anticapitalist, and anti-American content undoubtedly factored into the film's eventual ban, the constitution of balanced censorship committees, multiple reviews, and the KCIA's acknowledgment of the film's artistic merit point toward a judicious deliberative process motivated by diverse interests (political, educational, and cultural). What is particularly notable is that between the first and second meetings (July 1961 and January 1962), the jurisdiction of state film censorship was handed over from the MoE to the MPI.

The above-quoted KCIA opinion attests to the fact that *The Stray Bullet*'s unrelentingly pessimistic tone was as much responsible for the film's ban as the potentially subversive content singled out by the MoI's Security Bureau in April and May 1961. One of the cultural priorities of state censorship in the Cold War era was to inject a "cheerful" sensibility or affirmative attitude into Korean films. A cultural war was thus being waged against pessimism, despair, depression, and social malaise onscreen. As Pak Yu-hŭi states, "Since the 1950s, the 'bright, sound, and healthy' had been the consistent standard required of entertainment films.

The first clause of the MoE's 1958 performance art permit guidelines was 'to show the pleasure of the free world through pure artistic catharsis and entertainment.' This was a priority item throughout the 1960s as well."[57] Newspaper headlines of the 1960s reported the government's request to make "cheerful and constructive films" and its tendency to censor dark and erotic content.[58]

Perhaps this state-directed tonal control of national cinema should be understood as a sort of cultural policy rather than as repressive political censorship. Along with *The Stray Bullet*, *The Coachman* was also put on the aforementioned list of thirty-five "impure" domestic films that the new government reviewed for censorship. In this award-winning film (recipient of the Silver Bear at the 1961 Berlin International Film Festival), the titular widower Ch'un-sam (played by Kim Sŭng-ho) is injured in an automobile accident and gets unjustly laid off. A casualty of modernization and an obsolete relic of the past, the emasculated patriarch saves face due to the filial loyalty of his adult children and the selfless devotion of his romantic interest, Suwŏn-daek (Hwang Chŏng-sun), a maid in his ex-boss's household. The film's denouement shows the family happily reunited in snowy downtown Seoul, where they celebrate the family's hopeful future after receiving long-awaited news that the eldest son, Su-ŏp (Shin Yŏng-gyun), has passed his bar exam on his fourth attempt. In this film, natural lighting in the final exterior sequence is bright and crisp, and blocking of characters emphasizes familial bonding and solidarity. After spotting his name on the list of successful applicants posted on the wall of the Capitol building (Chungangch'ŏng, formerly Government General), the son turns around to find his disabled father watching him from afar and asking him if he passed. Su-ŏp rushes over to Ch'un-sam, who slips on the snow-covered road and falls. While still on the ground, father and son embrace and gaze at one other affectionately, holding back tears in the kind of tight close-up shot typically reserved for a Hollywood love scene. The shot widens as more characters enter the frame (Suwŏn-daek from the right side; the daughter [Ŏm Aeng-ran] and the younger son hand in hand from the left side) and form a joyful group. Su-ŏp asks Suwŏn-daek to be their mother from that day forward and Ch'un-sam exchanges shy yet consenting glances with the woman he loves. Against nondiegetic music rising to a crescendo, the final shot cranes up to a bird's-eye-view of five characters (whose back is turned toward the perched camera) marching forward side by side to their destination: home sweet home.

Set in a dimly lit taxi at night, the mise-en-scène of *The Stray Bullet*'s gritty final scene cannot be more different from that of the heartwarming exterior scene in *The Coachman*, which takes place in a city whitened by snowfall. Feeling nauseated and dizzy from a double tooth extraction (done against his first dentist's warning), Ch'ŏl-ho stumbles into an empty taxi he spots at a busy traffic intersection. To the question of the driver's assistant, "Where to?," the light-headed passenger replies, "Liberation Village." In a noir-like medium shot with heavy shadows and reflected lights from the outside traffic lights to provide

FIGURE 1.2 The uplifting dénouement of Kang Tae-jin's *The Coachman* (1961) shows the family happily reunited in snowy downtown Seoul, where they celebrate their hopeful future after receiving long-awaited news that the eldest son, Su-ŏp (Shin Yŏng-gyun: far right), has passed his bar exam.

FIGURE 1.3 *The Coachman*'s final bird's-eye–view shot captures an image of the family as a coherent support group united in the common goal of upward mobility and with a clear sense of destination.

high-contrast patterns similar to those in 1940s Hollywood B movies, Ch'ŏl-ho seems barely conscious, while his eyes are closed in pain. The camera then cuts to an exterior long shot of the dark streets outside the taxi. Partially lit with the neon contours of buildings and headlights, the shot shows the vehicle circling to change direction. A cut to another interior medium shot of Ch'ŏl-ho, who has regained consciousness and looks out the window, follows. He modifies his destination: "No, the university hospital," he says, indicating the place where his deceased wife and newborn son are located. This precedes another exterior long shot of the taxi turning around. Then the camera cuts back to Ch'ŏl-ho, who changes his mind once again and orders, "No, take me to Chungbu Police Station," which is where his brother is detained. From here, the spectator is taken to the hospital newborn ward where Myŏng-suk can be seen gazing at her baby nephew, who is being held in a nurse's arm across the window. Her voiceover fills the soundtrack along with the ambient noise of the wailing baby: "Brother, come back. Did you not say what you love most is the smiling faces of babies? Your baby will smile soon. I know he will. We have to do everything so that he will smile." Yu's camera dollies in and settles on a medium close-up shot of Myŏng-suk's teary face, but the scene switches back to the taxi, closing off the possibility of a potentially redemptive ending.

In a deeply staged medium shot (with the entire taxi interior captured from the stationary camera placed outside), Ch'ŏl-ho, in the background, is awakened by the driver's helper in the foreground. The latter reports that they have arrived at the police station. In a long take of the same shot, the driver can be seen casting furtive glances at the back mirror as if he were suspicious of his passenger. A cut to Ch'ŏl-ho in close-up as he looks out to the police station entrance follows. In another example of deep staging within the taxi interior, Ch'ŏl-ho closes his eyes, leans back, and feverishly utters, "Let's go! (*Kaja!*) Go." With their back turned to the camera (from Ch'ŏl-ho's point of view), the driver and his companion gossip about the passenger who might be drunk and grumble about how unlucky they are to be stuck with "an aimless bullet" (*obalt'an*, the original Korean title of the film). The camera cuts to another medium shot of Ch'ŏl-ho in the passenger seat, now with noticeable bloodstains on his white shirt. His voiceover soliloquizes, "An aimless bullet? I have to be a son, a husband, a father, a brother, and a secretary. So many things I have to be. Maybe you are right. I might be an aimless bullet made by the Creator. I don't know where I should go. But I should be going somewhere now." Ch'ŏl-ho's upper body sags to one side as he succumbs to the loss of blood. The final montage assembles a close-up of the changing traffic signal, a long shot of the city street, a high-angle deep-focus shot of the driver's assistant turning his head to inquire "Where to?," a medium shot of Ch'ŏl-ho shouting "Let's go!" with a bloody mouth, a close-up of the traffic signal, and a long shot of the traffic.

Unlike in *The Coachman*'s uplifting ending, where characters are mobile within an open exterior space, *The Stray Bullet*'s final scene accentuates feelings

FIGURE 1.4 In *The Stray Bullet*'s pessimistic ending, all characters are disconnected and distant from one another (separated by partitions, compartments, or borders). In the hospital ward, a "fallen woman," Myŏng-suk (Sŏ Ae-ja), gazes at her motherless baby nephew held in a nurse's arm across the window.

FIGURE 1.5 "An aimless bullet" is an apt metaphor not only for the protagonist Ch'ŏl-ho (Kim Chin-gyu) roaming the city without knowing which obligation he should attend to first, but also for his rehabilitating nation undergoing one political upheaval after another in the chaotic postwar era.

of entrapment and claustrophobia with visual motifs of partition, including glass, window frames, and vehicular compartments. In *The Coachman*, family members constitute a coherent support group united in the common goal of upward mobility and they have a clear sense of destination (as straightforward as the open boulevard ahead of them in the final shot). In *The Stray Bullet*, all characters are disconnected and distant from one another (separated by partitions, compartments, or borders in both taxi and hospital ward). Again and again, this loss of direction is verbally and visually emphasized. The protagonist changes his destination several times until he is unable to name a new one. The taxi circles around, constantly making detours. In the use of repeated shots, the traffic appears to be stuck in a constant circular movement. The taxi is as aimless as its occupant is in his life. As the final paragraph of Yi's original story describes, "Knowing no destination but caught in the moving stream, the car carrying Ch'ŏl-ho, too, had no choice but to move."[59] "An aimless bullet" is an apt metaphor, not only for the protagonist roaming the city without knowing which of his many obligations he should attend to first, but also for the nation that is attempting to rehabilitate itself, even as it undergoes one political upheaval after another in the chaotic postwar era. Out of the thirty-five Korean films recensored after the May 16 coup, only *The Stray Bullet* was banned: in contrast, *The Coachman* was allowed to resume its release. Leaving to one side its implicit anticapitalist message, *The Coachman*'s optimistic ending and wholesome sense of morality were likely seen to be in conformity with to the government's regulatory policy of encouraging a kind of "uplift cinema"; it is this conformity that saved the film from the fate of Yu's downbeat social-problem film, often compared with Vittorio De Sica's Italian neorealist classic *Bicycle Thieves* (*Ladri di biciclette*, 1948).

Appealing Censorship and Canon Formation: The Stray Bullet vs. The Coachman

Perhaps the most persuasive evidence of censorship as a dialogical process of cultural negotiations rather than a unilateral exercise of power by one party over another can be found in the appeal process. The MPI censorship file demonstrates that multiple parties—including Kim Sŏng-ch'un, the film's producer; Yun Pong-ch'un, the president of the Motion Picture Association of Korea (MPAK: Yŏnghwain hyŏp'oe); and the University of Southern California film professor Richard Dyer MacCann—put collective pressure on the government by requesting the lifting of the suspension of *The Stray Bullet* and allowing for its re-release. It is noteworthy that on August 21, 1963, the MPI not only issued an exhibition permit to Taehan Production but also sent a memorandum to the KCIA two days later, justifying its action.

In his petition to the ministry dated June 11, 1963, Kim repositions *The Stray Bullet* as an uplift film supportive of national reconstruction by critiquing social ills at the time of Syngman Rhee's corrupt regime. The producer reasons, "After recensorship, the film was suspended because of the concern that its dark exposure of social reality might harm the task of the May 16 Revolution.... However, now that the basis for national reconstruction has been achieved, I would like to motivate citizens to reject corruption and devote themselves to the national cause while enjoying an art film."[60] Furthermore, Kim lists self-censored revisions to the earlier print based on the feedback it had received from the ministry. First, the North Korean matriarch's mantra "Let's go! (*Kaja!*)" is clarified as "Let's go to green pastures along with a flock of sheep" in order to avoid a misunderstanding and to stress a humanistic yearning for a peaceful utopia. Second, a foreword was added praising the revolutionary government's bold policies and denouncing the corruption of the old regime that had brought misery and poverty. Third, an end credit caption was added highlighting the SCNR's pledge to end despair and hunger by restoring the national economy.[61]

It appears that the MPI was an accomplice, rather than an obstruction, to the lifting of the ban on *The Stray Bullet*, a major lobbying item of the South Korean film industry at that time. To advance this cause, the MPAK's president enlisted MacCann, a former film critic for the *Christian Science Monitor* and at that time a visiting professor at the Korean National Film Production Center (NFPC), whose letter of support was forwarded to the ministry.[62] In this undated letter addressed to Yi Sŏng-ch'ŏl, the NFPC director, MacCann recommends the submission of *The Stray Bullet* to the San Francisco International Film Festival (SFIFF), offering praise for its artistic merits and a defense of its negative portrayal of Korean society. The American academic states:

> I personally feel that it is one of the most impressive and moving films I've ever seen.... It may be said that the film presents Korea in a bad light. So do other prize-winning films from other countries present their countries in a bad light. But they call for a better life through emphasizing tragedy and poverty. The audiences and critics who see foreign films from other countries will not judge Korea as any poorer than they already know Korea to be. They will actually see the big buildings and the traffic of Seoul for the first time in a dramatic story. And they will see the problems presented here as universal problems, presented with great artistry and forces in a stunningly beautiful example of filmic technique. The story presents in part a negative and tragic philosophy, but no more than any other films and it is presented with strength and good taste.[63]

Later Yu gave full credit to MacCann's recommendation of *The Stray Bullet* as South Korea's entry for the SFIFF as the primary reason why the government lifted the ban on his film.[64] As Sangjoon Lee points out, Yu's film "was released for screening in Seoul only a few weeks before the festival for the specific purpose of making it eligible for entry in the festival."[65]

Based on her oral history interviews with the former staff in the MPI, Yi Sun-jin concludes that the lifting of *The Stray Bullet*'s ban was possible due to collaborative efforts between industry personnel who rallied behind Yu and government bureaucrats who were sympathetic to their cause.[66] What is fascinating about documents found in the film's censorship file is that the ministry initially approved the film's re-release in a letter to Kim, dated July 22, 1963, on the condition of cutting the demented mother's repeated line of "Let's go" in three different scenes and shortening a scene depicting an American soldier's sexual advance on Myŏng-suk. The ministry also prepared two interagency reports dated the same day, justifying this decision: one to the KCIA and the other to the MoI (two departments that probably played a key role in suppressing the film for political reasons). It can be inferred that these reports were not sent. On July 25, 1963, the ministry sent a rejection letter to Kim, simply explaining that "the time was not right" for permitting the film's exhibition. Inexplicably, the same producer sent a letter addressed to the MPI on August 20, less than one month after the rejection, petitioning for *The Stray Bullet*'s re-release again on the grounds that the film (along its director and stars) had received an official invitation from the SFIFF programmer earlier that month, and that Metro-Goldwyn-Mayer (MGM) Studios had expressed an interest in importing the film to the United States. Kim implored the minister to lift suspension so that the film could be sent abroad and contribute to opening overseas markets for the Korean film industry.[67] The following day, the ministry's Motion Picture Division circulated an internal memo (reviewed and signed by the minister himself), which sided with Kim and recommended the lifting of the ban, citing both overseas responses and domestic press opinion sympathetic to the film. Moreover, on the same day, the ministry sent a one-line letter to the film's producer, bearing the good news.

It is reasonable to conjecture that the ministry's staff (or perhaps even its leadership) was behind the coaching of the producer to resubmit his petition and solidify his case by citing an invitation from San Francisco and an import inquiry from MGM. It can be inferred that the ministry encouraged this action in order to strengthen its own excuse to the KCIA (in a report sent on August 23) as to why it permitted the film's exhibition despite the ideological suspicion previously raised by the MoI's Security Bureau head back in May 1961. As pointed by Stephan Haggard, Byung-kook Kim, and Chung-in Moon, the summer of 1963 was a crisis period for the Park regime, which was pressured by the United States government to stabilize the economy (as foreign exchange reserves decreased to U.S.$100 million in July 1963 from U.S.$193 million in June 1962) and rush the transition from the military junta to democratic rule. With the specter of currency devaluation and the Kennedy administration's withholding of foreign aid as a form of political pressure, the military government was pushed to "generate foreign exchange" and devise "several innovations in support of exporters, including new financing schemes, tax exemptions, and a system that linked the right to import to export proceeds."[68]

By July 1963, imports of foreign books were halted to save foreign currency. Import allowances for foreign films were drastically cut from U.S.$810,000 in 1962 to U.S.$450,000 in 1963. Due to currency shortages, only U.S.$130,000 of the 1963 quota could be filled and foreign movie specialty theaters (approximately one-third of 363 theaters nationwide) were forced to show domestic films to make up for reduced supplies.[69] Given Park's aggressive export-led economic policy to overcome the crisis, Kim's petition linking the lifting of the ban to the opening of a new export market for Korean films could not have been more politically potent. It would not be a surprise if he had insider advisors in the ministry tipping him off to send another petition directly addressed to the minister and advance this effective argument. Given the expedited processing of Kim's second petition and the brevity of the permission letter to the producer, one can reasonably conjecture that the ministry's Motion Picture Division staff was on board and the first petition was rejected on purpose to cite more persuasive reasoning for the film's unbanning to other branches of the government.

On October 12, 1963, *The Stray Bullet* was domestically re-released two years and three months after its original release, garnering a rather modest 50,000 admissions.[70] The following month, the film—along with its director, Yu Hyŏn-mok, star Kim Chin-gyu, and the MPI's Motion Picture Division chief, Kim Tong-sik—travelled to San Francisco, once again demonstrating a collaborative relationship between filmmakers and regulators. In his memoir, Yu recollects, "As an Asian film, *The Stray Bullet* did not appeal to foreigners at the SFIFF. They did not understand why the protagonist is starvingly poor although he has employment and why he does not go to the dentist despite his toothache. It was difficult for them to appreciate inferior printing and recording quality compared with their cinema as well as Eastern lifestyle, customs, and emotions."[71] Director Ha Kil-jong attended the festival as an MFA student in filmmaking at the University of California, Los Angeles (where he was a classmate of Francis Ford Coppola). According to his eyewitness account, most attendees walked out during the screening and those who stayed were baffled by the film, calling it "a Korea-specific text that is not suitable for the world stage."[72] In a seminar with jury members following the festival, complaints about the incomprehensible plot (along the line of what Yu describes) were made. Although its American proponent MacCann expected that the film's "cry against poverty, injustice, and aimlessness . . . would appeal to European and American critics,"[73] the opposite proved true. Yu's philosophical tendency and cerebral approach to social problems were an unwelcome departure from Italian neorealist cinema's overpowering affective appeal firmly grounded in traditional humanism and spiritual redemption. Some seminar participants even questioned whether *The Stray Bullet* was meant to be economic propaganda aiming at attracting more foreign aid by exploiting social misery.[74] Embarrassingly, this dismissive comment was corroborated by Yu himself, who told a reporter in San Francisco, "I hope President Kennedy will see this film and continue his aid to South Korea. Otherwise, the poverty will become worse."[75] In an oral history interview, another director, Pae Sŏk-in, testified that the Korean consulate general in San Francisco made a request that further examples of humiliating films depicting miserable conditions of contemporary Korea not be sent in the future.[76]

The cold reception that *The Stray Bullet* received in San Francisco contrasts with the critical success that *The Coachman* had garnered two years earlier in Berlin, where the latter Korean film had been awarded the Silver Bear Grand Jury Prize. In his July 19, 1961, contribution to *Tonga Ilbo*, Mun Han-gyu, a Korean medical student at the University of Berlin, reported on its the heartwarming European reception:

> Excited by the news of a Korean film screening, we [Koreans in Berlin] ran to the theater in Kurfürstendamm, only to be disappointed and saddened upon arrival. Naturally, we expected a large crowd, but there were only a few dozen people and the auditorium looked empty. My heart was filled with pathos as a citizen of a Third World country. I felt that we were shamed like that because of a lack of publicity and poor cultural diplomacy. However, as the film titles rolled and the story unfolded, audiences were aroused emotionally and gratified. The European woman sitting next to me was full of tears. . . . Although there were parts hard to understand for Europeans, they seemed to be moved by our Eastern virtues and morals. This is probably why *The Coachman* won the Silver Bear Award. Later I heard that an American juror actively advocated for the film. Many friends congratulated me after the award was announced and asked me where to see the film belatedly.[77]

Perhaps this contrasting international reception validates, to a certain degree, the South Korean government's effort to uplift the national sentiment. The message of hope was not simply a means of national propaganda but an affirmation of universal human values welcomed by international film audiences from around the world.

As illustrated by Christina Klein in her book *Cold War Cosmopolitanism*, neorealist works like Kim So-dong's 1958 film *Money* and Yu's *The Stray Bullet* represent the "culture of despair" forged as an alternative to more commercial films such as the melodrama *Madame Freedom* (*Chayu puin*, 1956) and the musical comedy *Hyperbolae of Youth* (*Ch'ŏngch'un ssanggoksŏn*, 1956). Directed by Han Hyŏng-mo, these two films manifested an "optimism about modernity" and a "Hollywood-inflected Cold War cosmopolitan style."[78] Klein goes on to state, "Realism was at once a product of the limited resources available to filmmakers, who turned to exterior locations, minimalist props, and stories about working people out of necessity, and also a sign of the creative influence of European cultural trends such as Italian neorealism and French existentialism, which gave intellectual cachet to expressions of despair."[79] *Money*, the film recommended by the industry's selection panel as South Korea's entry for the fifth Asian Film

Festival, was boycotted by the MoE because it was deemed to be "too dark." The government replaced the film with the lighthearted crowd-pleaser *Hyperbolae of Youth*. The director of *Money* protested, posing a series of rhetorical questions: "Does it mean that we have to make only comedies and cheerful films? Do we need to show tall buildings and construction sites to be able to show our films abroad?"[80] Despite this cynical retort, which was one likely shared by critics and industry insiders who supported Kim's dystopic tale of poverty in the countryside, there was a broader tactical consensus among government bureaucrats and filmmakers, as Kim Ch'ŏng-gang notes, that cinema "had to serve the national function with images beneficial to the nation."[81] In the words of Kang Hyŏng-ok, the producer of *Three Women* (*Sam yŏsŏng*, 1959), "The function of cinema should be showing 'dreams' to the masses" rather than exposing reality as it is.[82]

Korean audiences at that time were apparently in agreement with this commercial view of cinema as an escapist medium. According to the Chungang University Film School's survey of 1,210 college students from eight different campuses conducted in July 1963, the three favorite movie genres were, in order of preference, the romance, the thriller, and the musical comedy. With the exception of Elia Kazan's *On the Waterfront* (1954), respondents' top ten favorite foreign films—*Ben Hur* (1959), *Splendor in the Grass* (1961), *From Here to Eternity* (1953), *The Bridge on the River Kwai* (1957), *Waterloo Bridge* (1940), *For Whom the Bell Tolls* (1943), *On the Waterfront*, *A Farewell to Arms* (1957), *Gone with the Wind* (1939), and *Back Street* (1961)—are romance/melodramas, literary adaptations, and humanistic war/religious epics rather than overtly political films. Although *The Stray Bullet* impressively took the number seven spot in a list of favorite domestic films, the top six—*The Houseguest and My Mother* (*Sarangbang sŏnnimgwa ŏmŏni*, 1961), *Prince Yŏnsan* (*Yŏnsangun*, 1961), *Only for You* (*Akkimŏpsi churyŏnda*, 1962), *Evergreen Tree* (*Sannoksu*, 1961), *Sŏng Ch'unhyang* (1961), and *Romance Papa* (*Romaensŭ p'ap'a*, 1960)—are more conservative films in terms of their aesthetics and morality. Reporting on the survey outcome, journalist Kim Chŏng-ok observed, "There is no doubt that these [top-ranked] Korean films are outstanding, but their morals are Confucian and premodern. On the one hand, it is positive for college students to yearn for the Korean sentiment, but on the other hand, these rankings reveal conversative thinking."[83] In an April 14, 1966, editorial contributed to *Tonga Ilbo*, a professor of French at Seoul National University, Chŏng Myŏng-hwan, identified Hollywood's happy ending as a cinematic convention that externalizes American citizens' optimism and youthfulness. Despite his personal aversion to such a formulaic device (which compelled him to leave theaters twenty minutes prior to the end to imagine his own narrative closure), the academic expressed envy and imagined "how happy [he] will be if the day comes when Korean films likewise project wholesome civic philosophy consistently whether by public pressure or voluntarily."[84] Chŏng's indirect criticism of South Korean cinema's defeatist, pessimistic tendency echoed the concerns of the state film regulators. Collective evidence cited above points to the conclusion that Yu's dark cinematic vision in *The Stray Bullet* was a view held only by a minority of filmgoers. For this reason, what is significant about the prolonged contention over the film's ban is not whether or not some government officials were paranoid about the line "*Kaja!*" or other elements allegedly expressing procommunist sympathies. Rather, the censorship debate over South Korea's equivalent to *Citizen Kane* (1941), in terms of both its canonical standing and its use of innovative film language to convey uncompromisingly dark content, is meaningful precisely because it fostered public dialogue. This public discourse concerned the definitions and different functions of national cinema, as both artistic expressions and social practices, at a momentous historical juncture of regime change and national reconstruction.

Of course, *The Stray Bullet* got the last laugh. It is now considered an indisputable masterpiece of realist cinema by critics, scholars, and journalists. It topped the Korean Motion Picture Promotion Corporation (now the Korean Film Council)'s 1995 list of the "10 Best Korean Films" as well as the 1998 *Chosŏn Ilbo* poll of the "50 Best Korean Films."[85] More recently, Yu's film shared the top honor along with Kim Ki-yŏng's thriller *The Housemaid* and Ha Kil-jong's comedy *The March of Fools* (*Pabodŭlŭi haengjin*, 1975) on the 2014 KOFA list of "100 Korean films." There is little doubt that debates surrounding the banning and unbanning *The Stray Bullet* in the early 1960s raised its cultural status as a brave film that challenged the military government using subversive politics and underlying social critiques. During the 1980s, Yu's personal copy of the film was circulated in college underground screenings organized by student activists when it was reevaluated and therefore canonized. From Na Un-gyu's *Arirang* (1926) to *The Stray Bullet*, Korean film historiography has tended to favor resistant artists and their politically provocative art. However, as Steven Chung suggests, "The basic idea that political subversion in film was possible in any given historical period, and further that such practices were matters of personal volition, both skews the historical record and misconstrues the processes of film authorship and production."[86] In the context of postwar Korea, one cannot fully understand or construct film history without reassessing censorship as a complex process of cultural negotiations where both state regulators and filmmakers played active roles in shaping the new narrative or sentiment of the nation in the contested arena of screen culture during the Cold War.

2

From *Blackboard Jungle* to *The Teahouse of the August Moon*

Censoring Hollywood
in Postcolonial Korea

On August 3, 1969, Glenn Ford arrived at Kimpo Airport along with his son Peter and a representative of Screen Ventures International, Anthony Ward. The Hollywood star and his companions were greeted by a delegation of the South Korean industry's top stars, including Shin Yŏng-gyun, Nam Chŏng-im, and Yun Chŏng-hŭi. In his father's biography *Glenn Ford, A Life*, Peter Ford recollects the trip:

> By August 1969 there was a serious film offer for my father to consider. Tony Ward in Screen Ventures International wanted my Dad to star in a film about the April 14, 1969, downing of an EC-121 Constellation, an unarmed American reconnaissance plane shot down by North Korea. . . . We went to Seoul, Korea, and Tokyo, Japan, supposedly on a fact-finding trip. I think Tony's main goal was to introduce Dad to some investors in the Orient who might bankroll his project. . . . It was edifying to experience the colorful Ginza shopping and entertainment district in Japan, as contrasted with the stark and rather depressing military complex that was Seoul at the time.[1]

Although Screen Ventures International's project never materialized, the preliminary visit presented a rare opportunity for Korean press members and fans to see a famous Hollywood star up close. Of the eighty films Ford had appeared in up to that point, ten (including *Blackboard Jungle* [1955], *Random!* [1956], *The Teahouse of the August Moon* [1956], and *Cimarron* [1960]) had been released in South Korea. During a press conference, the Canadian-born star confided that he had not seen any Korean films yet but expressed an interest in exploring coproduction opportunities with a local company and promoting international cultural exchange. He shared his belief in cinema's function as an "escape from reality" and the imperative to "transcend politics."[2] When the Korean press asked Ford about his personal favorites among his movies, the prolific actor named two Metro-Goldwyn-Mayer (MGM) films, *Blackboard Jungle* and *The Teahouse of the August Moon*, betraying blissful ignorance of the controversy these films had caused earlier in the East Asian country.

As Christina Klein points out, the United States government actively promoted American motion pictures in South Korea since 1945 "for both economic and ideological reasons." Klein elaborates this point, stating, "Always eager to penetrate foreign markets, Washington during the Cold War particularly valued the ability of films to convey the values of democracy, freedom, individualism, and capitalism."[3] The U.S. Army Military Government in Korea (USAMGK) and the Supreme Command of Allied Powers (SCAP) worked closely with the Motion Picture Export Association (MPEA), a centralized export cartel of oligopolistic eight major studios (Paramount, MGM, Twentieth Century-Fox, Warner Bros., RKO, Universal, Columbia, and United Artists), to ensure the unrestricted importation and distribution of American motion pictures in the region. In April 1946, the Seoul branch of the Central Motion Picture Exchange (CMPE), MPEA's outpost, was open to directly distributing Hollywood productions in the former Japanese colony. Occupation authorities wished to mobilize U.S.-produced films as key tools of the "reorientation program of the people in their occupied territories, in particular to disseminate positive images of America and American liberal democracy."[4] Brian Yecies and Ae-Gyung Shim argue, "While many CMPE films approximated this model, an equal number offered a different view of America: one that depicted opulence, feisty and independent female characters, unrestrained love-making, violent themes and an exotic cultural milieu that was both thrilling and dangerous.... This suggests that CMPE was keen to select sensational films that would bring both locals and Occupation troops to the cinemas in droves, without carefully distinguishing between these two audiences."[5] To the delight of State Department officials and USAMGK bureaucrats in Seoul, movie-struck Koreans proved to be avid consumers of all things Hollywood (and by extension, American culture). According to an American political advisor's February 1948 report to the State Department, the most frequently asked question that U.S. troops received from locals upon arriving in the occupied zone south of the thirty-eighth parallel was how Shirley Temple and Deanna Durbin were doing in Hollywood.[6] Between November 1945 and March 1948, 422 American feature films and 289 American newsreels, as opposed to 17 Korean features and 35 Korean newsreels, were screened under USAMGK occupation.[7]

The indiscriminate influx of Hollywood cinema within the liberated southern half of the peninsula understandably elicited nationalist responses from both intellectuals and local filmmakers as well as exhibitors. In an editorial that he contributed to the October 13, 1946, issue of *Kyŏnghyang Sinmun*, Yi T'ae-u criticized American films for "lacking poetry and imagination" and bewitching the public with "provocative eroticism" and illusionistic magic. The commentator warned the audience against uncritically accepting Hollywood supremacy to the extent that one might neglect to reflect on the nascent local film industry.[8] In February 1947, the CMPE's monopolistic demand that Korean theaters take five films (two A features, two B features, and one ten-chapter serial), which they would distribute in blocks and advance book fifty-two days of a three-month period (ninety days), caused uproar among local exhibitors. CMPE also forced the sale of newsreels (packaged with their features), whether they were screened or not. Newspaper editorials condemned the CMPE for its "imperialistic ambition to deteriorate Korean theater culture and reduce Korean theaters to markets of American movies."[9] The CMPE eventually conceded and lifted the required number of days to screen their products only after major Korean theaters boycotted all American films for three months (filling their programs with live theater performances). As imperialistic as it might have seemed to foreign interests, CMPE overseas operations were modeled after stateside block booking and blind bidding practices that the eight major studios had forced on unaffiliated independent theaters during the studio system era of mature oligopoly in the 1930s and 1940s. In the landmark Paramount Decree of 1948, the United States Supreme Court outlawed such practices because they violated the 1890 Sherman Antitrust Act.

After the end of USAMGK occupation, the new South Korean government of Syngman Rhee (Yi Sŭng-man) put restrictions on American film imports to protect the domestic industry. In 1949, the CMPE's direct distribution ceased for an extended period due to the new foreign currency regulation that prevented the foreign company from wiring profits to the U.S. headquarters. From February to September of that year, American films disappeared altogether from Korean screens and were replaced by French and British counterparts. In October, CMPE distribution resumed under the negotiated term that profits would be reinvested locally. With the outbreak of the Korean War in June 1950, the CMPE withdrew from the Korean market (where direct distribution of Hollywood studios would not resume until 1988). By the mid-1950s, thirty-seven local traders (such as Segi Corporation [Segi sangsa or Century Trading Company], Puli Trading, Korean Arts [Han'guk yesul], Kukdo Theater, Tongyang, Kyoryŏ, Namsŏng, and Namyang, among others) supplied foreign films to Korean theaters. In 1955, the Rhee administration announced that American motion pictures would receive preferential treatment in biannual selections of foreign films to import in accordance with the trade agreement between the United States and the Republic of Korea (ROK). There was speculation in the industry that Twentieth Century-Fox president Spyros Skouras's recent visit to Seoul, where the Hollywood executive met with the ROK president and cabinet officials, around the same time had something to do with this American film–first policy. In 1959, 160 American films were imported (as opposed to 2 British, 10 French, 9 Italian, and 15 West German). Out of 203 foreign feature films released in South Korea that year, 78 percent were American. Between 1960 and 1975, out of 1,028 foreign films imported to South Korea, approximately 63 percent (652) were American.[10] Although annual statistics (import numbers by countries of origin) prior to 1959 are not available, it can safely be assumed that American films dominated Korean screens throughout the 1950s.

Perhaps Korean audiences' insatiable appetite for Hollywood was as much responsible as U.S. trade pressure and ROK compliance for continued American domination on Korean screens after the departure of the USAMGK. In his autobiographical novel entitled *The Life and Death of Hollywood Kid* (*Hŏlliiudŭ k'idŭŭi saengae*, 1992), renowned journalist-novelist Ahn Junghyo (An Chŏnghyo) describes intense Hollywoodphilia in postwar South Korea: "We chased dreams and escaped the sorrows of our ugly life through the films.... For us, going to the movies was a religious act, like going to Mass.... Absorbing diverse models of life manufactured in Hollywood ... we came to believe that the wide plains of the American West were our beautiful, lost home from some previous life. Denying our poverty-stricken home and dirty streets, we came to mistake the screen world as our idealized reality."[11] If teen boys in the 1950s (contemporaries of Ahn, who was born in 1941) imagined themselves as cowboys riding the high plains and cavalry soldiers occupying forts throughout the Wild West, city girls vicariously lived through the romantic escapades of Audrey Hepburn, Grace Kelly, Marilyn Monroe, Elizabeth Taylor, and other glamorous women while imitating the latter's hairstyles and fashion and buying American home appliances. As Yi Sŏn-mi points out, Korean women in the 1950s were "hailed as new subjects of consumerism in a capitalistic cultural environment mediated through the fantasies of American cinema."[12] Beyond simply consuming images and products, Yi notes, female audiences desired to be like American heroines onscreen and dreamed of living in a more egalitarian, affluent, and modernized society.[13]

In other words, as Hollywood's loyal consumers, Korean audiences were practitioners of what Klein calls "Cold War cosmopolitanism ... a *cultural style* [that] entailed the appropriation and indigenization of a range of stylistic elements derived from Western models ... a distinctly Free Asian aesthetic, showcasing the lifestyles that capitalist democracy promised to make possible."[14] According to Klein, proponents of Cold War cosmopolitanism "embraced the project of Western-style modernization optimistically and projected a vision of

South Korea moving boldly into the future [as] a full and equal participant" in the international network of the Free World.[15] Such a cosmopolitan celebration of Pax Americana, of course, hinged upon a neocolonial situation described by historian Bruce Cumings in the following way: "American influence in the South had reached new heights by 1950.... Americans kept the government, the army, the economy, the railroads, the airports, the mines, and the factories going, supplying money, electricity, expertise, and psychological succor.... At this time South Korea was getting more than $100 million a year from the United States most of it in the form of outright grants (The entire southern national budget for 1951 was $120 million)."[16] Therefore, it should not come as a surprise that South Koreans selectively accepted particular kinds of Hollywood cinema that supported utopian images of the United States as their aspirational country. According to Yi, Western auteur John Ford, best known for the many films he directed that starred John Wayne (e.g., *Stagecoach* [1939] and *The Searchers* [1956]), "was popular in both the United States and South Korea. But his critically acclaimed masterpiece *The Grapes of Wrath* was not released in South Korea." The main reason is that Ford's 1940 drama, an adaptation of John Steinbeck's novel of the same title, could be interpreted as being "critical of American society." In Yi's words, Hollywood motion pictures that showed "dark sides of [American] society and poverty were rejected by Korean audiences."[17]

Richard Brooks's *Blackboard Jungle* was one of those rare films about the seedier side of American society that was admitted to South Korea, though its release was met with significant resistance. The film was initially imported by Segi Corporation in 1960 under the Korean title "Violent Classroom" (*P'ongnyŏk kyosil*). The film's sensational depiction of North Manual Trades, an inner-city vocational high school in which teachers are routinely harassed, disrespected, and physically attacked by juvenile delinquents and teen gangs, sounded alarms across various sectors of Korean society, including those in which public educators and government officials figured prominently. As a result, its exhibition was suspended in July 1961. After several recensorship meetings in January and April of 1962, the ban was lifted in May and the film was re-released under the original title *Blackboard Jungle* that month. In the following pages, I offer a comparative analysis of the censorship file of the Korean Ministry of Public Information (MPI: Kongbobu) alongside the Motion Picture Association of America (MPAA)'s Production Code Administration (PCA) file. While Korean state censors and Hollywood's internal censors shared similar concerns over universal regulatory priorities such as sexuality and violence, the MPI file contains a document that demonstrates a decidedly local interpretation of MGM's film as a "purification" (*chŏnghwa*) story that echoes the stated aims of Park Chung Hee (Pak Chŏng-hŭi)'s new military government that came to power with the May 16 coup in 1961.

The second case study in this chapter—Daniel Mann's *The Teahouse of the August Moon* (another Segi Corporation import)—likewise demonstrates the role of postcolonial censorship debates as a generator of alternative meanings for Hollywood's lavish Orientalist productions. Ironically, MGM's painstaking efforts to depict Japan and its culture authentically backfired in South Korea whose national censors restricted the film under the unique regulatory category of *waesaek* (Japanese color). After its exhibition permit application was denied in November 1962 (on account of it being a *waesaek* movie showcasing the talents of several Japanese cast members), the suspension was lifted in August 1963, two years prior to the signing of the Treaty on Basic Relations between Japan and the ROK (on June 22, 1965), at a time of increased cultural exchange between the two countries. Drawing upon both archival evidence and press discourse analysis, I argue that *The Teahouse of the August Moon* functioned as a significant political symbol for nationalist producers and critics, a means through which to test the state's commitment to protecting the Korean film industry under the perceived threat of Japanese cultural invasion ahead of diplomatic normalization. Ultimately, the crisis was resolved when the interests of all three branches of the Korean motion picture trade (production, distribution, and exhibition) aligned in favor of the film's release and the MPI's own impulse to protect the industry outweighed any qualms there might have been (growing out of anti-Japanese public opinion).

Censorship History of *Blackboard Jungle* in the United States and Other Countries

Blackboard Jungle came out of the decade of paranoia and panic in McCarthy-era America. Along with what Robert G. Lee calls the "three specters [that] haunted Cold War America in the 1950s: the red menace of communism, the black menace of racial mixing, and the white menace of homosexuality,"[18] the menace of juvenile delinquency emerged as a major social problem. Throughout the decade, the Federal Bureau of Investigation (FBI) reported skyrocketing numbers of juvenile arrests. The FBI's 1959 crime report announced that "juvenile court cases had increased 220% from 1941 to 1957."[19] More specifically, the FBI announced that "51 percent of all arrests for crimes against property in the United States [in 1954] were of persons under twenty-one."[20] The Senate Subcommittee on Juvenile Delinquency was formed in 1953 to address these social concerns. In a series of televised congressional hearings in 1954 and 1955, the committee led by Tennessee senator Estes Kefauver directed its investigation at negative effects of mass media in triggering teen violence and antisocial deviance. In particular, crime and horror comic books (dubbed in the subcommittee's report as "short courses in murder, mayhem, robbery") and "excessive brutality, sadism, and illicit sexual behavior in motion pictures" were named by field experts (who testified in front of a congressional panel) as culprits for the increased number of crimes committed by young people.[21] Fredric Wertham, a German-born, New York–based psychiatrist and author of *Seduction of the Innocent* (1954), was the star witness for a 1954 hearing on comic books (which led to the formation of the Comic Code Authority and the industry's self-regulation, which in some respects was modeled after the MPAA's Production Code system). In June 1955 hearings on motion pictures, collective testimonies—both oral and written— by medical experts of clinical psychology proved to be damning. Frederick J. Hacker, a member of the Medical Correctional Association, vouched that "the description of violence in the movies may just act as a trigger mechanism and not be an essential cause. But we certainly do see in our clinical practice, without a question of a doubt, innumerable crimes are distinctly influenced in their conception, in their perpetration and even in some details by certain models that were gained by the mass media of communication—movies, television, comic books, etc." James L. McCartney similarly reported, "For several years, I was director of classification for the New York State Department of Correction, and during those years as a psychiatrist, I examined upward of 10,000 juvenile delinquents.... One cannot escape the conclusion that although there are many factors which influence the formation of personality, the printed page, movies, and television very definitely have an effect which is not at all healthy."[22]

From Capitol Hill to Main Street, USA, the problem of juvenile delinquency was turning into as a midcentury national obsession, gaining broad cross-media exposure as a moral panic in newspaper editorials, magazine articles, books, radio and television serials, newsreels, and motion pictures. The entire special issue of New York's *Daily News* dated March 5, 1954, was devoted to the topic of juvenile delinquency. Under the front-page headline "Crime Perils City Schools: Teachers Urge Mayor to Act," some of the shocking reports were as follows: "School lavatories have become laboratories of crime where students gamble, smoke, drink, deal in dope in a sort of clubroom atmosphere"; "In some schools, teachers estimate fully half of the pupils carry pushbutton switchblades or homemade zipguns"; and "In all parts of the city, public school teachers are being threatened and beaten, students are stabbed, and shaken down, and girls attacked, while the seriousness of the situation is suppressed by an educational dynasty apparently anxious to keep the complete picture of disorder from the taxpayers."[23] In addition to big studio fare such as Columbia's *The Wild One* (1953), MGM's *Blackboard Jungle*, and Warner Bros.'s *Rebel without a Cause* (1955), over sixty low-budget B pictures about juvenile delinquents were produced throughout the 1950s. This attests not only to the significance of juvenile delinquency as a headline-grabbing social phenomenon but also to the rise of teen audiences as Hollywood's newest loyal demographic. As Yannis Tzioumakis observes, "Unlike the rest of the potential film audience, who were deserting movie-going for other forms of cultural and recreational activities, teenagers emerged as the most frequent cinema-goers, refusing to follow the trends established by older generations."[24]

Teens reportedly made up 75 percent of *Blackboard Jungle*'s patronage during its theatrical run, worrying several theater owners who were growing increasingly concerned about disorderly behavior such as dancing in the aisles to the title song "Rock around the Clock" during the film's opening and closing credits.[25] In order to exploit the media buzz following the congressional hearings of 1954, MGM rushed the film through production within three months and released it in March 1955, well in advance of the planned schedule and three months prior to motion picture hearings. With a ballyhoo-style flair that would become a more glaringly obvious part of teenpics and exploitation cinema throughout the latter half of that decade, publicity taglines read "A drama of teenage terror" and "They turned a school into a jungle."[26] In the publicity brochure, the studio foregrounded sensationalistic statistics, capitalizing on public fears for the sake of box-office gains, stating, "The FBI's report covering 1953, from statistics gathered in more than 1,000 cities, disclosed that persons under 18 committed 53.6 percent of all car thefts, 49.3 percent of all burglaries, 18 percent of all robberies and 16.2 percent of all rapes."[27]

A social-problem film like *Blackboard Jungle*, in which a female teacher is nearly raped by a student in the library and her male colleague is threatened by a doped pocketknife-wielding hoodlum in the classroom, was not a typical release for MGM. With the motto "more stars than there are in heaven," MGM had been the most profitable and most politically conversative studio a decade earlier, earning a reputation (that stretched back even earlier) for producing glamorous star vehicles, extravagant musicals, and all-American franchises like the "Andy Hardy" series under staunch Republican Louis B. Mayer's leadership from 1924 to 1951. After his forced retirement, Mayer was replaced by his more liberal successor, Dore Schary, who had several socially conscious "message pictures" such as *Boys Town* (1939), *Crossfire* (1947) and *Bad Day at Black Rock* (1955) under his writer/producer belt. After purchasing the rights to Evan Hunter's novel *Blackboard Jungle* (based loosely on the author's substitute teaching experience at the Bronx Vocational High School) and hiring writer-director Richard Brooks to adapt it, Schary was approached by several industry leaders, including Paramount executive Y. Frank Freeman and MPAA president Eric Johnston, who unsuccessfully attempted to persuade him to drop the project. His own boss in New York, MGM president Nicholas Schenk, was concerned about the prospect of eliciting political scrutiny over a potentially communist slant in the controversial source material, which was critical of contemporary American society.

In the "Making of *Blackboard Jungle*" panel that reunited surviving cast and crew members (producer Pandro S. Berman, Brooks, Ford, Anne Francis, and Paul Mazursky among others) at the Samuel Goldwyn Theater of the Academy of Motion Picture Arts and Sciences on January 10, 1983, Berman recalled, "The New York office (of MGM) took a dim view of the project. They sent for me to come to New York and meet with the department heads for the purpose of dissuading me from doing it. They thought it was an outrage that America was exposing our own weaknesses on the screen."[28] Given the fact that two House Committee on Un-American Activities (HUAC) investigations of communist infiltration in Hollywood (first in 1947 and then from 1951 to 1952) left more than 300 creative personnel blacklisted for alleged "red" sympathies, the MGM executives' misgivings were not groundless. To Schary's relief, Schenk's conservative instincts were overcome by a projected profit of $9–10 million with an investment of under $1.2 million.[29] Fulfilling those promised figures, *Blackboard Jungle* went on to become MGM's most profitable film of 1955. During the aforementioned panel, however, Brooks remembered Schenk's nervousness even after greenlighting the project. The director and the producer had to talk the executive out of forcing them to insert "a similar classroom scene in Moscow" to prove their nonpartisan view of the Cold War.[30]

Paralleling MGM's regime change and liberalization from the Mayer era to the Schary era, Hollywood's internal regulation agency, the PCA, was undergoing a similar transformation during *Blackboard Jungle*'s production. In 1954, Joseph I. Breen, a former journalist and devout Irish Catholic, retired, bringing an end to his three-decade rein as the industry's chief censor who guided the morality of American cinema. He was succeeded by the PCA's second-in-command Geoffrey Shurlock, who, as Robert Sklar tells it, was "a Briton who took the iconoclastic view that the code should not stand in the way of scenes depicting real human behavior on the screen, if they were not gross or offensive to audiences."[31] Schary's first correspondence with the PCA was with Breen shortly before the latter's exit. In his September 20, 1954, letter to the MGM production head after lengthy script review, the outgoing chief first warns that "there are a number of elements in this story which . . . could not be approved." In particular, the industry censor opposed the "unsavory" storyline of "a high school boy criminally assaulting" Lois Hammond (Margaret Hayes), a rookie teacher, which is "unsuited for inclusion in that type of entertainment envisioned as being acceptable for general patronage." Second, Breen complains about the script's "over-all tone of viciousness and brutality which . . . exceeds the limits of acceptability from the Code standpoint." Singled out is a back-alley scene in which Richard Dadier (Glenn Ford), a Navy veteran and English teacher, and his buddy and math teacher Josh Edwards (Richard Kiley) get ambushed by a gang led by Artie West (Vic Morrow), an irredeemable delinquent. The students beat both teachers in revenge for their classmate's arrest for Hammond's sexual assault. Lastly, the PCA head notes that numerous uses of profanity such as "damn" and "hell" are unacceptable.[32]

The second correspondence between the self-regulatory agency and the studio in the following month was overseen by Shurlock. In his October 22 letter to Schary, the PCA's new head reiterates his predecessor's concerns in greater detail. As for the rape scene, Shurlock comments, "The entire sequence of the boy attacking Miss Hammond will have to be handled with extreme care to avoid offensive sex-suggestiveness. This action should not be handled so as to suggest an attempted rape, but rather the boy is merely attempting to kiss the woman. There should, of course, be no unacceptable exposure of her body as a result of her torn clothing."[33] In the finished film, it is clear that the action witnessed and interrupted by Dadier is a criminal sexual attack as suggested by a stray high heel in front of the library, the victim's scream, her torn top and disheveled hair, and the attacker's desperate escape attempt (by diving headlong into the closed window). In fact, the scene is a focal point of the film's advertising. Its theatrical poster foregrounds the terrified face of a middle-aged woman with exposed shoulders who covers her mouth with one hand and holds on to a bookshelf with another while being approached by an ominous shadowy male figure in silhouette. The copy reads, "The most startling picture in years!" The shameless marketing angle of "rape sells" is a telltale sign that Schary had no intention of exercising care and discretion despite repeated pressure from both Breen and Shurlock.

As for the alley attack scene, Shurlock insisted that "the action of boys attacking Rick and Josh appears to be excessively brutal both in quantity and quality of detail. Specifically, we have in mind the action of two boys holding Josh against the wall while a third one beats him. Staging of this action should be done more by suggestion than by actually photographing, and specifically, there should be no kicking or kneeing."[34] In the finished film, this shot of the math teacher pinned against the wall and punched in his abdomen is more than suggested and shown fleetingly twice, although fast cutting, the upbeat jazz soundtrack, and the low-key lighting of the scene soften the brutality and shock to a certain degree. In addition, the new PCA chief objected to uses of ethnic slurs such as "dago" and "pope-lovers" in the script, reminding Schary that such expressions "will undoubtedly give extreme offense to many people in the audience." Shurlock also cautioned against the sexual suggestiveness of showing spinster Hammond's flirtation with a married man, Dadier, in a scene where the two are left alone in school after extracurricular activities of Christmas show rehearsals.[35] One of the PCA's internal memos, dated February 7, 1955, summarizes a phone conversation between Eugene "Doc" Dougherty, Shurlock's assistant, and Robert Vogel, an MGM representative, in which the studio agreed to make requested deletions and edits as preconditions for a certificate of approval (without which MPAA members would not have been able to distribute or exhibit their films in first-run theaters). The PCA's list of demanded cuts or edits included the following: a few utterances of "hell" and "damn" should be eliminated; a shot of the student ripping Hammond's suit jacket and exposing her bosom should be eliminated; the alley attack scene should be reduced; and a shot depicting a student hoodlum wrapping a chain around his hand before hijacking a newspaper delivery truck should be eliminated.[36] It is safe to say that MGM passed in-house regulation with much of the controversial material left intact save for a few deletions of profanity and modest edits of the most violent scenes. As Shurlock admitted years later, "I was confronted with a situation that could make a joke of the censorship code sections on violence and brutality.... If I tried to block the movie solely because it dealt with juvenile delinquency, I would be saying that movies must not deal with contemporary problems. And yet, juvenile delinquents act brutally and talk coarsely. So I asked that brutality be toned down and the language be made less offensive. That was all I could ask for."[37]

After passing the stage of preemptive internal regulation relatively unscathed, the studio faced uphill battles with external censorship boards, both domestic and foreign. Before its operations were ruled unconstitutional in 1956 by the state court, the Pennsylvania State Board of Censors approved *Blackboard Jungle* with a provisional sheet dated March 31, 1955. The state censor warned MGM, "In the face of complete opposition on the part of officials of the Public and Parochial School Systems, the City Police, the Clergy, the Crime Prevention Association, and the Council of Churches, and because of certain legal limitations, we reluctantly issue a Seal of Approval on the film *Blackboard Jungle*. We call your attention to the Certificate of Approval which carries 'THE BOARD RESERVES THE RIGHT TO REVOKE THIS CERTIFICATE,' and advise that we will invoke this right if any instance directly connected to this film is reported."[38] In its reference to "legal limitations," the Pennsylvania board was alluding to the Supreme Court's 1952 "Miracle Decision" (*Joseph Burstyn, Inc. v. Wilson*, 343 U.S. 495), which granted First Amendment protection to motion pictures, reversing its 1915 *Mutual Film Corporation v. Ohio* ruling thirty-seven years later. As pointed out by Jack C. Ellis and Virginia Wright Wexman, "The 1952 Court did not rule on constitutionality of film censorship as such [but] simply stated that 'sacrilege,' particularly one faith's perception of it, was not sufficient grounds" for the New York Board of Regents' revoking the license of Roberto Rossellini's short film *The Miracle* (*Il miracolo*, 1948). Regardless, the landmark ruling opened the floodgate of anticensorship lawsuits in lower courts in which the position of the United States's highest court regarding free speech in motion pictures was upheld and reaffirmed. In other words, shocking expressions in *Blackboard Jungle* were indirectly protected under the First Amendment, at least in the U.S. context, despite universal opposition they provoked from nearly all key sectors of public communities (e.g., education, religion, public safety) in Pennsylvania.

Certain municipal censors were not as accommodating as the Pennsylvania state board. The Milwaukee City Motion Picture Commission threatened to revoke the operating license of Towne and Metro theaters unless cuts of objectionable scenes to *Blackboard Jungle* were made (MGM complied and made the four demanded cuts to appease the municipal censor). Police Inspector Hubert E. Dax was quoted as saying, "I don't like this film. It is grossly exaggerated."[39] Among the most outraged (and draconian) of local censors was Lloyd T. Binford, the insurance executive–turned–censor of Memphis who was notorious for banning films for a variety of capricious reasons—from Ingrid Bergman's out-of-wedlock pregnancy and Charlie Chaplin's alleged communist sympathies to depictions of train robberies in Westerns and themes of integration in comedies—during his long tenure from 1927 to 1955. The octogenarian chairman of the Memphis Board of Censors condemned *Blackboard Jungle* as "the vilest picture [he had] seen in 26 years as a censor" before "binfordizing" (an industry shorthand for stringent censorship or the outright banning of motion pictures) it. Afraid of a legal challenge, the mayor quickly reversed the ban but restricted screenings "for adults only." Teens responded by flocking to theaters in West Memphis outside of the city jurisdiction. The same pattern ensued when another city in the Deep South, Atlanta, banned the film. As observed by Jerold Simmons, "Suburban theaters beyond the ban reaped the benefit until a federal district judge overruled the censor."[40] Georgia governor Ernest Vandiver had a bigger fight than preventing his state's teenagers from seeing MGM's motion picture. In his 1960 address to state legislators, the segregationist governor cited the film set in an integrated northern school (of an unnamed city) as a cautionary tale of what would happen to Georgia's schools should they comply with the Supreme Court's 1954 *Brown v. Board of Education* ruling. Vandiver ominously predicted the proliferation of perilous situations laden with "switchblade knives, marijuana, stabbings, rapes, violence and blackboard jungles" across the South.[41]

Conservative southern backlash was not the only woe that befell the controversial motion picture. Many northern intellectuals and educators were also against it. *New York Times* film critic Bosley Crowther was one such detractor. In his March 27, 1955, contribution to the newspaper, he questions the film's authenticity, asking, "Is it a true and valid picture of conditions of any schools today? . . . Indeed, are there any schools where pupils are so arrogant and out-of-hand, so collectively devoted to disorder, as are the hoodlums in this film?" The movie critic contends that if the answer is no, *Blackboard Jungle* is "irresponsible and fraught with peril" despite the "most sincere intent of causing a 'public awareness' of problems and inadequacies in schools."[42] Crowther is particularly concerned that MGM's top grosser will negatively affect the career prospects for vocational school graduates and recruitment efforts for teachers in city schools, not to mention causing imitative acts of recalcitrant behavior among some impressionable youngsters. A disturbed Schary wrote to the journalist personally, arguing, "If *Blackboard Jungle* is seen by enough people it will eventually provoke and arouse committees and school boards to do something progressive and courageous about the problems of juvenile delinquency, rather than keep it in the area of forum discussions."[43]

Despite the studio chief's rebuttal, Crowther's criticism was shared by several readers who wrote to the *New York Times* to support his opinion piece. Edward N. Wallen, principal of Samuel Gompers Vocational and Technical High School in Bronx, was in full agreement, stating, "We educators . . . have been disturbed by the picture's exaggeration and its plausible effects upon the public attitude toward the students and teachers." Based on his thirty-year teaching career, the principal also answered Crowther's questions about the film's credibility with an "empathic NO," elaborating, "I have worked for the New York City School system since 1925. In that time I of course have seen some troublemaking students, but nothing remotely resembling the type of persons Evan Hunter has written about."[44] In his July 1955 interview with the trade paper *Variety*, Chicago's assistant superintendent of schools, Hobart H. Sommers, reiterated Crowther's claims about the film's potential harm (encouraging delinquency, perpetuating the damaging stereotypes of trade schools, and worsening a shortage of teachers), adding an international perspective by noting, "if shown overseas, it does irreparable harm to the United States in foreign eyes. Believe me, if the teaching profession were as well organized as the Catholic Church, the picture would have never reached the screen."[45]

Sommers was not alone in worrying about U.S. national prestige being undermined by *Blackboard Jungle*. In his review of an early script, Dave Blum, an executive at MGM's parent company Loew's Incorporated, sent a similar warning to his boss Arthur Loew, president of Loew's International. Concerned about the finished picture's potential to do a disservice to the nation by furthering communist propaganda, Loew's executive complained about the story's setting of an American school where "pupils, apparently without exception, are guilty of every conceivable crime ... [and] teachers are either helpless to combat the situation, or inefficient."[46] He further lobbied Robert Vogel, an MGM publicist, recommending an insertion of exploratory information such as "the present wave of unruly children is found in all countries," drawing special attention to juvenile delinquency problems in Russia.[47] After reviewing a rough cut, Schary brushed aside Blum's misgivings, assuring him that *Blackboard Jungle* is "an important emotional lift [and] a portrait of democracy at work" that demonstrates that social ills can be eliminated "with patience ... courage and understanding" exemplified by the all-American ex-serviceman hero.[48] As a guide to fend off local censorship objections, Loew's International prepared a special manual entitled "*Blackboard Jungle*: A Sociological Study and Box-Office Production Extraordinary and Its Relationship to Censorship" (dated October 17, 1955) and addressed to MGM managers abroad. Claiming *Blackboard Jungle* to be "a serious study of a major sociological problem of today's world ... a testament to the courage and liberty of cinematography [and] a tribute to the teaching profession," the literature denounces any attempt by censors to desecrate it with "careless shears."[49] Citing accolades of the foreign press from *The Sunday Express* of London to *Weekly Asahi* of Tokyo,[50] the booklet goes on to attack misguided champions of the film's suppression, who were called out for disregarding "the basic difference between free countries eager to proclaim its glories but not adverse to admitting the less desirable aspects of their culture, and Iron Curtain countries, whose productions ... 'show only happy, smiling peasants.'"[51]

Such extraordinary defensive efforts inversely belie the extent of the troubles that the controversial motion picture encountered in the foreign markets. Unfortunately, for Schary, neither State Department employees nor foreign audiences bought his self-serving view that a "self-critical" film such as *Blackboard Jungle* could contrarily serve as "enormous anti-communist propaganda" by demonstrating that "there is nothing wrong with a country that can make pictures examining some of its own problems."[52] In August 1955, U.S. Ambassador to Italy Clare Boothe Luce pressured organizers of the Venice International Film Festival to pull *Blackboard Jungle* from the official competition by refusing to attend a showing of the film, which she felt presented her country in an unfavorable light. Out of diplomatic courtesy, Italian authorities replaced the juvenile delinquent flick with *Interrupted Melody* (1955), an MGM musical biopic starring Eleanor Parker as polio-afflicted opera star Marjorie Lawrence and Glenn Ford as her doctor husband who helps to cure her. The incident drew considerable controversy of its own after Loew denounced Luce's action as "unwarranted personal censorship at the hands of our diplomatic representatives" and filed "a vigorous protest" with Secretary of State John Foster Dulles.[53] The State Department defended the ambassador and asserted that "MGM was having a field day for its own publicity."[54] According to the MGM interoffice communication sent to Schary, Berman, and Brooks (dated October 4, 1955), Eddie O'Connor, the MGM manager in Japan, enthusiastically exclaimed in his cable, "Long live Clare Luce. Vive le controversy. Banzai," crediting the Venice scandal for the film's strong box-office showings in Tokyo and other Japanese cities. The studio even attributed its passing without cuts by conservative Asian censors in Thailand and Hong Kong to the "Luce uproar."[55]

MGM did make a token effort to mitigate potential damage to the prestige of the U.S. educational system abroad by adding a foreword specifically designed for export prints. The foreword read, "We, in the United States, are fortunate to have a school system that is a tribute to our communities and to our faith in American youth. Today we are concerned with juvenile delinquency—its causes—and its effects. We are especially concerned when this delinquency boils over into our schools. The scenes and incidents depicted here are fictional. However, we believe that public awareness is a first step toward a remedy for any problem. It is in this spirit and with this faith that *Blackboard Jungle* was produced."[56] However, as pointed out by a trade commentor writing for *Variety*, "a foreword can hardly be expected to counterbalance the dramatic impression left by a film such as *Jungle* and that audiences abroad have a tendency to generalize, particularly if scenes in a film coincide with preconceived notions they may already hold of life in this country."[57] On January 19, 1956, Darryl F. Zanuck of Twentieth Century-Fox wrote to Schary, notifying his counterpart at MGM that leading left-wing or communist French newspapers such as *L'Humanité* "gave a big splurge to [*Blackboard Jungle*] on four consecutive days and they went as far as to indicate that U.S. State Department had insisted on the apologetic foreword." Regretting his own decision to distribute Fox's social-problem films such as *The Grapes of Wrath*, *Pinky* (1949), and *No Way Out* (1950) in Europe where communists exploited them as anti-American propaganda, Zanuck opined that "it would have been no great sacrifice on the part of MGM to have withheld the picture from foreign distribution."[58] The *Blackboard Jungle* controversy renewed an old debate whether or not "the industry, in cooperation with the U.S. State Dept., should voluntarily weed out and nix for export certain films which tend to show the U.S. in a bad light,"[59] when the issue of national reputation had become a major battleground for the Cold War. This, of course, was not a realistic expectation, given the primary purpose and utility of American motion pictures as profit-maximizing entertainment. While not denying such a commercial reality, proponents of free trade typically justified exporting a film like *Blackboard Jungle* with the argument that "even if a picture contains negative elements about American life, this in itself is a plus factor in foreign countries where audiences are bound to appreciate the American capacity for self-criticism."[60]

The international reception history of *Blackboard Jungle* proves that priorities of foreign audiences were elsewhere. As Adam Golub assesses, "In many countries around the world, MGM's 'portrait of democracy' was received more as a "portrait of delinquency' that threatened to corrupt children and undermine public order."[61] On March 24, 1955, the British Board of Film Censors (BBFC) informed MGM that *Blackboard Jungle* had failed to pass censorship review for its depiction of "irresponsible juvenile behavior... in scenes of unbridled, revolting hooliganism." The board felt that such a "spectacle of youth out of... control" was not counteracted by "moral values [that are] sufficiently strong and powerful." The BBFC further expressed their conviction that MGM's picture would "provoke the strongest criticism from [British] parents and all citizens concerned with the welfare of our young people, and would also have the most damaging and harmful effect on such young people, particularly those between the ages of 16 and 18, who even under an 'X' certificate, would be able to see the film."[62] After receiving MGM's appeal for reconsideration, the BBFC reviewed *Blackboard Jungle* for the fourth time in July 1955, only to stand by its earlier decision. Pressured by the American studio's persistent protests, however, the board offered to examine a cut version with "the most objectionable features of the story" removed in order to "reach... a conclusion more satisfactory" to both parties.[63] Throughout months-long negotiations with the BBFC, MGM representatives advocated the British public's right to see "a serious film of this kind" without its impact being damaged by drastic cuts (they were apparently prepared to "accept cuts [but] not an emasculated version of the film").[64] Furthermore, they saw the BBFC's outright rejection of *Blackboard Jungle* as unjust and inconsistent with the standards of other boards in the British Commonwealth (which passed the film with cuts or age restrictions). Ultimately, the American studio bowed to the British censor's authority by making five-minute cuts of various scenes that the BBFC suggested for the purpose of taming sexuality, violence, and language within the X criteria.[65] The recut version was released in Great Britain with an X certificate.[66]

The United Kingdom was not the only Commonwealth territory where *Blackboard Jungle* encountered censorship problems: it was banned in Alberta (Canada) and India. In Australia, it was extensively cut with most of the rape and alleyway attack scenes gone. In Toronto, women's organizations and city government members were agitated by Canadian teens applauding violent scenes (such as a climactic classroom confrontation in which West, under the influence of drugs, pulls a switchblade on Dadier, telling him to "go to hell"). Concerned parents and local politicians lobbied the Ontario Board of Film Censors (which placed the film in the "Adult Category"), calling for a province-wide ban. In his May 1955 interview with *Variety*, William Dennison, a Toronto alderman, made the following criticism: "Hollywood has succeeded, as usual, in glorifying in the minds of teenagers just the things it pretends to attack.... there is no good in glorifying the classroom development of criminal tendencies." Dennison also reported that the film's contrived foreword made good-humored Canadian audiences laugh rather than respecting the U.S. "capacity for self-criticism" as homegrown defenders expected of foreign audiences.[67] Dennison's view was shared by an American father and Hollywood producer, Ray Stark, who, in his congratulatory letter to Brooks, shared his own parental concern despite the film's artistic merits, "I cannot tell you what.... [trouble] this picture has been for not only my kids but all the kids in the neighborhood. If there ever was a blueprint for making kids obstreperous, this is it and I just hope it will make the studios realize one of these days how necessary it is to have an adult rating placed on pictures."[68]

In Japan, the Motion Picture Code of Ethics Committee or Eirin (founded in 1949 and modeled after the MPAA's self-regulatory system), like its British counterpart, believed the film was harmful to their nation's youth. However, unlike the BBFC, the Japanese committee was not free to reject American motion pictures, due to an unexpired occupation policy that put export selection power in the hands of Hollywood studios. As such, the *Blackboard Jungle* controversy in Japan was politicized differently than in other countries, as a single film was a much larger symbol that "reinforced the image of an unyielding, delinquent American culture that would not fully recognize Japan's independence" despite the official end of SCAP occupation in 1952.[69] Locally, the Kanagawa Prefecture barred admissions of minors to theaters showing the MGM film, while the Chiba Prefecture Association of Motion Picture Theatre Owners refused to distribute it. Parent-teacher organizations in Fukuoka, Kyushu, and Utsunomiya lobbied their local officials to ban the film in their cities.[70] As observed by Golub, Japanese reception of the MGM film was "transnationally mediated by local discourses about juvenile behavior, concerns about the corrupting effects of American popular culture, and resentment of lingering policies from the U.S. occupation."[71]

FIGURE 2.1 Canadian parents' organizations lobbied to ban MGM's *Blackboard Jungle* (1955) after witnessing their teens rooting for Artie West (Vic Morrow: left), an unredeemable juvenile delinquent who curses and pulls a switchblade on the all-American hero Richard Dadier (Glenn Ford: right).

A Story of Purification: Korean Film Censors as Interpreters of Hollywood Texts

Examining the MPI film censorship file on *Blackboard Jungle* (available at the Korean Film Archive [KOFA: Han'gukyŏngsang charyŏwŏn]), along with the Korean press discourse from a cross-cultural perspective, offers us an opportunity not only to expand previous scholarship on the censorship history of the MGM film but also to conceptualize international censors as adaptive local audiences who reinterpret Hollywood texts within their own unique cultural contexts. Although *Blackboard Jungle* had already encountered many problems with local, state, or national censors, not to mention parents and educators, inside and outside of the United States, there was an additional reason for Korean state censors to oppose the motion picture's distribution. Unlike Hollywood's Production Code, which was in effect from 1930 to 1968 (and which was segmented into categories related to sex, vulgarity, obscenity, profanity, costumes, dances, religion, locations, national feelings, and titles), Korean film regulation codes had a separate clause about education.

Five years prior to the proclamation of the Korean Motion Picture Law's enforcement regulations (*sihaenggyuch'ik*) in July 1962, which first legalized the ROK's motion picture censorship, the Ministry of Education (MoE: Mungyobu) enacted public performance censorship bylaws (*kongyŏnmul kyŏmyŏlsech'ik*) for both motion pictures and stage plays. This most detailed set of formalized regulatory rules in Korean modern history (divided into six areas of nation/law, religion/education, public morals, sex, cruelty, and others) was created primarily to restrict undesirable foreign films and protect a nascent domestic film industry.[72] Since the ROK government was pressured by trade associations to curb CMPE's monopolistic dominance in the market, it would have been a logical response to strengthen the censorship process, targeting morally objectionable foreign films while maintaining preferential accommodations for motion pictures from the United States for diplomatic reasons. Under the religion and education section, the 1957 bylaws prohibited deliberately mocking or insulting the democratic educational system or educators and other content that might hinder the edification and guidance of adolescents. This clause was rephrased in the 1962 law's enforcement regulations as a prohibition against "mocking or insulting educators under the democratic system." Although Shurlock blamed *Blackboard Jungle* for making "a joke of the censorship code sections on violence and brutality" more generally, Korean regulators must have had more culturally specific concerns about the representation of educators and the educational system that were outside of the PCA's purview in the United States.

In July 1960, foreign film distributor Segi Corporation signed a contract with MGM to distribute *Blackboard Jungle* in South Korea for a period of five years. On August 24, 1960, the MoE recommended the importation based on a screenplay synopsis (included in the censorship file) that shamelessly misrepresented the film's plot. According to this fictive synopsis, the film is set in middle school, not high school. Richard takes an interest in two troublemaker students (named George and Jim) who are initially aloof and evade the teacher's caring overtures. After both students skip school one day, Richard makes house visits and discovers that they are living within dysfunctional families (George is rebellious toward his stepmother and Jim's parents are separated). With his wife's consent, the teacher invites the two students to move into his house and treats them with parental love. Richard's tireless devotion not only reforms the delinquent boys but also earns the respect of their classmates. Archival evidence suggests that the import permit was issued on false information deliberately fabricated by the distributor (except for the names of Richard and his wife Anne, none of the above narrative events matches the actual film).

When *Blackboard Jungle*'s trailer was screened in theaters in December 1960, the National Parent Teacher Association (NPTA: Chŏnguk sachi'nhoe) threatened to file a lawsuit should the film's exhibition be permitted. In an interview with *Seoul Sinmum*, Kwŏn Sun-yŏng, a court official for juvenile protection, opposed the film's release based on what he had seen in the trailer and opined that no benefits could possibly come from exposing minors to such unwholesome material.[73] The National Motion Picture Ethics Committee (NMPEC: Yŏnghwayulli chŏngukwiwŏnhoe), a new civil regulatory board, officially requested the film's suspension for scenes of sexual and physical violence that had been looked upon unfavorably by censors and citizens in other countries. An opinion piece in the February 2, 1961, issue of *Kyŏnghyang Sinmun* admonished MoE officials for allowing the importation of infamous juvenile delinquent films such as *Blackboard Jungle* and *Beat Girl* (1960) that had been deemed harmful to minors, whose rate of criminal offenses was steadily on the rise (in 1960 alone, 9,779 juvenile crimes were prosecuted).[74] Faced with negative public opinion, the government blamed transitional authorities immediately following the April 19 Revolution of 1960 (which ended Rhee's autocratic rule and birthed the democratic Second Republic) for permitting the film's import. While this is not exactly true, considering the fact that Chang Myŏng's parliamentary administration was fully in place when *Blackboard Jungle* was imported in August 1960, the month was indeed a chaotic period in motion picture regulation. The NMPEC, founded earlier that month, was still in the preparation stage. While motion picture censorship was nominally unconstitutional under the Second Republic's constitution, the MoE continued to review foreign import applications in a more permissive environment. As discussed in chapter 1, it was not until October 1960 when the MoE strengthened censorship for foreign motion pictures due to the scandal of European "adultery films" such as Louis Malle's *The Lovers* (*Les amants*, 1958).

After the May 16 military coup of 1961 and the transfer of power to Park Chung Hee's military junta, the Supreme Council for National Reconstruction (SCNR: Kukkajaegŏn ch'oegohoeŭi), *Blackboard Jungle*, along with twenty-one other foreign films and thirty-five domestic films, was subject to recensorship review by the new government. The list of "impure" (*pulsun*) films was compiled by the Ministry of the Interior (MoI) and submitted to the MoE with a request for bans on May 23, 1961. The MoI prefaced the list as follows: "With the outlawing of censorship in the wake of the April 16 Revolution, some profit-driven businessmen drew widespread social criticism by producing or importing morally or ideologically unhealthy films with no regard to national and social damage. We are submitting the following list of criticized films in consideration of public opinion that demands wholesale recensorship and screening bans or confiscation and disposal of prints."[75] On July 18, 1961, the suspension of *Blackboard Jungle*'s exhibition was decided after an initial round of recensorship review. Between January 26 and 29 of 1962, an interagency censorship panel with representatives from the MoI, the MoE, the MPI, and the Korean Central Intelligence Agency (KCIA: Chungangjŏngbobu) met again to review *Blackboard Jungle*, along with ten other films suspended the previous year. Out of the eleven films, bans on four films (two domestic films, *Kobau* [1959] and *The Housemaid* [*Hanyŏ*, 1960] and two foreign films, *Blackboard Jungle* and *Beat Girl*) were lifted.

Of the regulators from the four state agencies, only those from the KCIA voted against lifting the suspension of the MGM film's exhibition. In their rationale, the KCIA regulators Ch'oe Yu-hŏn and Pyŏn Yŏng-sŏk elaborated, "Although the film is good for educators of democracy and adults, it would be appropriate to suspend the film since there are risks of imitation by minors."[76] On the other hand, Yi Ch'un-sŏng, the head of the MoE Culture Division, defended the lifting of the suspension, classifying *Blackboard Jungle* as an "education film" (*kyŏuk yŏnghwa*). The state bureaucrat reinterpreted the story as a cross-cultural cinematic rendering of the "revolutionary education policy" of the new ROK government, focusing on "purification of school" (*hakwŏnjŏnghwa*) as a cheerful, democratic institution. Yi particularly applauded Richard's pursuit of "creative" educational methods (such as showing an animated cartoon of "Jack and the Beanstalk" for ethics debates) in lieu of "passive, formal, and ineffective" ones. The MoE regulator went on to praise the film as a beneficial "lesson for teachers, leaders, and parents," supporting its public exhibition.[77]

This Korean regulatory view coincides with Brooks's own interpretation that his movie was not about "juvenile delinquents with knives in a classroom," but instead about "a teacher who wants to teach where the students have no stake."[78] As the writer-director had intended, *Blackboard Jungle* "is supposed to shock [as] it isn't something Hollywood dreamed up. The situation exists—and the picture will have people sitting up and saying, 'We better do something about it.'"[79] In the script development stage, MGM sought to transform Hunter's novel about "society's failure" into a "story of the triumph of a sensitive idealistic man over almost insuperable obstacles,"[80] a narrative arch that would resonate with Korean state censors. For the sake of constructive storytelling, the most depressing event had to be modified from Brooks's earlier script, in which Dadier's distressed wife miscarries their baby boy after receiving West's harassing phone calls and letters falsely alleging his infidelity. In the revised script, the premature baby miraculously survives emergency delivery, giving the grateful father a reason to continue his fight with the renewed hope that he will learn from his own child how to be a better teacher.[81] This crucial change was specifically implemented to shape "a story of positive achievement" that dramatizes Richard's "joint and parallel triumph" (both as a teacher and father) over the "tremendous obstacles,"[82] not unlike the uplifting stories encouraged by Korean state film censorship of the Park era.

In his reply to Lionel DeSilva, executive secretary of the California Teachers Association, who had raised concerns about MGM's adaptation of *Blackboard Jungle* (which was described by the educator as "a very violent and shocking story [and]a serious injustice [to public school teachers]"), Schary shared his conviction that the film "will add up to a plus rather than a minus view and that perhaps [it] will provide some people with a spur to *clean up* conditions that should be cleaned up."[83] In his interview with *Variety*, the MGM executive similarly expressed that "we grant that no one picture is a panacea. We can only offer *Blackboard Jungle* as a report on the problem, and honestly suggest that something be done about a situation that can, if not controlled, become a menace."[84] Schary's authorial intention is clearly aligned with Yi's regulatory interpretation of the MGM story as that of "purification" of corrupt forces in the education sector.

Before lifting the suspension, the MPI (the ministry that took over film regulation operations from the MoE in 1961) took extraordinarily cautious steps, commissioning yet another censorship review by nine external regulators. They voted 7-2 in favor of unbanning following a two-day period of meetings in April 1962. The exhibition permit was finally issued on May 22, 1962, on the condition that Segi Corporation change its Korean release title from *Violent Classroom* (which had attracted negative press during the earlier release attempt in 1960) to the original *Blackboard Jungle* and that admissions of minors be strictly prohibited. Additionally, the MPI demanded that six controversial scenes (such as the rape attempt in the library, alleyway occurrences of teachers being beaten, and knife wielding in the classroom) be eliminated or shortened. A progressive regulatory request was made to eliminate West's racial epithet ("black boy") aimed at another student, Gregory Miller (Sidney Poitier), who assists Dadier in disarming the violent classmate and taking him to the principal's office toward the narrative's end. Interestingly, the most cited reason for regulatory restrictions on the MPI's list is "education impairment" (*kyŏuk changae*), a category unique to Korean film censorship.[85] Segi Corporation made a three-minute cut before releasing a ninety-seven-minute version in Academy Theater in June 1962.

Archival evidence suggests that the MoE's repositioning of *Blackboard Jungle* as a "school purification" story was a winning argument against the KCIA's concern about the film's negative influence on Korean minors, which is precisely the reason why the film had been so controversial in other countries. "Purification of school" became a major social issue after the toppling of Syngman Rhee's corrupt government by the April 19 Revolution of 1960. While corruption was widespread across various sectors of public life, from politics to business, one surprising bastion of social ills under the ruling Liberal Party (Chayudang) of the Rhee administration was schools. In his opinion piece entitled "How Should We Purify School?," published in *Tonga Ilbo* on September 20, 1960, Kim Kyŏngt'ak, a faculty member at Korea University, painstakingly detailed the extent of the shocking corruption in virtually every area of the education system, from grade schools and college campuses to local school districts and MoE leadership under the Rhee regime.

In elementary schools, mothers' clubs (led by Liberal Party elite families) collected donations for teachers and administrators from well-to-do parents whose children received favors in the form of grade boosts. Upper-grade homeroom teachers earned extra income by moonlighting as private tutors for wealthy students. Some of these illegitimate earnings were gifted to principals who enjoyed steady side incomes from both parental donations and teacher bribes. In turn, principals shared some of their profits as bribes to district officials to keep their lucrative posts. The MoE willfully turned a blind eye to school corruption since ministers and vice ministers themselves accumulated small fortunes through bribes. In middle schools and high schools, trustees (aka "school profiteers" [hakwŏn moribae]) embezzled registration fees rather than supporting school finances as they had been entrusted to do. Trustees and principals made additional profits by illegally readmitting failed or expelled students through the backdoor in exchange for large cash donations from their parents. Teachers were disempowered and silenced as trustees and principals could hire and fire them at will. Higher education was not exempt from corruption, and most private universities admitted "extra auditors" beyond their allotted student quotas for increased profits. Concluding that "school under Liberal Party rule was nothing more than an institution of elite power and profiteering under the ruse of education," Kim called for wholesale purification of the education sector by dismissing all principals, trustees, and university presidents appointed under the Rhee administration and replacing them with honest teachers and faculty members.[86]

It is important to understand this popular desire to purge many corrupt elements of Korean society in order to make sense of the reason why Park Chung Hee's military junta, launched with the expressed goal of "purifying" Korea, was broadly supported by the masses. As Bruce Cumings observes,

> If . . . you had neither an effective bureaucracy nor an enterprising business community, no growth, and no political stability, with every politician thinking it his birthright to be supported and have his every opinion heard, above all a historically obsolescent landed class of would-be aristocrats who had lorded it over the common people for centuries and now claimed to be principled democratic opposition—that is, the South Korean system in the 1950s—then one can understand how different the junta's dictatorship was from, say, a French junta shutting down parliament, why it was popular with many ordinary people, and why, far from paralyzing the streets in mass rebellion, the coup was almost entirely bloodless. . . . So, for a nation of current and recent peasants to watch the political class cashiered for a few months or years, by someone instantly recognizable as a son of the peasantry, was doubtless met with much mirth and silent approbation.[87]

In March 1962, the SCNR promulgated the "political activities purification law," under which four thousand purged politicians were banned from politicking for six years. In the sphere of politics, purification was a self-serving mechanism to eliminate competition and consolidate power under Park's Democratic Republican Party (Minjugonghwadang), which was founded in February 1963 and succeeded the SCNR in December of that year.

In the domain of education, however, the military junta's purification program served public interests. On May 10, 1962, *Chosŏn Ilbo* ran an editorial that assessed the "revolutionary" government's educational policy and its achievements over the past year. The newspaper article opens, "There was no other area where the storm of revolution hit harder. Big surgeries were required to cure the corrupt education sector sick with the corporatization of education, profiteering in schools, illegal admissions, and school disorder."[88]

FIGURE 2.2 It would not have been difficult for Korean state regulators at that time (in the early 1960s) to notice cross-cultural parallels between Richard Dadier, the fictional character, and Park Chung Hee, the general–turned–self-made politician. Both were soft-spoken novice leaders with military backgrounds and idealistic visions.

The SCNR was compared to a surgeon whose "scalpels" purified schools by removing cancerous elements: licenses for corrupt foundations, boards of trustees, and schools were revoked; sixty-one principals and twelve university presidents mired in various scandals (illegal profiteering or admissions) were dismissed; collections of unapproved private fees from parents were outlawed; and extracurricular exam prep classes harmful to the physical development of young children were disallowed. One major outcome of Park's school purification program was the abolishment of the NPTA, which was behind the lobbying against *Blackboard Jungle*'s release in 1960. In March 1962, the MoE ordered all NPTA groups across the country to disband after the SCNR's audit revealed that the organization had collected 400 million hwan (U.S.$615,400) in fees between 1953 and 1961 and had spent 70 percent of the money for teacher benefits instead of children's education. Although the revised education tax law of 1958 had already prohibited private fees beyond taxes and official fees, the NPTA continued to collect "temporary operation fees," increasing parents' financial burden.[89]

It would not have been difficult for state regulators at that time (in the early 1960s) to notice cross-cultural parallels between Richard Dadier, the fictional character, and Park Chung Hee, the general–turned–self-made politician. Both were novice leaders with military backgrounds and idealistic visions. They were equally determined to "purify" and reform a corrupt environment where violence, disorder, apathy, and cynicism were ways of life. They fought crimes and poverty, restored social order, and strove for mental health reforms. In the

January 8, 1975, issue of the *New York Times*, Korean American businessman Hancho C. Kim described Park as a "tough-minded, strong-willed, soft-spoken" leader who was "sick and tired of violence, of the incredible waste of manpower and of the hunger and wretchedness that had appalled him as a native of rural Korea and as young teacher in rural districts."[90] Although Richard arrives in an urban, rather than rural, school, he too is appalled by lack of discipline among unmotivated students from low-income families, uncaring senior colleagues accustomed to school crimes and dysfunctions, and low standards of living for teachers who have few incentives to endure unsafe working conditions (a weary older teacher who regards his school as a "garbage can" warns new arrivals, "Never turn your back on the class") or resources to initiate structural change.

Although the ex-Navy man almost fails his interview for an English teacher's job at North Manual Trades for being "soft spoken," the first-time teacher proves to be "tough minded" and "strong willed." Entering the classroom for the first day's class, Dadier is met with disrespect from West, a thuggish saboteur who retorts "Why?" to the teacher's demand to break up the loitering in the back of the room. Richard firmly articulates his order "Sit down" to the troublemaker, who sluggishly complies. While his back is turned to spell out his last name, a baseball is thrown at the blackboard and makes a deep dent. Without losing his cool, the teacher turns around and defuses the tension, looking out at a sea of stoic faces and responding, "Whoever threw that, you will never pitch for the Yankees." His straight-faced yet subtle joke brings a smile to Miller, who is more mild tempered and conventionally intelligent than his peers. The teacher then asserts his authority by instructing the class to call him "Mister Dadier" (correcting West's ungrammatical address "Mister Teach") and emphasizing the importance of correct pronunciation. Noticing West's disrespectful body language and glances, Dadier gives an order as if he were a military officer (in a close-up shot against the background of an American flag): "Take off your hat in this classroom." With his face lowered and eyes glued to a notebook, West challenges his teacher in a low voice: "You ever try to fight thirty-five guys at one time, Teach?" The resolute educator scans his classroom quickly and approaches West, who stands up in a confrontational manner. Dadier repeats his order in a low yet forceful voice: "Take your hat off, boy, before I knock it off." West glances at his classmates, seeking backup, but everyone looks away. The rebel backs down and takes his hat off before sitting down.

The new teacher resumes his class introduction in a more upbeat voice once the confrontation is averted: "The subject you learn in this class is English. Some of you may wonder if English can help you get a job as a carpenter, a mechanic, or an electrician. The answer is yes. In fact, it may even surprise you to find that English is your favorite subject." Rolling his eyes, Miller cynically responds, "I will be surprised alright." The ex-serviceman corrects the unruly behavior: "There will be no calling out. If you've got any questions to ask, just raise your hand." Unlike his well-intended but weak-willed fellow teacher Josh, who quits (after delinquent pupils vandalize his prized collection of jazz records in class), Richard perseveres and eventually inspires students in the face of hooliganism, anarchy, and intimidation inside and outside of the classroom. He appears to be a natural-born leader who educates his demoralized colleagues about labor equity during a teachers' meeting: "Now listen. A congressman and a judge are $9.25 an hour. Policemen and firemen, $2.75 an hour. Carpenter, $2.81. Plumber $2.97. Plasterer, $3.21. You know, a household cook gets more money than we do, and they get room and board. Oh, yes, I know, a teacher gets as much as a babysitter or a soda jerk."[91]

Ultimately, as Steve Benton argues, "Dadier's persistence, his good faith, and his genuine interest in betting on the lives of his students" motivate his class to support his struggle to disarm West and his pal in the climatic knife confrontation.[92] The united team effort makes classroom "purification" possible by rooting out poisonous elements. In the final scene set at the school gate, Miller reminds Dadier of their earlier pact that neither will quit school if the other stays and confirms that they will see each other tomorrow. The film's happy ending indicates that the disfranchised students of North Manual have come to believe again in the formerly forsaken American Dream thanks to one teacher's inspirational leadership. Such benign progression is ironically achieved through what Benton refers to as a "Cold War formula" of "brutal force" and martial masculinity (displayed in Dadier's violent banging of West's head against the blackboard after accusing him of distressing his pregnant wife with "foul letters" falsely alleging his infidelity that nearly cost the life of their unborn baby).[93] This contradictory formula resonates with another military man (Park)'s relentless pursuit of economic growth and social purification by any means and at the expense of civil liberties.

For Whom the Censor Prohibits?: Mediating Industrial and Public Interests through the Regulation of *The Teahouse of the August Moon*

My biggest takeaway from doing archive-based research on the MPI's regulation of Hollywood and Korean motion pictures from the 1960s to the 1980s is that there were strong correlations between the interests of the state and the industry despite the common assumption of their adversary relationship (as the so-called regulator vs. the regulated). It was the MPI's responsibility to accommodate a wide range of public opinion from different political, religious, and social groups (including varying agendas of other ministries) in their administration of content regulation of motion pictures to serve the nation's collective good. However, it was also their mission to protect the ROK's film industry and ensure its corporate growth, fiscal well-being, and international competitiveness. Therefore, the last thing that the MPI wanted was to cause significant material losses to production or distribution companies by prohibiting sales of their products for abstract reasons (moral, political, ideological, or religious). It was particularly undesirable and wasteful to suspend international film releases after valuable large sums of foreign currency had been paid to Hollywood or European studios for print imports.

If one reads between the lines of documents in the *Blackboard Jungle* file, it is apparent that the MPI carefully engineered the lifting of the suspension by bolstering a defense aimed at the film's naysayers and detractors. The censorship file includes the first draft of an internal memorandum dated March 22, 1962, that proposes to permit *Blackboard Jungle*'s exhibition contingent upon shortening three universally objected scenes (the library assault, the alleyway attack, and the knife fight). The memo does not seem to have advanced beyond the MPI Motion Picture Division as the signature line of the minister is blank. It can be assumed that the division decided to subject the film to another review by guest civil regulators commissioned outside of the four state branches involved in the January review to preempt potential controversy and public backlash. One target audience of such a prudent procedure was apparently the KCIA, the only branch that voted against unbanning MGM's juvenile delinquency picture. The second MPI memorandum, approved by the minister and dated April 17, 1962, has an attached interagency memo to the intelligence agency, informing that the lifting of the suspension has been decided by the "consensus" (*hapŭi*) of concerned government branches as well as the specialized consulting panel (*pungwa woewŏnhoe*) of industry personnel and cultural experts working in an advisory capacity for the MPI.[94] In a press interview with *Kyŏnghyang Sinmun* on May 27, 1962, the Motion Picture Division chief further defended their decision publicly: "We have cut all harmful scenes and made the release conditional to strictly restricting admissions of minors."[95] It is also notable that the ministry instructed Segi Corporation to cut or reduce three additional scenes and one racially offensive line than what they had originally planned in March because of their consulting review board's suggestions.

Two months after *Blackboard Jungle*'s exhibition was suspended in July 1961, Segi Corporation signed a contract with MGM to import *The Teahouse of the August Moon*, a lighthearted comedy about Captain Jeff Fisby (Glenn Ford)'s effort to Americanize the small village of Tobiki in occupied Okinawa by teaching native people to elect community leaders and boost the local economy with various entrepreneurial projects (from souvenir craft production to an organic brandy distillery). At the heart of the film's intercultural humor is Fisby's relationship with Japanese-speaking Lotos Blossom (Kyō Machiko), a young geisha whom grateful villagers "gift" to their occupation commander. Mistaking her as a prostitute, the American officer is at first mortified but soon learns through his interpreter, Sakini (Marlon Brando), that she is an entertainer and will lose face if he returns her. Pressured by a ladies' league demanding equal footing with Lotus in the eyes of men, Fisby reluctantly approves of geisha lessons to other

FIGURE 2.3 MGM's lighthearted comedy *The Teahouse of the August Moon* (1956) embodies Cold War Orientalism in celebrating a humorous yet harmonious integration between the United States (represented by Captain Jeff Fisby [Glenn Ford: right]) and noncommunist Asia (represented by Japanese-speaking Lotos Blossom [Kyō Machiko: left]).

women. In turn, the men of Tobiki demand a new teahouse where geishas entertain customers with songs and dances, and which is built and then demolished by order of Fisby's superior Colonel Prudy (Paul Ford), who misconstrues the nature of the establishment. The colonel belatedly changes his mind when he hears the news that congressional members are planning to visit Tobiki for an inspection tour after the American press has promoted the village as a success story of democratizing Japan. To the delight of the officers, Sakini explains that the villagers feigned destroying the teahouse and distillery, which are reassembled instantly. The film ends on a utopian note, with happy occupiers and villagers celebrating their common success in the titular establishment (a local signifier of maturity and wisdom). This seemingly harmless, middlebrow comedy based on Vern Sneider's semiautographical novel is exemplary of what Christina Klein calls "Cold War Orientalism" in that it narrates "the knitting of ties between the United States and noncommunist Asia" with an emphasis on "the values of interdependence, sympathy, and hybridity."[96]

Upon its release in Japan in 1957, *The Teahouse of the August Moon* drew the ire of Japanese critics for the racially offensive "yellowface" acting of Marlon Brando and the film's exotic representation of Japanese women as geishas, displayed for the pleasure of American occupiers-oglers.[97] However, it was a commercial hit in Japan, raking in an opening-day gross of 2.4 million yen (U.S.$6,700) at the Yuraku-za Theater in Tokyo alone, the single-day record for any picture in any theater in Japan.[98] According to a report by the Japanese newspaper *Mainichi*, Japanese audiences broke into gales of laughter when Captain Fisby calls villagers' custom of sharing bank accounts "communism."[99] In contrast with the Japanese critical reception, which looked unfavorably at Hollywood's Orientalist representation through the lens of race, and unlike some local audiences' subversive pleasure derived from laughing *at* (rather than with) the satire of American occupation, Koreans resisted the comedy owing in part to postcolonial reasoning. Notably, the film's Korean title was modified to *The Teahouse of August 15 Night* (*P'al.il.o.yaŭi ch'ajip*) to emphasize the date of national independence from Japanese rule. Segi Corporation's attempt to release this MGM film with a Japanese cast, settings, and themes was rejected multiple times as a part of nationalist cultural policy barring the circulation of the Japanese language and imagery after the 1945 liberation.

As Kim Sŏng-min points out, postcolonial Korean intellectuals called for "cultural independence" (*munhwajŏk toknip*) by erasing remnants of Japanese culture broadly labeled as *waesaek* or "Japanese color" in direct translation.[100] This postcolonial policy was retrospectively countering Japanese cultural control in the colonial era (1910–1945) when the imperial assimilation policy strictly censored the Korean language, press, and popular culture. Everything from Japanese signs and expressions to Japanese songs and motion pictures was deemed taboo as cultural pollutants of the new, independent nation. Film scholar Jinsoo An analyzes this phenomenon in the context of 1960s Korean film culture. As he states,

> Key to understanding the cultural politics of Korean-Japanese film exchange was the heated and protracted controversy surrounding the concept of "Japanese color" (*waesaek* in Korean), the perceived threat of the encroachment of Japanese popular culture into South Korean society, that persisted throughout the 1960s. The increasing cultural visibility of Japan gave rise to this defensive discourse, which tied directly into South Korea's troubled relationship with its colonial legacy. Further, the repression of postcolonial reflection on colonialism as a cultural system was bound up with a new Cold War order in which South Korea and Japan were allies and partners. Cinema, in particular, was an arena for contestation, for it was where an "acceptance" of Japan challenged the mandate of disavowal or negation that had effectively established discursive parameters on ways of imagining, remembering, and narrating the colonial experience for the people of South Korea.[101]

As a regulatory item, the amorphous concept of *waesaek* posed a challenge to state authorities in charge of administering motion picture censorship based on an established set of rules and regulations. For example, there is no clause that would justify forbidding "Japanese color" in the 1957 public performance censorship bylaws or the 1962 Motion Picture Law's enforcement regulations. On the contrary, the latter prohibited content that "might harm international relations by disrespecting customs of Free World allies and their national feelings."[102] Given Japan's official ally status in the U.S.-supported network of Free Asia united against communist enemies (including North Korea and Red China), imposing bans on images of Japanese allies and their culture on Korean screens could be construed as a violation of this diplomatic principle. More significantly, such cultural exclusion was in essence contradictory to Park Chung Hee's friendlier foreign policy toward Japan, which culminated with the 1965 normalization of diplomacy between the two countries. As Jung-Hoon Lee contends, however, Park's pro-Japanese maneuvering of international relations failed to achieve broad social consensus in South Korea, where there were, and still are, persistent demands for a "'genuine' Japanese apology and repentance for colonial wrongdoings." Unlike his predecessor Syngman Rhee, a former freedom fighter who encouraged anti-Japanese sentiment for both personal gratification and political gains, Park was a pragmatist who "broke the shackles of the past and put the bilateral relationship on a more positive and mutually beneficial course for the first time in the twentieth century... despite vociferous domestic opposition."[103]

The Rhee administration's MoE sent a notice of regulatory suggestions to the Korean Film Producers Association (KFPA: Hang'ukyŏnghwa chejakjahyŏp'oe) on March 12, 1959, which, among other things, discouraged filmmakers from including *waesaek* content (such as Japanese dialogue, music, costumes, etc.) in their productions.[104] Although now nostalgically viewed as South Korea's first democratic government, under which censorship was ruled unconstitutional, the Second Republic inherited Rhee's anti-Japanese cultural policy and rejected, in March 1961, import applications for five Hollywood motion pictures casting Japanese actors and/or featuring locations shot in Japan: MGM's *The Teahouse of the August Moon*, Warner Bros.' *Sayonara* (1957), Paramount Pictures' *The Geisha Boy* (1958), Twentieth Century-Fox's *The Barbarian and the Geisha* (1958), and the independently produced sci-fi–horror film *The Manster* (1959). Although there are no surviving documents of NMPEC civil regulation, according to a newspaper report, the NMPEC rejected *The Teahouse of August Moon* based on the MoE's "internal rules" that prohibited domestic screenings of "communist films, immoral films, or *waesaek* films."[105] After his earlier attempt to import *The Teahouse of the August Moon* was foiled under the Chang Myŏn administration, president Wu Ki-dong of Segi Corporation saw a new opportunity with the rise of Park's military junta after the May 1961 coup, which "freed South Korea from Syngman Rhee's stubbornly anti-Japanese posture as well as Chang Myŏn's political drift and administrative ineffectiveness."[106] With renewed hope, Wu sent yet another application to the new regime's MPI in the fall of 1961 only to be turned down again. In an internal memo filed on October 31 of that year, the

MPI's Motion Picture Division reported that "although *The Teahouse of the August Moon* is MGM's comedy in which an American military officer indoctrinates Okinawan natives and propagandizes what true democracy is through specific measures, due to the casting of several Japanese actors and villagers, it would be inappropriate to present it to our citizens given the current political situation with Japan and we will reject its importation." In particular, the ministry notes that there are only four main American characters as opposed to seven Japanese.[107]

Patience and persistence paid off, however, and Wu succeeded in acquiring the MPI's import recommendation on October 27, 1962. As Yi Hwa-jin points out, a series of new developments inside and outside of the film industry around that time gave Segi Corporation an incentive to try again to bring to light the import print from MGM that had been stored in the customs warehouse for an extended period. In May 1962, Shin Sang-ok's *Sŏng Ch'unhyang* (1961) became the first Korean film to be released in hundreds of theaters throughout six Japanese cities. In September of that year, the MPI permitted location shooting in Japan for underwater special effects in Yi Hyŏng-p'yo's *Tale of Simchŏng* (*Tae Simchŏngjŏn*, 1962) and exterior scenes of Kim Sŏng-min's anticommunist espionage action film *Black Gloves* (*Kŭmŭn changgap*, 1963) set in Tokyo.[108] In the summer of 1962, *Private Tutor* (*Kajŏng kyosa*), the Korean translation of Ishizaka Yojiro's novel *A Slope in the Sun* (*Hi no ataru sakamichi*, 1958), became the number one best seller in South Korea. In July 1962, CBS, a Christian radio station, broadcast serialized readings of the novel. Two months later, actress Ŏm Aeng-ran visited Tokyo to seek Ishizaka's permission to adapt the novel in the Korean film industry. The Japanese novelist's gracious letter to Ŏm, in which the bestseller author declined a copyright royalty and encouraged Koreans to make a good film instead, was shared publicly.[109] Kim Ki-yŏng's *Private Tutor* (1953), starring Ŏm, became the first Korean big-screen adaptation of a Japanese novel. Unthinkable only a few years before, several domestic films thematizing interethnic romances, friendship, or surrogate family relations between Korean and Japanese characters—such as *The Sea Knows* (*Hyŏndaet'anŭn algoitta*, 1961), *Happy Solitude* (*Haengbokhan kodok*, 1963), and *The Overbridge of Hyŏnhaet'an Strait* (*Hyŏnhaet'anŭi kurŭmdari*, 1963)—were released in the early 1960s.

On the political side, eager to share the financial burden of assisting the ROK's economic development with Japan, the Kennedy administration intervened when normalization talks were suspended for five months in 1962 due to opposition from the antitreaty forces in both countries. Washington urged Japanese prime minister Ikeda Hayato's cabinet to "[reach] a quick settlement with South Korea" in order to stabilize "a triangular East Asian security alignment between the United States, Japan, and South Korea."[110] A landmark breakthrough came on November 12, 1962, when KCIA director Kim Chong-p'il, Park's envoy for settlement negotiations in Tokyo, reached an agreement with Ikeda's foreign minister, Ohira Masayoshi. Known as the Kim-Ohira Memorandum, the clandestine agreement specified terms and amounts of the compensation package (U.S.$300 million in direct grants and another U.S.$300 million in a combination of development assistance and private loans) that the ROK would receive in exchange for signing the normalization treaty. Although the secret handling of negotiations provoked anger from oppositional forces, which saw Park's Japan policy as a kind of "humiliation diplomacy" (*kulyok oegyo*) lacking genuine reconciliation, and nationwide demonstrations stalled bilateral talks for the better part of 1963–1964, the Kim-Ohira Memorandum represented significant momentum on the path of normalization.

Even after getting the coveted import approval, Segi Corporation had to wait another ten months, until August of 1963, before the MPI's exhibition permit was belatedly issued. This delay is perhaps unsurprising, since Park's junta was coping with public backlash against his administration's capitulating to Japan with the Kim-Ohira agreement and allowing the importation of pro-Japanese films such as *The Teahouse of the August Moon*. When the upcoming MGM attraction's promotion began in the 1,900-seat Taehan Theater (designed by Twentieth Century-Fox and owned by Segi Corporation) in early November 1962 shortly after the MPI's import approval, protests ensued. In a press interview, KFPA president and respected filmmaker Shin Sang-ok sounded an alarm, saying, "I am surprised that the film was recommended to be imported. The MPI's directionless policy with no set rules about *waesaek* imports at a time when domestic films are not clearly protected is unsettling and disappointing."[111] Although Yi Wŏn-u, a cornered minister of the MPI, assured the public that the import permission was separate from the exhibition permission and that his ministry would deliberate on the latter seriously, the KFPA called two emergency meetings and declared "public struggles" (*konggae t'ujaeng*) against a commercialism that was exploiting "cheap curiosity for Japanese color" at the expense of the nation's cultural integrity.[112]

Not everyone was against *The Teahouse of the August Moon* and other so-called *waesaek* films from Hollywood. In his interview with *Chosŏn Ilbo* on November 10, 1962, Yi Chong-hyang, secretary of the Literary Society, opined, "If the quality of movies is good, it is okay to cast Japanese actors. It is too timid to think Korean films will be harmed if such films as *The Bridge on the River Kwai* (1957) and *The Teahouse of the August Moon* are imported. On the contrary, they will become a stimulus to improve Korean films. However, the government should implement more active policies to foster domestic productions through such measures as tax cuts or permission of location shooting in Japan."[113] On the same day, the MPI Motion Picture Division head, Paek Hyŏng-gi, said in a different interview, "We take *The Teahouse of the August Moon* seriously as a model case and the decision for its exhibition permission will be based on our survey of public opinion from various sectors. Our preliminary studies point to the majority being in favor of permission on the condition that the sweeping Japan 'boom' be tempered with effective policy about Japanese culture."[114] In other words, the MPI's hands were tied once a single film emerged as a symbol for a contentious culture war in the court of public opinion. State bureaucrats' self-protective procrastination, following highly publicized KFPA opposition, must have made Wu Ki-dong impatient as his prized MGM import's release date was put on indefinite hold.

Most likely what enraged him further was the MPI's inconsistency in favor of another domestic *waesaek* film: Sin Kyŏng-gyun's *Happy Solitude*, based on the memoirs of Akashishi Tokiko, a Japanese woman who married a Korean man and became naturalized as a Korean after immigrating to her husband's country. On September 4, 1962, the MPI approved Tongsŏng Film Corporation's production application on the condition that Japanese scenes be shot in South Korea. On January 24, 1963, the film received an exhibition permit on the condition that seven scenes be cut or shortened for Japanese color.[115] Four scenes were composed of inserted shots of the Tokyo city view and three were Japanese dance performances at an upscale bar/restaurant. In regulating other domestic *waesaek* films, the MPI's effort was similarly directed at cutting authentic representations of Japanese images and sounds. For example, for Kim Ki-yŏng's *The Sea Knows* (a wartime interethnic romance between a Korean student draftee and a Japanese woman set in Nagoya in 1944), the MPI instructed the producers to remove images of a film-within-the film showing samurai fights and reduce the volume of a Japanese military marching song so as to make the lyrics incomprehensible.[116] As Jinsoo An points out, state regulators must have been concerned about not only the "visible images of Japan [triggering] memories of forced assimilation and [implying] the failure of cultural decolonization" but also the harmful effect of the Japanese language on "older Koreans [who] would be called on to react ... much as they had done when they were subjects of the colonial era."[117]

Despite such regulatory intervention to minimize objectionable elements, *Happy Solitude* drew considerable controversy for its settings, characters, music, and costumes, which together foregrounded postwar Japan in an unprecedented way. When its promotional posters, which featured enlarged images of the kimono-clad heroine (played cross-ethnically by Miss Korea Sŏ Yang-hŭi, a performer with no prior acting experience), covered boulevard tree trunks and telephone poles throughout central Seoul in January 1963, the Seoul Metropolitan Police ordered the removal of "blatant *waesaek* advertising detrimental to the national spirit" and announced that they would summon representatives of the production company for lower court proceedings.[118] *Happy Solitude*'s release sharply divided KFPA leaders. Some strongly opposed it, since rallying behind the local production after having boycotted foreign *waesaek* films would be a publicity debacle for their trade organization. Others supported it, arguing that shelving a completed Korean film would be wasteful. As An indicates, "The controversy tarnished the reputation of the KFPA, for it had been vocal about the corrupting influence of Japanese color on the minds of Korean viewers."[119]

The MPI responded to the ruckus, insisting that they would decide "case-by-case" and continue to restrict excessive *waesaek* content.[120]

On March 20, 1963, just shy of two months after the MPI had approved of *Happy Solitude*'s release, a frustrated Wu sent a strongly worded petition to the ministry complaining about the groundless withholding of *The Teahouse of the August Moon*'s exhibition permit for months after his company had already spent a large sum of precious dollars for its importation.[121] The president of Segi Corporation detailed the reasons why its exhibition should be allowed without any further delay: (1) It is a "pure" MGM film (not a coproduction with Japan) about deprogramming Okinawan natives of the Japanese empire's totalitarian propaganda and converting them to American-style democracy through enlightenment programs; (2) The ministry has already permitted the distribution of local productions with greater Japanese color than the Hollywood import in question; and (3) Its suspension contradicts the current government's effort to normalize diplomacy with Japan and promote Korean-Japanese cultural exchange as well as friendship between two countries. Wu ended his letter with a pointed reminder that, due to recent foreign currency shortages and slowed importation, new Hollywood releases were in high demand and theaters specializing in foreign films were threatened by the potential for financial losses.[122]

It appears that Wu received no immediate response from the ministry, and he filed another petition with a shortened summary of his arguments on May 14, 1963. This time, he got a relatively prompt, if brief, reply from the MPI, stating that the exhibition permission could not be granted until rules for screening *waesaek* films in South Korea were established.[123] That vague response must have been devastating to Wu, particularly after he had witnessed the MPI-approved release of *Happy Solitude*, whose flashy *waesaek* advertising had even provoked the ire of city police units. The executive producer did not give up and sought assistance from three key trade associations—the KFPA, the Korean Foreign Film Distributors Association (KFFDA: Hang'ukoegukyŏnghwa paegŭphyŏp'oe), and the National Association of Theater Owners (NATO: Chŏngukgŭkjangju yŏnhap)—whose presidents cosigned his third appeal to the MPI, submitted on July 25, 1963.[124] Although the main contents of Segi Corporation's last petition were similar to those of earlier versions, albeit with more embellished details, the support of three main trade organizations as cosignatories made a difference by signaling the aligned interests of producers and exhibitors (i.e., opening the door for more Japanese themes in Korean films, filling in the schedules of theaters specializing in foreign films) with distributors. Considering the KFPA's indignation over the MPI's import recommendation for *The Teahouse of the August Moon* in the fall of 1961, this about-face united front of the industry's three branches over the contentious title (which had previously divided their interests) was no doubt a winning strategy in persuading the ministry in charge of developing and protecting that trade.

Yi Hwa-jin further conjectures that the KFPA and the NATO aligned with the KFFDA's bidding in 1963 partly because "that year's revision of the Motion Picture Law consolidated production and foreign film distribution sectors, converging disparate interests."[125] Exactly fifteen years after the United States government broke up the studio system by forcing the vertically integrated majors (Paramount, MGM, Warner Bros., Twentieth Century-Fox, and RKO) to divest their theater chains following the Paramount Decree, the ROK government was shepherding their industry toward the opposite direction. The 1963 amendment to the Motion Picture Law not only reduced the number of production companies (that had to meet stricter registration requirements of equipment and the increased annual production quota) from twenty-one to six but also strengthened the link between production and foreign film distribution by establishing a merit-based import quota reward system for producers.[126] As Yecies and Shim elaborate, "This forced merger between its production and distribution arms consolidated the industry even further, an important development in view of the government's attempt to establish vertical integration within the system."[127] Unlike its American counterpart, whose primary objective was to bust the oligopolistic control of the trade by removing unlawful barriers to fair competition, the Park government aimed to create the developmental state's "late studio system," as Sangjoon Lee labels it,[128] by rewarding powerful cartels such as Shin Film, Hanyang Film Corporation (Hanyang yŏnghwagongsa), T'aech'ang Entertainment (T'aech'anghŭnghyŏp), and Segi Corporation for the rapid expansion of the Korean film industry.

After all three branches of the Korean film industry had come together and consented to the release of *The Teahouse of the August Moon* for common benefit, there was no reason for the MPI to stand in the way. On August 19, 1963, an internal memo of the MPI's Motion Picture Division recommended exhibition permission for the MGM film citing the following reasons: (1) The film's continued suspension would be a "national loss" at a time when import specialty theaters were struggling to get new films due to a foreign currency crisis; (2) Lifting barriers to *waesaek* films would help reduce spectatorial curiosity and contribute to international cultural exchange; (3) It was unlikely that this particular film would cause social disturbance, given prior releases of other Japan-themed Hollywood features (*The Bridge on the River Kwai, Hell to Eternity* [1960], *Marines, Let's Go* [1961], etc.); and (4) Produced by MGM, the film propagandized the American military's effort to construct a democratic society with Okinawan natives (corresponding to the ROK's Cold War messaging).[129] Incorporation of the arguments of Wu's petition in the MPI's internal report attests to the fact that the state and the trade had reached a point of seeing eye to eye as to what was best for both parties. After Segi Corporation's epic battles for over two and a half years under two different regimes, on August 21, 1963, the MPI approved *The Teahouse of the August Moon*'s exhibition, contingent upon shortening three scenes of geishas putting on makeup and/or performing traditional songs and dances, as well as cutting two scenes of villagers interacting with the geisha where Japanese customs or language (without the mediation of English-speaking Captain Fisby) are foregrounded.

Ironically, MGM's aspiration for "authenticity" in the depiction of Japan was the principal grounds for objection on account of the importance of *waesaek* in South Korean censorship. MGM's coproducing partner, Daiei Motion Picture Company, loaned its contract star Kyō Machiko (who had first attracted Western fandom following the release of Kurosawa Akira's *Rashomon* [1950], the winner of the 1951 Venice International Film Festival) as well as Kyoto studio facilities to assist in location shooting for *The Teahouse of the August Moon*. The set for the Okinawan village of Tobiki was constructed in Ikoma, ten miles from Nara, and two hundred local residents were hired as extras.[130] As the MGM press book for *The Teahouse of the August Moon* proudly announced, "MGM sent its stars and a large production unit to Japan, where a greater part of the footage was filmed against authentic and picturesque settings, with a number of Japan's prominent actors and actresses taking part in the picture."[131] Thirty-eight studio crew and cast members (including producer Jack Cummings, director Daniel Mann, and stars Marlon Brando, Glenn Ford, and Eddie Albert) collaborated with fifteen Japanese artists (including Kyō, Kiyokawa Nijiko, and Negami Jun) to capture Japanese scenery in CinemaScope and MetroColor. The production team hired Fujima Masaya as its choreographer and technical advisor to ensure the accurate depiction of Japanese music, dance, costumes, and customs. Kanai Kikuko, an expert in Okinawan music, was enlisted to compose and orchestrate Okinawan musical sequences.[132]

When the MGM delegation left, they "packed up tons of sets, wardrobe, props, and equipment" and flew them back to Hollywood.[133] The press book also references a humorous episode in which U.S. Customs officials were puzzled by a shipment from Japan labeled as "60 cricket cages," bamboo-made local crafts to be used as props in *The Teahouse of the August Moon*.[134] It is notable, though, while talking up MGM's painstaking efforts to recreate Japan on the American screen as authentically as possible, the press book misidentified Tobiki as an impoverished and small "Korean village" on several occasions, reflecting MGM publicists' Orientalist imaginary (mixing up different East Asian nations, ethnicities, and cultures).[135] From a postcolonial perspective, such a conflation of Japan and Korea would have been an insult to citizens of the former Japanese colony, unjustly divided in August 1945 as a direct result of the imperialist rivalry between the United States and the Soviet Union to expand their respective spheres of influence in postwar Asia. Perhaps it was fitting, in that historical context, that MGM's efforts to increase the film's authenticity via location shooting and casting of Japanese acting talent backfired in South Korea on the political grounds of decolonization, not Orientalism or race.

As Yi aptly sums it up, stakes were exceptionally high for both the MPI and the Korean film industry in the censorship case of *The Teahouse of the August Moon*:

> The question of approving the American film's import and exhibition was not a bilateral affair between the censorship applicant and state regulators. It was not simply the question of prohibitions and violations. In the process of three-year censorship, *The Teahouse of the August Moon*, labeled as a *waesaek* film, was in the eye of the storm caused by conflicts within the industry and divided public opinion. The government's handling of its censorship was not deemed simply as permission or rejection of a single film but as an indicator for policy-in-making regarding the representation of Japan and Japanese film imports.[136]

It was challenging for both the government and the industry to navigate the uncharted territory of films with Japanese content while treading on a delicate national sentiment deeply troubled by the unreconciled colonial past. After the 1963 approval of *The Teahouse of the August Moon*'s exhibition, the MPI took more cautious approaches to *waesaek* films in the wake of mass antitreaty demonstrations such as the June 3 resistance movement of 1964 (when one hundred thousand students and citizens participated in street protests nationwide, prompting the declaration of martial law).[137] As a result, the release of another Segi Corporation import, the French-Japanese coproduction *Typhon sur Nagasaki* (1957), was delayed for three years until 1967. The vertically integrated company's ambitious attempt at the first Korean-Japanese coproduction, Cho Kŭng-ha's *The Governor's Daughter* (*Ch'ongdokŭi ttal*, 1965), starring the Japanese actress Michi Kanako, met a harsher fate and was shelved indefinitely until it finally received a theatrical premiere more than half a century later in March 2017 at the KOFA. The censorship file of Richard Fleischer's *Tora! Tora! Tora!* (1970) contains an internal report by the Ministry of Culture and Public Information (MCPI: Munhwagongbobu, formerly MPI) that voices concern for the continued suspension of *The Governor's Daughter* while a war spectacle from Twentieth Century-Fox with extended Japanese sequences was being imported for U.S.$100,0000 at a time when the government was restricting foreign currency spending.[138]

As I have argued elsewhere with regard to Hollywood cinema, "Film censorship is never an exercise of absolute repressive power by one party over another. It is a complex, discursive process of negotiations and compromises through which Hollywood studios modify, transform, and fine-tune their commodities to respond to various market demands and restrictions. This regulatory feedback structure is essential for the industry's long-term fiscal well-being, enabling it to achieve the primary goal of maximizing the market potential of their multimillion-dollar investments."[139] This dynamic still holds true in the history of South Korean cinema despite the intermediary role of the MPI, a state agency, as the chief administrator of motion picture regulation. On the surface, the MPI/MCPI appears to represent what Hollywood's PCA regulators and studio executives called, in the vernacular of the business, "political censorship" external to the industry. Upon closer scrutiny of archival evidence, the ministry can be better understood as a double agent whose role was to mediate industrial and public interests for the greater good of the nation. They prohibited certain types of screen content, withheld issuance of exhibition permits, and, in very rare cases, indefinitely suspended completed motion pictures such as *The Governor's Daughter*. Despite such authoritative measures, primary documents available for research at the KOFA reveal that state regulators were far from being impartial guardians of public morality and always had the trade's commercial interests in mind.

3

Myths of Martyrs and Heroes in a Godless Land

Interagency Regulation of
1960s Anticommunist Films

Historian Michael Robinson has identified 1988 as a landmark year in South Korean history—a year when the first peaceful transfer of power took place by direct presidential elections, opening up "a space for more diverse and creative cultural production." The relaxation of censorship and the rise of apolitical popular culture in the late 1980s to early 1990s, according to Robinson, emancipated South Korean cinema from three "political, cultural, and social obsessions": namely, the national division (1945) and the Korean War (1950–1953), anticommunism and nationalism, and the memory of Japanese colonialism.[1] Citing such contemporary blockbusters as Kang Che-gyu's *Shiri* (1999) and Park Chan-wook (Pak Ch'an-uk)'s *Joint Security Area* (*Kongdong kyŏngbiguyŏk*, 2000), the historian argues that the postdemocratization era enabled "a huge step away from the master narrative of the Cold War and the demonization of the South's Northern brethren" by humanizing North Koreans *for the first time*.[2] Corroborating Robinson's thesis, Park Yu-hŭi, in her Korean-language scholarship on Golden Age auteur Yu Hyŏn-mok's films, identifies the Korean Central Intelligence Agency (KCIA: Chungangjŏngbobu)'s collaboration in interagency film censorship as a catalyst for solidifying the bifurcated cinematic narrative of the North/communism/evil/hell vs. the South/capitalism/good/heaven in the name of national security throughout the 1960s and 1970s.[3] Film scholar

Daniel Martin echoes Robinson's periodization, noting that contemporary South Korean cinema, free from censorship laws and control by military dictatorship, openly "interrogates the causes and consequences of the Korean War without demonizing the North." Martin names, however, precedents of sympathetic, humanized North Korean characters such as Agent Margaret (Yu In-ja), a northern spy-bargirl who falls in love with a southern intelligence officer in Han Hyŏng-mo's *The Hand of Fate* (*Unmyŏngŭi son*, 1954), and who resembles her counterpart Yi Pang-hŭi/Yi Myŏng-hyŏn (Kim Yun-jin), a revived enemy/lover archetype, in *Shiri*.[4]

What should be noted is that how communism and communists were depicted in South Korea's Golden Age cinema (1955–1972) was consistent with global trends of Cold War film culture. Even without the United States federal government's direct involvement in film censorship, Hollywood's Korean War films demonized and dehumanized Soviet, Chinese, and North Korean enemies as grossly caricatured, villainous brainwashers torturing heroic American prisoners of war (POWs) in such films as MGM's *Prisoner of War* (1954), Columbia's *The Bamboo Prison* (1954), and United Artists' *The Manchurian Candidate* (1962). The Red Scare and the blacklisting culture of the McCarthy era constituted an oppressive political backdrop in which a score of anticommunist films vilifying communist spies and lionizing U.S. law enforcement were made. Examples include *I Was a Communist for the FBI* (1951), *My Son John* (1952), and *Kiss Me Deadly* (1955). Furthermore, a wide range of 1950s Hollywood genre films from Westerns (e.g., *High Noon* [1952], *The Searchers* [1956]) to science fiction (e.g., *It Came from Outer Space* [1953], *Invasion of the Body Snatchers* [1956]) contain pervasive Cold War allegories pitting "good" against "evil" and "us" against "them." As many scholars have observed, the fervor and intensity of anticommunism in the United States was rooted in a religious (mis)interpretation of the Cold War. According to Kenneth D. Wald, "American anticommunism took the form of a moralistic crusade in which the object of disdain was invariably described as 'atheistic.'"[5] Thomas Aiello likewise observes, "Demonizing opponents was a recurring practice throughout the Cold War period. Regardless of logical merit, attacks on the godlessness of Communism habitually referred to Satan and the Antichrist."[6]

In South Korea, the anticommunist film (*Pangong yŏnghwa*) developed as an institutional genre, endorsed by both the state and the industry, with more secular political objectives. According to Hana Lee (Yi Ha-na), the label "refers to films produced with the goal of arousing anticommunist consciousness or films with anticommunist themes, but the concept did not have clear stipulations upon inception."[7] Cho Jun-hyoung (Cho Chun-hyŏng) defines the genre as affect-oriented films that "emphasize disillusionment with communist ideology or encourage the fighting spirit against communists."[8] Cho elaborates that it is a "parasitic" genre that can graft onto or mutate into any existing film genres with new rules. As David Scott Diffrient points out, the anticommunist film can be better understood as an "umbrella genre" that encompasses "everything from war films and division dramas (narrative centered on divided families and ideological conflicts) to espionage thrillers and melodramas."[9] Similar to American film noir, the generic anticommunist film label emerged retrospectively. Han Hyŏngmo's action melodrama *Breaking the Wall* (*Sŏngbyŏkŭl ttulgo*, 1949), revolving around the family conflict between an army officer and his communist brother-in-law, is now considered the first film of the genre, one that was supported by the Ministry of National Defense (MND: Kukpangbu) and financed by the Ministry of Public Information (MPI: Kongbobu). However, at the time of its original release, it was categorized as a "military drama" (*kunsagŭk*) or "policy film" (*kukch'ek yŏnghwa*), rather than an anticommunist film, in press reviews.[10]

Lee argues that the term "anticommunist film" entered the popular discourse in the mid-1950s following public controversies surrounding Yi Kangch'ŏn's *Piagol* (1955), "which based its scenario on a press release from the North Chŏlla Province Police Department on the capture of the Ppalch'isan communist guerrillas, had heavy backing and support of the military and police during production, but experienced difficulties in its premiere over growing differences in opinion within the government."[11] Despite the film's blatant efforts to expose the cruelty and inhumanity of communist ideology, members of the Security Bureau of the Ministry of the Interior (MoI: Naemubu) felt that it did not qualify as an anticommunist film for it was seen as misleading the public (by depicting South Korea as a communist-infiltrated "place with no military or police").[12] Along with the MND, the security branch pressured the Ministry of Education (MoE: Mungyobu, the ministry that administered state film censorship from 1955 to 1960) to cancel the film's exhibition permit at the last minute. The film had to undergo another round of censorship review and was allowed to be exhibited only after additional cuts were made. Notably, a superimposed image of an oversized South Korean flag was added in the background of the final shot to make explicit the final destination of the female partisan (No Kyŏng-hŭi), who has left the guerrilla hideout in the Chiri Mountains near the end of the film.

Although anticommunist films were not unique to South Korea during the Cold War, no other country, as Diffrient puts it, "went so far as to institutionalize anticommunism as a categorical imperative through the implementation of industry-wide standards and protection policies."[13] Prior to the rise of Park Chung Hee (Pak Chŏng-hŭi)'s military regime with the May 1961 coup, the anticommunist film was a minor genre. Between 1948 and 1961, only 36 such films were produced. Between 1962 and 1969, the genre rose to prominence and 125 films, which represented over 9 percent of the entire industry's output (1,342 narrative features), were produced. In 1966 alone, 25 anticommunist films were made.[14] The same year, the Grand Bell Awards (Taejongsang), South Korean cinema's highest honor, officialized the genre within the industry by adding two new awards for "Best Anticommunist Film" and "Best Anticommunist

Screenplay." From 1967, the producers of "Best Anticommunist Film" winners were rewarded import quotas for lucrative foreign motion pictures, further incentivizing the genre. Throughout the 1960s, war spectacle/combat action was the dominant mode of anticommunist films. Examples include *The Marines Who Never Returned* (*Tolaoji annŭn haebyŏng*, 1963), *YMS 504 of the Navy* (*YMS504 subyŏng*, 1963), *Red Muffler* (*Ppalgan majura*, 1964), and *The North and South* (*Namgwa puk*, 1964). This trend demonstrates that the genre was firmly rooted in the commercial logic of entertainment and populism, not simply Cold War ideology and state directives. When the genre fell into decline throughout the 1970s, it was largely submerged in the backwaters of B-movie espionage action, awash in James Bond knockoffs that used global geopolitics as an excuse to display sex and violence in exotic locales such as Hong Kong and Thailand. The last year the Grand Bell Awards honored anticommunist films was 1987. This institutional shift, as well as broader political changes, both domestic (partial democratization) and international (the end of the Cold War), explains why the anticommunist film as a distinct genre began to vanish in the late 1980s, although the theme of division and inter-Korean relations remained crucial to many subsequently produced war and action films with mainstream appeal, from Kang Che-gyu's *Tae Guk Gi: The Brotherhood of War* (*T'aegŭkgi hwinallimyŏ*, 2004) to Chang Hun's *Secret Reunion* (*Ŭihyŏngje*, 2010).

In this chapter, I investigate the various censorship discourses surrounding two largely overlooked 1960s anticommunist films set in North Korea: Yu Hyŏnmok's *The Martyred* (*Sungyoja*, 1965), based on Korean-American writer Richard E. Kim (Kim Ŭn-guk)'s 1964 English-language novel of the same title, and Kim Su-yong's *Accusation* (*Kobal*, 1967), based on the real-life story of Yi Su-gŭn, a North Korean journalist–turned–high-ranking official who defected to the South only to be prosecuted and executed for being a double agent two years later (having unlawfully expatriating in a failed attempt to seek asylum in a third country). Despite the elimination of the bluntest passages in Kim's novel (sections of prose that critique the hypocrisy of both organized religion and military propaganda), the narrative of Yu's film is largely faithful to the controversial plotlines of its source material, including the pastor-hero's open admission of his disbelief in God's existence (delivered to the atheist narrator) as well as a colonel's complicity in creating the myth of martyrs out of collaborators and cowards to advance his anticommunist propaganda program. It is hard to imagine such material—had the novel been adapted within the American film industry—passing without fierce objections on the part of Hollywood's internal regulator and stateside censorship boards, which were particularly sensitive to flagrant sacrilege and nonpatriotic messaging. The MPI censorship file housed at the Korean Film Archive (KOFA, Han'gukyŏngsang charyŏwŏn) demonstrates that a modest level of regulatory feedback related to military morale was given to the producers of *The Martyred*, allowing them to freely explore polemical content about religion, which angered Korean Protestants when the film came out.

Interestingly, in an interagency collaborative effort of regulatory review, only the KCIA objected to several potentially controversial narrative events such as a Christian mob's killing of a clergyman and a military doctor's insubordination against his retreat order. However, none of the three government branches involved in film regulation (the MPI, the MND, and the KCIA) made any heavy-handed interventions to control the images of North Korea and its communist ideologues. The case study of *The Martyred* indicates that state film censorship was a flexible, accommodative process in which the artistic merits of Kim's international best seller were respected by government regulators who minimized their bureaucratic meddling to matters of greatest national import. Archival evidence conflicts with Robinson's characterization of pre-1988 representations of North Korea and North Koreans as being completely devoid of any humanity due to authoritarian film censorship. This point is clearer in the case study of *Accusation*, which depicts family life and the workplace under Kim Il Sung (Kim Il-sŏng)'s Stalinist rule. Precisely because the state-sponsored anticommunist genre facilitated the unprecedented allocation of screen time to everyday life in North Korea (a subject rarely seen in contemporary Korean media, with a few exceptions such as the Netflix-distributed Korean rom-com series *Crash Landing on You* [*Sarangŭi pulsich'ak*, 2019–2020]), it was nearly impossible *not* to develop noble North Korean characters who suffer, resist, or transcend unjust purges and human rights violations in order to deliver the desired political messages. Whereas state cultural policy guided and fostered the development of the anticommunist film as an institutional genre, moral polarization of good vs. evil, democracy vs. communism, and oppression vs. freedom in film diegeses could be attributed as much to (melo)dramatic imperatives of commercial genre films as to regulatory input (either restrictive or permissive) from government censors.

I wish to challenge my own thesis of reasonable, if bureaucratic, film censorship under Park's military dictatorship (1961–1979) in the second half of the chapter, which is devoted to a combined contextual-textual analysis of *Accusation*. This biopic of the highest-ranking North Korean official to have defected to the South to date was an overt anticommunist propaganda project sponsored by the KCIA. After passing the MPI's censorship review with minor revisions, its exhibition permit was invalidated in February 1969 when the KCIA intentionally masterminded mass deception by announcing that the film's real-life protagonist, Yi Su-gŭn, had been identified as an infiltrated North Korean spy (based on falsified evidence extracted through torture). The aim of this fabricated political scandal was to turn the KCIA's mishandling of the most valuable defector to a fiction of counterespionage triumph. In July of that year, Yi was hurriedly executed after being convicted for violations of the National Security Act (Kukka poanbŏp) and the Anticommunist Law (Pangongbŏp) in a rushed trial. In this case, the KCIA had absolute power to make and unmake a hero out of Yi (diegetically and extradiegetically), killing both the subject and the film about him. The censorship history of *Accusation* is a sobering reminder that South

Korea was under a rather unforgiving dictatorship prone to enforcing draconian laws, far from being the land of hope and freedom as portrayed in the anticommunist genre of the Park era.

From an Existential Novel to an Anti-Communist Film: Adaptation of *The Martyred*

A best seller of 1964 and nominee for the National Book Award, North Korean native and immigrant writer Richard E. Kim's first novel, *The Martyred*, centers on the experiences of college instructor–turned–army intelligence officer Captain Lee (Nam Kung-wŏn in the film). More specifically, it focuses on his investigation of Minister Shin (Kim Chin-gyu), one of the two survivors of a mass communist execution of captured Christian reverends in Pyongyang on the day of the Korean War's outbreak (June 25, 1950). Once the northern capital is occupied by United Nations forces, Lee's commanding officer, Colonel Chang (Chang Tong-hwi), is determined to promote the martyrdom of twelve murdered clergymen as fodder for the South Korean army's anticommunist propaganda. Instead of clearing his name by denying suspicion of his collaboration with the enemy, Shin keeps silent about what happened and cites "divine intervention" as the reason for his survival. Colonel Chang presents Major Jung (Ch'oe Myŏng-su), a captured police bureau officer, as a witness to testify to both the heroism of the martyrs and the innocence of Shin and Hann (Kim Kwang-yŏng), another survivor who has succumbed to madness while in communist captivity. The communist prisoner goes rogue and testifies in front of a group of religious leaders summoned to Colonial Chang's office that the twelve Christians died in a cowardly way, betraying one another, denouncing their God, and begging for mercy. Major Jung explains that he did not kill Shin, out of respect for the defiant minister's courage to spit in the enemy's face, nor Hann, because of his mental illness. Chang kills Jung later and plans to dispute Shin's forthcoming corroborating testimony of what really happened. To the officer's surprise, the reverend supports the army's mythmaking by falsely admitting his guilt in betraying the martyrs to save his own life. As Josephine Nock-Hee Park observes, "*The Martyred* constructs a series of parallels between the minister and the colonel: both are singularly devoted to their calling.... At the heart of the contest between Chang and Shin is a problem: the supposed purity of the martyrs.... Colonel Chang is a skeptic, disdainful of Christianity, but his political interest requires the perfect piety of the martyrs; Reverend Shin, the only sane witness to the martyrs' last days, seeks to protect their virtue."[15]

Shin's confession lights the fire under an evangelical lynch mob, which destroys his house and directs violence toward Hann, who is killed in the attack. The disgraced minister turns public opinion around by delivering a powerful sermon, identifying himself and his congregation as fellow sinners while glorifying the persecution and bravery of saintly martyrs who died for their sins. As Park describes, "in publicizing their suffering, Shin delivers his martyrs to the propaganda campaign" of Colonel Chang, who privately claims that the twelve men are "good and saintly... *because* they were murdered by the Reds" regardless of their (mis)conduct.[16] Paralleling Shin's conflict and reconciliation with the community is his rocky friendship with the narrator, Captain Lee, an atheist who constantly challenges the minister's faith. After Chang is transferred to lead an underground espionage mission, Lee takes over his command and is ordered to evacuate Pyongyang as the tide of war turns with the Chinese intervention. The captain extends an offer of safe transportation to the South to Shin, who chooses to stay in the abandoned city with the weak who are being left behind (old men, women, and children). Before their parting, the minister not only acknowledges that he "searched for God" all his life but "found only man with all his sufferings... and death," but also confesses that he does not believe in an afterlife, the resurrection of the flesh, or the eternal Kingdom of God.[17] Nevertheless, Shin vows to take his secret to the grave and to harness Christian faith as a means of comforting people suffering from wars, poverty, and despair. The guilt-ridden minister confesses to having failed twice to guard his truth, bringing misery to those closest to him: his wife died with a broken heart after his declaration that there is no afterlife to let them see their dead son again, and Minister Hann was driven mad from the shock of learning his mentor's atheist (non)beliefs on the execution ground. After relocating from Pyongyang to Pusan, Captain Lee visits a chaplain from the North (Pak Am) running a tent church on a refugee island and hears a mysterious rumor that a dozen northern refugees claim that they have seen Minister Shin (who is presumed to be dead) everywhere in North Korea from the Manchurian border to a remote fishing village. The novel ends with the captain, now uplifted "with a wondrous lightness of heart," joining a group of refugees who sing "a song of homage to their homeland."[18]

For the most part, Yu's screen adaptation faithfully follows Kim's original story, which is dedicated to French existential writer Albert Camus, whose "insight into 'a strange form of love'" helped the Korean author overcome "the nihilism of the trenches and bunkers of Korea" during the war, in which he served as a South Korean army liaison officer after migrating from the North.[19] In his introduction to the 2011 Penguin Classics reprint of *The Martyred*, Heinz Insu Fenkl describes how "Kim's characters are what Camus would term men of 'balance' [*mesure*], who know their limitations as men. Kim's world in *The Martyred* ... could be characterized as one that illustrates the godless indifference of the universe—the nihilism attributed to Camus's early work. And yet, like Camus, Kim is able to move beyond nihilism by embracing and transcending the many enigmas portrayed in *The Martyred*."[20] Kim opens his novel with the same epigram from Friedrich Hölderlin's unfinished drama *The Death of Empedocles* (1846) that Camus used for *The Rebel* (1951): "And openly I pledged my heart to the grave and suffering land, and often in the consecrated night, I promised to love her faithfully until death, unafraid, with her heavy burden of

FIGURE 3.1 Richard E. Kim sitting at a desk with books. ca. 1964. Kim's debut novel, *The Martyred* (1964), was influenced by the immigrant author's experience as a South Korean army liaison officer during the Korean War. Photo Credit: University Photograph Collection. Special Collections and University Archives, University of Massachusetts Amherst Libraries.

fatality, and never to despise a single one of her enigmas. Thus did I join myself to her with a mortal cord."[21]

The critical consensus on Yu's adaptation upon its original release was that the film was overly faithful to Kim's novel. One reviewer opined, "Those who read the novel will feel like they have already seen the film.... It feels like a 'video film' of a theatrical performance."[22] Another commented, "The novel is more 'cinematic' and the film is more 'novelistic.' Despite the difference of two mediums, director Yu was extremely faithful to the original, page by page."[23] However, Yu's film version makes strategic alterations to the opening and closing passages of the novel to reinforce the Park regime's policy of anticommunism and nationalism. Kim's novel begins quietly with its narrator documenting the earliest flickerings of the war with cool objectivity: "The war came early one morning in June of 1950, and by the time the North Koreans occupied our capital city, Seoul, we had already left our university, where we were instructors in the History of Human Civilization. I joined the Korean Army, and Park [Captain Lee's close friend and son of one of the martyrs] volunteered for the Marines Corps."[24]

The film narrator is much more forceful and dramatic in his condemnation of the northern invasion. After opening credits roll over a close-up shot of a trembling military net against a sonic backdrop of artillery explosions and aerial bombings, the screen transitions to a nondescript view of drifting clouds with continued sound effects associated with war. The grave voiceover intones with an air of indignation and indictment befitting the anticommunist genre: "June 25, 1950, a most atrocious war to be fought among the same people started by the blood-thirsty North Korean communists. The South Korean Army and the UN Forces launched an immediate counterattack. They overrode the thirty-eight parallel and the northern territory has succumbed to an angry wave of the onrushing forces of freedom." The first scene following the opening narration is an event that is presented as a flashback on page fifty-eight of Kim's novel, where Captain Lee is first introduced to Minister Hann. The demented young man's emaciated face brings back the memory of a dying survivor of the mass execution of political prisoners in the cave by retreating communists. After digging up the skeletal man (with hollow eyes and oozing mouth infested with flies) from the cave, Captain Lee is consumed by anger when a phalanx of photographers, both Korean and foreign, competitively flash their cameras to take better shots of the survivor. When asked by the photojournalists to move out of their cameras' view, the officer snaps and smashes those photographic instruments with a shovel.

The film's opening scene segues from the sky to the cave, where a group of prisoners in civilian clothes enter, along with communist soldiers in padded winter uniforms. Captain Lee's narration omnisciently intones, "Just before they withdrew from the city, the North Korean communists led a number of politicians and religious leaders to a cave and mercilessly massacred them there." A medium close-up shot of a religious man kneeling in prayer is followed by a medium shot of Red soldiers machinegunning offscreen prisoners. The camera pulls back to reveal a long-shot view of the cave, where executed men fall to the ground (in the foreground) and a North Korean officer and his enlisted men flee the scene (in the background). An explosion rumbles offscreen and the camera cuts to a close-up of rubble as the narrator's voice returns: "And the entrance to the cave was sealed off by a dynamite blast." A cut to a black screen, accompanied by the sound of Captain Lee continuing his narration, provides this sound bridge: "Four days later we reopened the seal." A long shot of the cave returns with most of the frame shrouded in darkness save for the background, where the entrance is cracked open, admitting light. Against a tense musical backdrop, a close-up shot of a hand lifting up to the ceiling among the dead is foregrounded, just before there is a cut to a long shot of South Korean soldiers entering the cave. Captain Lee immediately attends to the man in the center who is still breathing and holds on to his hand in a show of compassion. The officer's humanity is accentuated in close-ups of his hands and eyes, setting him apart from cruel communist soldiers whose faces are rendered indistinguishable in the distance. Unlike his counterpart in the novel, Lee merely chases away a group of reporters rushing into the cave to take pictures (calling them "inhuman" and "merciless") rather than destroying their cameras.

This altered opening undoubtedly establishes Yu's *The Martyred* as an anticommunist text by vividly visualizing a massacre occurring in real time instead of embedding it as a geographically distant flashback to the aftermath of the event witnessed by the narrator. While the novel remains locked into a first-person mode from its first page until its last, the film's point of view shifts between focalized narration and omniscient narration (for example, the opening moments capture images of atrocities that the captain, who is not present, has not witnessed). The barbarity of communists is once again emphasized during the sermon scene, which presents a montage of gruesome torture lasting seven days and nights and rendered as a flashback. In the novel, the corresponding scene is described in a removed, abstract way. Captain Lee narrates it as follows: "To my surprise—and uneasiness—Mr. Shin, for the next twenty minutes or so, described to the congregation in the minutest detail how each minister was tortured, one after another, all twelve of them. Mr. Hann, said Mr. Shin, collapsed after three days and nights of torture and became ill."[25] Presenting the passage as an inserted montage flashback, the film adaptation does not leave the "minutest detail" of communist torture to the audience's imagination.

When Shin asks his congregation, "You know how they tortured the martyrs?" the camera dollies in on a close-up of the minister's face. The next shot provides a flashback, which shows a line of six martyrs being tortured by communists whose hands are shown pouring water on the faces of their victims (from the top of the frame). Then there is a cut to another shot of martyrs lined up in a distressed position with their hands in ropes propped up in the back. The camera tracks laterally to the action and stops at the agonized face of a prisoner on the far right, none other than Shin himself. The minister's voiceover indicates that "the bodies of the martyrs were nothing but the maimed hunks of meat from torture beyond human tolerance." At this point, the camera cuts to a low-angle long shot of the prison cell, where a group of battered men are shown standing in a circle, wracked by pain, until some fall to the ground. Shin's narration explains, "Their bones are crushed and arms and legs are twisted." A cut to two men lying on the ground unconscious with blood gushing from their mouths is accompanied by Shin's offscreen voice: "Some of them fell on their own vomited blood." This forty-second torture montage reaches its crescendo with a close-up shot of an iron rod in a bucket—blazing hot atop burning coals—that is scored to an ominous orchestral cue. The camera tracks right alongside the communist officer's leather boots as the torturer approaches his roped victim to brand a thigh covered with thin cotton pants. A high-pitched shriek brings an abrupt halt to the flashback and the scene returns to the church, in which a female parishioner is seen passing out in a pew. As a palpably gruesome opening scene, this montage of medieval-style communist torture as acts of religious persecution serves to bolster the film's identity as an anticommunist text.

Perhaps the most notable change is the film's patriotic ending, in which Captain Lee recites a slight variation of the novel's above-quoted epigram. Following an oral flashback of Shin's plea ("Love the people and assist them. Fight despair and have pity on the mortals. And bear your cross with courage"), the captain's soliloquy mixes into the soundtrack, which plays "Patriot's Song" (Aegukka), the Korean anthem. Lee declares, "I promised to the land of darkness and suffering. May her be the land of heavy burden of misfortune in the night full of sacrifice, I will love her until my death without fear and with all my sincerity. Thus, there was born a fateful bondage between me and my motherland." Hölderlin's abstract land of many enigmas is turned into a specific locality/nation with a particular fate as a symbol of the superpowers' confrontation. Yu's closing remark evokes a melancholic metanarrative of the Korean nation and people as victims of the Cold War. The solemn mood in the cinematic ending contrasts with the novel's final statement, in which Captain Lee expresses "a wondrous lightness of heart" that, as Fenkl notes, is "entirely antithetical to" the storyline of "tragic bitterness and pessimism" leading up to it.[26] This paradoxical emotion can be best explained by Kim's embrace of Camus's literary philosophy of the absurd. Lee resembles Camus's heroes of absurd reasoning, such as Meursault in *The Stranger* (*L'Etranger*, 1942), who demonstrate contradictory impulses of "one man's awareness of [the] nihilist void" and "the need . . . to affirm some value, some vitality driving him on, in spite of the void."[27]

In Kim's novel, the captain experiences a strange feeling of relief after two older men, unlikely conspirators in creating the fictional martyrdom, have perished: Colonel Chang is killed in action and Minister Shin, who is diagnosed with an advanced stage of tuberculosis, is in all probability dead (although he remains a mythical immortal figure in the collective minds of North Korean refugees). As Josephine Nock-Hee Park notes, "In *The Martyred*, those who love the land 'faithfully until death' do not survive: Chang's devotion to the state dooms him, as does Shin's devotion to the people. . . . By contrast, Lee is ultimately a figure of retreat. . . . Captain Lee is a renegade who remains aloof from the novel's 'plots and counterplots'. . . . Lee understands that to bind himself to occupied land would be utter folly."[28] His cinematic counterpart is a more

FIGURE 3.2 Compared with his nihilist literary counterpart, Captain Lee (Nam Kung-wŏn) in Yu Hyŏn-mok's *The Martyred* (1965) is a more relatable humanist hero who is reborn as a committed Cold War warrior through empathy and catharsis toward the end.

relatable humanist hero who remains deferential to the memory of his seniors (Chang and Shin) and vows to follow their lead to be loyal to his nation and compatriots. The narrator/protagonist is reborn as a committed Cold War warrior through empathy and catharsis, thus departing from the absurdist tone of the original ending.

Of War and Religion: A Two-Pronged Approach to Censoring *The Martyred*

There are two dimensions of censorship issues related to *The Martyred* that are worth noting. In a screenplay censorship report dated March 20, 1965, the MPI raises concerns about two items tied to national security or military images and one about religion. The state censor demands that (1) the scene in which Captain Lee destroys journalists' cameras be deleted or rewritten; (2) the line that North Korean prisoner Major Jung was shot be removed in consideration of military morale; and (3) the producers be cautious not to mock or incite hatred of religion or insult religious consciousness.[29] As mentioned earlier, in the film version the captain merely kicks reporters out of the cave with a shovel raised in his hands rather than breaking the private property of press members, which would have been inappropriate conduct for a military officer. The colonel's confession of shooting a POW in violation of the Geneva Convention would have been a more serious offense as far as the government is concerned. In the revised script and release print, Colonel Chang informs Captain Lee that Major Jung has been sent to a POW camp. The ministry's caution for overall religious representations is based on "enforcement regulations" (*sihaenggyuch'ik*) for the Motion Picture Law of 1962, mandating that motion pictures be censored (either deletions of offensive materials or denial of exhibition permits) for "depicting religion as an object of sarcasm, mockery, or hatred" or for "deliberately mocking or vilifying clergy."[30] However, apart from paying lip service to this regulatory principle, the ministry demanded no specific revisions or deletions of objectionable scenes or plotlines, and there is little evidence that producers heeded this generalized advice in revising their scripts.

The Martyred passed a censorship print review on June 16, 1965, on the condition that Colonel Chang's antiwar line, which was lifted verbatim from Kim's novel ("You have licked the sweat and sucked the blood of this war"), be deleted.[31] After issuing its exhibition permit to Hapdong Film (*The Martyred*'s production company, established in 1964), the MPI responded to the feedback from its interagency regulatory partners (the MND and the KCIA) with advice favorable to the production company. Having assisted the film's production with military supplies, the MND made modest suggestions in a report to the MPI dated June 17, 1965: (1) the deletion of a gruesome scene in which a mummy-like, heavily bandaged soldier collapses and dies in agony; and (2) revisions of army branch names in dialogue (for example, replacing "Counter Intelligence Corps" with "army authorities").[32] In a memo circulated internally, Motion Picture Division staff in the MPI opined that it would be implausible to reshoot or reedit a released film (whose exhibition started in Seoul's Academy Theater on June 18) to accommodate the suggested changes. Acting diplomatically, the ministry advised that the military branch leverage their sponsorship for the production and negotiate directly with Hapdong Film for their desired revisions.[33] One can conjecture that the film company talked the MND out of this demand, citing the exorbitant costs of postproduction reedits, since the objected scene and dialogue can be still found in the print available for on-demand viewing (with burnt-in English subtitles) through the KOFA's website.

In *Hollywood Diplomacy: Film Regulation, Foreign Relations, and East Asian Representations* (2020), I dispute a widely held perception of the Pentagon's "technical advising" of Hollywood productions as a form of government censorship.[34] After the 1949 establishment of the Motion Picture Section of the Pictorial Branch within its Office of Public Information, the United States Department of Defense (DoD) exerted a moderate degree of negotiation muscle as individual filmmakers were obliged to submit their scripts and preview prints in exchange for free access to military bases, equipment, personnel, and stock footage. However, without command of jurisdiction over the private industry's distribution and exhibition sectors, the Pentagon had no means of penalizing producers for neglecting its desired messages. Based on archival research in the DoD Film Collection housed at Georgetown University, I have argued that Pentagon-sponsored technical advising on Hollywood's midcentury anticommunist films cannot be simply reduced to a "propaganda model" aimed at force-feeding governmental ideology and interests to the public. Undoubtedly, anticommunism is a political slant found in some of the advisory comments provided by military script reviewers, but the primary impulse of military technical advising was to strive for the realism and authenticity often lacking in Hollywood's fanciful scripts.

Compared with the copious, specific notes sent to producers of Korean War POW films such as *Prisoner of War* and *The Bamboo Prison* by Pentagon reviewers (as detailed in *Hollywood Diplomacy*), South Korea's MND provided minimal regulatory feedback for *The Martyred*. Even those minor items were not adopted by Hapdong Film, which was free to release its film without the MND's approval. The MPI was the government agency in charge of issuing exhibition permits, thus downgrading the MND's position as a secondary state reviewer, which was consulted in a nonbinding capacity as evidenced by the above-quoted correspondences. South Korea's MND was in the shoes of its American counterpart as far as its relationship with the film industry was concerned. Both government branches supported film productions, desiring positive publicity for the military, and provided suggestions for revising scripts or finished prints in accordance with their policy. However, without any enforcing power, they were dependent on the willing cooperation of individual filmmakers, who were free to adopt their advice selectively, if at all. Given the sensitive subject matter related to the army counterintelligence corps' propaganda war against communists and a commanding officer's campaign to bury the truth told by an enemy informant, the MND's comments are surprisingly meek and passive. In particular, their adherence to technicality (such as names of armed services) indicates an awareness of their disempowered position vis-à-vis the private industry, which benefited from military sponsorship without clearly defined reciprocal obligations.

In other cases, the MND's regulatory input was elevated to censorship precisely because the MPI was on board for enforcing its implementation to film producers prior to permitting exhibition. An illustrative example is Yi Man-hŭi (Lee Man-hee)'s Vietnam War film *A Spotted Man* (*Ŏllungmuniŭi sanai*, 1967), based on the real-life story of Yi In-ho (Kim Sŏk-hun), a marine captain who died heroically by using his body as a shield against a grenade thrown by a Vietcong combatant—an act of bravery that saved the lives of his squad men during a cave search mission in August 1966. The location shooting of combat action in CinemaScope (featuring the actual marine special forces unit under Yi's command and 1,000 Vietnamese extras) was fully supported by the MND and the Headquarters of Republic of Korea Forces in Vietnam. Given the film's military significance as a combat picture about a posthumously decorated hero and the ongoing war, it is not surprising that the MPI solicited the opinions of the MND on both the screenplay and the preview print. Unlike the case of *The Martyred*, the defense branch provided a lengthy list of detailed script changes and substantial scene deletions for *A Spotted Man*.

The KOFA's MPI censorship file on *A Spotted Man* includes an undated list of script revisions demanded by the MND (presumably sent immediately after the MPI sent a memo on December 10, 1966, requesting a prompt report on the screenplay forwarded on November 3). Several items of suggested alterations target direct or indirect references to war deaths in song lyrics, dialogue, and facial expressions. For example, defense reviewers demanded that the numbers of deaths and injuries reported by a radio signal man in two scenes be lowered (in one scene, from nine deaths and two injuries to two deaths and three injuries; in another scene, from nine deaths and twelve injuries to three deaths and seven injuries). A shot of marines shedding tears for their fallen buddies was singled out as something to be cut, as was a lieutenant's line that he is going to "spit in the face of anyone who talks about tomorrow in the battlefield." Two items pertained to representations of American soldiers. The MND disapproved of an unruly bar brawl scene in which a Korean sergeant gets into a physical fight with an American soldier over a Vietnamese bargirl while the men in his squad stand by, cheering for him. Military reviewers suggested that the scene be rewritten with the Korean marine withdrawing after casually apologizing, saying "I am sorry" to his U.S. counterpart. Another significant change involved a scene in which Captain Yi hesitantly gifts a mercy bullet to a fatally wounded, pleading American captain stranded in the coastal area where his division has been annihilated following a beach landing. The MND proposed that the scene be rewritten so that Korean allies offer first aid and several bullets for self-defense to the ill-fated captain. Other miscellaneous revisions on the list addressed the use of ranks and salutations in dialogue and an illiterate staff sergeant's line, "I can't read" (which advisers felt should be cut).[35]

In addition to extensively cleansing the script in accordance with wartime public information policies, the defense ministry requested further edits upon reviewing the preview print in a memo to the MPI on August 18, 1967. Four scenes were objected to and became the subject of a request for removal: (1) a scene of Vietcong prisoners' mass suicide; (2) a scene in which marines are blocking with bayonets Vietnamese protestors demanding the release of prisoners; (3) a scene in which a mortally wounded soldier discusses death while donating blood to an injured Vietnamese child; and (4) a scene in which a marine is brutally killed in ambush by Vietcong guerrillas during a search mission.[36] Although *A Spotted Man* is a lost film and therefore unavailable for viewing, the MPI's internal memo attached to the letter from the MND indicates that the "voluntary" revisions of these scenes were requested to the production company.[37] It is not entirely clear what was or was not included in the release print, but based on a copy of the revised script available for research at the KOFA, it can be inferred that most of the objected items were removed.

What is particularly notable is how the American captain plotline was rewritten. In the revised script, Yi's unit successfully rescues a parachuted American pilot captured as a Vietcong prisoner and evacuates him to safety.[38] This incident was relocated toward the beginning of the narrative so that it might act as a catalyst for dramatic conflicts between Yi's well-meaning unit and Vietnamese villagers (who lose their family members and neighbors to Vietcong revenge killings after Captain Lewis's rescue). This new storyline follows the familiar "rescue narrative" formula of anticommunist films in which South Korean soldiers save American GIs, symbolizing the Cold War security alliance between the two countries (as shown in such films as Chŏng Ch'ang-gŭn's *The Hill of Immortal Bird* [*Pulsajoŭi ŏndŭk*, 1955] and Yi Yong-min's *A Cross in Gunfire* [*P'ohwasokŭi sipjaga*, 1956]) and stoking the national ego of Korean audiences.[39] Furthermore, it eliminates controversial elements in the earlier script by shifting the Korean hero's role from that of a reluctant accomplice to the American captain's suicide to that of the latter's valiant savior. Although Yi Man-hŭi's production team did not exactly follow the MND's suggestion for the scene's revision, the military censor's objection likely prompted a creative solution that could better serve both dramatic and commercial purposes.

Returning to our discussion of *The Martyred*, the MPI's privileging of national prestige over religious matters is precisely where Korean film censorship distinguishes itself from its American counterpart. Religion was intrinsic to the principles of content regulation conducted by both Hollywood's self-regulation agency, the Production Code Administration (PCA: 1934–1968) and external boards at state, municipal, and local levels in the United States. The Motion Picture Production Code of 1930, which governed the industry's "self-cleansing," was cowritten by religious authorities, Jesuit priest Father Daniel A. Lord and Catholic trade publisher Martin Quigley. As Thomas Doherty notes, "Conceived in faith and invested with a sacred aura, the Code would be likened to another text, the Bible, and metaphors of print-based religiosity waft around it like incense: the commandments, the tablets, and the gospel."[40] Enforcers of Hollywood's self-regulation were carefully chosen to boost the industry's respectability and credibility in the eyes of Protestants and Catholics. Will H. Hays, the president of the Motion Picture Producers and Distributors of America (MPPDA, now the Motion Picture Association [MPA]), was a Presbyterian elder from Indiana, and Joseph I. Breen, the head of the PCA, was a devout Irish Catholic with powerful friends in the Church. The 1933 formation of the Legion of Decency, a Catholic pressure group that pointed a damning finger at "sinful" Hollywood movies (which were handed a "C [condemned]-rating") and organized a nationwide boycott campaign, posed a serious economic threat to the Depression-hit industry. Hollywood responded to the crisis by strengthening its self-regulation and monitoring religious offenses on screen under the PCA's watchful eyes.

On the surface, the language of provisions related to religion in Hollywood's Production Code is no more stringent than that of its Korean counterpart. The Code mandates, "(1) No film or episode may throw *ridicule* on any religious faith; (2) *Ministers of religion* . . . should not be used as comic characters or as villains; (3) *Ceremonies* of any definite religion should be carefully and respectfully handled."[41] However, its implementation would not have been as lax and half-hearted as the MPI handled the subject in their censorship review of *The Martyred*. Undoubtedly, this matter would have been the highest priority for those who worked for the PCA and on stateside censorship boards had it been a Hollywood production. From a constitutional perspective, motion picture censorship based on Christian doctrines could be accommodated in the United States, as the federal government had no part in it. In South Korea, however, a state ministry, an official branch of the government, was responsible for administering film censorship. Therefore, Article 20 of the 1948 constitution of the Republic of Korea (ROK) reads, "No state religion shall be recognized, and religion and state shall be separated,"[42] a sentiment that was certainly applicable to the MPI's handling of religious representations in motion pictures.

While not being overly pushy about the "correct" way to depict any one religion throughout the censorship review process, the ministry was responsible for answering to grievances from *all* religious leaders about any perceived blasphemy, sacrilege, or mockery of ministers, priests, nuns, Buddhist monks, and so on. For example, the MPI mediated disputes between Shin Films and the Chogye Order of Korean Buddhism over Shin Sang-ok's *Dream* (*Kkum*, 1967), which contained controversial scenes (absent in Yi Kwang-su's original novel of the same title) showing a monk character performing an obscene song and seducing an innocent girl. The enraged national Buddhist organization demanded that the film—an insult to them—be banned by the MPI, which arranged negotiation meetings between the two parties (the producer agreed to make cuts to offensive scenes).[43] Similarly, the Korea Evangelical Holiness Church petitioned to the MPI to suspend the exhibition of *The Martyred* for depicting atheism, insulting ministers and martyrs, and portraying a holy congregation as a violent mob. In this case, the ministry defended the film, insisting that it was faithful to the original novel rather than expressing independent opinions about religion of its own.[44]

In *Hollywood Diplomacy*, I highlight the role of audience boycotts and protests over offensive images detrimental to their group's self-esteem as a third kind of motion picture censorship—one that complemented external censorship (by state, municipal, or foreign boards) and self-regulation (in-house PCA censorship or MPA ratings). In that book I argue that, "as a 'third kind of censorship,' such media advocacy of ordinary citizens and consumers opens up a dialogical space that has been referred to by Heather Hendershot as 'competing censorships'.... The power of activism lies not in its ability to bring radical change to representational politics of oligopolistic media giants but in its ability to attract the public's attention to the hegemony, inequality, and inauthenticity manifested in their mainstream productions and call for collective action (boycotts, picketing, etc.)."[45] Of course, in the above quote, I am referring to different power dynamics between Hollywood studios and minority or foreign audiences resisting the racially regressive representational politics of global blockbusters.

On the surface, these power differentials appeared to be inversed in the antagonistic relationship between Yu Hyŏn-mok, an artistically minded auteur (who struggled to find producers to invest in noncommercial films such as *The Stray Bullet* [*Obalt'an*, 1961] and *The Martyred*) and the Korean Protestant church, which denounced his film. In his 1995 memoir, Yu recalls, "I too grew up as a devout Christian and still firmly believe in God, so it was a difficult situation. In small city theaters, Bible-toting Christian protestors blocked the entrance. To someone as poor as me, [the boycott] translated to more debts."[46] Despite the constitutional principle of the separation between state and religion, conservative factions of the church were fully behind Park's military dictatorship and its anticommunist campaign, expanding its social power in the 1960s and 1970s.[47] Regardless, Korean Christians' organized boycotts of *The Martyred* and the ensuing public debate about the film reaffirm Hendershot's argument that, in an ironic twist, competing censorships coming from all ideological directions—from the religious right to the progressive left and everything in between—can collectively function as democratic enablers of "critical thought, discussion, and activism."[48] In the final analysis, "Censorship and free speech are competing, heterogenous, and nonbinary cultural constants."[49]

The strongest condemnation of the film and its original novel came from offended ministers, reverends, and Christian commentators. In Sunday sermons, many parish leaders openly labeled the text as "anti-Christian" and blamed it for staining the history of the Korean Protestant church. In his June 1965 interview with *Tonga Ilbo*, Minister Cho Tong-jin of Huam Church fiercely opposed the film for featuring a North Korean officer as a truth-telling witness against martyrs and depicting Christianity as a cult organization. Hwang Kwang-ŭn of Yŏnggwang Church echoed the resentment, stating, "Literary and religious dimensions are different. There could be fiction in literature. However, this text is set in Pyongyang during the Korean War. Therefore, it should have been faithful to historical facts of martyrdom. We take this as an outside challenge to our church. We could debate about Camus and his explicit atheism. But this type of 'humanism' that denies the existence of God is a bigger problem as far as Christianity is concerned. I fear that young Christians might lose their spiritual anchor."[50] In an opinion piece contributed to the June 26, 1965, issue of faith-based newspaper *Christian*, renowned screenwriter and film critic O Yŏng-jin criticized *The Martyred* for distorting the "truth of martyrdom" in his native city Pyongyang and overstepping the boundaries of fiction.[51]

This collective religious backlash against the film should be contextualized in relation to the centrality of the Korean War to Christian martyrdom. Out of the 254 martyrs officially identified and recognized by the Korean Christian Martyrs Memorial, 189 (approximately 75 percent) were victims of communist atrocities during the civil war.[52] Minister Son Yang-wŏn, a saintly martyr who adopted a communist who was responsible for the deaths of two of his biological sons, is a symbolic figure whose memory is engrained as an integral part of Korean Christian persecution by savage communists. The minister refused to abandon his church (doubling as a leper house) in the coastal city of Yŏsu and to flee retreating communist forces. Son was captured by North Korean troops and sent to a prison where he was interrogated and tortured for two weeks. According to an eyewitness account, on September 28, 1950, Son and 120 other political prisoners were dragged to an orchard hill where they were shot, bayonetted, and stoned to death in groups of ten. Minister Son's corpse "had two bullet wounds on his shoulder and two fingers. His mouth had a blunt force trauma and teeth were broken. Probably they shot his lifted shoulder and fingers while he was singing a hymn to spread the gospel and hit his mouth with a stone while he was praying."[53]

Although atrocities were widely committed by both sides (communist and anticommunist) throughout the fratricidal war, northern Christians who migrated to the South believed that they had a good reason to hate communists as both religious and political foes. During the Japanese colonial period (1910–1945), Pyongyang was a hub of Christian missionary activities in the colony, earning the nickname the "Jerusalem of Chosŏn." In 1915, with approximately 10 percent of its entire population of 60,000 attending churches and studying bible teachings, the many of the major thoroughfares of Pyongyang were deserted on Sundays. By 1924, the Presbyterian Church had grown to 120 chapels, 21,000 members, and thirty schools in Pyongyang and its vicinity. In addition, there were sixteen Methodist churches with 2,300 members.[54] With the rise of communism and its antireligion movement among North Korean intellectuals in the 1920s, the church responded with a campaign to promote Pyongyang as a historic holy city where the first Protestant martyr, Robert Jeramin Thomas, a Welsh missionary working as an interpreter for the American trade ship *General Sherman*, had been killed in 1866. The wartime mass migration of northern Christians seeking religious freedom contributed significantly to the postwar revival of Christianity in South Korea. Of the 2,000 new churches built by the mid-1950s, 90 percent were for North Korean refugees.[55] For the most part, Northerners constituted the most devoted and evangelical members of Protestant churches in the South, united in their hatred of communism and defense of the southern system that enabled their accumulation of economic and social capital. Given this context, it is not hard to imagine why *The Martyred*, a film in which a North Korean persecutor literally laughs at martyrs and belittles their cowardice and indignity in his spiteful testimony, stirred the indignation and antagonism of many Christians, particularly those from the North.

The controversy over *The Martyred* generated productive conversations about the meaning of religion among believers and nonbelievers alike. For example, an editorial in *Chosŏn Ilbo* sought to reason with incensed Christian readers in the following way:

> While it is understandable that Christians disagree with the atheistic declaration 'There is no God' (although the novel does not say it explicitly), attempting to blacklist the film among congregations or ban its showings entirely is excessive. Not only is it laughable to confuse the artistic 'reality' with our real-life 'reality' but also this columnist does not feel that the novel or its film adaption damaged the reputation of Christianity or clergy.... I do not believe

that the film will drive people to atheism; rather, *The Martyred*, novel and film, might very well serve as a skybridge to faith for modern people who want to believe but find it difficult.... Today, atheist humanism has more power to battle human despair than anything else. It can be an ally in the ideological battle against church destroyers, not an enemy. It is fine for the church to criticize this attitude but unwise to reject it altogether.[56]

Support for the film also came from the Christian community itself. On June 22, 1965, the monthly magazine *Christian World* (*Kidokkyo segye*) hosted a discussion panel entitled "Analyzing Faith in *The Martyred*" to which original novelist Richard E. Kim, film director Yu Hyŏn-mok, and Christian leaders were invited. Kim clarified that he never denies the existence of God in his novel and his character Shin merely confesses that he could not "find" Him in his subjective struggle regardless of the objective truth.[57] Chaplin Pyŏn Sŏn-hwan of Ewha Woman's High School opined that instead of insulting members of the clergy, the film explores the inner domain of human beings, as it shows that ministers and priests can experience doubts in their minds despite their holy occupation. Minister Mun Ik-hwan of Han'guk Theological Seminary likewise argued that the film "deals with different human approaches to finding God," foregrounding two conflicting ideas—"loveless God" and "love without God"—in modern Christianity.[58] Ultimately, calls for censorship opened a dialogical space in which communications between Christians and atheists or agnostics, as well as among churchgoers who held different interpretations of faith, were facilitated.

Accusation and the KCIA's Role in Film Regulation

Alongside the MND, there was another branch of the government that weighed in on *The Martyred* via censorship report: the KCIA. The institution was founded on May 20, 1961, as an investigative intelligence arm of Park Chung Hee's military junta following his bloodless coup four days before. The special agency was responsible for collecting both domestic and foreign intelligence, investigating crimes related to national security and communism, and monitoring or supervising intelligence or investigation activities of other branches of the government, including the military. According to sociologist Paul Y. Chang,

> Designated the central organ in Park's strategy to defend South Korea from communist threats, the KCIA's power to investigate individuals and organizations accused of antiregime activities was nearly unlimited.... So many dissidents were taken to be interrogated in the KCIA facilities in the Seobinggo district, at the foot of the South Mountain (Namsan) in central Seoul, that activists would joke that they were checking into the "Seobinggo Hotel VIP room." The euphemism belies the terror that the KCIA represented

as it frequently spied on, harassed, investigated, detained, and tortured participants of the democratic movement. The KCIA was responsible for the most egregious human rights violations in the 1970s ... It was, simply put, the most feared and despised institution during the Park Chung Hee era.⁵⁹

While the KCIA's role as a chief antagonist in the struggle for democracy under the Park regime is well documented, its involvement in film regulation has thus far not received much scholarly attention.

According to Cho Jun-hyoung, between 1969 and 1979 (prior to the handover of censorship print review operations to the semiautonomous Public Performance Ethics Committee [Kongyŏn yulliwiwŏnhoe]), the KCIA was a "regular censor" (*sangsi kyŏmyŏlja*) for motion pictures along with the Ministry of Culture and Public Information (MCPI: Munhwagongbobu, formerly MPI) and the Security Bureau of the Ministry of the Interior.⁶⁰ From 1962 to 1969, the KCIA participated in film regulation in an advisory capacity as needed by the MPI/MCPI. In particular, the KCIA's opinions were sought on the matters of national security and division. According to Yi Nam-gi, who was a staff member for the MCPI's Motion Picture Division in the 1970s, there were rarely conflicts among film regulators from different government branches. In an oral history interview with the KOFA, Yi elaborates as follows:

> We generally followed KCIA regulators' opinions for items related to national security. However, after cutting this and that, we would also ask, "Can we perhaps allow this much?" We deliberated together and negotiated. Then we would say, "Okay. That will do as long as we can remove this excessive item." Like that, there were never conflicts or fights among regulators. And these people [regulators from other branches] did not take ultimate responsibility. They deferred general matters to the MCPI. "This is our view but you decide" was their attitude. All responsibility was on the MCPI and we had to watch and rewatch films several times because of the burden.⁶¹

This oral history testimony on the KCIA's limited power in film regulation controlled primarily by another ministry can be verified in the censorship file of *The Martyred*.

Dated June 22, 1965, the memorandum sent by the KCIA to the MPI expressed national security concerns over several plot elements of *The Martyred*, which had been screening at the Academy Theater. The intelligence agency demanded that a few harmful scenes and dialogue passages be eliminated from the release print: (1) a scene in which a Christian congregation lynches Minister Hann, suspecting his betrayal in captivity; (2) a scene in which a starving mother eats mud alongside her child at the seaside; (3) scenes in which a medic leaves intensive care patients behind only to return to his hospital against his retreat order; (4) dialogue related to Colonel Chang's fabrication of martyrs' heroism; and

(5) dialogue reporting the rumor that Minister Shin is free and has been spotted throughout North Korea, where Christianity is prohibited.[62] In their response four days later, the MPI defended the film on the grounds that it was a faithful adaptation of an international best seller widely circulated and favorably received around the world, and that the KCIA had already participated in joint regulation wherein consensus had been reached to allow its exhibition in its current form.[63] To readers who are familiar with U.S. film regulation documents (e.g., PCA files, DoD Film Collection files, the Bureau of Motion Pictures files for the World War II propaganda agency the Office of War Information), the KCIA's demands might come across as standard responses to controversial or sensitive materials such as religion, poverty, war, the military, and enemy nations. It is rather surprising that the MPI and the MND did not express concerns about such objectionable elements as a Christian mob's lynching of a minister and the military cover-up of truth that the apparently savvier KCIA regulator picked up, albeit belatedly. The MPI's rejection of the KCIA's proposal to order further cuts of the released film indicates that state film regulation was a malleable, accommodative process that balanced trade and public interests while respecting the artistic integrity of literary adaptations (*munye yŏnghwa*).

Evidence of the KCIA's productive regulatory contributions can be also found in the KOFA censorship file on *A Spotted Man*. Some of the KCIA's comments on the film's screenplay share the MND's concerns discussed earlier. Melancholic song lyrics mourning war deaths had to go, as did the undiplomatic scene of a bar fight between a Korean marine and an American GI. The KCIA also objected to lines in which Vietcong prisoners attest to atrocities of the ROK army. Other responses were original insights and likely responsible for improving the film script. The KCIA regulator objected to an officer encouraging his enlisted men's gambling and joking about adopting it as a part of marine corps training. The intelligence agency also objected that the episode about an American captain, a lone survivor of the failed amphibious landing of two entire divisions, grossly exaggerates the incompetency of the U.S. military. As analyzed previously, the revised plotline addresses this criticism. The marine captain is transformed into a pilot who is captured by the enemy after bailing out from his plane alone. The final item on the KCIA list showcased the professionalism and attentiveness of its regulator who pointed out a continuity error that placed a Christmas scene before an event taking place on December 20.[64]

While it behooves us to acknowledge the KCIA regulators' capacity to offer helpful suggestions for producers and collaborate harmoniously with other ministries such as the MPI and the MND based on both archival and oral history evidence, it would be naive to conclude that the KCIA was purely a productive or beneficial regulatory force in the era of authoritarian media control. Another, more sinister face of the KCIA was exposed by the spy scandal of Yi Su-gŭn and the suppression of his biopic *Accusation*. Yi was vice president of North Korea's Central News Agency (CNA: Chosŏn chugangt'ongsinsa) when he defected to

South Korea on March 22, 1967, through the Demilitarized Zone (DMZ) during a press visit to escape an impending purge by the Workers' Party of Korea (WPK: Chosŏn Rodongdang).[65] After his security clearance by the KCIA, the former North Korean official was hired as an intelligence analyst and put on an anticommunist lecture circuit. Although Yi had a wife and three children in North Korea, he married another woman, Yi Kwang-wŏl, a physical therapy professor, in August 1968. The KCIA continued to surveil the defector closely, wiretapping all his communications and monitoring his everyday activities through their spies planted as Yi's domestic workers. Harassed constantly by the agency and estranged from his new wife, Yi realized that the freedom he had longed for in South Korea did not exist and decided to defect once again to a third country, where he hoped to be reunited with his northern family.

On January 31, 1969, en route to Cambodia (his temporary asylum destination before reaching Switzerland), Yi arrived incognito at Saigon's Tan Son Nhut Airport with a forged passport and wearing a fake mustache and wig. At the airport, he was ambushed by Korean embassy staff dispatched by the KCIA and forcefully repatriated to Seoul. Following literally torturous forms of coercive interrogation, Yi falsely confessed to being a North Korean spy disguised as a defector. His trial began on April 10 of the same year and a death sentence was handed to him on May 2. On July 2, his execution was performed merely two months after sentencing. It was unprecedented to execute a death row inmate while his codefendant (Pae Kyŏng-ok, his North Korean wife's nephew who helped his uncle's illegal expatriation and accompanied him to Vietnam via Hong Kong) was still in the process of challenging the death sentence. Pae's sentence was commuted to life in prison at the end of an appeals trial and he was released from prison in 1989. One can speculate that Yi gave up his appeal because he was in solitary confinement under the KCIA's prison surveillance. For his final words before execution, the condemned man is reported to have said, "I wanted neither the North nor the South. I intended to go to a neutral country where I could write a book about reunification plans for the Korean Peninsula based on my experiences of living under both regimes. I am not a communist."[66]

According to a 2006 report by the Truth and Reconciliation Commission (which, between 2005 and 2010, independently investigated post-1945 state crimes and human rights violations), "This incident was an undemocratic human rights abuse by the embarrassed KCIA that framed Yi Su-gŭn as an undercover spy and deprived his right to live after the defector left South Korea due to excessive surveillance and concerns about his family in North Korea."[67] As recommended by the commission, Pae and Yi were granted retrials (in 2008 and 2018, respectively) and both of them were found not guilty. Posthumously exonerating Yi and vacating his erroneous conviction nearly half a century later, the Seoul Central District Court declared, "It is time to sincerely ask for forgiveness of the defendant and his family for the mistake committed by the state in the age of authoritarianism."[68] Throughout the 1960s and 1970s, the KCIA fabricated several spy scandals as psychological warfare against North Korea and political distractions to quell antigovernment protests. In 1967, for example, it made an announcement that 169 Korean immigrants and students in Europe (including well-known artists such as composer Yun I-sang in Berlin and painter Yi Ŭng-no in Paris) had received espionage training in the Democratic People's Republic of Korea (DPRK) embassy in East Berlin. In 1968, KCIA agents kidnapped thirty-four overseas Koreans residing in West Germany (who had visited the North Korean embassy out of curiosity or to be reunited with divided family members or friends in the North) and extrajudicially transported them to Seoul for imprisonment and interrogation. In 1970, the government released all remaining detainees in response to diplomatic pressures from Germany and petitions of European artists and human rights activists. As noted by Chang, "The KCIA exercised extraordinary powers and its activities often went beyond legally defined objectivities and jurisdiction."[69]

The KCIA's involvement in the production and suppression of *Accusation* chillingly parallels how the agency first used Yi as a tool for anticommunist propaganda and then discarded him as if he were an obsolete object when his daring escape overseas brought risks of reputation damage and a publicity disaster. Directed by Kim Su-yong, a modernist stylist sometimes referred to as the "Korean Antonioni," *Accusation* is a powerful propaganda film that creatively mixes documentary footage and dramatized scenes. As an anticommunist film, it purports to expose North Korea's oppressive regime of terror under which many innocent men and women became victims of groundless purges, forced labor, imprisonment, and murders for speaking their minds, disobeying the WPK, or simply posing challenges to their political foes. Kim wastes no time in setting up this central theme by opening his film in the train compartment where Yi (Pak No-sik) meets an old woman (Song Mi-nam) with three dozing grandchildren (one kindergarten-age girl and two elementary school–age boys, just like the protagonist's own children) sitting across from him. The woman confides to the fellow passenger that her son and daughter-in-law are missing after being purged. The family misfortune has left her with no choice but to take her parentless grandchildren to a collective farm in Kaesŏng. The grandmother asks Yi where he is going. The camera dollies in on a close-up shot of Yi's face that expresses discomfort as he averts his gaze and looks out of the window. The voiceover narration fills the soundtrack, externalizing his inner thoughts: "Where am I going? To tell you the truth, I am going to the ROK. I might be able to defect through the DMZ ... Nine out of ten odds, I will be a dead corpse, but I might have a ten percent chance of survival. So why should I do this kind of risky gamble? Is it okay to leave my family to save my own life? 'Are you not a husband and father?' people might ask and be baffled by my decision. Would you like to hear an absurd story that forced me to do an absurd thing?"

The freeze-frame of Yi in close-up segues to a flashback to ten years earlier, when the vice president was a poor country reporter who takes turns in cooking dinner with his wife Kyŏng-suk (Chu Chŭng-nyŏ) as they struggle with long working hours (from dawn to dusk) and meager food rations. When his pregnant wife returns home from work, she silently joins her husband and two sons at the dinner table with no greeting or smile. Yi's narration explains, "Because we were hungry and overworked, we always looked angry as if we were fighting." In his office, however, Yi is a hardworking, promising writer who is reputed to be as efficient as five of his colleagues combined. Ambitious and upwardly mobile, the young reporter opportunistically prints precisely what the WPK wants to hear even if he knows it to be untrue. For example, he spins the "no lunch" movement, the state's latest work efficiency program, by writing a false narrative about alleged benefits such as reduced chances of stomach disease and increased appetite for breakfast and dinner. "Even children know that skipping lunch is bad for health," confides Yi, but "because the Party gave me an order, I was a faithful reporter." His loyalty is rewarded with a medal and the chief editor post at *Kaesŏng Minbo*, a city newspaper.

The first test of his resolve to succeed by any means comes when he is called as a witness during the purge meeting for his mentor, Song Tal-hyŏng (Kim Tong-wŏn), a cultural propaganda head, who is accused of being a counterrevolutionary for not making speeches against American imperialists and the South Korean government and not visiting the graves of fallen communist soldiers although he frequented sites of historical memorials of the old society. To save himself and his career, Yi keeps silent while Song is unjustly attacked by his enemy and taken away to the forced labor camp. Yi's voiceover narrates, "Yes, a forced accuser on demand. For someone I respect most and who loved me most—if I disobey, all my achievements will turn into nothing and my ideology as a Party member will be suspected. That amounts to suffocation. My heart was dark and heavy as I had to betray my teacher. It was the most shocking event of my life." Despite such a sharp sting at his conscience, Yi is handsomely compensated for this betrayal and promoted to vice president of the CNA in the capital city of Pyongyang. The high-ranking post comes with perks such as well-tailored suits and coats, high-quality food rations, a private car with a chauffeur, and a spacious modern house, one of the best in North Korea.

Yi immediately becomes a political target of another vice president, Pak Kŭn-ung (Ch'oe Sŏng-ho), a Moscow-trained elite who is eyeing promotion and eager to eliminate any threat to his prospects. In the meanwhile, Kyŏng-suk is promoted to a managerial post in the powerful audit department and invites Pak (who has requested her husband's audit report in hopes of digging up dirt) to the couple's house to show off her family's loyalty to the WPK. After the dinner party–turned–loyalty test, the wife privately warns her husband of Pak. Selected as the only female recruit for the Central Party School's training program for future leaders, the careerist woman pursues her own ambitions, leaving household duties to Yi for three months. Our hero's attachment to Song, now a common laborer at the port construction site, becomes his weakness, which Pak's eagle eye does not miss. After accidentally reencountering his mentor during a work visit, Yi tracks down Song's daughter, a textile factory worker named Hyŏn-ok (Nam Chŏng-im), and looks after her well-being. When Hyŏn-ok elopes with her fellow worker Myŏn-hun (Han Sŏng) to escape sexual harassment at the hands of the widower foreman, the desperate young couple turns to Yi's house for an overnight hideout. Security guards come to search for factory fugitives, but Kyŏng-suk's knack for shaming soldiers for failing to follow rules and procedures (during a search in a high-ranking official's residence) saves the day. Threatened by her husband's association with a "reactionary" family, Yi's wife takes the couple to Song's ramshackle seaside cabin against the father's wish not to reveal his whereabouts to the daughter. Seeing an opportunity, Pak approaches Hyŏn-ok, offering long-term hospital treatment for her ill father and arrangement of her marriage to Myŏng-hun. Pretending to be altruistic, Pak badmouths Yi for betraying Song in hopes of recruiting Hyŏn-ok for his political machinations.

When Hyŏn-ok is called as a witness to Yi's purge meeting in the same auditorium where Song was purged two years before, everyone expects her to denounce the man who betrayed her father. In a surprise twist, the virtuous young woman denounces the "poisonous purge culture spreading like wild mushrooms in the DPRK" instead. She beseeches her audience, who are booing hysterically at her and calling for her purge, "I already wrote a petition to Premier Kim Il Sung. I argued that friendship and love are what we need. Arrest me. I am not afraid of dying. I don't hate you. I love you. You will remember what I said." This moment of honesty costs Hyŏn-ok's life, hardening a wavering Yi's resolve to defect. As vice president of the CNA, Yi enjoys access to South Korean media that has given him a window to observe the capitalist development south of the DMZ (as shown in previous scenes). After witnessing Hyŏn-ok's death-defying bravery, however, Yi grapples with a more resolute reckoning while going through South Korean newspapers and magazines in his home office. A frontal close-up of Yi's dour face cuts to newsreel footage of Park Chung Hee's visit to Manila for a regional summit and Lyndon B. Johnson's visit to Seoul. Yi's enthused voiceover provides political commentary: "It's clear that the ROK is a leader in Asia and undoubtedly secured political status. This is what communists are afraid of most. President Johnson's visit to Seoul on October 30, 1966. The leader of the Free World brought the world's attention to South Korea, pledging the strengthened alliance between two countries and signing an economic treaty that binds them closer. It showed South Korea's international prestige in front of the whole world. It proved that the DPRK is inferior to the ROK militarily, diplomatically, and economically."

The film's most propagandistic scene segues to its most melodramatic one: Kyŏng-suk confronts his plan to defect to the South the next morning when he is ordered to visit the DMZ as a press representative. In tears, the understanding wife gives her permission for him to go: "I know that it is very difficult for you to survive in this land. I wanted you to be like many men here, loyal to the Party and pretending to be cheerful. Go for your freedom as you wish." After the couple shares an emotional embrace, the scene cuts to an image of the moon in the sky and then to the dimly lit bed where the bare-chested husband is awakened by his wife in long johns next to him whispering, "It's time, honey." After kissing and caressing his sleeping children (reminiscent of the orphaned children in the train compartment scene), Yi shares his final moments with his wife at the gate of their house. Kyŏng-suk sends her husband off with a brave face and a touching message (holding her tears until he disappears out of her sight): "Let's meet again when Korea becomes united. Letting you go is the biggest love I give to you. Forgive me for times when I was harsh to you. If I don't see you again, be well." After recreating Yi's dramatic defection at the DMZ with a mixture of newsreel footage and reconstructed scenes, the film closes with a reenactment of the defector's public address to welcoming citizens of Seoul: "I have to say one sentence: I am free. I am free. I am a free man. I implore to fathers of the world: let me live with my family. . . . Please return my family, my beloved wife and children left in North Korea, on humanitarian grounds. Please return them."

The censorship file on the film is devoid of any documents issued by the KCIA, and the MPI's regulatory restrictions on the censorship print were minimal. One scene in which a DPRK flag was raised was ordered to be cut. Three passages of dialogue (referencing Kim Il Sung's name and glorifying his government branch) had to be removed. Granting the exhibition permit conditional on these revisions, the MPI positively assessed the film as an "anticommunist drama that exposes the inhuman society and politics of terror in North Korea" produced with the KCIA's support.[70] Comparing the original and censorship review scripts (both available for research at the KOFA) offers insights into the sponsor agency KCIA's guidance, whether direct or not, in shaping the film as an exemplary anticommunist work. In the original script, the old woman in the opening scene is by herself. Conversely, in the censorship review script, she is with young grandchildren whose parents are victims of a purge and presumed to be in a political prisoner camp if not dead.[71] The alteration is instrumental in foreshadowing the recurrent theme of purges as evidence of the Kim regime's brutality, irrationality, and lawlessness. In the original script, after the defiant speech, Hyŏn-ok disappears and her fate is unknown to Yi.[72] In contrast, the finished film foregrounds her martyrdom explicitly and amplifies its anticommunist message through an inserted close-up shot of her bloodied body (an image that was accentuated as a symbol of communist atrocities in the film's promotional poster printed in newspaper ads).

In the original script, Kyŏng-suk expresses her communist dream as a wish to send her children to Kim Il Sung University and to study abroad in Moscow.[73] The line is removed in the censorship review script. This is consistent with the KCIA's policy of avoiding on-screen references to the Soviet Union in an admiring way. For example, in their script review report on another anticommunist literary adaptation by Yu, *The Descendants of Cain* (*K'ainŭi huye*, 1968), based on Hwang Sun-wŏn's 1954 novel set in North Korea immediately after the 1945 liberation, the KCIA advocated for censoring lines such as "modeling after the Soviet Union, an advanced country" and "our liberator, the Soviet Red Army" as well as minimizing shots of Kim Il Sung's and Joseph Stalin's portraits.[74] In the original script of *Accusation*, Kyŏng-suk's farewell speech includes the line, "If I don't see you again, get another wife in the South."[75] The second part of this line is eliminated in the revised script and the release print. In an interview with journalist Cho Kap-je (who first published a special report maintaining Yi's innocence in a March 1989 issue of *Weekly Chosŏn*, nearly twenty years prior to his exoneration in court), a former intelligence official complained about Yi's womanizing and identified it as one of the personality flaws that led to his rift with the KCIA (which tried to match him with several different women in support of his settlement in the South).[76] The removal of this line, which is suggestive of inter-Korean polygamy, was strategic as a means of sanitizing the anticommunist hero and making him more likeable. In *Accusation*, Yi is depicted as a model husband who takes up various household chores (from cooking to laundry) to support his career-oriented wife despite his lofty status in the public sphere.

There is a good reason why the newsreel footage of Park and Johnson over Yi's propagandistic voiceover feels out of place and contrived. In both scripts (original and censorship review), this scene does not exist. Right after Hyŏn-ok's testimony in Yi's purge meeting, the film would have segued more logically to explanatory narration set in his workplace: "I barely dodged the peril of the purge by luck or divine help. Ironically, my enemy Pak was reprimanded for forming factions. But I was so deeply moved by Hyŏn-ok's holy and beautiful last act that my thoughts were distracted and I couldn't focus on my work."[77] This original voiceover, rather than the non sequitur political monologue that compliments South Korea's international standing, would have made more sense in the context of the narrative flow. Inserted archival footage and a new voiceover disrupt narrative causality and coherence to serve the didactic purposes of the anticommunist genre. Even if the change was not instructed by the KCIA, it is far more likely that the scene was added to please the sponsor agency than the paying audiences. Similarly, for Kyŏng-suk's graduation scene, Yi's voiceover narration (absent in the original and censorship review scripts) is inserted in the final print to make its political message more explicit. In the scenario, the scene is simply described: "The graduation auditorium of the Central Party School. Singing Party members. Kyŏng-suk's face. Lectern. Kyŏng-suk's enthusiastic face."[78] In the finished film, Yi's heavy-handed voiceover contextualizes pantomime images of a seemingly fanatic group of graduates and instructors singing in unison with militaristically syncopated arm and foot movements: "My wife received three months' indoctrination and was awarded Kim Il Sung's medal on graduation day. The Party demanded from its members blind obedience and superhuman loyalty. In other words, this was a process of dehumanization and mechanization."

Accusation was honored with the Best Anticommunist Screenplay and Best Actor prizes at the Grand Bell Awards on December 4, 1967. The KCIA's fabricated spy scandal put everyone involved in the film's production in an embarrassing position one year and two months after the awards ceremony. The lead star, Pak No-gŭn, expressed outrage at having been duped into playing the title role in a motion picture whose exhibition permit was officially cancelled on February 13, 1969. In his interview with the daily *Chosŏn Ilbo*, Pak confided his wish to invalidate the award and return the trophy, an unwanted reminder of the much-maligned "spy." The shamed star lamented, "We made so much effort to make the film. For the sake of realistic action, while shooting the escape scene, our sedan really broke through the barricade, and shattered glass pieces injured two American soldiers sitting in the front seats."[79] Pak's interview is demonstrative of the barely pent-up resentment that the "betrayed" public felt against Yi at that time. Singer Kwŏn Hye-kyŏng, who had dated the defector briefly before his marriage to another woman, condemned him in colorful language, saying, "A betrayer like Yi Su-gŭn who deceived thirty million citizens of South Korea should be executed publicly in Kwanghwamun Square."[80] Newspaper reports likewise resorted to sensational rhetoric as part of his character assassination, thereby intensifying readers' emotions. According to the February 14, 1969, issue of *Kyŏnghyang Sinmun*, "Heinous spy Yi Su-gŭn is not only a traitor who betrayed the nation and the Free World but also a subhuman who trampled a woman and her family."[81] A *Tonga Ilbo* article from February 13, 1969, was titled "Citizens Enraged by Deceptive Behavior of 'Red Devil' Yi Su-gŭn Who Wore the Mask of Defector." A thirty-five-year-old entrepreneur is quoted in the piece as saying, "It makes my teeth tremble. To think that the whole nation warmly welcomed this vicious spy makes me explode in anger." A twenty-three-year-old student interviewee opined, "I realized what the phrase North Korean atrocities means through this incident. It's shocking. The government and our people should use this incident to raise anticommunist consciousness and strengthen security. Yi should be executed according to the law." And a thirty-five-year-old housewife stated, "Something was fishy from the beginning. He made a fuss about leaving his beloved family and then got married not long after that. It made me suspect him."[82]

Perhaps the most disconcerting reports concern schoolchildren's demonstrations against Yi. On February 15, *Kyŏnghyang Sinmun* reported that 500 students of Yŏngdong Girls Middle and High School ceremoniously burned effigies of Kim Il Sung and Yi Su-gŭn. Children demanded the execution of the undercover spy and delivered their petition to local government officials. In addition, 700 students of Sunch'ŏn High School held a rally denouncing Yi and calling for his immediate execution. High schoolers read their message to President Park and unanimously adopted a resolution that pledged to (1) destroy devilish invasion activities of Kim Il Sung and his Party; (2) instantly annihilate infiltrated communists; and (3) defend the nation and democracy.[83] The fanatic anticommunist zeal of South Korean teenagers is ironically reminiscent of the destructive antagonism toward counterrevolutionaries (*pandong*) that Yi's primary school children display in *Accusation*. In one scene, to his father's chagrin, the eldest son boasts of his dream of becoming a DPRK army officer and destroying counterrevolutionaries in the South. As pointed out by Hana Lee,

> In fact, the Yis reflect the South Korean society like a mirror. Yi's children resemble their South Korean counterparts who give speeches saying "Let's get them, commies!" under the counterespionage banner.... When Yi Su-gŭn goes to work in a private car and comments on the "poor life of the masses [being] radically different from that of high-ranking elites," North Korean streets outside of the window are in reality shot in a shantytown of Seoul. Although the two systems are different, North and South Korea are mirroring one another in a typical "anticommunist film" like this.... The more one portrays another society realistically to criticize it, [the more] the inner workings of that society previously concealed to audiences are revealed. Paradoxically, "anti-communist films" expose that North Korea is also a sovereign nation, a place where people live, and its appearance is not that different from South Korea.[84]

In this respect, *Accusation* can be compared to Ernst Lubitsch's romantic comedy *Ninotchka* (1939), in which Greta Garbo's stern Soviet official falls in love with an easy-going capitalist in Paris. Despite its unfavorable portrayal of the Stalin regime's political repression and drab living conditions in Moscow, according to Jeremy Mindich, Lubitsch's film "does suggest that there are certain qualities to be admired about the Soviet Union and its people." Mindich singles out "social responsibility and devotion" as positive attributes of communism depicted in the film.[85] Before she succumbs to the seduction of capitalism and romantic love, the titular character is thoroughly devoted to the Soviet Union, communist ideals, and the Russian people. Both *Ninotchka* and *Accusation* depict their female characters as productive members of a revolutionary society where women participate equally in various public sectors, from industrial factories to government administration. It is indeed rare to see a patriarch partaking in domestic duty such as cooking dinner, hand-washing laundry, and ironing family clothes in 1960s films set in South Korea (as Yi's character does in *Accusation*'s North Korea). From a feminist perspective, *Accusation* depicts gender equity in a manner that is relatively progressive, hinting unwittingly at women's superior status in North Korea. Both Kyŏng-suk and Hyŭn-ok are stronger characters than Yi, surpassing the male protagonist's political acumen or moral courage.

These unintentional representational consequences attest to the paradox of anticommunist films set in North Korea. In *Accusation*, a film produced over three decades before *Shiri*, *JSA*, and other seemingly more "enlightened" political thrillers, we encounter North Koreans as sympathetic, ordinary people (who endure dirty office politics for the sake of family and children, the source of parental joy and pride). When Kyŏng-suk tells Yi, "I wanted you to be like many men in this land, loyal to the Party and pretending to be cheerful," if the "Party" is replaced with the "company," the situation widely applies to South Korean business culture then and now. The ultimate irony, though, lies in the final scene set in Seoul, where Yi euphorically celebrates his newly found freedom. Before being red-baited, witch hunted, and legally lynched in that "free land," Yi explained himself to Yi Tae-yong, a Saigon embassy minister/KCIA operative in Vietnam who captured him: "Yes, South Korea is one hundred times better than North Korea. If there is a hell in this world, North Korea is it. That's why I escaped but the South is wrong too. There is no freedom and it is a dictatorship. I wanted to go to somewhere neutral like Switzerland."[86] Such an idealistic pursuit of neutrality in the polarized world of the Cold War was heavily censored in "free" countries and on their media platforms from the United States to South Korea where anticommunism served as (to borrow the words of Edward S. Herman and Noam Chomsky) "a national religion and control mechanism."[87] There is no archival evidence in the censorship file that the KCIA directly interfered with the MPI's approval of *Accusation*'s exhibition with specific regulatory comments. However, because of the KCIA's unlawful act of framing Yi as a spy to censor the truth about his escape from South Korea, *Accusation* was permanently taken out of theatrical circulation in 1969 and is currently only available for research viewing or special screenings at the KOFA.

A Director's Take on the "Freedom of the Silver Screen"

Throughout this book, I have made deliberate efforts to avoid lensing the regulation history of motion pictures through individual directors' perspectives or an auteurist lens. The established filmmakers responsible for the main case studies in this chapter—Yu Hyŏn-mok (*The Martyred*), Yi Man-hŭi (*A Spotted Man*), and Kim Su-yong (*Accusation*)—are habitually named as key victims of authoritarian censorship of the Park era in both journalistic and scholarly accounts of Korean film history. In the 2019 press conference for the KOFA's public exhibition of film censorship documents, Kim went as far as saying, "Had there not been censorship, Korean films would have advanced thirty to fifty years ahead. Bong Joon-ho [the director of Oscar-winning *Parasite* (*Kisaengch'ung*, 2019)] would have arrived fifty years earlier. If I reattached all my film footage cut by censors, it would be as long as the distance between Seoul and Pusan [201 miles]."[88] The ninety-year-old veteran director's estimates on both counts are not just questionable but exaggerated to the point of self-parody, but the point is well taken. From film artists' perspective, censorship in any form (self-regulation, external boards, or audience boycotts) is an inherently negative obstacle to overcome in pursuit of freer creative expression. However, it is simplistic to assume that censorship single-handedly sabotaged

South Korean cinema's international recognition or that it was possible for commercial motion pictures (of any national context in any given period) to go completely uncensored in the first place.

Even in the United States, where the First Amendment is revered as the most important protection of American civil liberties, classical Hollywood pictures were rigorously censored within the industry even before they were presented to external boards, stateside and foreign. According to Doherty, after Breen and his staff systemically solidified the PCA's regulatory apparatus by the mid-1930s,

> what rankled filmmakers most was his invasive scrutiny of the micro, not the macro, matters. All conceded that crime must not pay and the wages of sin were death, but was it really necessary to eliminate the sight of a baby in diapers or the plosive sound of a street urchin blowing a "raspberry"? . . . By fighting tenaciously not just for the Big Picture arc but pea-brained minutiae, the Breen Office soon acquired a reputation not for grand vision but squinting myopia. It paid a scrupulous, not to say fetishistic, attention to the tiniest cinematic details. It banned titles . . . It demanded translations of all foreign words, uttered, printed, or sung . . . It blushed at the most innocuous exposures.[89]

Were Golden Age Korean filmmakers subject to harsher or stricter censorship? The answer—based on archival, not anecdotal, evidence—should now be apparent to the reader.

As stated previously, it is hard to imagine that *The Martyred* could have passed PCA muster with a mere two "big picture" revisions about officer conduct despite inflammatory materials on religion and army propaganda. *Accusation* similarly got a nearly free pass despite its sensitive subject matter (e.g., communism, violence, sex, and strong language/dialects) and sympathetic portrayals of North Korean characters, including WPK members. There is even a motel lovemaking scene involving an unmarried couple, Hyŏn-ok and Myŭng-hun, which passed without any cautionary mention in the MPI review. Of course, the camera cuts away from their passionate foreplay kiss, as it does during another lovemaking scene between Yi and his wife, which transitions from an embrace in the living room to a postcopulatory bedroom shot of the following morning. Regardless, this premarital love scene might strike us as overly permissive not only from a moralistic perspective (as it would have been primarily viewed in Hollywood regulation) but also politically speaking. The KCIA, for example, objected to the "unrestrained lifestyle" of excessive drinking, bountiful feasting, and unconventional heterosexual affairs (a ménage à trois love triangle among a landowner, his cohabitant maid, and her estranged communist husband) in another North Korea–themed film, *The Descendants of Cain*, set in 1945 under Soviet occupation before the founding of the DPRK.[90] Of the three censorship files that I closely examined throughout the writing of this chapter, only that of *A Spotted*

FIGURE 3.3 Two years after delivering a controversial presentation critiquing the absence of freedom for the Korean silver screen in 1965, Yu Hyŏn-mok was prosecuted for filming a six-second nude shot, which was cut in the release print of *Empty Dream* (1967), an erotic art film.

Man contains documents requesting changes of "the tiniest cinematic details" à la PCA censorship (such as death totals and song lyrics) due in part to sensitivity toward wartime portrayals of allies and enemies and the feelings of the real-life war hero's bereaved family.

On May 23, 1965, about one month prior to the release of *The Martyred*, Yu Hyŏn-mok gave a presentation on the topic "Freedom of the Silver Screen" in a cultural seminar hosted by the South Korean branch of the International Association for Cultural Freedom. In it, the director criticized censorship with the following words:

> To tell you the truth, Korean film artists today are not basking in "the freedom of the silver screen." What I mean is that artists' creative activities are interfered in by a third party, an external bureaucratic force—"those with absolute power" in a Third World country. Creators and censors are naturally on bad terms. Moreover, our nation's reality adds another delicate situation (semiwartime) that complicates the original meaning of conflicts between two parties.... There is a saying that best arts and best politics go hand in hand. If we depict North Korean soldiers as lifeless mannequins because 'anticommunism' is the national policy, how can we create conflicts and drama to lift the stature of film arts? It would not be possible to indoctrinate and enlighten the national policy without the highest expressions of film arts.[91]

Yu had reason to be frustrated by "those who have absolute power" in blocking the way of artistic freedom, as his colleague Yi Man-hŭi had recently been prosecuted for a violation of the Anticommunist Law by showing favorable images of North Korean troops in *Seven Female Prisoners* (*Ch'ilinŭi yŏp'oro*: recut and renamed as *Returned Female Soldiers* [*Tolaon yŏgun*, 1965]), a Korean War film in which a gallant DPRK officer saves ROK army nurses from Chinese rapists. After Yi's imprisonment in February 1965 sent a shock wave across the industry, Yu joined his peer members of the trade organization Motion Picture Association of Korea (Yŏnghwain hyŏp'oe) in defending *Seven Female Prisoners* as a misunderstood anticommunist film and demanding Yi's release in the name of all Korean artists. Yi was released after forty days on a suspended sentence thanks in part to the trade pressure that had been applied to the prosecution.

Ironically, Yu faced a similar fate two years later in February 1967 when he was prosecuted for a double charge of obscenity (for a nude scene in *Empty Dream* [*Ch'unmong*, 1967]) and a violation of the Anticommunist Law (for the above-quoted speech on the "Freedom of the Silver Screen," excerpts of which were printed in several daily newspapers). He received a suspended sentence of a year and a half for the former charge but was found not guilty of the latter one. In a press interview, Yu lauded the second verdict as evidence of "the democratic growth of our country."[92] As observed by the much-celebrated Golden Age auteur, this competing presence of anticommunist authoritarianism and fair processes of petitions and appeals aptly captures the contradictory political atmosphere of "Korean-style democracy" (*Han'guksik minjujuŭi* as Park Chung Hee famously labeled his system) under which the motion pictures highlighted in this chapter were censored.

4

Cinematic Censorship as Sentimental Education

Indoctrinating Gaiety as National Emotion in Yushin-Era Youth Comedies

The sentimental orientation of *myŏngnang* ("gaiety") literature—a unique East Asian genre that was popular in Japan and Korea from the 1930s to the 1970s—has long been linked to state policies of cultural regulation. During the colonial period, Japanese authorities encouraged *myŏngnang* novelists to harness their storytelling abilities for the purposes of indoctrinating docile, complacent colonial subjects. Inheriting the colonial cultural policy, the postcolonial authoritarian regimes of Syngman Rhee (Yi Sŭng-man: 1945–1960) and Park Chung Hee (Pak Chŏng-hŭi: 1961–1979) promoted *myŏngnang* as a wholesome, productive national sentiment through public campaigns and media regulation. During Rhee's presidency, radio broadcasters adopted a state policy known as *myŏngnanghwa* (translated as "becoming or making cheerful") and mass-produced lighthearted and cheerful comedy programs. In December 1955, the popular entertainment magazine *Myŏngnyang* was launched, which helped usher in the heyday of *myŏngnang* novels focusing on humorous stories revolving around the mundane everyday lives and romances of optimistic characters who rise above adversity, misunderstandings, and conflicts to achieve happy endings. The laughter-inducing genre was responsive to not only the top-down cultural policy but also the bottom-up desire among many members of the citizenry for survival and self-preservation in postwar society.¹

The early years of Park's administration saw *myŏngnanghwa* become a key philosophical element of state film censorship administered by the Ministry of Public Information (MPI: Kongbobu, or the Ministry of Culture and Public Information [MCPI: Munhwagongbobu] after 1968), so much so that any production that did not at least attempt to inject levity into the proceedings or find a way to put a positive spin on depressing scenarios was subject to editorial revision and other forms of government intervention. For example, Yi Man-hŭi's *Holiday* (*Hyuil*, 1968), a minimalist film that—over the course of a single day—follows a penniless young man who steals money from his friend to pay for his girlfriend's abortion (during which the pregnant woman dies), was banned because state regulators found it too downbeat and hopeless. The MCPI urged the filmmakers to switch out the ending with a more upbeat, less disheartening one, but the film's creators rejected the government's proposal and were ultimately denied an exhibition permit.

In this chapter, I explore the role of state film censorship in shaping the tone of screen comedy during the Yushin period (1972–1979), which has sometimes been referred to by cultural historians as the "Dark Age" of South Korea's cinematic output. As Kim Chi-yŏng argues, the *myŏngnang* sentiment in novels of the 1950s, 1960s, and 1970s cannot simply be seen as a "subordination to state pressures" but represents a widespread longing for "deviation and resistance."² Son Yŏng-nim echoes this view in his study of 1970s youth films, stating that examples of that emergent genre "were laden with conflicting desires and fracture points created by its double strategy of critiquing society and accommodating state demands at the same time."³ Focusing on director Ha Kil-jong's *The March of Fools* (*Pabodŭlŭi haengjin*, 1975) and drawing upon the Korean Film Archive (KOFA: Han'gukyŏngsang charyowŏn)'s digitized files of censorship documents, this chapter demonstrates how censorship contributes to the creation of a sophisticated text that balances effervescence and gravity in tonal duality. On the surface, the Yushin-era comedy appears to uphold the government's *myŏngnanghwa* policy through carefree images of college students and their youthful pastimes (blind dates, inebriation, sports, misdemeanors, etc.). However, it also resists such top-down sentimental indoctrination by exposing youth discontent, depression, and despair in authoritarian culture.

The Colonial Origins of *Myŏngnang* Sentiment

In the Korean language, *myŏngnang* has two meanings. First, it refers to fair, sunny weather and cloudless skies lacking the gloom that is sometimes associated with rainy, overcast days. Second, it denotes the mental state of someone whose cheerful or lighthearted emotions are clearly visible, physically embodied in the person of an optimistic individual. The first use of the term dates back hundreds of years, but the second use is a modern phenomenon that emerged in the 1930s. According to So Rae-sŏp, two major forces were behind the rise of *myŏngnang* culture at this particular juncture of history. The first was the Government General of Korea (GGK: Chosŏn ch'ongdokpu)'s "affect politics" (*kamjŏng chŏngch'i*), which aimed to "reform Korea to be conductive to the colonial system and to control the bodies and brains of Koreans." The second was "affect capitalism" (*kamjŏng chabonjuŭi*), which compelled individuals to "modernize" emotions with self-management conducive to social mobility.[4] As So points out, the urban gentrification project of making Seoul cheerful (*tosiŭi myŏngnanghwa*) was an extension of cultural control, including creating "exemplary human beings" (*mobŏm ingan*) via the educational system and censoring subversive content in popular media such as newspapers, magazines, musical recordings, and motion pictures.[5] In other words, manufacturing gaiety was a deliberate political policy to suppress what colonial authorities saw as the opposite manifestations of modern living, such as "uncleanness, delinquency, contamination, crime, decadence, regress, vulgarity, disorder, unrest." The GGK promoted *myŏngnang* as a synonym of wholesomeness in order to "suppress resistance to the colonial system ... by labeling obstacles to colonial management as 'vulgar, disorderly, decadent, or seditious.'"[6]

The Japanese colonial policy was succeeded by postcolonial authoritarian regimes in the South backed by the United States. For example, in the State of Union address of 1966, President Park Chung Hee implored citizens from different walks of life—across political divisions and within various business sectors—to spare no effort in constructing a "society of faith" and a "society of gaiety" as a propeller of the nation's modernization (*kŭndaehwa*) efforts. After touting his administration's achievements in security (having sent ground troops to Vietnam to support U.S. allies in the global containment of communism) and the economy (having successfully wrapped the inaugural year for the aid-supported Five-Year Economic Plan), Park singled out several divisive, harmful elements that not only threatened to "darken" Korean society but also chained the nation to poverty and underdevelopment. Among the named culprits were political corruption, bureaucratic inefficiency, and violent demonstrations.[7] The MPI was fully behind administering the state policy in commercial motion pictures and encouraged filmmakers to make "cheerful and constructive movies fitting a nation at war and under reconstruction."[8] Much like the former colonial master, the dictatorial military regimes of Park and Chun Doo Hwan (Chŏn Tu-hwan: 1980–1988) used the rhetoric of militarization and modernization to suppress dissent and indoctrinate gaiety as a sentiment of compliance.

In 1981, the year after the Kwangju Uprising and the massacre of an estimated 2,000 protesters in the capital city of Chŏlla Province, the so-called Cheerful Movement (*Myŏngnanghwa Undong*), which was driven by various media, cultural, and educational campaigns, took hold of the region with the goal of making residents light-hearted, affirmative individuals resistant to negative emotions, such as jealousy, slandering, and criticism. As So puts it, "The movement was the most ambitious in human history ... aiming at no less than changing human personality."[9] Given the strong connection between *myŏngnanghwa* initiatives and undemocratic regimes, it is not coincidental that the term *myŏngnang* disappeared from popular parlance in the early 1990s, around the same time that South Korea transitioned to civil rule, returning to a stable state of representative democracy that it had not seen in more than three decades. So speculates, "It may be because the totalitarian atmosphere relaxed with systematic democratization that the use of *myŏngnang* discontinued since the 1990s."[10] In other words, the term is oxymoronic, insofar as any outward gaiety that might be expressed by indoctrinated or willing subjects is predicated on a sense of hopelessness that comes from being confined to a depressing period in Korean politics and history.

However, it would be rash to define *myŏngnang* purely as a top-down propaganda tool that was concocted to serve the interests of colonial authorities, military officials, bureaucratic elites, and members of the capitalist class. As Michel Foucault explains, "Where there is power, there is resistance," and the existence of power relationships "depends on a multiplicity of points of resistance."[11] The bottom-up, counterhegemonic impulse of the indoctrinated subjects either resisted the state order to be cheerful with depression and cynicism or appropriated the word to express their own social desires. The former group is represented by poet and college professor Kim Kwang-sŏp, who, in his contribution to *Chosŏn Ilbo*'s 1960 column on cultural expressions of *myŏngnanghwa*, wrote, "Writers or artists are usually depressed individuals.... Historically they rarely raise their hands in delight and be cheerful.... I do sometimes get out of my dark room and engage in pleasant conversations with various groups.... The problem is whether or not the reflection of our reality allows us to be cheerful even temporarily. Can this society, this age fill even our tiny rooms with gaiety? Cheerfulness belongs to dogs and reflects the will of those who trample on smiles [of others]."[12] In the final analysis, Kim concluded, "True *myŏngnang* only comes to those who are owners of their emotions, not slaves."[13]

Kim Ki-rim, a poet and cultural critic of the 1930s, had a more positive outlook on *myŏngnang*, a concept that he believed was instrumental to his early modernist poetry. Kim's philosophy is stated in the introduction of his first poem collection, *Sun's Custom* (*T'aeyang ŭi p'ungsok*, 1939): "Let us reject causeless tears, the unsalvageable obsession with the past, and uncontrollable sentimentality and despair. Let us learn from the Sun's cheerful, wholesome custom."[14] His vision of cheerfulness rejects the hypocrisy of the disingenuous smiles and positivity forced by colonial and capitalist mandates. The poet saw subversive potential in nonsentimental gaiety as a dynamic, affirmative state of mind that is unafraid of challenging and destroying the status quo. For him, it is a spirit of resistance and denial (*pujŏng*), not compliance and acquiescence as encouraged by the colonial government and capitalist elites.[15] Kim's modernist poetry embraces *myŏngnang* as an uplifting yet iconoclastic emotion in pursuit of modern subjecthood, self-determination, and social change, resisting not only the oversentimentality of his literary peers but also state discourses prioritizing the transformation of exterior rather than inner domains. This positive, dynamic sentiment of *myŏngnang* permeates Ha Kil-jong's youth comedy *The March of Fools*, which was made nearly four decades later, amid a very different set of contextual factors.

Park Chung Hee's Film Policy and the Creation of Youth Ideals

Seung Hyun Park's 2002 article, "Film Censorship and Political Legitimization in South Korea, 1987–1992," offers a predictable assessment of oppressive censorship under successive military regimes of the Cold War era: "Censorship has been the greatest barrier to the development of Korean cinema since its inception.... The military governments... further decreased the capacity for creative expression.... Until the end of 1986, it was possible for political authorities to control virtually every facet of a film through economic censorship of producers, whose primary concern was to ensure that no film got made that authorities presumed would be 'offensive' or 'detrimental' to the government."[16] Fortunately, the availability of the MPI's censorship documents of the period through the KOFA digital archive gives historians an opportunity to challenge earlier accounts and reevaluate the complex role of film censorship in Cold War Korea. While political suppression existed inside and outside the motion picture industry during this period, film censorship was not simply a tool for authoritarian dictatorship. Archival evidence makes it possible for scholars to resist the temptation to conflate the national (or macro) policies of oppressive regimes with the industry-specific (or micro) operations of film censorship, which in fact involved many different players (e.g., the MPI/MCPI, the Security Bureau of the Ministry of the Interior, the Ministry of Education, the Ministry of National Defense, the Korean Central Intelligence Agency [KCIA], the United States CIA, film producers, and trade associations).[17] These discursive agencies and organizations were involved in a multilayered process of regulating individual motion pictures with different agendas in mind (including but not limited to national security, public morality, suppression of obscenity, protection of children, and market demands) and appealing such decisions. One of the most noteworthy contributions that state censorship of the Cold War era made was to inject a cheerful attitude or sensibility into Korean films (exemplified by tacked-on optimistic endings to melodramas of the 1960s and a cycle of light comedies and youth films during the 1970s). A cultural war was thus being waged against pessimism, despair, and depression or social malaise onscreen. As discussed in chapter 1, the MPI censorship file on *The Stray Bullet* (*Obalt'an*, 1961) reveals that the film was banned primarily because of its defeatist, hopeless dénouement, which was contrary to the affirmative *myŏngnang* culture embraced by the new regime.

This policy is in essence not far removed from World War II film policies in Great Britain and the United States. For example, Franklin D. Roosevelt's propaganda agency, the Office of War Information (OWI: 1942–1945), discouraged the mass production of war films and urged Hollywood producers to provide more escapist entertainment to boost public morale. Nelson Poynter, the Chief of Hollywood Office of the OWI's Bureau of Motion Pictures, informed the *Hollywood Reporter* in 1943, "As life has become grimmer and more upset, there is greater need for pictures that offer the public escape from the realities of page one.... *More people than ever before will go to the movies*—to get away from the war. Hence war should not crowd escape pictures from the screen. The point cannot be emphasized more strongly that there should *not be too many war pictures*."[18] Similarly, in the 1970s, Korean censorship reviewers were given a list of "encouraged directions of domestic productions" along with the Motion Picture Law as regulatory guidelines. In addition to content that dealt with the nation's development, its economic and military self-reliance, anticommunism, modernization of national consciousness, traditional arts, and moral lessons for adolescents, wholesome entertainment that "cheers up everyday life" (*saenghwal ŭi myŏngnanghwa*) was encouraged.[19] In 1974, the Korean Motion Picture Promotion Corporation (Yŏnghwa chinhŭnggongsa) was established to subsidize "government policy films" (*kukch'ek yŏnghwa*). Along with content that encouraged patriotism, rural renewal (the New Village Movement), the export push, science, and positive images of police and civil servants, "depictions of the bright, cheerful future of youth" were among sought-after scenarios for government production subsidies.[20]

With the 1972 proclamation of the Yushin constitution,[21] which lifted limits on Park Chung Hee's executive power and cleared the way for a more draconian form of governance throughout the second half of that decade, college students became a core constituency to voice dissent and demand democratic reform. The student population grew considerably from 13,000 in 1960 to 28,000 in 1975.[22] Politically, they staged publicly visible demonstrations and class boycotts to protest against Park's full-fledged authoritarian Yushin system. Socially, they embraced countercultural signifiers, letting their hair grow long, appropriating the hippie fashions popularized years earlier in Europe and the United States, drinking draft beer, and strumming acoustic guitars (1970s icons of Korean youth featured prominently in *The March of Fools*). For Park's regime, young people were looked upon as targets of both control/discipline and courting/flattery. With cultural regulation and media censorship, the government attempted to indoctrinate ideal images of youth as agents of modernization and national rebuilding. In the 1970s, the Park administration defined model citizenship among the nation's youth by singling out people who were "competent, sincere, and responsible" enough to fulfill South Korea's needs.[23]

While the government focused on cultural reform or the remaking of youth, filmmakers catered to young audiences' tastes and interests in hopes of reviving the declining industry (pushed to the margins by powerful competitors such as Hollywood imports and domestic television broadcasts). The Korean situation in the 1970s was not very different from Hollywood's predicament in the 1950s. The American film industry experienced the same three problems: the political oppression of anticommunist blacklisting, dwindling box-office revenues in the television age, and the rise of youth audiences and their rejection of traditional culture and values. Like their Hollywood predecessors, who churned out lighthearted escapist youth entertainment such as Elvis Presley's rock-'n'-roll musicals, "Beach Party" movies starring Frankie Avalon and Annette Funicello, and low-budget exploitation science fiction or horror flicks directed and produced by Roger Corman and William Castle, Korean filmmakers responded to their own crisis with *myŏngnang* youth comedies such as *The March of Fools* and *Yalkae, A Joker in High School* (*Kogyo yalgae*, 1976) in an attempt to win back the hearts and minds of youth audiences, including college students and teenagers.

Censorship History of *The March of Fools*

The director of *The March of Fools*, Ha Kil-jong, is a legendary figure in the Korean film industry, an iconoclast whose death at the age of thirty-seven (in 1979) only immortalized his fame. After graduating from Seoul National University, Ha went to the United States and studied filmmaking at the San Francisco Art Academy and the University of California, Los Angeles (UCLA) for seven years. He was a classmate of Francis Ford Coppola, a Film School Generation New Hollywood auteur. His debut film, *The Pollen of Flowers* (*Hwabun*, 1972), is an experimental work in which a mysterious young drifter arrives in a "blue house" (an oblique, allegorical gesture toward South Korea's presidential residence) and engages in sexual affairs with all of its occupants—the businessman owner, his mistress, and her sister—driving bourgeois characters into self-destructive jealousy and rage. This first feature by Ha has a strikingly similar story to Pier Paolo Pasolini's *Teorema* (1968), so much so that he and the film became embroiled in a plagiarism controversy. Having explored stylistic experiments and thematic ambiguity rivaling those of New American Cinema and European art cinema in his dark debut thriller, Ha had a low opinion of his third feature and commercial breakthrough, *The March of Fools*, adapted from a newspaper serial novel by Ch'oe In-ho (the best-seller author who, in adapting his own work for the big screen, was paid an unprecedented 3 million won [U.S.$9,400], the largest fee given to any Korean screenwriter to date). Ha's film was released at Kukje Theater on May 31, 1975, and garnered 174,000 admissions in forty-nine days.[24] The film's freshness and semidocumentary realism, owing partly to its two male leads being played by a college junior and a recent graduate with no screen acting experience and 200 student extras recruited by Ha himself from various university campuses, garnered critical accolades.[25] After the film's preview at

FIGURE 4.1 UCLA film school graduate Ha Kil-jong had a low opinion of his light-hearted third feature and commercial breakthrough *The March of Fools* (1975), adapted from a newspaper serial novel by Ch'oe In-ho.

Tangsŏngsa Theater on April 28, 1975, veteran director Kim Su-yong praised his junior colleague, telling him, "You now know the power of the public, the essence of popular culture. It's not that there are merely Pasolini's films. Pasolini and Bergman had European traditions, and there are things you can learn in Korea. That is [our] art." The Pasolini-inspired auteur (who regarded *The Pollen of Flowers* as his masterpiece) reportedly contested these remarks, saying, "Director Kim, I am sorry to hear this. It's a fake. I just helped Ch'oe In-ho blow his nose. I just tickled Ch'oe so that he can make some money."[26]

These divergent, conflicting views of cinema held by Kim (who advocated for popular entertainment that might please the masses) and Ha (who believed in the power of art cinema, which is problematically thought to be controlled single-handedly by visionary auteurs) are crucial to evaluating the role that state film regulation played in reshaping *The March of Fools* as a potentially mainstream text through cultural guidance to suppress didactic political content and amplify the effervescence of youth images. For Ha, who was forced to compromise his original vision in the process of both government and market censorship, *The March of Fools* was a pale counterfeit of what he considered "true" or ideal cinema. In an opinion piece published in the Kongju National University newspaper in October 1975, the disappointed film director elaborates by asking,

Are recent popular box-office successes such as *Heavenly Homecoming to Stars* (*Pyŏldŭlŭi kohyang*), *Yŏng-ja's Heydays* (*Yŏng-ja ŭi chŏnsŏng sidae*), and *The March of Fools* movies? Definitely not. They are just efforts to approximate filmmaking. Why are they not movies even though they broke box-office records and served social functions of filmmaking? I am not trying to disparage the birth of new, trendy films because some thirty minutes of my film were cut by censors in accordance with state film policy. I am not merely referring to the fact that audiences saw my work in a crippled form. Why are the aforementioned titles not movies? I am inclined to believe that the goal of film and media should be showing the beautiful or ugly doings of our realities truthfully. What I want to call a movie is a work that is clear and pure in creative themes, nurtured by the author's vision and poetic spirit to reflect and probe into the inner core of realities, and which succeeds in establishing a cosmopolitan order ... [After returning from the United States] I decided to wait until a Bergman, a Godard, or a Costa-Gavras arrives in South Korea even if it takes ten or fifty years. But I came to realize that in this country, cinema is not a personal art that can be achieved by individual talents.[27]

Ha's absolute faith in the unadulterated form of auteur cinema as a truth-telling medium to represent reality and express a deeply personal vision—like the films made in New York City by John Cassavetes, whose pioneering, low-budget experiments such as *Shadows* (1959) and *Faces* (1968) must have influenced the Korean auteur during his formative years at UCLA—is precisely why film historians should take an objective stance by balancing perspectives of multiple agents and decision makers in the highly collaborative, deliberative process of producing, distributing, and exhibiting motion pictures. Prioritizing the views of exceptionally talented mavericks (from Orson Welles in Hollywood to Ha Kil-jong in South Korea) who had trouble in adjusting to the profit-driven entertainment industry that aimed at mass-producing and widely distributing commercial products to the broadest spectrum of market constituents is an auteurist fallacy that erects a faulty binary between heroes and heavies, that is, brave artists who fought for artistic freedom and meddling obstructionists who were in the way of that noble cause, be they greedy executives of commerce or prohibitive watchdogs of censorship. Such a myopic perspective, as Thomas Schatz warns, is responsible for "transforming film history to a cult of personality" rather than acknowledging "a melding of institutional forces, that reduces "any individual's style" to "no more than an inflection" in the massive gestalt of the filmmaking machinery intrinsic to any national cinema.[28]

Moreover, one cannot correctly take the pulse of the general public at a given historical juncture by examining socially progressive texts exclusively filtered through the political consciousness of independently minded auteurs. As Stuart Hall famously puts it, "Popular culture is one of the sites where this struggle for and against a culture of the powerful is engaged.... It is the arena of consent and resistance.... It is partly where hegemony arises, and where it is secured.... That is why 'popular culture' matters. Otherwise, I don't give a damn about it."[29] In other words, the popular is collectively constructed by the complex network of social actors involved in the production and consumption of media texts, not simply by their individual authors. For this reason, to extend Hall's argument further in relation to this study, state film censorship *matters* as an arbiter of the popular and a defender of public interests, whether or not one agrees with particular rules and applications. For director Ha (and to a lesser degree, Catholic screenwriter Ch'oe, whose modestly ambitious serialized work targeted a large readership of sports fans and consumers of literary magazines), regulatory interventions were acts of impairment and obstruction to their creative impulses. But for others with different social beliefs or interests, they served to defend and preserve their values, ideologies, attitudes, and way of life.

The ultimate irony is that along with *The Housemaid* (*Hanyŏ*, 1960) and *The Stray Bullet*, *The March of Fools*—a lighthearted comedy about youth culture and college dating based on presold popular literature—was named as the greatest Korean film of all time in the KOFA 100 Film List that was compiled in 2014. The consensus in Korean film historiography is that Ha was a victim of draconian Yushin censorship, which, according to Youngju Ryu, controlled "what the public could read, hear, and see ... from the pages of daily newspapers to reels of film to broadcasts over the airwaves."[30] A catchy headline such as "Ha Kiljong's genius cut by the scissors of censorship" is typical when the topic is retrospectively covered in the contemporary press.[31] There are even trade rumors that Ha's early demise following a fatal stroke was indirectly caused by the stress that resulted from the oppressive conditions of Korean filmmaking during the final years of the Park administration. As observed by Chŏng Chong-hwa in the KOFA booklet accompanying the Blu-ray release of *The March of Fools*, the surviving print of the film is 102 minutes. This is fifteen minutes shorter than the 117-minute censorship review print submitted to the MCPI. Chŏng further speculates that the actual running time of the release print would have been two minutes and twenty-nine seconds shorter than the existing print.[32] That censored footage has been reattached and restored to the 2014 Blu-ray release and is presumed to have been absent from the final release print in 1975.

In the supplemental booklet to the film's Blu-ray release, KOFA researchers comment on the role of censorship in disrupting the diegesis or narrative flow of Ha's film. Cho Jun-hyoung (Cho Chun-hyŏng) notes, "From the first draft ... through the complete production, censorship continuously sought to ruin the film, and many scenes and set-ups that Ha had intended were rendered useless."[33] Chŏng chimes in, stating, "It has been incredibly hard for me to summarize the synopsis of the film.... It is impossible to write a synopsis unless you can talk about deleted scenes."[34] However, before making a rushed judgement that authoritarian film censorship ruined the UCLA graduate's masterpiece (which, according to the director, was a "fake film" catering to the lowest common denominator but, despite its regulatory mutations, is reputed to be one of the greatest films in Korean film history) by enforcing the removal of some fifteen to seventeen minutes of footage, it is important to examine archival evidence with analytical objectivity. In their review of the first draft of the screenplay submitted on December 27, 1974, the MCPI recommended an overall caution to the producers at Hwach'ŏn Trading (Hwachŏngongsa) so that the completed film would not cause controversy over the "problematic" subject matter of disempowered college students. Specifically, government censors demanded deletions and revisions of several scenes, including three scenes of student demonstrations.[35] In the preview print review dated May 13, 1975, the ministry approved the film's release on the condition that five scenes be cut, three scenes be reduced, and four lines of dialogue be eliminated.[36]

The first set of deletions or revisions concerns the opening military exam sequence. The film begins with a medium-long shot of potential draftees (naked save for underwear) marching forward to the offscreen physical exam room. There is no sound of march orders or replies. The credit sequence has been edited (and presumably sound had to be removed to solve a continuity problem) to accommodate the state censor's demand to cut a scene of college students mocking the private giving their march orders. In the opening scene of the censorship review scenario housed at the KOFA, the private encounters difficulty in instilling discipline in a ragtag group of young students who exhibit countercultural attitudes such as smoking and talking back. The military man encourages new conscripts with a patriotic prep talk, telling them, "You are preparatory soldiers who plan to serve proudly. Do you understand that you are rankless soldiers of the great Republic of Korea?" An apathetic youth in the crowd retorts, "Not understood." The irritated private probes, "Who is this? Raise your hand." Another youth jokes mockingly, "He is dead."[37] The regulatory cut of this scene is ironically responsible for creating an experimental feel in the silenced opening shot, which tracks backward and then zooms in on a random character's red underwear (singling him out in the line of other young men who wear white or gray briefs). The lack of verbal anchoring draws our attention more empathically to visual symbols, including those rooted to color-based associations, carefully planted by Ha.

The pantomime credit sequence segues to a fast close-up/reverse shot montage of physical examinations zeroing on different body parts (mouths, rear ends, groins, and eyes). The medic asks a young man what is wrong with his penis and receives a candid answer: "Syphilis." This exchange of dialogue about venereal disease (included in the 102-minute restored print but presumed to be missing in the release print) is listed as a to-be-deleted scene in the ministry's report of the preview print review. Given the fact that Hollywood's Motion Picture Production Code, a set of detailed guidelines of self-censorship within the industry that were in effect from 1930 until 1968 (around the time of the introduction of the Motion Picture Association of America [MPAA]'s rating system), had the prohibitive provision, "*Abortion, sex hygiene and venereal diseases* are not subjects for theatrical motion pictures,"[38] it is not surprising that such a standard was upheld as part of the Korean motion picture industry's stringent content regulation during the 1970s.

Other regulatory demands concern indecent exposure (related to a public bath scene in which two main characters wash their crotches), foul language (including that which references male genitalia), and illicit sexuality or winking innuendo—all common subjects of film censorship around the world. One particular scene objected to by state regulators is when protagonist Pyŏng-t'ae (Yun Mun-sŏp)'s blind-date partner Yŏng-ja (Yi Yŏng-ok), a French major enrolled in a nearby university, visits her professor's home at night to flirt with him, begging him to raise her grade on a failed exam. While the college student plays her charm on the visibly uncomfortable middle-aged man (who hurriedly escorts the young woman to the door after reluctantly giving her a chance to make up her low class score with a report), Pyŏng-t'ae waits outside at a makeshift street-food stand. The scene has been shortened and close-up shots of Yŏng-ja's most flirtatious interactions with the professor have been eliminated (though they can be still viewed in the 102-minute version). This editing is not necessarily harmful to the narrative, as the whole scene is based on the far-fetched misogynistic premise that female students would do anything, including stalking their male professors and invading their homes at night, to raise their grades. Yŏng-ja's lie to Pyŏng-t'ae, a man she met earlier that night, that she is checking on a friend afflicted with cancer is indicative of the shame and illegitimacy associated with her behavior. The reduction of this baffling scene cannot salvage the shallow characterization of Yŏng-ja but perhaps serves the purpose of downplaying any implication of an illicit affair between the (presumed) old bachelor with no show of a wife or children at home and a student half his age.

Some regulatory intervention was explicitly political. For example, there is a scene in which Pyŏng-t'ae and his best pal, Yŏng-ch'ŏl (Ha Chae-yŏng), are chased by a bumbling policeman who has spotted their long hair during a street patrol. After the 1973 proclamation of the Misdemeanor Law (which prohibited dance lessons in covert locations, spitting or being drunk on the streets, growing male hair long [beyond what was recognized as being consistent with purportedly biological "norms"], and wearing obscene clothes), Yushin police made street arrests of long-haired men and "punished" their minor misdemeanors with free military crew cuts. In 1973, 12,000 cases of long-hair control took place. In one week of June 1974 alone, the Seoul Metropolitan Police enforced 9,841 compulsory haircuts and sent 262 noncompliant violators to small-court proceedings.[39] Against Song Ch'ang-sik's whimsical trot song "Why Do You Call Me" (Wae pullŏ), the dressed-up duo on their way to a group blind date seeks to escape unwanted haircuts that might ruin their chance of appealing to the girls.[40] Ambushed by two policemen, who approach from opposite sides of a pedestrian bridge in a slapstick manner, the student fugitives finally give in and are arrested.

As Han Sang Kim points out, this deceptively light pantomime chase scene is emblematic of the film's maverick spirit as an "answer to the despotic rule ... in its depiction of the disciplinary facets of everyday life under the Park Chung Hee regime."[41] It is clear that the state found the film's message to be subversive, since it banned the ostensibly harmless love song "Why Do You Call Me" (along with 221 other songs including "Whale Hunting" [*Korae sanyang*], another item from Song's repertoire used in Ha's film) in 1975 specifically for its use as a soundtrack for the scene of civil disobedience to long-hair policing.

While being interrogated in the precinct station, Pyŏng-t'ae and Yŏng-ch'ŏl implore one of the clownish officers to allow them to go on their blind date without haircuts, reminding the older man of his youth as a college student. The MCPI objected to the disciplinarian officer's reaction close-up, which draws attention to his own long hair hidden under the police cap. The shot (which survived in the 102-minute version) is no doubt satiric and humorous, while its perceived offense to law enforcement is hard to miss from a censors' perspective. In March 1973, the MCPI issued revised "enforcement regulations" (*sihaenggyuch'ik*) for the Motion Picture Law. It included a clause that prohibited "ridiculing or slandering just law enforcement or depicting law-enforcing officers as incompetent and powerless figures."[42] Hollywood's Production Code shares this concern and explicitly states, "Law, natural or human, shall not be ridiculed, nor sympathy be created for its violation."[43] In fact, it is not unreasonable to conjecture that a similar scene in a Hollywood studio film would have been regulated by the Production Code Administration [PCA], the American film industry's centralized self-cleansing house prior to 1968 (when the Classification and Rating Administration [CARA] took over to implement a new rating system).

Perhaps the most authoritarian way that the filmmakers' free expression was suppressed is apparent in the ministry's demand that any allusions to political unrest be deleted from the film. As a result, a fleeting shot of college students carrying protest placards was replaced by a still frame of a random anticommunist rally whose non sequitur presence is puzzling in the context of a drinking contest sequence (with inserted shots of students in the library and the science lab). Toward the end of the film, Pyŏng-t'ae goes to campus, only to catch a glimpse of a bulletin board, affixed to which is a notice of the faculty council's decision to cancel all classes indefinitely. That scene is among the deleted ones on the state regulatory list and was probably eliminated from the release print despite its inclusion in the restored print. On a deserted college campus, the directionless protagonist sits alone on a bench, listening to a PA announcer repeat, "Can you hear me?" The PA announcement is another deleted element on the ministry's list. There is no doubt that these scenes had to be removed because they obliquely, if not explicitly, reference political opposition to Park's Yushin constitution.

One can argue, though, that their elimination does not make fundamental changes to Pyŏng-t'ae's characterization. In an earlier scene, he decides not to leave the classroom when the professor allows students to skip his lecture to attend a "cheer practice" for campus sports teams. Even after the professor and the other students leave the room, the philosophy major stays until sunset, solitarily meditating rather than joining his peers for a group activity. In the original scenario available at the KOFA, the activity that Pyŏng-t'ae refuses to join is anti-Japanese student demonstrations, more decisively identifying the loner protagonist's aversion to political activism.[44] In this sense, the Korean student hero is akin to Dustin Hoffman's Benjamin in Mike Nichols's *The Graduate* (1967), a young man who emphatically responds "no" to his prospective landlord's question if he is an "agitator" (i.e., a political activist or dissident). Indeed, the titular character is searching for a rental apartment in the University of California, Berkeley campus area to pursue a romantic, not political, goal. Neither Ben nor Pyŏng-t'ae is politically engaged and both remain detached from politics despite the passion for youth activism that has become so pervasive in their immediate environment (the Berkeley campus of 1967 and the Korean campus of 1975). These deleted scenes from *The March of Fools* are indexical references to campus activism (both student and faculty) of the Yushin era, and their elimination serves to decouple the narrative from its sociopolitical setting, perhaps not that differently from how the Berkeley campus is decontextualized in *The Graduate*. This common maneuver, motivated by either commercial interests or political mandates, ultimately makes both texts universal and timeless. *The March of Fools* could therefore be said to deserve credit as one of the greatest Korean films ever made, not merely one of the greatest Yushin-era productions.

One of the most significant interventions that MCPI film regulators made is regarding Yŏng-ch'ŏl's suicide scene. After suffering one rejection or humiliation after another (by the military, by his love interest, and by disciplinarian paternal figures), this lost soul heads out to the East Sea in search of a mythical whale, a Hemingway-like dream the character had professed to repeatedly in earlier scenes. Accompanied by Song Ch'ang-sik's upbeat song "Whale Hunting" on the soundtrack, the scene is oddly evocative of the *myŏngnang* sentiment despite the tragic outcome that follows. Yŏng-ch'ŏl's face brightens with a happy smile when he gazes at a magnificent sea vista from the top of a cliff where his bicycle is temporarily parked. The camera zooms in on the ocean waves as if foretelling the young whale hunter's final destination. As Chŏng states, "This is the most representative scene of the film, along with the one of Pyŏng-t'ae and Yŏng-ja kissing at the end. [The jumping scene] was deleted when the film was released, and the audience only watched the scene where Yŏng-ch'ŏl takes his foot off the brake and steps on the pedal."[45] In other words, what state regulators disallowed is not the act of suicide but an explicit showing of the falling body and bicycle off the cliff in an extreme long shot. The 1973 enforcement rules of the Motion Picture Law prohibit films that might "encourage suicide."[46] A precedent for a similar provision can be found in the 1938 amendment to the Production Code's crime regulations: "Suicide, as a solution of problems occurring

FIGURE 4.2 After suffering one rejection or humiliation after another (by the military, by his love interest, and by disciplinarian paternal figures), Yŏng-ch'ŏl (Ha Chae-yŏng: left) heads out to the East Sea in search of a mythical whale, a Hemingway-like dream the character had professed to repeatedly in earlier scenes.

in the development of screen drama, is to be discouraged as morally questionable and as bad theater—unless absolutely necessary for the development of the plot."[47] In this particular instance of Korean regulation and compliant cutting, the suicide scene is remade so that it is suspended in time, much in the way that another liberating death scene is depicted in Ridley Scott's *Thelma & Louise* (1991). Arguably, this could be construed as a poetic transformation, one that taps into the audience's imagination and, thus, serves as evidence of an enabling, not purely restrictive, function of censorship.

Another deleted scene from the censorship review copy appears to be persuasive evidence supporting the established trade narrative that Yushin-era film censorship inflicted artistic and political injuries on extraordinarily gifted, cosmopolitan auteurs such as Ha, who was well versed in the experimental traditions of New Wave cinema in Europe and the United States. This cinema verité–style, self-reflexive scene is framed as television news interviews with random college students (including Pyŏng-t'ae and Yŏng-ch'ŏl) idling on the campus lawn. A member of the television crew introduces himself as a reporter for a new program called *Youth Chorus*, which aims to show young people's aspirations and dissatisfaction with the older generations. Requesting support for his report, the journalist poses a series of questions to nonresponsive students off-screen: "Do you have plans for this fall as a college student? You must not want to answer. Then next student. What are your recent favorite movies? What do you want to be in the future? Anyone who wants to answer?" A frustrated reporter approaches Pyŏng-t'ae to ask, "What do you think about youth culture? Which one do you believe is better? A love marriage or an arranged marriage?" Our hero is aloof and nonchalant in his reply, saying, "I don't know." Giving up on getting any talking-head footage, the television reporter suggests taking a group picture and demands that everyone smile. No reactions, just stoic faces. The journalist tells his cameraman, "No use. They don't listen. Let's go."

Undoubtedly, the audacious scene, which couples Brechtian techniques of direct address and poignant social commentary on youth disillusionment, would have delighted cinephilic critics and intellectuals who appreciated comparable interludes in Jean-Luc Godard's *Weekend* (1967), Haskell Wexler's *Medium Cool* (1969), and Robert Altman's *M*A*S*H* (1970). Although its depressing and gloomy content appears to be in violation of *myŏngnang* policy, this scene is surprisingly not on the ministry's list of objectionable items to be deleted or recut. If I were to speculate based on archival evidence, I would say that the most reasonable scenario is that the production company voluntarily removed it from the preview print after making an excuse to Ha that state censors demanded the cut along with several others (notably, the director blamed government censorship for cutting thirty minutes, rather than fifteen or seventeen minutes, of his film in the aforementioned student newspaper). It is unclear whether this decision was motivated politically or commercially. It is logical, however, to conjecture that producers at Hwach'ŏn Trading were not fully on board with Ha's innovative film language and would have preferred to avoid a digressive, non sequitur–style scene that might have puzzled mainstream moviegoers with a predilection for more traditional, immersive narration. As critic Kang Sŏng-ryul notes, the film's disconnected narrative owes as much to its original source's episodic structure (nearly half of the serial novel's thirty episodes were abandoned in the screen adaptation) and to "Ha's directorial inventions in radically reordering Ch'oe's story and inserting or deleting episodes to make it his own story" as it does to censorship deletions or revisions.[48] As elaborated by Hall in the above-quoted passage, popular culture is a contested "arena of consent and resistance" governed by many conflicting or converging interests of powerholders and decision makers. In this case, the state policy of *myŏngnang* serendipitously advanced the commercial interests of Korean film producers, whose primary goal was and still remains maximizing profits by pleasing, rather than alienating or offending, as many audiences as possible.

The Duality of *Myŏngnang* in a Censored Narrative

In her study of 1960s comedy and film censorship, Park Sŏn-yŏng describes the paradox of comedy as both a permissive genre and a restrictive genre. On the one hand, the government welcomed the use of comedy as a tool for constructing a *myŏngnang* society. But in order to maintain the state-sanctioned narrative of a cheerful, wholesome nation, comedic vulgarity or deviation had to be carefully monitored and suppressed.[49] Another paradox of the genre is that the sentiment of *myŏngnang* in a fractured text like *The March of Fools* could simultaneously reinforce the state narrative of Yushin-era South Korea and resist such national propaganda. As a censored text, Ha's film walks a fine line between conforming to the "affect politics" of the Yushin regime and subverting it through the self-reflexive parody of *myŏngnang*. One particular scene is illustrative of the film's sophisticated tonal duality wherein deceptively uplifting emotions thinly veil deeper anxiety, crisis, and discontent.

The scene is framed as a flashback of Pyŏng-t'ae as he meditates in an empty classroom. The lecture hall has been deserted by his classmates, who have opted for *myŏngnang* sports spectatorship and cheering (signaled by offscreen crowd noises/band music and inserted shots of baseball, soccer, and basketball games) over a philosophy lecture. Before his own departure, the professor asks our hero—the final student in the classroom—to erase the blackboard on which "Aristotle's Utopia" is written. Next to the English phrase is the Korean translation *isanggukga* ("ideal state"). The lone student playfully erases some of the Korean letters and uses chalk to modify the phrase into *sakura*. The primary meaning of the Japanese word is "cherry blossom." However, Pyŏng-t'ae's silent wordplay invokes another meaning (a fake customer or shill), thus questioning the concept of "ideal state." A documentary montage of soccer and basketball games is intercut with static shots from various angles of Pyŏng-t'ae, who appears to be lost in solitary thought. A profile close-up of his pensive face fades out of focus and transitions to another close-up of Yŏng-ch'ŏl aiming a pool shot (in a flashback). Three other students who are with Pyŏng-t'ae and Yŏng-ch'ŏl begin to debate about what their country needs most today. Two materialistic answers (money and oil) are given. A medium-long shot follows to expose the background of the billiard club, where professionally dressed office workers are seen playing pool in a leisurely way in the rear while a group of casually clothed college students engage in a heated philosophical discussion in the front. Declaring his opposition to money, Yŏng-ch'ŏl tells his peers that "trust among fellow men" is what he believes South Korea needs most. The camera cuts to a low-angle medium two-shot of Yŏng-ch'ŏl and Pyŏng-t'ae as the latter cynically retorts that everything in the world is fake and not to be trusted. This misanthropic line is listed among the four dialogue passages to be deleted in the MCPI's preview print review, dated May 13, 1975.

Another classmate tests Yŏng-ch'ŏl's "trust theory" and puts up 500 won (US$ 1.6) as bet money. The group gives the money to a newspaper delivery boy in the club and asks him to break the bill and bring change from outside. The boy offers to leave a bunch of fresh newspapers as collateral, but the older students let him go with no strings attached. Everyone but Yŏng-ch'ŏl believes that the paperboy will not return and the money is gone. Pyŏng-t'ae is particularly vocal about his mistrust, asking his friend if he is "waiting for Godot, who doesn't come." Half an hour later, everyone else gives up and is ready to leave. Maintaining his faith in humanity, Yŏng-ch'ŏl insists on waiting for the boy's return. A tense montage builds suspense, cutting between a close-up of the clock and shots of the waiting faces. Finally, the door is flung open and the boy bolts in, excusing himself for being late and explaining that he jaywalked and was detained by police for nearly an hour. In a medium shot, Yŏng-ch'ŏl pats the newspaper boy's head, thanking him for "saving his life" in front of smiling classmates (except for Pyŏng-t'ae, who is seen scratching his head awkwardly in the back). The camera cuts to a close-up that registers the young boy's look of surprise at Yŏng-ch'ŏl's overstatement. A reverse close-up centers on Yŏng-ch'ŏl's emotive face as he asks his younger counterpart, "Selling the paper makes you happy?" A cut to another close-up of the boy, whose sweaty face radiates with a smile, follows, and he replies, "Of course." In another medium shot, Yŏng-ch'ŏl acknowledges the boy on behalf of the whole group (everyone adoringly gazes at him except for Pyŏng-t'ae, who lowers his head with a somber expression), declaring, "You are our big brother. You are the better man." In an exaggerated burst of *myŏngnang* joviality, the paperboy lifts his right hand, shouting "Newspaper! Newspaper!" and leaving the group in an exhilarated state. The boy's *myŏngnang* sentiment seems infectious to Yŏng-ch'ŏl, who gleefully embraces his nonresponsive pal Pyŏng-t'ae (whose head remains down) in a childlike display of happiness.

The screen fades out to a blur, which transitions back to the profile shot of Pyŏng-t'ae's serious, depressed face against the black background. He closes his eyes and lowers his head as if in pain against the sonic counterpoint of cheerful band music from the offscreen sports field. The flashback scene closes with a John Ford–like door shot that frames the deep, chapel-like interior space of the dark lecture hall (which is only partially lit with natural light from four windows in the upper left corner of the frame). The solitary hero is dimly lit, ensconced in shadows, and seated at the farthest end of the stadium-seating classroom. As in the final shot of *The Godfather* (1972), directed by Ha Kil-jong's UCLA classmate Coppola, the closing door engulfs the distant character in the utter darkness. Ha's concept of editing in this sequence is furthermore reminiscent of legendary Soviet filmmaker Sergei Eisenstein's notion of dialectical montage, which is defined as "an idea that arises from the collision of independent shots—shots even opposite to each other."[50] In particular, the jarring contrast between the newspaper boy's theatrical performance of *myŏngnang* in high-key lighting and the framing profile close-up of Pyŏng-t'ae's gloomy face in low-key lighting undermines the cause-and-effect coherence of continuity editing with colliding images, emotions, and ideas. One can assume that Pyŏng-t'ae appears uncomfortable and disengaged in the flashback because he is ashamed of himself for having doubted the honest boy. However, it is still baffling why he looks so desolate and moody after remembering the heartwarming episode about children's innocence and goodness.

It is particularly noteworthy that the child actor who plays the newspaper boy is Yi Sŭng-hyŏn, best known for appearing in the "Yalkae" series, a *myŏngnang* high school comedy series that started with the 1976 film *Yalkae, A Joker in High School* (theatrically released one year after *The March of Fools*). Yi's brief yet memorable appearance in Ha's film prefigures his iconic role as "Yalkae," a nickname for the titular troublemaker (Na Tu-su), who transforms from a delinquent

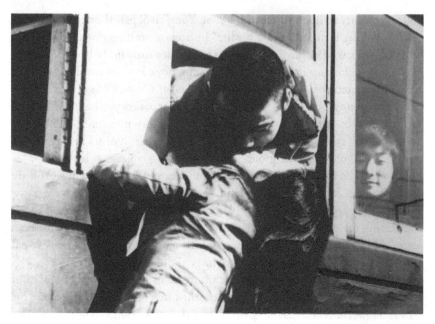

FIGURE 4.3 Protagonist Pyŏng-t'ae (Yun Mun-sŏp: upper), a pensive philosophy major, enlists in the military after struggling to woo Yŏng-ja (Yi Yŏng-ok: lower), a bubbly French major from a nearby university.

prankster to a pious model student after bonding with Ho-chŏl (Kim Chŏng-ŭn), a nerdy classmate from an underprivileged background whom he has bullied earlier in the narrative. After indirectly causing the latter's leg injury by breaking his eyeglasses in a practical joke and forcing him to deliver milk without corrected eyesight, Yalkae (who lives a comfortable life as a professor's son) visits Ho-chŏl's humble rooftop apartment to apologize. Like the newspaper boy who bursts into performative *myŏngnang* euphoria in Ha's flashback scene, the parentless high schooler (who barely makes more than a meager living along with his factory worker sister) is another young cheerleader for hard work and an affluent future promised by the state. As if he were a mouthpiece for the Park administration's developmental policy, Ho-chŏl passionately insists that "poverty is never something to be ashamed of. It's just inconvenient. Yalkae, we have a bright and hopeful future. To achieve a better future, we students must work hard." Unlike Pyŏng-t'ae, who remains detached from the paperboy's *myŏngnang* spectacle, Yalkae is nearly brought to tears by Ho-chŏl's emotive speech, which literally turns him into a new person who not only studies hard in classes to take notes for his bedridden friend but also secretly delivers milk in his place to raise money for Ho-chŏl's replacement glasses and hospital fees. In his review of *Yalkae*, director Ha complained about the commercialism and oversentimentality of Korean teenpics as demonstrated by the second part of this film, in which Yalkae transforms from a mischievous kid to a model student through a trite plot twist.[51]

Although *The March of Fools* precedes *Yalkae, A Joker in High School*, the common presence of the child star Yi Sŭng-hyŏn and his embodiment of *myŏngnang* ideals make it difficult not to make connections for retrospective viewers. Ha's Soviet montage–style juxtaposition of the newspaper boy's *myŏngnang* and Pyŏng-t'ae's depression critically draws attention to the constructedness or fakeness of the "ideal state" and its policy of sentimental education. Yu Sŏn-yŏng compares Park Chung Hee's *myŏngnang* film policy to that of the Nazis during the mid-to-late 1930s, when half of German cinematic productions were "cheerful films" such as comedies and musicals.[52] While this is a persuasive analogy, historical film censorship in democratic—not just fascist or totalitarian—states likewise tended to suppress excessive bleakness, brutality, and pessimism with no constructive moral lessons. In addition to the OWI's wartime encouragement of lighthearted, morale-boosting entertainment as referenced earlier, Hollywood's internal regulatory agency, the PCA, was gravely concerned about the postwar rise of film noir, which, according to film historian Thomas Doherty, not only "sabotaged the sunny optimism of Hollywood cinema" but also "incited an upward spike in censorship battles with state boards and city czars." Doherty goes as far as to declare (with tongue planted firmly in cheek), "Film noir was the un-American activity in Hollywood that the U.S. Congress should really have been investigating."[53]

The omniscient narrator of *Yalkae, A Joker in High School*'s trailer (whose script is included in the KOFA's collection of censorship files) explicitly markets the sentiment of *myŏngnang* with this invitation to the audience: "Let us laugh. Laugh heartily. Laugh and laugh. And if that is not enough, let us cry heartily. Let us all laugh heartily marching to Yalkae's song. Please look forward to *Yalkae, A Joker in High School*, a film our theater presents confidently with the promise of a hopeful and bountiful tomorrow." Released on January 29, 1977, the teen comedy garnered 258,000 admissions (84,000 in excess of *The March of Fools*'s box-office record), spurring several sequels and spin-offs, including *High School Champ* (*Kogyo uryanga*, 1977), *Mischief's Marching Song* (*Yalkae haengjingok*, 1977), and *Tomboys of School* (*Yŏgo yalkae*, 1977). This indicates that the sentiment of *myŏngnang* was very much in tune with the popular desire and market capitalism of the Yushin era, not merely a fascist tool of national propaganda akin to Nazi film culture in Third Reich Germany.

Yalkae, A Joker in High School and *The March of Fools* targeted two different groups of youth audiences. The former's exhibition was allowed to anyone above elementary school age while the latter's exhibition was restricted for minors. In the 1970s, Korean movie audiences were, on average, younger than in previous eras, consisting mostly of teenagers and twenty-somethings. When films were permitted to be exhibited to minors, teenagers were nearly 80 percent of the audience, whereas college students were the primary patrons of adult-only films.[54]

This may explain different portrayals of *myŏngnang* as a vehicle for comedy and entertainment (in *Yalkae*) vs. a mode of social introspection or criticism (in *The March of Fools*). In a 1974 audience survey conducted by the Korean Motion Picture Promotion Corporation (Yŏnghwa chinhŭnggongsa), 18 percent of the respondents named "entertainment" as the primary reason for going to movies while 29.8 percent reported that they patronized motion pictures because "there is something to learn."[55] The bifurcated tonality of *The March of Fools* oscillates between these two impulses, capturing the double desire of youth audiences to be entertained and educated.

Waiting for the Sun in Hell Joseon

Scholars like Kang Suk-gyŏng echo the trade consensus that Ha Kil-jong's masterpiece became the unfortunate casualty of extreme political oppression. Kang observes that while Ha's film adaptation has a stronger tendency toward social criticism (expressed through the added character of Yŏng-ch'ŏl, who is absent in Ch'oe's less political original centering on universal themes such as existential crises and generational conflicts), Yushin-era film censorship ultimately caused "signs of 'resistance' to dissipate."[56] This evaluation is understandable in the broader context of the film's release date (May 31, 1975), eighteen days after the Park administration's Emergency Decree Number 9 was proclaimed. According to sociologist Paul Y. Chang, the infamous decree "illegalized all forms of criticism of the government, legalized direct imprisonment without due process of law, and was worded vaguely enough to be applied to almost all protest situations."[57] In particular, this final edition of the series of presidential emergency decrees (declared between 1974 and 1975) prohibited not only public gatherings and demonstrations but also the distribution of "documents, books, recordings, or other expressions" for the purpose of "denying, opposing, or distorting" the Yushin constitution or "insisting on, petitioning, or agitating its revision or abolition."[58] It goes without saying that *The March of Fools* was introduced to the public during one of the darkest periods of South Korean history. In her PhD dissertation on 1970s Korean film censorship, however, Song A-rŭm contends that the MCPI's regulation of *The March of Fools* was far from being oppressive (as one expects from the aforementioned political context) but was protective of college-age youth as a privileged group. An uncomplimentary line such as "Who were not college students in the past? There are so many of them" was requested to be removed. Instead of being concerned about youth rebellion, state regulators were sensitive to the cinematic depression of young people who should be full of hope and positivity.[59]

Ironically, this same worry has kept many Korean politicians and presidential candidates awake at night in recent years, nearly fifty years after the film's release. According to a 2016 survey of 3,173 college students and corporate employees (jointly conducted by JobKorea and Albamon, two of the many employment service websites), 90 percent of respondents in their twenties and thirties said that they have adopted the damning rhetoric of "Hell Joseon" at various times in their young lives.[60] For most young Koreans, their home country (formerly known as the Chosŏn [Joseon] Dynasty [1392–1910]) is a *Squid Game*–like serial of "mini hells" (taking them from college-entrance hell to job-seeker hell to real-estate hell and so on) and inequality, unemployment/underemployment, and diminishing prospects for basic human rights (getting married, buying homes, having children, etc.) depress and discourage them. In the past decade, neologism after neologism, such as *samp'o sedae* (a generation who gave up courtship, marriage, procreation), *op'o sedae* (a generation who gave up courtship, marriage, procreation, homeownership, career), and *isaengmang* (this life is ruined), has captured a culture of desperation and despair among Korean adolescents and young adults. Despite their country's lofty global standing as a powerhouse exporter of consumer electronics, automobiles, K-pop, and films/dramas, and its robust civil democracy (which allowed the 2017 impeachment of a corrupt, disgraced president, Park Geun-hye [Pak Kŭn-hye], none other than Park Chung Hee's daughter, by the will of the people), *myŏngnang* seems as elusive for today's South Korean youth as it was for their predecessors of the 1970s whose sentiments could not be easily modified through cultural programs or cinematic censorship.

As Won Kim states, "The popular culture of the times cannot be reduced to the self-identity of terms such as *censorship*, *oppression*, *subordination*, and *domination*. Poised between subversion and decadence, and often crossing the boundary between the two, popular culture of the period richly reveals the numerous fissures in the seemingly uniform surface of Yushin rule."[61] This assessment is even more true for motion picture censorship, which is always a complex process of negotiations and compromises between regulators and the regulated. As KOFA chief researcher Cho Jun-hyoung notes, previous scholarship has erected a false binary between the oppressive state/censor and film artists who, much like sacrificial lambs, saw their work and vision cut up and undermined by a hegemonic apparatus imposing anticommunism, nationalism, and other official ideologies of Cold War military regimes.[62] This abstract construction of film censorship as a propaganda tool of the authoritarian state, as Cho points out, neglects the microlevel, procedural process of "complicity, collaboration, bargaining, and negotiation" between censors and the censored that universally applies regardless of macrolevel political systems (democracy, socialism, military dictatorship, etc.) under which motion pictures are regulated.[63] *The March of Fools* was the second highest-grossing domestic film of 1975 (following *Yŏng-ja's Heydays*) and remains a beloved cultural artifact in the minds of both the public and critics. The version that theatergoers saw was not the 117-minute censorship review print, closer to Ha's original vision, but a censored recut of the film running under one hundred minutes.

In the final analysis, *myŏngnang* is the sentiment that both the Yushin government wished to indoctrinate and ordinary Koreans pursued on their own to brighten their dark times. *The March of Fools* represents an accidental synthesis or convergence of these otherwise divergent interests. Ultimately, the film strikes a remarkable balance as not only a "wholesome" text that received the MCPI's approval but also a "resistant" text which intermixes laughter and lightness with pathos and somberness. It captures the era's zeitgeist brilliantly even after more explicit political allusions have been deleted. For many Koreans living during the Yushin period, *The March of Fools* might have been the much-needed sun's rays as described in Kim Ki-rim's colonial-era poem written thirty-six years before: "The sun's beauty my poem cannot surpass. The sun's being my poem cannot be, so it turns to grief, so I use it to keep the light on inside my gloomy sickroom, and, Sun, I am waiting for you to come, staying up through this night."[64]

5

Censors as Audiences and Vice Versa

Sex, Politics, and Labor
in 1981

In the January 1977 issue of *Ethics for Performing Arts* (*Kongyŏnyesul*), the Public Performance Ethics Committee (PPEC: Kongyŏn yulliwiwŏnhoe)'s monthly publication, stage performance regulators Yu Min-yŏng, Yi Myŏng-wŏn, and Ko Myŏng-sik categorize performing arts into two categories: "Those that observe reality in a positive way and affirm our moral and national values; and those that observe reality in a negative way and present social absurdities that we are trying to eliminate in an accusatory manner." Yu, Yi, and Ko acknowledge that the second group of works can have positive functions if they serve collective moral values and national interests by suggesting solutions to exposed social problems. If critical observations are "misused" purely for the negative purposes of harming morality and national interests, according to them, that is when the PPEC's regulation is most needed and its guidelines of performance ethics can best serve public interests.[1] The PPEC regulators recognized the difficulty of protecting public morality and national interests without compromising the artistic integrity and imagination. Censorship, in other words, was a balancing act of administering set moral guidelines with flexible interpretative room to allow maximum artistic freedom within reasonable social boundaries. Although articulated by stage performance regulators, this philosophy of censorship can easily apply to motion picture regulation.

With the 1975 proclamation of the Public Performance Law (Kongyŏnbŏp), the PPEC succeeded the Art and Culture Ethics Committee (ACEC: Yesulmunha yulliwiwŏnhoe) in 1976 as a legalized regulatory entity for stage plays, musical recordings, and motion picture scripts. In 1970, the ACEC (founded in 1966) had taken over the task of preproduction script reviews from the Korean Film Producers Association. Between 1976 and 1979, the PPEC only reviewed scenarios in the preproduction stage and from April 1979, the organization was also entrusted with the authority to review finished prints on behalf of the Ministry of Culture and Public Information (MCPI: Munhwagongbobu). The 1976 inaugural ethics committee consisted of seventeen members representing such professions as journalism, education, filmmaking, lawmaking, and broadcasting regulation. Under the general committee, there were three specialized areas of review committees (motion pictures, stage performances, and songs/recordings) with their own members.[2] Some PPEC motion picture regulators were directors and/or producers (Ho Hyŏn-ch'an, Kim Ki-dŏk, Yi Kang-chŏn, Ch'oe Ha-wŏn, Yu Hyŏn-mok, Cho Mun-jin, Han Hyŏng-mo, Kwŏn Yŏng-sun, etc.) or film critics (Im Yŏng, Son Ki-sang, Chŏng Ŭng-t'ak, Yi Yŏng-il, Kim Chong-wŏn, Hŏ Ch'ang, Yu Chi-na, etc.).

In the May 1977 issue of *Ethics for Performing Arts*, the PPEC motion picture regulator Ho Hyŏn-ch'an (who had produced critically acclaimed masterpieces of Korean cinema such as Kim Su-yong's *A Sea Village* [*Kaetmaŭl*, 1965] and Yi Man-hŭi's *Late Autumn* [*Manch'u*, 1966] and who had served on the regulatory board for the national broadcaster KBS [Korean Broadcasting System]) reflected on his first-year task of reviewing 197 screenplays. While Ho admitted that PPEC script regulation might have caused mental distress to those filmmakers who desired unrestrained artistic freedom, he defended the process as a "moral shield" (*yullijŏk pangp'ae*) that protects audiences and families by "eliminating polluting elements [from] popular culture." Declaring that there would be no future for South Korean cinema unless filmmakers were motivated to upgrade their productions (beyond cheap action fare or teen melodramas), Ho partially credited the PPEC regulatory feedback system for diversification of subject selections and for the improvement in quality of screenplays submitted for review throughout the first half of 1977.[3]

In the February 1982 issue of *Ethics for Performing Arts*, film critic and producer Kim Kap-ŭi took Ho's ideas further and mounted a persuasive defense of censorship as an act of critical spectatorship. According to Kim,

> There is a saying that directors are the first audiences of films. In a similar vein, censors are the first objective audiences. What is the difference between these important first audiences and regular audiences? There is no such difference.... There are very few countries with no censorship. But if there are no conflicts somewhere else it is because filmmakers move, overwhelm, amaze, and bring censors to tears. Filmmakers should not think that there are different

audiences out there if they cannot even move and overwhelm a handful of censors. People are saying that censorship became lax lately, but I do not think so. In the process of undergoing numerous censorship procedures film producers and directors came to understand the intents and reasons for cutting and uplifted their cinematic expressions. As a result, censors simply could not find scenes to cut.... For morally upright filmmakers and directors, the film regulation body is a great advisor, collaborator, and companion. To filmmakers and directors who may still believe that vulgar films are the only means to expand their wealth, the PPEC will remain an uncomfortable existence to the end.[4]

In the June 1982 issue of the same publication, Son Ki-sang, an editor of *Chungang Ilbo* and a PECC motion-picture regulator, admits his own allergic reaction to the word "censorship" (*kŏmyŏl*), which connotes to him, as a journalist, "ideological control" (*sasangt'ongje*) of the press, publications, broadcasting, theater, and motion pictures. Defining his role with the softer term "regulation" (*simŭi*), Son shares a few things he had recently learned about motion picture censorship, including film producers' contradictory demand for a minor admissions (*ch'ŏngsonyŏn ipjangga*) rating while inserting scenes that would make even adults blush. The journalist-film regulator confides that "there are times when it is confusing whether our role is censoring or directing. When there are lengthy and frequent scenes of sex, albeit not violating regulatory rules significantly, it bewilders regulators. It is our belief that inducing [filmmakers] to shorten unnecessarily long and repeated sex scenes is desirable even if there are not direct violations. Most discussions we had were about sex scenes, not violence or other matters."[5]

These collective observations, positionings, and theorizations of film censorship published by civil PPEC regulators operating under the auspices of the MCPI offer valuable contextual frameworks for approaching state regulation documents preserved at the Korean Film Archive (KOFA: Han'gukyŏngsang charyŏwŏn) and available for research. Their insights into the various roles of censors—from defenders of national interests and moral shields for the public to "first objective audiences" and surrogate directors who edit out gratuitous sex scenes—resonate with revisionist literary and cultural studies scholarship on censorship, referred to by Matthew Burn as "New Censorship Theory." Influenced by the writings of French theorists Michel Foucault and Pierre Bourdieu, New Censorship theorists, including Richard Burt, Laura Gilbert, Sue Currey Jansen, Annette Kuhn, and Annabel Patterson, have collectively "recast censorship from a negative, repressive force, concerned only with prohibiting, silencing, and erasing, to a productive force that creates new forms of discourse, new forms of communication, and new genres of speech."[6] As Burn points out, some New Censorship theorists have interrogated state censorship "as a form not distinct from civil society, a repressive sub-species in a sea of constitutive structural censorship, but as largely created by the same sorts of forces." The reevaluation of state censorship as a productive, if also "contingent, contested, and unpredictable," force, is only possible when "historians shift their focus from the 'upper reaches' of power to examine the functioning of censorship" in the proverbial trenches (i.e., attending to "the quotidian life of writers, censors, editors, and publishers").[7]

In his study of press media control in the German Democratic Republic (GDR), for example, Dominic Boyer challenges the preconceived notion of censorship as the anthesis of creativity and intelligence, or simply put, "a crude business: punitive, petty, anti-humanitarian." Instead, he recuperates East Germany's party-state censorship as a "productive intellectual practice" or an "intellectual vocation."[8] Contrary to much of the Western prejudice against authoritarian political censorship in Soviet-bloc states, for the GDR's Agitation Division functionaries, "'censorial practices' (among them, the editing, licensing, and criticism of media texts) were treated as truly vocational activities since even minute textual and lexical calibrations were believed to contribute to the greater welfare of the *Volk*." In fact, as Boyer notes, "The everyday life of censorship in the GDR, from the perspective of its practitioners, was suffused with a gentle, progressive aura not unlike the elusive vestiges of professionalism present in any intellectual vocation embedded in an institutional context."[9] Boyer's insight is eminently applicable to the Republic of Korea (ROK)'s state-private (*kwan-min*) hybrid film censorship from the 1970s to the 1980s—the harshest period of the successive authoritarian regimes of Park Chung Hee [Pak Chŏnghŭi]'s full-fledged Yushin dictatorship and Chun Doo Hwan [Chŏn Tu-hwan]'s much-hated Fifth Republic.

In the July 1979 issue of *Ethics for Performing Arts*, Son Se-il, an editor for *Tonga Ilbo* and a PPEC film regulator, declared, "State censorship should be abolished in motion pictures and other areas as soon as possible." While welcoming the transfer of print review operations from the MCPI to the PPEC earlier that year as a step forward in the right direction, Son felt compelled to point out the imperfections of this new system, which nominally granted autonomy to the commissioned committee performing film censorship on behalf of the MCPI. Regardless, the journalist-film regulator expressed confidence in his vocation, saying, "Given the constitution of the committee, I do not think serious creative activities of talented filmmakers will be restricted. On this earth, there is no perfect country without contradictions and absurdities, and it is the nature of the modern arts to expose social imperfections. Therefore, such freedom of expression should not be restricted."[10] Despite Son's liberal articulation of "antiscissoring" principles (an attitude that apparently was shared by most or all of his colleagues), his insider account of committee operations from April to July of 1979 showcases the dilemma that PPEC regulators with high credentials (such as journalists, professors, lawyers, lawmakers, and film critics) faced when reviewing disappointing entertainment-based films catering to the lowest common denominator.

Son chronicled the committee's long discussions while trying to balance freedom of expression and enterprise with the public duty to curb the harmful effects of exploitative or gratuitous images of sex and violence on theatergoers, particularly minors. Although some members went as far as threatening to quit should tighter restriction of lower-quality products not be implemented, the committee as a whole was permissive and kept their cutting to the most obvious elements (such as a close-up of the bloody knife blade after a victim is attacked in the abdomen, to use Son's own example), despite their dissatisfaction with the overall quality of submissions. A major turning point came when the new committee made the bold decision to reject their approval (*pallyŏ*) for the husband-wife gender role reversal comedy by writer-director Kim Ŭng-ch'ŏn, *You Are a Woman, I Am a Man* (*Nŏnŭn yŏja, Nanŭn namja*, 1979). As Son explained, it was not because that particular film was more offensive than others but because the committee felt compelled to take action in coercing future cooperation and compliance of producers.[11] According to the MCPI censorship file accessible at the KOFA, the PPEC passed Kim's screenplay on April 10, 1979, on the condition that profane dialogue be changed to something more palatable and that vulgar actions and lines in scenes of men serving women be purified. On June 22, 1979, the PPEC informed the MCPI that *You Are a Woman, I Am a Man* had failed the censorship by the unanimous decision of fourteen members (including famous director Han Hyŏng-mo) who were present and voted against passing the preview print.[12] An attached review report states that the producers did not make the requested revisions after the PPEC's screenplay review. The message was loud and clear. Hanjin Enterprises (Hanjinhŭnghyŏp), the film's production company, promptly made the necessary cuts and its exhibition permit was issued on July 5 without further requests for revisions. This little-known anecdote—one that had remained buried in the hinterlands of Korean film history until recently—affirms Boyer's assertion that there should be greater effort to shift the locus of censorship studies from "the victim's perspective" to the understudied "censor's point of view" in order to reconstruct history in all its complexities.

With these contexts in mind, I spend the remaining pages of the chapter investigating two social-problem films from 1981—Yi Wŏn-se's *A Little Ball Launched by a Dwarf* (*Nanjangiga ssoaollin chakŭn kong*) and Kim Su-yong's *The Maiden Who Went to the City* (*Tosiro kan chŏnyŏ*)—with particular attention to censorship as audience feedback and generative participation. Both texts underwent significant revisions during the production and postproduction stages to accommodate progressive censorship demands (from PPEC reviewers and/or trade unions) for more respectable representations of marginalized social identities: the disabled, evictees, and underclass working girls. It is tempting to read these films as evidence of nefarious cultural control by Chun's new military regime which massacred hundreds of innocent protesters or bystanders of Kwangju in May 1980 (commemorated as *o-il-p'al*, or May 18). What else can we expect from a dictator who ordered the mass killing of his own citizens for the "crime" of demanding democratic reforms? After all, is it not because of his "making-citizens-fools" (*uminhwa*) policy that mindless sex was encouraged on the screen in the 1980s and any explicitly political topics were avoided at all costs? In her PhD dissertation on Korean erotic films of the 1980s, Yun-Jong Lee points out the bias of "rigid, puritanical, doctrinal leftism" on the part of film critics who blamed Chun's notorious "3S [sport, screen, sex] policy" for the eroticization and degeneration of Korean films over that decade. According to Lee, "Chun wanted to divert national attention, which was naturally drawn to political issues in the wake of the Kwangju incident to something non-political ... particularly to, sport, screen (cinema), and sex (sex industry).... Although the policy was never codified or promulgated by Chun and his administration, it was tacitly in effect throughout the 1980s."[13] It is beyond the scope of this chapter to debate whether such a policy was truly in effect and responsible for the rise of the soft-porn genre in the 1980s, as many critics have argued, after the enormous success of Chŏng In-yŏp's *Madame Aema* (*Aema puin*, 1982).[14] This sensational erotic fantasy dwells on the sexual awakening of Yi Ae-ma (An So-yŏng), who, after her businessman husband's imprisonment for involuntary manslaughter, fantasizes having sex with strangers; engages in a rape–turned–perverted affair with her ex-lover, a married man living upstairs in her apartment complex; and pursues a part-time romance with an innocent young artist. Taking advantage of the abolition of the national curfew system (which restricted civilian outings between 12 A.M. and 4 A.M. from 1945 to 1982), this first Korean "midnight movie" reserved for adult-oriented late-night screenings was a commercial hit that was followed by eleven sequels and numerous spin-offs.

Archival evidence makes it clear that, in their everyday operations of regulating motion pictures, neither the PPEC nor the MCPI subscribed to the so-called 3S policy (even if such an informal principle existed in the upper echelons of the presidential Blue House). As quoted above, PPEC regulators of the late 1970s to early 1980s made concerted efforts to *curtail* gratuitous sex scenes and encouraged producers to uplift their films by aiming for something higher than the stimulation of basic human instincts. For example, in July 1979, Son Se-il articulated the PPEC's evolving policy in the context of the universal liberalization of sexual expression in Hollywood and beyond, stating, "In the future, in restricting sexual expression, a one-size-fits-all approach of the past should be avoided and selective customization case by case should be made." According to Son, "A prohibitive clause against 'exposing breasts and other parts of the body' should be eliminated. Depending on the nature of films, even more explicit expression might need to be permitted. On the other hand, pure commodification of sexual expression without narrative causality should be strictly restricted to protect citizens from the toxins of 'faulty products.'"[15]

This principle was upheld in the PPEC regulator Ho Hyŏn-ch'an's scenario review of *Madame Aema* dated October 15, 1981. What particularly seems to have bothered the reviewer was not the screenplay's candid exploration of female sexual desire for multiple partners (including exchanges of queer gazes, or lesbian looks, with her close friend/confidante) but instead the repeated pornographic sex scenes catering to male heterosexist rape fantasies. Ho found two disturbing scenes objectionable. One is the upstairs neighbor's illegal entry into Ae-ma's bedroom through an open veranda and violation of the sleeping occupant, whose body—barely clothed in seductive lingerie—is conveniently exposed and responsive to the intruder's sexual touch after initial resistance. Another is the janitor's attempted rape of the same woman in the elevator of his workplace. The latter scene was eliminated, along with a few other expendable sex scenes, after the MCPI, based on the PPEC's feedback, requested that the production company, Yŏnbang Films, overhaul their first draft of the screenplay, which caused "concerns about harming sexual morality and family ethics with pornographic and decadent narration."[16] Given such carefully delineated regulation of acceptable and unacceptable sex on the screen at a time of increasing liberalization (at least with regards to sexuality) across global cinema,[17] it would be a gross simplification to assume that Chun's elusive 3S policy was the primary culprit responsible for unleashing a proliferation of erotic films (ero yŏnghwa) and suppressing political content.

Far less frequently discussed than the 3S policy, but perhaps more relevant to the day-to-day activities of state bureaucrats and their civil partners, was Chun's "New Culture" (saemunhwa) policy, which was announced by the MCPI minister (Yi Kwang-p'yo) in June 1981. The policy defined culture (munhwa) as "the spiritual foundation for creating a new history of democracy, welfare, and justice." Its top three objectives were (1) the development of an autonomous and creative national culture; (2) the equal distribution of cultural benefits and materialization of cultural welfare to all citizens regardless of their regional and economic differences; and (3) the improvement of financial support and social infrastructure to enhance artistic activities of culture industry professionals.[18]

Cynics might be quick to point out that this policy was nothing more than a calculated political move to boost the legitimacy of Chun's dictatorial regime, particularly in the eyes of Western observers, as Seoul was preparing to host major international sporting events: specifically, the 1986 Asian Games and the 1988 Summer Olympics. Such skepticism is warranted. However, it does not alter the fact that Chun was the first ROK leader who put culture at the forefront of his policies, prioritizing it as one of the strategic areas in the nation's five-year plan for economic development. Chun's administration shifted the focus from the preservation of dynastic national treasures (munhwaje) prioritized in the Park era to investments in the creation of new arts and cultural programs.[19] A humorless military dictator with a shameful record of human rights violations may not be the typical candidate for "culture president," but Chun apparently aspired to be one, and he made significant inroads by not only solidifying the nation's cultural infrastructure through building projects (e.g., museums, concert halls, art schools) but also relaxing regulations to foster creativity. Did he do it for his own political gain? Probably yes (after all, he was a politician). Were MCPI bureaucrats and PPEC committee members (civilian elites) Chun's political lackeys who surreptitiously pushed more sex on screen as a means of social distractions and killed any messages of dissent? Most definitely not. Even entertaining such a possibility would be an insult to the intelligence of both regulators and audiences, whose agendas, goals, and political views were heterogenous, fragmented, and sometimes surprisingly progressive in terms of protecting the rights of the socially marginalized (as demonstrated in the ensuing case studies).

"They Are Smart People": Censorship as an Intelligence Test Game

The MCPI censorship file on *A Little Ball Launched by a Dwarf* (hereafter *A Little Ball*), contains an interagency memo from the Security Bureau chief of the Ministry of the Interior (MoI: Naemubu) to the MCPI dated September 3, 1981. Citing an *Ilgan Sports* article reporting new actor Yi Hyo-jŏng's casting in Yi Wŏn-se's latest film, the MoI official rang the alarm to a fellow bureaucrat. The security chief elaborated by noting that *"A Little Ball* is a collection of stories by Cho Se-hŭi first published on June 5, 1978. On March 15, 1979, publisher Literature and Intelligence [Munhakgwa chisŏng] reprinted 150,000 copies of this seditious book that was primarily used by troublemaking university clubs for the purpose of student radicalization. We recommend an inquiry into the production company's motivation to adapt the book and thorough review of the screenplay to eliminate subversive elements."[20] Perhaps the MoI's concern, while born out of a paranoia that came with living under authoritarianism, was not entirely groundless since *A Little Ball* is a representative work of leftist "labor literature" (*nodong munhak*) of the 1970s and exemplifies what literary critic Ha Chŏng-ill calls the "narrative of resistance" (*chŏhaangŭi sŏsa*).[21] Cho's celebrated anthology creatively blends a modernist narrative structure (twelve fragmented, interrelated stories that weave together the lives of a capitalist family, a middle-class family, and an underclass family headed by the titular patriarch) with realistic social themes related to urban poverty, labor struggles, forced eviction, real estate speculation, and the sexual exploitation of women living in slum areas. As reported correctly by the MoI, *A Little Ball* was a must-read for student activists and dissident intellectuals of the late 1970s and early 1980s.

It would be difficult to explain how such risky material could have been made into a commercial motion picture at a time of political repression and cinematic escapism without understanding Yi's grand design when he proposed the project to Hanjin Enterprises (which previously had censorship trouble for *You Are a Woman, I Am a Man*). In his 2017 interview with the KOFA research team, the director detailed the process of the film's inception:

There are two types of original materials for film adaptation: one group is very easy to translate into cinematic language and the other is hard to adapt even if they are famous and highly acclaimed. *A Little Ball* belongs to the latter group. When that book came out, there were no producers or directors who were interested in adapting it.... Looking back, subjects that I pursued were all dark... and had to do with the socially disfranchised.... So *A Little Ball* was something I personally liked regardless of what others thought.... I was looking for a producer who understands the work and is willing to take responsibility to the end. I took the novel to Han Kap-jin, president of Hanjin Enterprises, since I was close to him and could see him without getting anyone's approval... I told him that I would like to test the ability of hypocritical politicians with power... I wanted to test whether or not they had brains to appease us rather than deterring us with a question like "Is that so? You want to make a film based on that book?" when we submit our production application. You see, at that time, Chun Doo Hwan was in power. So this was what was going on in the back of my mind. President Han listened to me and said, "Let's do it."[22]

Yi's take on censorship as an intelligence test or game is intriguing. British-born Hollywood director Alfred Hitchcock also used a game metaphor to describe his relationship with censors. The master of suspense reportedly compared "the spirited give-and-take" in his negotiations with Hollywood's internal censor, Joseph I. Breen of the Production Code Administration (PCA), to "the thrill of competitive horse trading."[23] In contrast, the Korean director's proposed game with state censorship is clearly politically motivated. There is an underlying demonization of the censor as well as an equation between the macropolitical structure of military dictatorship and the microadministrative operations of film regulation in Yi's assumption. This is consistent with what Boyer, in the context of GDR press censorship, regards as flawed tendencies to define the censor as "the absence of morality and ethics, the inversion of standards and norms, the immersion in the abyss of power onto which the writing of (good) intellectuals should always instead seek to cast light" rather than an intellectual vocation that administers "a complex configuration of both restrictive and productive textual practices."[24]

By the time that the MoI sent the above-quoted memo to the MCPI, Hanjin Enterprises had already made two rounds of revisions to the original screenplay submitted with the production registration application on July 21, 1981. In 1980, preproduction screenplay review was nominally abolished, although the production registration system gave the MPCI power to prescreen scripts and give feedback to producers after consultation with PPEC regulators. The MCPI censorship file includes Ho Hyŏn-ch'an's handwritten note that details problems he found in the original script. The PPEC regulator expressed concerns about the screenplay's magnification of the anger and despair of the poor without suggesting any positive vision. He flagged scenes in which class divisions and conflicts are foregrounded, such as the collective protest of union workers (led by the dwarf family's eldest son, Kim Yŏng-su [An Sŏng-gi]) for their employer's failure to pay overtime wages although its president makes a generous charity donation to help flood victims for the sake of corporate publicity. Both Yŏng-su and his younger brother Yŏng-ho ([Yi Hyo-jŏng], who has lost two fingers in a machine accident) are laid off from the Ŭngang Textile factory for their union activities. Yŏng-ho holds a grudge against family friend Chi-sŏp, a law student–turned–labor activist, for having encouraged their involvement in the union and, in the deleted scene of the original screenplay (available for research at the KOFA), punches him while delivering this protest speech: "You educated people made us this way. You knocked us. How do you, who went to college luxuriously, know our suffering? Look at my [disfigured] hand, this is reality. What you preached was nothing but sleep talk. We don't need a dream. What we need is work."[25]

In response to Ho's regulatory feedback, the production team eliminated the union plot as well as Chi-sŏp, a secondary character whose background history can be found in other stories of Cho's collection. Instead, they created a new storyline of Yŏng-ho pursuing the dream of becoming a professional boxer while working as a car washer. In his debut match, the inexperienced boxer is defeated but recognized as a promising new talent. In the original script, Chi-sŏp buys meat (with the proceeds from selling his books after being chastised by Yŏng-ho) for the evicted family's last barbeque meal in their condemned structure right before demolition. In the finished film, Yŏng-ho pays for the meat through the hard labor of his bruised body in the boxing contest. The youngest son vows to his brother, "I am going to be the champion [and] will solve all our family's problems with my fist," demonstrating the kind of affirmative can-do spirit that state censors promoted from the 1960s to the 1980s (as alluded to in earlier chapters of this book).

In addition to the representation of the poor and labor relations, Ho problematizes unflattering portrayals of two "fallen women" (Myŏng-hŭi [Chŏn Yŏng-sŏn], the love interest of Yŏng-su, and Yŏng-hŭi [Kŭm Po-ra], the Kim family's daughter) who trade sex with men for economic survival. In Cho's novella (the namesake fourth story of the anthology), Myŏng-hŭi's fate is not explicitly spelled out and is left to the reader's imagination. Yŏng-su ambiguously narrates, "When she was older she became a tearoom waitress, an express bus conductress, and a caddy. . . . Later, Mother said whenever Myŏng-hŭi came home her stomach was big. Myŏng-hŭi breathed her last at a suicide prevention center, the kind that deals with poisonings."[26] In Yi's film, on the other hand, her cinematic counterpart is clearly identified as a bar hostess serving foreign seamen in the port city of Inch'ŏn four minutes into the opening sequence. Myŏng-hŭi's suicide scene is embellished for the big screen and her first love dramatically carries her to an emergency clinic when the despairing woman takes poison in her mother's home near the Kim residence. After the funeral, Yŏng-su explains the cause for her suicide to his mother (Chŏn Yang-ja): "She was pregnant but the man returned to his home country without a word." Specifically, Ho objected to Myŏng-hŭi's line identifying herself pejoratively as a "hostess who got promoted to a local mistress [*hyŏnjich'ŏ*]" for her foreign lover. In the finished film, this line has been softened to eliminate self-derogatory terms. She simply tells Yŏng-su that she is going to enter a domestic relationship (*sallim ch'arida*), a "promotion" that her peers desire. As for the other plotline of seventeen-year-old Yŏng-hŭi's sexual encounter with a rich real estate broker (who purchases her family's occupancy rights [*imjukwŏn*] to a new apartment unit in the redevelopment zone), the filmmakers self-censored in their revisions an oral and visual reference to the use of a lidocaine-soaked gauze to anesthetize the virgin teen's postcopulatory pain.

The PPEC regulator's most progressive intervention was his criticism of the screenplay's treatment of disability for potentially inducing prejudice against and humiliation of little people. Ho cautioned, "There could be harm to people with disabilities and these portrayals should be taken seriously."[27] Although the small-statured patriarch Kim Pul-i professes his fantastical dream of traveling to the moon and building the Lilliput town of dwarfs for his wife, his suicidal flight from the chimney of a brick factory along with a paper plane brings the film to a bleak, hopeless sense of closure. As Ryu Kyŏng-dong argues, the dwarf, a recurrent character throughout Cho's anthology, is a "symbol that represents scrubby human beings who are maladjusted to the modern industrial society." The literary critic further points out, all of Kim's past occupations ("selling bonds, sharping knifes, washing windows in high-rises, installing water pumps, and repairing waterlines") are affiliated with outdated preindustrial menial labor lacking the "'normality' of capitalism," a form of "deformity" metaphorically suggested by the character's small-sized body (at least within ableist contexts).[28] The appropriation of disability (both physical and mental) as an allegorical stand-in for the oppressed class has been a long tradition in Korean film and literature. In Na To-hyang's 1925 short story "Deaf Sam-ryong" [*Pŏngŏri Sam-ryong-i*] (which was adapted into films in 1929, 1963, and 1974), the titular servant (a deaf-mute with short stature) remains loyal to and protective of his master's seventeen-year-old son, who harasses and abuses him regularly. His loyalty is tested when the family arranges a child marriage by buying the spoiled teen a beautiful, well-bred bride from a noble family whose fortunes have declined. The spiteful groom beats the bride daily, driving her to a suicide attempt. Sam-ryong, who develops tender feelings for the young mistress, prevents her from hanging herself in the private chamber, but soon a vicious rumor of the two's illicit affair brings them more misery and suffering. After being whipped and beaten to a pulp, the disabled servant, unable to speak or to defend himself, is expelled from the house. That night, the master's house is mysteriously engulfed by flames and Sam-ryong returns to look for the mistress. After neglecting the young master's cry for help and spotting his death-wishing bride covered in bedding, the severely burned and injured servant takes her in his arms to the roof, where he dies peacefully with a smile.

In Cho's novella, the Kim patriarch is identified as "the offspring of a hereditary slave," not unlike Sam-ryong. As with Sam-ryong's muteness, Pul-i's dwarfism functions as a symbol of social marginality, and both characters face protest-like death at the site of capitalistic exploitation and class oppression. In the ninth story of Cho's collection, entitled "The Fault Lies with God as Well," Yŏng-su narrates, "Just because Father was small was no reason for the life allotted him to have been so small. Through death Father had rid himself of the suffering that was larger than his body.... He worked hard but forfeited a life of human decency.... Father sought economic, social rights, his injuries didn't heal, and he fell into the smokestack of a brick factory."[29] Placing aside the potentially potent political metaphor of the little-person laborer putting an end to his abject suffering by falling from the top of a tall capitalist structure (which dwarfs him), Ho's concern about the film's potentially negative effect on audiences with physical disabilities facilitates an alternative interpretation of the otherwise socially progressive text. Cho's novella "A Little Ball" opens with Yŏng-su's first-person narration: "People called Father a dwarf. Their perception was correct. Father *was* a dwarf. Sad to say, that was their only correct perception of Father. They were wrong about everything else."[30]

While the original story begins with an indictment of able-bodied people's prejudice against persons with disabilities, Yi's opening scene highlights the shame the father's deformity brings to his young children. The precredit flashback sequence opens with a long shot of two children (Yŏng-su and Myŏng-hŭi) with schoolbags walking on the muddy saltern field against a misty mountain backdrop. In the voiceover narration, the dwarf's eldest son argues, "If you cultivate a small pea with a big pea, it is bound to produce only big peas." Myŏng-hŭi rephrases his argument: "So you're saying that if you get married and have a kid, you're going to be able to have a normal kid, not a dwarf like your dad." Yŏng-su replies, "Yes, and I'll know more for certain once I study eugenics." The next shot shows Yŏng-su fighting, in front of his sister Yŏng-hŭi, with another boy who has called his father "a dwarf." In the third long shot, Yŏng-su's younger brother Yŏng-ho is measuring Yŏng-hŭi's height against the door in the foreground while their older brother is erasing the children's graffiti on the cement wall in the background. Yŏng-ho reports proudly to his sister that she is now one centimeter taller than their father. To Yŏng-hŭi, who breaks into tears out of pity for their father, Yŏng-ho yells, "Do you want to be short like dad? I hate it! I am tired of hearing the word 'dwarf.'" After Yŏng-su censures his younger sibling with the words "Why do you utter the word 'dwarf' yourself, then?" Yi's camera cuts to a close-up of the teasing graffiti ("Dwarf's place") on the wall.

In the original screenplay, Yŏng-su's opening line is "Hereditary forms and traits are divided into dominant and regressive genes. When these two are crossbred, only dominant genes manifest in the offspring."[31] The above-quoted pea example (that is retained in the finished film) follows this eliminated line. Also gone is Myŏng-hŭi's incredulous reaction to a fellow grade-schooler's amateur eugenics lesson: "You're treacherous. Do you think I don't know what you are calculating?" Although Yŏng-su shows respect for his father by fighting another kid and scolding his own brother (calling him a "dwarf"), he too resorts to the discriminatory rhetoric of eugenics in order to impress a girl he is fond of. Given the conspicuous placement of a politically incorrect line (in which a child protagonist gives a pseudoscientific justification for overcoming the "inferior" chromosomes of his disabled parent) in the film's first scene, Ho's sensible advice to take the issue seriously protects more than the feelings of disabled audiences. It also safeguards the social respectability of both the production company and the regulatory institution (the MCPI/PPEC). A compliant self-censoring edit mitigates the affront just enough without obscuring the original meaning entirely.

Hanjin Enterprises submitted the revised script with a new plot summary to the MCPI on August 4, 1981. Along with it, the production company enclosed a table showing the contrasts between the first and second drafts of the screenplay. Four main categories of revisions are noted in the table: relocation of the story to a new setting, change of the eviction authorities from the city to a private company, elimination of union references, and a shifted focus in the Kims' family drama (away from the social exposé focalized through the activist character of Chi-sŏp).[32] As in Cho's novella, the original screenplay is set in an urban shantytown where poor families live in squalor inside an unauthorized shack built on city-owned land (i.e., they built it without procuring a permit). The revised version, on the other hand, is set in the Kunja salt pond (located in Sihŭng between Inch'ŏn and Suwŏn) on the western seaside. The new setting is personal for Yi Wŏn-se, who as an elementary student (about the same age as the Kim children in the opening scene) grew up in the saltern town after his family crossed the thirty-eighth parallel and migrated to the South from North Korea in 1946. In the above-quoted KOFA oral history interview, Yi recollects, "The landscape of the town is imprinted in my head vividly . . . desolate fields with windmills, waterlines, and white salt mountains, silent workers who do not say a single word. . . . There were wildflowers whose name I do not remember. . . . Seasonal red flowers in desolate mudflats were incredibly beautiful. . . . [My childhood memory] is why I often used the salterns as my film's setting."[33]

Yi also defended this change of setting against the critiques of his detractors, who saw it as capitulating to censors at the expense of toning down Cho's original message. The director elaborated, "In the original, *A Little Ball* is set in the city's shantytown. I had my own story of *A Little Ball* to tell. . . . In every country and every society, there are always dwarfs and giants. My characters have dreams and ideals. . . . I had my own idea about the background to set their ideals . . . and that place for me was the salterns. . . . It was not a careless choice made to avoid censorship.... My own *A Little Ball* was blossoming inside me."[34] We can only speculate whether Yi would have altered the setting of his own accord without a preproduction regulatory intervention pressuring him to shift narrative focus away from class conflicts. Ultimately, the new setting seems to have satisfied Yi's artistic vision and helped him claim ownership of the story by combining the eviction storyline of Cho's original with the saltern landscape, the director's own aesthetic signature.

This marriage of two visions is particularly effective in the climactic demolition scene, wherein a bulldozer tears down the walls of the Kims' residence while the family is cooking and tasting barbecue at their dinner table. The preceding montage crosscuts from an aerial extreme long shot of the bulldozer arriving in the saltern field road and a long shot of waterbirds peacefully lighting on mudflats to a medium frontal shot of the bulldozer menacingly approaching an off-screen structure (presumably the Kim family house) and a long shot of the birds flying away from the salterns. The soundtrack mixes the competing ambience noises of the machine engine and bird shrieks, amplifying the clash between industry and nature. By resetting Cho's story in the salt pond town (a location dear to director Yi's heart), the film expands its social commentary to the cinematically coded environmental message that subtly indicts corporate greed destroying not only evictees' homes but also the natural habitat of wildlife.

There are conflicting accounts as to how many times the screenplay was revised. Yi cites eight in his KOFA interview, whereas archival documents in the MCPI censorship file reference three revisions (and three drafts of scenarios are also available for research in the KOFA scenario collections). That discrepancy can be reconciled when counting additional internal revisions supervised by Hanjin Enterprises' administrative team, which, according to Yi, sent staff members to the set to advise on desired changes in the review scenarios annotated by the PPEC.[35] Regardless, it is safe to say that the story underwent multiple alterations in which scenes of collective protests (of factory workers and evictees) were removed while melodrama (Yŏng-su and Myŏng-hŭi's love story) and family drama (the Kims' struggle with prejudice, poverty, and eviction) were reinforced. After the second revised screenplay was submitted on August 26, 1981, both Ho of the PPEC and Sŏn Yŏng-mun of the Agency for National Security Planning (ANSP: Kukkaanjŏngihoekbu, which succeeded the Korean Central Intelligence Agency [KCIA] in 1981) reviewed it on the MCPI's behalf. Ho expressed his approval of the filmmakers' effort to address problems in the earlier drafts. He still found the revised script pessimistic and wished it to be further modified as a humanistic drama.[36] The ANSP regulator opined, "This scenario vividly depicts slices of life on the bottom rung of society and as an exposé fiction, it should not be viewed as a problematic work whose exhibition needs to be restricted. However, there is the potential to unnecessarily provoke negative views among some minors and elicit feelings of unbelonging among citizens in a similar situation. Perhaps this administration can display its confidence by instructing the filmmakers to uplift the ending and inspire hope and courage in our citizens. Once the film is complete, perhaps strict censorship should be applied to readjust content."[37]

The MCPI's consultation with the ANSP perhaps makes sense, given the MoI's report on subversive elements in the original book and the potential political risks involved in approving the film production based on it. Given the ANSP's notoriety for torturing student and labor activists and fabricating spy scandals during the Chun regime, its regulatory feedback was surprisingly level headed and permissive about "an exposé fiction." In his 2017 oral history interview, Yi recalls his frustration with repeated revisions and his desire to confront the man in power (President Chun Doo Hwan) to ask him, "Who do you not understand [this work]? You should encourage something like this if you want to be a great politician." The director goes on to complain about being attacked by the "institution underneath [Chun]" for critiquing the system (*ch'eje*) in his film. Somewhat cynically, Yi did acknowledge that censors are "smart people" capable of seeing through directorial intentions and red-penciling all the subversive parts in review scripts.[38] Documents in the MCPI file tell a different story. Consolidating feedback from both the PPEC (a civil board) and the ANSP (a state agency), on September 17, 1981, the MCPI advised Hanjin Enterprises not to depict society too darkly, not to provoke negativity in minors and feelings of disharmony between different classes, and to uplift the content to that of a heart-warming family drama. To achieve these larger goals, the ministry requested that the following elements be revised or eliminated: (1) soon-to-be bargirl Myŏng-hŭi's postcoital line (after her loss of virginity to Yŏng-su), "I feel relieved to lose something burdensome"; (2) dialogue and actions of mocking the dwarf; (3) the scene of a protesting crowd leaving the precinct office; (4) Myŏng-hŭi's transformation to a local mistress and her ensuing suicide; (5) Yŏng-hŭi's trading of her body to retrieve her family's occupancy right to a new apartment; and (6) the suicide of the dwarf.[39] Of these flagged items, only the third one was entirely removed in the finished film and hence can be read as an example of "critiquing the system" (the singular censorship agenda for his film according to Yi's recollection). Other restrictions governed issues of sexual morality and disability from a regulatory perspective that was no more repressive or distinctive than the universal standards of pre-ratings content regulation imposed on other historical and contemporary national cinemas.

Although the ANSP suggested strict censorship interventions at the postproduction stage, they were not necessary because Hanjin Enterprises successfully cleansed their product prior to the print review, after which any extensive revisions would have required costly reshooting or reediting. The preview print of *A Little Ball* uneventfully passed PPEC censorship review on October 6, 1981, contingent upon removal of a shot of Yŏng-hŭi's virginal blood on the bedsheet after her loss of virginity and shortening of "rhythmic" body movements in the steamy sex scene of Yŏng-su and Myŏng-hŭi. It would be fruitless to debate whether or not Yi's film could have become a more progressive text without regulatory cuts in the original screenplay (including disparaging remarks directed toward the disabled and women) or preview print (more explicit sexual expression). Such binaristic thinking, as Michael Holoquist criticizes, erects the "illusion that . . . there either is censorship or not . . . that a complete absence of censorship is somewhat possible. . . . To be for or against censorship as such is to assume a freedom no one has. Censorship *is*."[40]

Comparing the original novella and the screen adaptation of *A Little Ball*, Ch'oe Kang-min argues that, although protest scenes (set in the Ŭngang factory and the precinct office) were removed in the process of censorship review, symbolic signifiers of resistance are visible in Yi's codified cinematic language. As Ch'oe elaborates, "Director Yi Wŏn-se narrates resistance through a close-up of the kitchen knife that the dwarf sharpens, an enlarged close-up of Yŏng-ho's angry fists on the boxing gym monitor . . . and the [stolen] jackknife that indicates Yŏng-hŭi's willingness to kill the man who bought the family's occupancy right."[41] In the penultimate story of Cho's book ("The Spiny Fish Entering My Net"), Yŏng-su is tried for assassinating the brother of the Ŭngang group owner (having mistaken him as the owner) with a knife as revenge for violating the human rights of factory workers. The dwarf's eldest son is condemned and executed for the crime. Although this politically motivated interclass murder was eliminated in the film adaptation process, recurrent images of knives (particularly in the imaginary scene of Yŏng-hŭi killing the real estate broker with a stolen jackknife from his safe) function as stand-ins for the likeable protagonist Yŏng-su's radical action, which was apparently self-censored for commercial reasons. The film's final voiceover is a telepathic conversation between Yŏng-hŭi and Yŏng-su when the family picks up the dwarf's corpse to take home. The sister pleads silently, "Brother, doesn't this make you angry? Let's kill all evil people who called dad a dwarf." Yŏng-su turns his resolved gaze to Yŏng-hŭi and responds internally, "I promise. I will kill them." The incongruous mixing of conspiratorial dialogue and the conventional sappy music on the soundtrack brings narrative to uneasy, open closure.[42] In this foreshadowing ending, Yŏng-su's fate is sealed for viewers capable of filling in the gaps or narrative ellipses. Although Ch'oe grumbles that censorship has weakened Yi's resistant messages, which "are hardly detectable to lay audiences,"[43] one could argue that inhibitions paradoxically enhance, rather than hinder, a film's textual complexity, sophistication, and poeticism. As Holoquist puts it, "The patent aspect of a censored text is only part of a totality that readers must fill in with their interpretations of what was excluded." In other words, censorship inadvertently "creates sophisticated audiences" and adept interpreters of the "ineluctably dual structure of the censored text, the simultaneity of a manifest and a suppressed level of meaning."[44] As such, the ending of *A Little Ball* serves the dual functions of both censored humanistic drama (overtly spotlighting the resilience of the Kim family united by a tragedy) and resistant narrative (insinuating the gentle protagonist's silent metamorphosis into a wrathful avenger of class oppression).

Recollecting the censorship history of *A Little Ball* in the aforementioned KOFA interview, Yi Wŏn-se stated, "I believe censors and scenario reviewers had very special, unusual, probing eyes. I am not sure what they are doing right now but they had exceptional intelligence. They may be regretting their work with the passage of time and defending themselves with an excuse such as 'It was excessive back then. We could not help it.'"[45] Unbeknownst to Yi, the PPEC reviewer Ho (who raised objections to the film's earlier scripts) went on to become an influential film critic who published the book *Korean Film 100 Years* (*Hang'ukyŏnghwa 100nyŏn*) in 2000. In this sweeping historical account covering a century of transformations in national cinema, Ho cautiously distances himself from the history of film censorship in the 1980s, an era of dictatorship. The former regulator writes as if he were an impartial observer rather than an active player, stating, "As a film that spotlights the lives of poor, disfranchised class in the dark age of political instability and postindustrial ills, *A Little Ball* garnered interest and attention of many but censorship authorities viewed it unfavorably."[46] Referring to *Madame Aema*'s censorship, Ho even mocks the now-legendary censorial intervention that homophonetically transformed the Sino transcription of the heroine's name from "horse lover" to "linen lover" (a heavy-handed attempt intended to censor the suggestion of bestiality).[47] Yet, the MCPI file on the film includes a document with Ho's signature that makes this very suggestion. Such self-conscious closeting on the part of a former censor attests to the pervasive cultural bias that champions victims of state censorship as political heroes while maligning vocational regulators as servants of dictatorship, as Boyer's scholarship observes in another national context.

Ultimately, the PPEC professionals commissioned to review motion picture scripts and prints on the MCPI's behalf were far from being automatons passively following the marching orders of corrupt political power. They were elite civilians who were concerned about cultural representations on the big screen for a variety of social and moral reasons. They were indeed smart, but not because (as Yi sarcastically insinuates) they were gifted with special abilities to detect and remove politically subversive elements from progressive texts such as *A Little Ball*. Rather, their intelligence is best exemplified by Ho's insightful feedback to producers that images of disability and prostitution should be taken seriously lest they bring humiliation or hurt to the most vulnerable members of the audience in movie theaters.

Union as Censor: Protecting Trade Prestige in *The Maiden Who Went to the City*

The Maiden Who Went to the City (hereafter *The Maiden*) is another significant case study with which to test the idea that censors are audiences and vice versa.

Produced by Yim Wŏn-sik and directed by Kim Su-yong, the film spotlights three bus-guide girls (*annaeyang*), a popular vocation among uneducated rural migrant women from the 1960s to the 1980s. The most virtuous of them is Yi Mun-hŭi (Yu Chi-in), who refuses to participate in the common practice of *ppingttang* (petty theft of collected cash fares to supplement low wages) and is awarded a prize for exceptional ethics and performance. The model employee falls in love with a swindling peddler and transforms him into a law-abiding sailor under her moral guidance. Toward the end of the film, the bus company betrays Mun-hŭi's trust and subjects her to a humiliating naked body search in a harsher crackdown on *ppingttang*. Both protesting against this inhuman treatment and seeking atonement for her vocation's collective corruption, the righteous woman jumps from the rooftop of her workplace and is crippled (in the original script/print, she is killed from the fatal fall). As a counterpoint to Mun-hŭi, who is an innocent country girl, there is a street-smart tomboy, Yŏng-ok (Yi Yŏng-ok), who has no qualms about *ppingttang* and ends up purchasing a private taxi with her savings from the illegitimate source of income. The sunniest member of the trio falls for a married driver (without knowing his marital status) and is left heartbroken at the end. Falling in the middle of these two opposite archetypes is Sŏng-ae (Kŭm Po-ra), a meek, kind-hearted girl who reluctantly steals from collected bus fares to support her extended family. She develops tender feelings for a high school–aged passenger and eventually asks him out for a date when he enters college, only to be jilted by the middle-class man.

Before being replaced by automatic fare machines in the late 1980s, bus guides or conductresses (*ch'ajang*) were entrusted with three main tasks: (1) greeting boarding passengers and helping them into overstuffed vehicles, (2) collecting accurate fares from exiting passengers, and (3) signaling drivers when to stop and depart. According to a May 1974 union survey of 1,609 bus guides working for 55 bus companies, 62 percent were under the age of twenty; 79 percent did not complete formal education beyond middle school; 86 percent came from fishing villages or agricultural towns; 68 percent chose the vocation because they came to Seoul with no other plans (like Mun-hŭi in the film's opening); and 50 percent quit within the first year.[48] Out of the many harsh working conditions (low and delayed wages, long working hours with poor benefits, cramped unsanitary boardinghouses, humiliating treatment from passengers, etc.), what distressed these women most was daily body searches for stolen fares. Even the most private parts of female anatomy—body parts otherwise shielded by brassieres and panties—were violated during those invasive rituals. Some of the humiliated victims spoke back to this organized cruelty with acts of suicidal self-harm. On January 5, 1976, Yi Yŏng-ok, a twenty-year-old conductress for T'aegwang Transportation, attempted to commit suicide by stabbing her abdomen twice with a knife after being suspected of stealing approximately 4,000 won (U.S.$8.25) from collected fares and then subjected to a body search.[49] On October 19, 1978, Kang Mi-suk, a twenty-four-year-old, took acetic acid and

Censors as Audiences and Vice Versa • 157

FIGURE 5.1 Kim Su-yong's *The Maiden Who Went to the City* (1981) spotlights three bus-guide girls (*annaeyang*), a popular vocation among uneducated rural migrant women from the 1960s to the 1980s. The most virtuous of them is Yi Mun-hŭi (Yu Chi-in: center), who refuses to participate in the common practice of *ppingttang* (petty theft of collected cash fares to supplement low wages).

killed herself after being bullied into receiving naked body searches—performed by both female and male inspectors—at her workplace (Samhwa Commerce Transportation).[50]

In his 2005 memoir, director Kim reminiscences about the controversy surrounding *The Maiden*:

Because of the trouble I experienced [with the film] ... I became skeptical about socially conscious filmmaking.... Maidens from the countryside preferred the bus guide job for easy [untrained] employment. Hundreds of them boarded together in the terminals and their human rights were blatantly violated with poor working conditions and *ppingttang* crackdowns.... Novelist Kim Sŭng-ok collected real-life episodes from his research trips to bus terminals and based his screenplay on them.... However, there was an incident in the morning of *The Maiden*'s opening in Chungang Theater. Three hundred conductresses flocked to the theater for demonstrations and some radical women climbed to the roof to take down the sign. They claimed that the film insulted them.... Protestors rose to 500 [in number] and bus operations without conductresses aggravated traffic delays throughout Seoul. The government stopped film screenings that afternoon. Later I found that the incident was agitated by the pro-state union to cover up their own corruption. The guiltless film was dormant for three months in the storage before being rereleased.... I was furious and resentful but there was nothing I could do under military dictatorship except for consoling myself, "Sure, so much for social consciousness in movies. Let us put aside messages of exposure and protestation until the better days. Let us just make movies about lovemaking or tear jerking until then."[51]

As Song A-rŭm points out, Kim's authorial interpretation, echoed by industry personnel (screenwriters, directors, film critics, etc.) who collectively denounced the arbitrary infringement on their artistic freedom, insinuates that a kind of abstract, amorphous "state violence" was behind the unruly boycotts of conductresses who disrupted the lawful exhibition of *The Maiden*. "The simplified understanding of the subject of censorship" as well as "the schematization of the state as the perpetrator and artists as victims," as Song observes, begat conspiracy theories that scapegoated the government for any obstructions to free expression and commerce of motion pictures.[52]

Evidence from both press reports and archival documents in the KOFA collection discredits much of Kim's account of the event quoted above. It was neither the government nor the pro-state union that stopped the film's exhibition. Rather, the censorial impetus came from the bottom up: from undereducated, young female transport laborers who were enraged by unflattering images of their screen surrogates who steal cash, have affairs with married men, and stalk passengers obsessively. According to Yi Chung-sik's December 11, 1981, report printed in *Chosŏn Ilbo*, "Bus guides exerted their force (*sillyŏk haengsa*), but this time not to protest against labor relations such as body searches or unpaid wages.... They are agitated and angry because of the film playing in Chungang Theater ... [that] was supposed to be based on their stories but so absurd and bizarre that they feel ashamed to ride the bus again. Their human rights declaration made officials of the Federation of Korea Trade Unions [FKTU: Hang'uknodongjohap ch'ongyŏnmaeng, or noch'ong], the Ministry of Labor [MoL: Nodongbu], and the MCPI sweat while trying to calm agitated conductresses."[53] The news reports favorably portray rational workers strategically leveraging their union representation, not a hysterical mob destroying private property and paralyzing city traffic (as suggested in Kim's recollection). On December 9, 1981, six days after the film's release, 200 conductresses gathered in the headquarters of the Korea Automobile and Transport Workers' Federation (KATWF: Chŏngukjadongch'a nodongjohapyŏnmaeng) to file a complaint. Pressuring trade union leaders to stop screenings of *The Maiden*, they dangled the prospect of taking more radical measures such as a strike or box-office picketing should their demand not be met. The union's response was immediate. On the same day, the FKTU, the KATWF's umbrella organization, sent an official letter to the MCPI, demanding the suspension of the controversial picture's exhibition. The federation's chairman, Chŏng Han-jun, pleaded with the ministry, accusing *The Maiden* of not only featuring "decadent" content harmful to public morality but also defaming and "trampling human rights of 150,000 drivers and conductresses belonging to the KATWF and our union."[54] The following day, the MCPI also received an interagency memo from the MoL, supporting the FKTU's request and expressing concern about "new labor disputes and mass protests" that might ensue should screenings of *The Maiden* continue.[55]

Bus guides won their battle when the FKTU and the production company, T'aech'ang Entertainment (T'aech'anghŭngŏp), reached a speedy agreement that the film's prints would be withdrawn on December 11 (within one week of its release) in an apparent attempt to contain a scandal that was injurious to both parties. T'aech'ang voluntarily returned the exhibition permit to the MCPI, vowing to reapply after recuts in accordance with the union's demands. Although the premature withdrawal was ostensibly voluntary on the part of the film's producer (with the MCPI acting as an impartial, silent observer of the two parties' negotiations whose paper trail is preserved in the film's censorship file), the motion picture industry was resistant to what they saw as a threat to artistic freedom imposed by the extrajudicial force of special interest groups. Producer Yim grumbled in his interview with *Tonga Ilbo*, "How can we do artistic activities if subject matters are restricted in an open society? I would like to invite social dignitaries to a public screening and let them judge if this film only shows the darker side of society." Director Kim Su-yong added, "My movie is for enlightenment, not social exposé even though the latter should not be excluded either." Screenwriter Kim Sŭng-ok put forth his own realism-based defense: "I stayed in a motel in Tobonggu [a precinct with many bus terminals] for three months to write a screenplay based on facts."[56] Members of the Motion Picture Association of Korea (Yŏnghwain hyŏp'oe) staged their own protests in the court of public opinion. The Screenwriter Division of the trade organization called for urgent meetings and held overnight discussion sessions for three consecutive days following the film's withdrawal. In a collective statement, the writers declared, "Regardless of reasons for its suspension, *The Maiden* was produced and exhibited after undergoing the legal process. Therefore, it should not be subject to pressure from a special interest group beyond expressions of critical opinions. Motion pictures are intellectual properties of our society and nation. Violence against films like *The Maiden* exposes us as a backward country of culture." The last comment specifically alludes to the fact that the incident attracted attention from members of the foreign press, including the Associated Press and the Japanese broadcaster NHK (Japan Broadcasting Corporation). On December 15, the Association for Film Critics of Korea (Yŏnghwap'yŏngnonga hyŏp'oe) issued a statement, echoing a similar sentiment: "Creative freedom and free expression should not be infringed as long as no law is broken. Audiences should not overinterpret parts of fiction as if they represent the whole [group of people]."[57]

In his book *Korean Film 100 Years,* Ho sides with the industry's take on the incident. Describing it as "a disgraceful affair caused by violent resistance on the part of certain vocational members," the former PPEC regulator compares it with other infamous cases (such as Im Kwŏn-t'aek's *The Monkess* [*Piguni*], whose production was stopped in 1984 due to accusations of obscenity and blasphemy from Buddhist groups that filed a legal suit against the production company, T'aehŭng Production) and notes, "There were drivers and conductresses who stole bus fares in real life but the problem was that it was depicted in a motion picture." He then poses the rhetorical question, "We cannot make films about characters with no names and vocations, though, can we?"[58] For anyone who is familiar with the creative dilemmas of dramatizing human failings without offending specific social groups, it would be hard not to sympathize with such a defense of artistic freedom by industry insiders. However, it is important to acknowledge the commercial reality of motion pictures in the context of South Korea's mainstream culture industry, whose primary aim was—and still is—to entertain audiences and to turn a profit for investors. In other words, films should serve the interests of theatergoers (and home video/streaming audiences in more recent decades), whose satisfaction and patronage are key to the survival of not only individual producers but also the industry at large. If the trade's goal is unrestricted access to the broadest market to distribute products intended for mass entertainment, creative entitlement to uncensored expression is a luxury that filmmakers oftentimes cannot afford, even in the United States where First Amendment rights are taken seriously as a core principle of its citizenry. The scandal of *The Maiden* can be attributed as much to T'aech'ang Entertainment's unwillingness to take what Hollywood studios call "technical advising" from professional bus guides (to ensure authenticity and respectability of vocational representation) during the production stage as to the alleged oversensitivity of transport workers.

As reported in the December 11, 1981, issue of *Chosŏn Ilbo,* conductresses brought a complaint to the production company as early as June of that year, when they first saw a promotional still of the bedroom scene depicting an illicit affair between a married driver and his assistant advertised in a magazine. To their dismay, T'aech'ang's representatives were dismissive of their concerns and assured them that the production would be lawfully overseen by the MCPI. In her newspaper interview, Kŭm Ryŏng-ja, a female officer of KATWF, confided, "It was difficult to understand the production company's behavior" of rejecting union workers' proposal to attend the film's preview before its general release.[59] If this report is true, T'aech'ang's "don't-tell-us-what-to-do" response to unionized workers whose lives serve as the main subject of their film was tactless at best and arrogant at worst. At the very least, state regulators paid lip service to encouraging more positive representation of the transportation trade and its employees, as evidenced by the ministry's letter to the production company dated January 23, 1981. Accepting the production registration of *The Maiden*, the MCPI urged its producer to refrain from "accusatory, negative portrayals, such as bus guides' *ppint'ang* practices and prevention measures of transportation companies" that were harmful to "national unity."[60] Such a well-intended yet halfhearted push, however, appears to have elicited no compliance on the part of the creators (both screenwriter and director) bent on exposing what they deemed realistic social problems in their picture. In the PPEC's review report for the finished print dated June 24, 1981, only three scenes were flagged to be modified: (1) multiple slappings of a driver who attempted to rape Mun-hŭi by seven or eight different employees, (2) exposure of Mun-hŭi's nipples and crotch in the body search scene, and (3) a shot of the shocked crowd and a cut to Munhŭi's fallen body on the ground.[61] Ultimately, the PPEC/MCPI's regulation zeroed in on universal representational issues of violence, indecent exposure, and suicide rather than vocation-specific concerns about the trade prestige of KATWF members.

In the context of American film historiography, the multiplicity and prevalence of censorship has been accepted as a precondition for operating the world's most profitable film industry (dominating 85 percent of world screens for most of the twentieth century). What Hollywood insiders have called "political censorship" external to the industry included seven state boards, thirty-one municipal boards, 200–250 ad hoc local boards, and foreign censorship boards mostly controlled by their governments. Before the transition to the Motion Picture Association of America (MPPA)'s rating system in 1968, all source materials, treatments, screenplays, and final prints were thoroughly cleansed and censored within the industry by the self-regulatory Production Code Administration (PCA) in preparation for external reviews. The hundreds of official boards were not the only agents of censorship and regulation for Hollywood producers. When there were substantial amounts of representations of foreign places and citizens, it was customary to clear scripts or prints through official diplomatic channels (i.e., embassies and consulates) in Washington, DC, New York City, and Los Angeles in order to eliminate potential national or racial offenses that might hinder exports of finished prints. Although federal censorship of motion pictures theoretically never existed in the United States, various government agencies (including the State Department, the Office of War Information, and the Department of Defense) were involved in "advising" studios on the content of their motion pictures for diplomatic, political, or security purposes. To enhance the verisimilitude of their productions, Hollywood studios often employed paid experts in vocational areas (historians, linguistics, scientists, doctors, lawyers, diplomats, etc.) as technical advisors. In addition, various special interest groups and cultural watchdogs (church groups, women's clubs, civil rights organizations, immigrant societies, etc.) pressured producers and studio executives with boycotts, picketing, negative media publicity, and lobbying to local censors for insulting images detrimental to a given group's self-esteem.

Although South Korea's equivalent to Hollywood (the Ch'ungmuro film industry) was minuscule in the 1980s and almost exclusively catered to the domestic market (with far fewer stakeholders and agents involved in production, distribution, and exhibition of local motion pictures), the case of *The Maiden* was a wake-up call for Korean producers, especially those with a myopic understanding of censorship as merely passing state regulatory reviews and receiving exhibition permits. The second round of censorship review for the reapplied exhibition permit was essentially handled outside of the established regulatory regime. KATWF union members representing conductresses' interests were the main subjects of censorship this time round. In an attempt to appease offended trade audiences, T'aech'ang hosted two previews on January 13 and February 6, 1982. Having received no feedback from the union after the first preview, the production company voluntarily cut a few controversial scenes (which depict a rape attempt, *ppingttang* practices, and a search raid in the locker room that involves not only company administration but also union representatives). They also changed the tragic ending to an uplifting one in which the virtuous heroine survives the fall from the rooftop and, after being released from the hospital, rides the bus with a crutch and assistance from her reformed lover. The happy couple smiles at the sight of a trade slogan inside the bus that reads "Don't forget Yi Mun-hŭi" (implying that the protagonist's exemplary conduct and sacrificial act sparked industry-wide self-cleansing and moral reforms).

On February 15, 1982, nine days after the second preview, the KATWF sent an official notification to the production company, acknowledging that the recut print had successfully eliminated all problematic parts objected to by trade representatives. On February 20, five days after the KATWF's green light to the filmmakers, its parental organization, the FKTU, reported to the MCPI that unions no longer had any objection to the film's rerelease "for the sake of advancing motion picture arts."[62] The MCPI file on *The Maiden* painstakingly chronicles the multiple steps that the ministry took to ensure that due process was followed in the voluntary suspension of the film's exhibition and its rerelease permission. As a part of that process, MCPI officials testified in front of the Culture and Public Information Committee of the National Assembly (Kukhoe) on December 11, 1982, and verified that there was no state pressure to stop the film's screenings. Following that testimony, the ministry hosted a private screening of the film for seven lawmakers serving the committee, who found "no particular problems" in the withdrawn print.[63] After getting the KATWF/FKTU's permission in writing, the MCPI formally consulted the MoL and the PPEC before issuing a second permit on March 4, 1982, without demanding any further revisions of its 105-minute, voluntarily recut version.

FIGURE 5.2 Pressured by trade unions representing bus conductresses, T'aech'ang Entertainment changed the tragic ending of *The Maiden Who Went to the City* to an uplifting one in which the humiliated heroine survives the fall from the rooftop and reunites with her love interest.

Song summarizes the lesson of *The Maiden* controversy:

Many censors were involved in the process of *The Maiden*'s rerelease and they included filmmakers themselves. Because each party represented [its own] self-interest, censorship was smooth and devoid of troubles. In order to recuperate financial losses caused by the film's suspension, the producer voluntarily asked for recensorship as an opportunity for revival. It was an already negotiated process with no room to debate countercensorship principles such as free expression or the distinction between reality and representation. . . . There were no more problems after the film was reedited according to the demands of conductresses whose objection created the whole incident to begin with. . . . Although the PPEC's censorship continued [throughout the 1980s], independent of this process, civil groups began to . . . respond sensitively to filmic representations of themselves and demanded revisions of unwanted images. . . . In the 1980s . . . new forces operating outside of state policy were asserting their power over censorship.[64]

What Song defines as "new [civil] forces" of motion picture censorship existed prior to the 1980s and originated in different social sectors, from the religious right opposing "atheist films" such as Yu Hyŏn-mok's *The Martyred* (*Sungyoja*, 1965) to concerned parents boycotting foreign "adultery films" such as Louis Malle's scandalous *The Lovers* (*Les amants, 1958*), as discussed in earlier chapters of this book. What differentiates the role of the transport workers' union in reshaping the narrative and characterizations of *The Maiden* from previous interventions is that this labor group advocated for the human rights of the weakest members of society (poor, undereducated young girls of rural backgrounds), not hegemonic institutions such as churches and schools or traditional practices such as monogamous matrimony. In many ways, this resembles so-called good censorship in the U.S. context where, as Ellen C. Scott reminds us, "society's weakest members [have used] censorship as a tool for ethnic or gender equality" from the silent era to the age of blockbusters.[65] Nearly half a century prior to the arrival of the civil rights era in the 1960s, activist groups started to function as unofficial censors or public crusaders who condemned Hollywood's problematic portrayals of racial minorities and foreign nationals, as evidenced by the National Association for the Advancement of Colored People (NAACP)'s nationwide campaigns to ban D. W. Griffith's racist epic *The Birth of a Nation* (1915) and the California-based Japanese immigrant community's organized protests against Cecil B. DeMille's *The Cheat* (1915), in which a Japanese villain (Sessue Hayakawa) attempts to rape a married white woman.

A more analogous case in American film history is what happened with the release of *Salt of the Earth* (1953), an underground film directed by Herbert Biberman, a member of the infamous Hollywood Ten (who was blacklisted after being subpoenaed by the House Un-American Activities Committee [HUAC] in October 1947 and cited for contempt of Congress). The documentary-like, low-budget film was commissioned by Local 890 of the International Union of Mine, Mill, and Smelter Workers (consisting primarily of Mexican American zinc miners) and chronicles their months-long strike from October 1950 to June 1951 against Empire Zinc Company in New Mexico. As Benjamin Balthaser points out, *Salt of the Earth* is a rare instance of "worker-artist collaboration," which struck a balance between the grander political agendas of the Hollywood left (represented by Biberman and his blacklisted collaborators/writers Paul Jarrico and Michael Wilson) and the more pressing local concerns of labor activists who were not as invested in "exposing the scope of the international cold war and finding a cultural front, from which to critique its multiple sites of exploitation."[66] Local 890 representatives vetoed several of the original plotlines addressing larger social problems such as "the collusion of the Catholic Church, the D.A., the sheriff, local businesses, and the zinc mine" as well as "explicit links between the culture of anticommunism and racism, sexism, and imperialism" suggested by references to the Korean War and the U.S.-Mexico War.[67] In his analysis, Balthaser concludes that the complete film is "perhaps less radical in

FIGURE 5.3 Directed by Herbert Biberman, a blacklisted filmmaker, and commissioned by Local 890 of the International Union of Mine, Mill, and Smelter Workers, *Salt of the Earth* (1953) is a rare instance of "worker-artist collaboration," which struck a balance between the grander political agendas of the Hollywood left and the more pressing local concerns of Mexican American labor activists.

some ways than the pre-production script,"⁶⁸ which was closer to the authorial vision of Biberman, Jarrico, and Wilson, since the union disapproved of both blatant critiques of U.S. foreign policy and unflattering portrayals of their leadership (a subplot depicting the infidelity and chauvinism of their leader, played by real-life Local 890 president Juan Chacón, was requested to be eliminated). Similarly to Local 890 miners who challenged the blacklisted creators' political vision and asserted ownership of *Salt of the Earth* as *their* story in the collaborative rewriting process, three decades later, Korean bus conductresses succeeded in gaining control of their screen images and altering them to their satisfaction, even though it meant compromising the creative independence of older male cultural producers with greater social power. As Balthasser argues, "Resistance is always culturally and materially located not only within the realm of the possible but within the immediate needs of disempowered groups."⁶⁹ In the cases of both *The Dwarf* and *The Maiden*, censorship ironically enabled this resistance by intervening to protect the weak and vindicate their immediate needs over the artistic entitlement of a few privileged members of society.

6

Beyond Oral Histories and Trade Legends

A Bourdieusian-Foucauldian Deconstruction of Anti-Censorship Myths

In his introduction to *The Censorship System inside Korean Film History* (*Han'guk yŏnghwa sok kŏmyŏl chedo*, 2016), an edited volume of Korean-language essays utilizing the Korean Film Archive (KOFA)'s censorship document collection, Cho Jun-hyoung (Cho Chun-hyŏng) singles out the deficiency of methodology, along with the shortage of researchers working in film policy studies and the difficulty of accessing archival documents, as reasons for the underdevelopment of censorship studies in Korean film historiography.[1] The KOFA's public opening of digitized files for on-site research in 2016 and subsequent online release of selected archival documents for the films of major Golden Age auteurs (e.g., Kim Ki-yŏng, Kim Su-yong, Shin Sang-ok, Yi Man-hŭi [Lee Man-hee], and Yu Hyŏn-mok) solved the access problem to a certain degree, despite the fact that trade files that might corroborate that material are either lost or currently unavailable for public viewing. The KOFA's continued effort to increase access to archival censorship documents in their digital collections is encouraging news to researchers armed with Korean-language proficiency and a vested interest in generating empirical scholarship on material history and film culture during Park Chung Hee (Pak Chŏng-hŭi)'s and Chun Doo Hwan (Chŏn Tu-hwan)'s regimes.

However, the methodological question needs to be addressed before I bring this book to an end, in hopes of taking Korean film censorship studies to the next stage and guiding new researchers in the field as they attempt to interpret and make sense of primary documents with critical insights shared by seasoned censorship scholars in both literary and film studies.

Prior to the KOFA's opening of its censorship archive, earlier critical histories of the subject typically relied upon hearsay and speculation in the absence of publicly released primary documents of actual industry and government communications. The earlier methodology of mobilizing directors' interviews and often-biased testimonies as evidence of censorship was inherently flawed, as it often generated "inaccurate information, [distortion] of the entire censorship system, or [exaggeration] of damage."[2] Unlike in the case of the self-regulation of industry standards in the United States, Korean directors were not participants in day-to-day censorship administration as communications with state censors were exclusively handled by production companies. As such, the reliability of secondhand accounts by directors (who often had artistic or political agendas of their own, hence their antagonistic stance vis-à-vis the censors) is compromised and questionable. Oral history–based approaches to censorship studies turned film history into a kind of free-for-all space of speculative fiction, one that tended to lionize directors as creative visionaries and villainize state officials as cruel persecutors armed with ever-snipping scissors.

Consider the following snapshots of legendary stories involving Korean film censorship: (1) a superimposed patriotic image of the South Korean's flag was tacked on in the final scene of *Piagol* (1955), which received a reissue permit following a national security controversy and temporary suspension of the film's exhibition; (2) an adulterous kiss scene between a married heroine and her playboy neighbor was cut in *Madame Freedom* (*Chayu puin*, 1956) due to moral panic; (3) *The Stray Bullet* (*Obalt'an*, 1961) was banned by Park's military junta, which was suspicious of the pro-North message in the North Korean refugee mother's repeated line, "Let's go!"; (4) after being imprisoned for forty days on the charge of violating the Anticommunist Law with favorable North Korean images in *Seven Female Prisoners* (*Ch'ilinŭi yŏp'oro*: renamed as *Returned Female Soldiers* [*Toraon yŏgun*, 1965]), director Yi Man-hŭi faced more harassment and investigations for casting matinee idol Shin Sŏng-il (apparently too handsome and fashionable) as a communist officer in *Soldier without a Serial Number* (*Kunbŏn ŏpnŭn yongsa*, 1966); (5) director Yu Hyŏn-mok was prosecuted and found guilty of obscenity for filming a six-second female nude shot on the set of *Empty Dream* (*Ch'unmong*, 1965), although the image was cut in the release print; (6) director Ha Kil-jong smuggled an uncensored print of *The March of Fools* (*Pabodŭlŭi haengjin*, 1975) into the projection room on the day of the film's premiere in protest against the Yushin government's excessive cuts; (7) an unprecedented one hour of footage was ordered to be cut from *The Last Witness* (*Ch'oehuŭi chŭngin*, 1980) by Chun's dictatorial regime; and (7) the same regime did not allow director Yi Chang-ho (Lee Jang-ho) to originally title *Declaration of Fools* (*Pabosŏnŏn*, 1983) as *Children of Dark Streets II* and suggested the nonsense title as a political distraction.

As an in-depth investigation of archival evidence from the censorship files of *The Last Witness* and *Declaration of Fools* demonstrates in this chapter, some of these legends are not even factual, although they have been repeatedly circulated and reprinted in both academic and journalistic film history accounts. The situation is reminiscent of a line spoken by the reporter Maxwell Scott (Carleton Young) after hearing the confession of Ransom Stoddard (James Stewart), a senator whose political career was built on the myth of killing the titular outlaw, in John Ford's *The Man Who Shot Liberty Valance* (1962): "This is the West, sir. When the legend becomes fact, print the legend." While there are a handful of Korean scholars who have begun the process of demythologizing trade legends and reshaping film censorship studies based on empirical documentation, critical consensus within and outside academia still hinges upon the metanarrative that South Korean cinema became more creative and was able to attract international attention in the twenty-first century, due partly to the replacement of state content regulation with the civil rating system in 1997. This convenient narrative fails to explain why Korean cinema's Golden Age peaked in the 1960s during Park's authoritarian regime and why an anarchist, experimental film such as *Declaration of Fools* (irreverent toward both Korean society and commercial film language) came out during the harshest period of Chun's military dictatorship.

Applying the Censorship Theories of Foucault and Bourdieu to a Korean Context

In her book *Better Left Unsaid: Victorian Novels, Hays Code Films, and the Benefits of Censorship*, Nora Gilbert argues that the "central liberal allegations" directed against censorship—including the belief that it "leads to fewer and duller representations of human sexuality," that it "squelches political protest," and that it "destroys art"—are paradoxical and problematic. This wholesale presupposition, as the author observes, "gives the censor both too much and too little credit—too much because it assumes that the censor is shrewdly omnipotent, controlling and restricting the artist's every move, too little because it assumes that the goals of the censor are necessarily at odds with the goals of the artist."[3] On the contrary, Gilbert defines the relationship between the censor and the artist as collaborative in the creation of "an allusive, subtextual system of storytelling that is, in many ways, precisely the style best suited to telling tales of both sexually and socially subversive desire."[4] Gilbert, like other New Censorship theorists, is indebted to Michel Foucault's conception of power as productive and enabling rather than simply repressive and inhibitive. For Foucault, censorship is not simply a "mode of subjugation" or "a general system of dominance," as one might presume. Rather, in a way that is indicative of the French philosopher's notion of discursively constructed power, censorship can be understood as a generator of discourse encompassing "the multiplicity of force relations immanent in the sphere in which they operate" or, in other words, "the process which, through ceaseless struggles and confrontations, transforms, strengthens, or reverses them."[5] The existence of power relationships not only "depends on a multiplicity of points of resistance" but also kindles "the pleasure... at having to evade this power, flee from it, fool it, or travesty it."[6]

In the context of Korean motion picture censorship as in other national industries, this Foucauldian dynamic is clearly traceable in both parties: the censor and the censored. In his interview with KOFA researchers, Yi Nam-gi (who served as a film censor in the Ministry of Culture and Public Information [MCPI: Munhwagongbobu] from 1974 to 1979) explains how he and his colleagues approached censoring motion pictures.

> When we censored, we did not simply watch images. We studied screenplays first and understood overall narrative contexts,... We considered various factors [such as artistry, morals of the time, comedy, violence, objectivity, etc.] and film censorship is not an easy task for its comprehensiveness.... Film techniques made a difference as well. For example, we did not have problems with scenes of violence and sex if they were not repulsive in the larger context of narrative flow.... We did not cut, for example, a violent scene skillfully shot from the side angle without a close-up.... If scenes appeared at the right time to advance the plot... there was no repulsion. It was a different story when gratuitous scenes were inserted to stimulate basic instincts such as excessive sexual contacts unnecessary to the plot.[7]

This former state censor's advocacy for "an allusive, subtextual system of storytelling" that is arguably more artistic and mature vindicates Gilbert's Foucauldian defense of the "benefits" and "joy" of censorship.[8]

In 1979, the MCPI transferred the film censorship operations of reviewing scripts and preview prints to the Public Performance Ethics Committee (PPEC: Kongyŏn yunlliwiwŏnhoe), a semiautonomous body consisting of ten to twenty members appointed by the minister (mostly civilian elites such as professors, journalists, writers, and filmmakers along with four officials of the MCPI). This transfer was partly in response to a bribery scandal involving ministry officials and filmmakers four years earlier. In May 1975, several ministry employees in the Motion Picture Division were arrested and prosecuted for a corruption charge. They had taken cash bribes from famous film producers such as Shin Sang-ok and Kim T'ae-su in exchange for expediting censorship reviews, extending exhibition permits, and nominating their films for state-sponsored "Good Film" (*Usu Yŏnghwa*) awards. The division chief was given a two-and-a-half-year sentence; three of his underlings received suspended sentences. In the aforementioned KOFA interview, Yi attests to government bureaucrats' fear of "strong-willed" (*tŭsaen*) civilians in the film industry and discusses his effort to transfer censorship power to a civil committee before quitting the ministry in 1979. He explains,

> At that time, film censorship was mainly conducted by the Korean Central Intelligence Agency [KCIA: Chungangjŏngbobu], the Security Bureau [Ch'ianbonbu of the Ministry of the Interior], and our ministry. The KCIA was only interested in national security affairs and Security in matters related to children and adolescents.... Because there were only a handful of censorship reviewers in our ministry, we were easy targets and shouldered the weight of responsibility. That's why we thought of transferring the duty to an independent committee and started to prepare for it.... Later the PPEC took over film censorship and their committee members were private experts. The industry folks did not dare to touch them because there were fifteen of them. It was not possible to try to bribe all of them and that was the end of problems.[9]

This interview exposes rarely discussed dynamics between Korean state censors and filmmakers that support Foucault's theory of power, repression, and resistance alluded to earlier in the chapter. As Cho explains, "From a layman's perspective, government bureaucrats in charge of censorship were transparent agents of the state ... they embodied the government's authority over the society/market. This leads to a perception that government censors had more power than filmmakers. Of course, this assumption is not entirely incorrect. However, in specific contacts of two parties, the power relationship between censors and the censored could be ambiguous or capsized and the former was not necessarily on the side of power."[10] Cho's insight confirms that South Korea's state film censorship was part of the complex constellation of social structures, or what Pierre Bourdieu identifies as habitus, that governs acceptable and unacceptable modes of expression on the national screen. As Bourdieu contends, "All linguistic expressions are, to some extent, 'euphemized': they are modified by a certain kind of *censorship* which stems from the structure of the market, but which is transformed into *self-censorship* through the process of anticipation [of the likely reception of his or her linguistic products]."[11] As elaborated by Matthew Burn, "Discourse constitutes a kind of euphemization, where speakers compromise the expressive content of their message in accordance with the norms of the field in which they are communicating, which Bourdieu calls 'censorship.'"[12] As administrators of such societal norms, the power of state regulators is necessarily limited (as attested in Yi's interview quoted above) and even secondary, as their interventions are only required when the most ideal form of structural censorship (i.e., self-censorship) fails. "The state can put one impetus for this behavior [of strategic euphemization]," as Burn notes, "but it is the not the only one: in fact, the market is the most dominant one in contemporary societies."[13] Lessons from Foucault and Bourdieu previously applied to reconceptualize censorship within Western democratic systems by New Censorship theorists are equally relevant to the state-private (*kwan-min*) hybrid system of motion picture regulation in the Fifth Republic led by military dictator Chun Doo Hwan, whom historian Bruce Cumings identifies as "the most unpopular in postwar Korean history, reviled as much for his lack of imagination and his slavish attempts to mimic Park Chung Hee's politics as for his draconian measures."[14]

Setting the Record Straight: State vs. Market Censorship of *The Last Witness*

In his 2016 presentation at the University of California, Berkeley (which was discussed in the introduction), Cho singled out the case of Yi Tu-yong's *The Last Witness* (*Ch'oejuŭi chŭngin*, 1980) to demonstrate the fallacy of reconstructing censorship history based strictly on directors' recollections.[15] Rediscovered as a "lost classic" when its restored 154-minute director's cut was screened at the Korean Cinema Retrospective of the 2002 Jeonju International Film Festival, Yi's film has frequently been cited as Exhibit A of the Chun regime's draconian censorship measures. Legend tells us that the authoritarian government ordered an excessive number of cuts (totaling anywhere from forty minutes to one hour of screen time) due to sensitive themes and images, including representations of North Korean partisans, corruption of the judicial system, and victimization of the socially weak or vulnerable.

Adapted from Kim Sŏng-jong's 1974 murder mystery of the same title, the film follows the investigative road trip of Detective O Pyŏng-ho (Ha Myŏng-jung), who is in search of clues that might help him solve the murder case of Yang Tal-su (Yi Tae-gŭn). The victim was a rich local brewer who lived with a younger mistress, Sŏn Chi-hye (Chŏng Yun-hŭi), and their out-of-wedlock daughter in the provincial town of Munch'ang. In Yang's hometown of P'ungsan (where his legal wife and son live), O finds that the deceased man was a leader of an anticommunist youth association, a vigilante group that hunted North Korean guerrillas in the Chiri Mountains during the Korean War. His investigation leads him to Kang Man-ho (Hyŏn Kil-su), a former guerrilla captain who surrendered to Yang after the death of his commander (who is none other than Chi-hye's father). Before being executed by his underlings under the order issued from Pyongyang, Commander Sŏn (Ch'oe Sŏng-ho) entrusts Kang with a map showing the whereabouts of hidden family treasures and asks the captain to take care of his teenaged daughter. After her father's death, Chi-hye is gang-raped by guerrillas. Earlier, she had been secretly impregnated by Captain Kang, who turned a blind eye to the sexual violence of his men to hide his own. The only person who is protective of Chi-hye is Hwang Pa-u (Ch'oe Pul-am), a middle-aged servant with a heart of gold whom guerrillas kidnapped as a forced laborer. Because of Kang's bargain with Yang, the guerrilla hideout (a school basement) is exposed. After a violent skirmish with crackdown troops, only

FIGURE 6.1 A labyrinthine flashback in *The Last Witness* (1980) reveals that North Korean guerrilla leader Captain Kang (Hyŏn Kil-su: right) had secretly impregnated his dead commander's teenage daughter during the Korean War. Hwang Pa-u (Ch'oe Pul-am: left), a middle-aged servant with a heart of gold whom guerrillas kidnapped as a forced laborer, protects the abused teen and claims her "bastard" son as his own.

four of thirteen people—Kang, Hwang, Chi-hye, and Han Tong-ju (Han T'ae-il), another civilian abducted by guerrillas—survive. In the process of escaping the burning school with Chi-hye, Hwang attacks Han and knocks him unconscious in self-defense. Before being taken to prison, Kang gives the commander's map to Hwang and Chi-hye who, after being cleared of wrongdoing, set up a humble home and live as husband and wife with the baby (Kang's "bastard son," whom Hwang accepts as his own).

The day after the couple finds Chi-hye's inheritance fortune buried in the Chiri Mountains (an excavation made possible thanks to a government permit that Yang helped the couple to obtain), Hwang is taken away on the false charge of murdering Han (who allegedly died in the hospital of the injury Hwang inflicted during the escape). The sham murder charge is a dastardly scheme concocted by Yang, who enlists Han to fake his own death and conspires with Kim Chung-hyŏp (Han Chi-il), a corrupt prosecutor who coerces a sexual favor from Chi-hye in exchange for saving her husband's life (instead, he requests the death penalty in court, framing Hwang as a communist). Sentenced to life imprisonment, Hwang tells his eighteen-year-old wife to give the baby to his

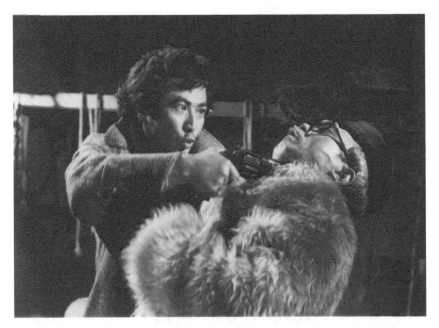

FIGURE 6.2 *The Last Witness* follows the investigative road trip of Detective O Pyŏng-ho (Ha Myŏng-jung: left), who fatally shoots himself after a self-defense killing in the final scene.

sister in the countryside and marry another person for her own sake. Yang takes advantage of the heartbroken, defenseless woman and becomes the entrepreneur of a brewery built with Chi-hye's fortune. Twenty years later, Hwang is released from prison and reunited with the grown-up son, T'ae-yŏng (Kang Pyŏm-gi), whom his sister raised. Shortly thereafter, the youth disappears after being spotted with a stranger. It is later revealed that T'ae-yŏng was incited by Han into the vengeful act of murdering the two men who wronged his father (this comes after Han blackmailed and extorted money from Yang and Kim). The traumatized killer goes mad and is institutionalized in an asylum while Chi-hye (who now works as a bar hostess after Yang's death) and Hwang reunite. After Detective O confronts the ill-fated couple about the truth, the old man takes his own life, leaving a suicide note in which he claims responsibility for the mentally ill son's crime. At the funeral, Chi-hye follows the self-sacrificial husband and ends her own miserable life. Consumed by guilt, Detective O fatally shoots himself while being taken into police custody for his self-defense killing of Han's brother.

In the postscreening question-and-answer session at the Cinematheque Friends Film Festival in January 2008 (where the restored director's cut of *The Last Witness* was screened), director Yi Tu-yong stated, "The film was made from May 1979 to April 1980 when the democratic movement was forming in the city of Kwangju.... I was told that '[my] ideology was suspicious' because of this movie. Without consulting me, the censors cut fifty minutes. Later, when it opened at Myŏngbo Theater, the timetable showed ninety minutes. There were too many deleted scenes and I ended up leaving the screening. That was a dark age for filmmaking."[16] Voice actor Yang T'aek-jo, Yi's longtime collaborator who was present at the session, corroborated the director's statement with his own recollection:

> I worked with Director Yi on postproduction dubbing for most of his films. Perhaps because it was the longest project, I was most attached to *The Last Witness* out of all those films and regard it as the highest artistic achievement. I saw it at Myŏngbo Theater too and one hour was cut out. "Don't ridicule law enforcement." Cut. "A prosecutor shouldn't be lustful toward Chŏng Yun-hŭi [Sŏn Chi-hye]." Cut. Cutting here and there ruined the whole film and it really angered me. Among the victims of censorship, *The Last Witness* and director Yi Man-hŭi's *The Wildflowers in the Battlefield* [*Tŭlguk'wa nŭn p'iŏtnŭndae*, 1974] were the most wasteful to me and I am so happy to see the former revived [in its original form].[17]

In a 2016 interview with *Han'guk Ilbo*, a daily newspaper, Yi reaffirms his account, stating, "After an industry preview, someone reported to the Blue House [presidential palace]. Called it a 'communist film.' I was called to the prosecutor's office many times. Later I saw [the ninety-minute cut] at a theater and it was in a wretched form. It made me consider quitting filmmaking. 'This is not my film,' I thought and never looked back [until the restoration of the director's cut]."[18]

There are contradictions as to how many minutes and scenes were removed by censorship. Even in the same question-and-answer session, Yi claimed fifty minutes as opposed to Yang's one hour. The KOFA's DVD liner notes claim that "the censored version with a running time of one hundred minutes," not ninety minutes as Yi remembered, was released at Myŏngbo Theater on November 15, 1980.[19] Any cursory look at Internet search results (in both English and Korean) on *The Last Witness* reveals uniform references to censorship that allegedly eliminated 30–40 percent of the film's original running time. Moreover, both Yi's and Yang's oral histories implicitly link this notorious case of Korean film censorship with political oppression during the Chun regime via allusions to Kwangju—where the massacre of an estimated 2,000 citizen protestors by Chun's paratroopers took place in May 1980, six months prior to the film's release—and insinuated political motivations behind the censoring of scenes. It is also alleged that dictatorial strong-arm tactics not only butchered Yi's masterpiece (noted for its self-conscious use of nonlinear narration, *Citizen Kane*–like puzzle flashbacks, experimental sound bridges, expressionistic low-key lighting, tilted angles, whip pans, fast zooms, elliptical montages, subjective *pansori*/folk opera narration, etc.), but also nearly destroyed the artist's will to continue honing his craft and pursuing future work in the industry.

The MCPI censorship file on *The Last Witness*, however, tells a different story. According to the primary documents, a 158-minute preview print of the film (four minutes longer than the restored director's cut) was submitted on September 6, 1980. It passed censorship review ten days later on the condition that four scenes be cut: Chi-hye's gang rape during the war, two scenes that depict Prosecutor Kim's misconduct (taking a cash stack from Yang for Hwang's conviction and sexually harassing Chi-hye in his house, respectively), and a scene in which a court clerk openly demands a bribe in exchange for granting Detective O access to public documents. In the restored print (presumably with these four censored scenes eliminated or reedited, cutting four minutes from the 158-minute preview print), Chi-hye's gang rape scene is gone and the audience only sees a glimpse of the victim's brutalized face as an aftereffect; the scene in which Yang drops a wad of cash on Prosecutor Kim's desk is eliminated altogether; the prosecutor's sexual harassment scene is still there, but only partially, and does not show the coerced sex act; and Detective O's brief interaction with the corrupt court clerk (who shows him court records) is present but there is no mention of bribery. Ultimately, the difference between the censorship review copy and the director's cut is minor. Caution against the gang-rape scene coincides with universal standards, and while the scene is abruptly halted with a cut, it is not difficult for mature viewers to conjecture what has transpired based on the dialogue and a close-up of Chi-hye's bloody and bruised face. The court clerk is such a minor character, appearing only fleetingly, that the depiction of his corruption would have been an irrelevant plot point distracting from the main investigation narrative. As for the scene that depicts Yang's bribery of Prosecutor Kim, one could argue that it would have made their criminal connection clearer, but suppression of that information can be also said to have strengthened the film's mystery as the linkage between their separate murder cases is revealed much later in the narrative.

The explanatory note found in the film's censorship file elaborates that the reason for eliminating the three corruption scenes was not that portrayals of unethical behavior of government officials were disallowed. Rather, nine reviewers of the PPEC, which conducted film censorship reviews under the MCPI's jurisdiction, found such scenes dramatically implausible and contrived.[20] The PPEC's objection to Prosecutor Kim's sexual misconduct scene on the grounds of narrative implausibility is not unfounded, as it is puzzling why Yang takes the woman whom he himself is lusting after to another man's house at night. One can assume that he is either offering Chi-hye to the prosecutor as a human bribe or pretending to be her advocate—someone who makes an effort to free her husband by introducing her to a big shot (later, after Hwang's conviction in court, Yang feigns fury over Prosecutor Kim's deception to his mistress-to-be). Regardless, the whole scene is gratuitous and contrived. A soft-focus, glamourous close-up of actress Chŏng Yun-hŭi—a screen goddess of the 1970s and 1980s (in the narrative she plays an innocent, faithful wife who even brings her baby to the scene)—ostensibly framed by the perverted harasser's erotic gaze, verges on sexploitation and is out of place in this artistically rendered neonoir.

Cynics might point out the disingenuousness of the PPEC/MCPI's excuse, seeing it as a thinly veiled cover-up for the Chun regime's more sinister intent of suppressing any expression of political dissent, including the aforementioned Kwangju Massacre. However, an objective investigation into archival evidence would lead to the conclusion that the PPEC's demand for the elimination of those corruption scenes was not inconsistent with similar regulatory acts in a more democratic context. For example, Hollywood's Motion Picture Production Code states, "The courts of the land should not be presented as unjust. This does not mean that a single court may not be represented as unjust, much less that a single court official must not be presented this way. But the court system of the country must not suffer as a result of this presentation."[21] While the PPEC upheld a corresponding clause in the Korean Motion Picture Law that prevents films from depicting "law-abiding citizenry or courts of law in a slanderous way,"[22] its explanatory comment goes further than simply forbidding the subject and opens up productive creative dialogue about the narrative logic and characterization of court officials.

In the original script housed at the KOFA, the narrative circumstances leading up to and after Prosecutor Kim's rape scene are even more contrived and exploitative. In the earlier script, there is a scene in which Chi-hye, Yang, and Hwang's lawyer openly discuss why the prosecutor is not being lenient in court despite their bribe. Chi-hye agrees to pay the corrupt official more money according to the lawyer's advice. In her temporary absence, Yang and the lawyer confirm that the bribe is to give the death penalty to Hwang, not to acquit him as the defendant's wife believes. Moreover, Yang reluctantly acquiesces when the lawyer tells him that the prosecutor is demanding a sexual favor in addition to cash. In the scene following the harassment at Prosecutor Kim's house, Chi-hye is once again brutally raped by Yang, who threatens the resisting young woman with the words "Stay still, bitch. You listened to the prosecutor but why not me? If you don't listen to me, you will be executed as well."[23] Undoubtedly, censorship review was responsible for cleansing the disturbing content of Chi-hye's double rape. In the released print, the elaborate sequence depicting Yang's collusion with the lawyer and the prosecutor's corruption was cut. Yang initiates his sexual relationship coercively, but not through brutal force as described in the original script. After Hwang's conviction, the double-crosser sweet-talks a heartbroken Chi-hye in a gentler manner, saying, "I was deceived by [Prosecutor Kim]. But what can we do about spilled water? Forget everything and make a better living with me, will you?"[24] It is notable, though, that in the censorship review script submitted to the MCPI (and available for research at the KOFA), Yang's rape had already been softened into seduction, demonstrating that the self-censorship mechanism was in place for controversial sexual content. These changes are consistent with Bourdieu's notion of censorship as a self-regulatory

FIGURE 6.3 Yang Tal-su (Yi Tae-gŭn: left)'s character in *The Last Witness* has been softened from a brutal rapist to a deceitful double-crosser in the self-censoring revision process filtering controversial sexual content. This accommodation is consistent with Pierre Bourdieu's notion of censorship as a self-regulatory system of euphemizing potentially offensive materials in anticipation of negative market reception.

system of euphemizing potentially offensive materials to preempt negative market reception.

If the PPEC/MCPI only demanded minor cuts amounting to four minutes, why was *The Last Witness* shortened so dramatically in its final release print shown at Myŏngbo Theater in November 1980? According to documents available in the KOFA digital archive, the film's producer, Kim Hwa-sik, resubmitted a shortened 120-minute print to the MCPI on November 6, 1980, requesting censorship re-review. Forwarding this request to the PPEC, the ministry explained that the production company had "requested recensorship of a 38-minute shorter version because the original running time [was] too long for the purpose of booking theaters."[25] Censorship documents suggest that Sekyŏng Films voluntarily cut as many as sixty-eight scenes in order to condense the film's length to 120 minutes, a standard "feature" length more likely to be favored by exhibitors whose profits would increase if turnovers were quicker and more screenings were scheduled per day.[26] The MCPI approved the voluntarily cut version on November 13, 1980, two days prior to the film's release. Considering this striking discrepancy of Yi's oral history and censorship documents, Cho Jun-hyoung considers different scenarios, including the fabrication of official documents to avoid a public scandal over excessive censorship. Ultimately, though, he settles on a more plausible explanation: the production company transferred blame to censorship so as to preempt the director's protest against cutting nearly seventy scenes for commercial reasons.[27] As Cho concludes, the case study of *The Last Witness* exposes the risk of basing censorship scholarship on directors' testimonies without considering the perspectives of multiple players such as PPEC reviewers, MCPI bureaucrats, distributors, exhibitors, press representatives, and audiences, all of whom directly or indirectly participated in the complex process of film censorship.[28] More importantly, archival evidence from the *Last Witness* highlights the most common fallacy of free speech crusaders whose myopic construction of censorship as a form of external coercion and repression, as Burn points out, "results in the erasure of structures that control the production and dissemination of texts, especially the market."[29]

The Pleasurable Battle of Censorship in the Creation of *Declaration of Fools*

Yi Chang-ho's experimental black comedy *Declaration of Fools* (*Pabosŏnŏn*, 1983) is another oft-cited victim of censorship, with a legendary anecdote about the inception of its unusual title. The film was originally planned as a sequel to the director's commercial breakthrough, *People of Dark Streets* (*Ŏdumŭi chasikdŭl*, 1980), and its earlier title was *People of Dark Streets 2*. From the onset, Yi was determined to craft a non sequitur experimental narrative as a form of rebellion against the foreign-film quota system, which incentivized producers to make four domestic films a year in exchange for an import quota for one foreign film, resulting in hasty productions of "import quickies." In his interview with film critic Kim See-mu, he stated, "In those days, a film cost about 150 million won [U.S.$227,300] on average to make, but *Declaration of* [*Fools*] was made for just 50 million won [U.S.$75,800]. I wrote a fake script for it, with a 'reward the good, punish the bad' moral in it that the government would like."[30] The MCPI censorship file on *Declaration of Fools* includes this treatment (submitted on March 17, 1983), which Yi later called a "scenario intended for the mentally challenged" (i.e., duped censors).[31]

The story contained in the treatment has nothing to do with the completed film except that the protagonist in both versions has the same name: Tong-ch'ŏl. In the version submitted to the ministry, he is a petty criminal who spent most of his adolescence and young adulthood in different correctional facilities. After being released from prison as an adult man, he continues to mix with sketchy people in the underworld until he encounters someone from his past: Kong Pyŏng-su, an ex-pickpocket who has been rehabilitated as a pastor. Tong-ch'ŏl's lost soul oscillates between Kong's moral mentoring and criminal girlfriend Kyŏng-ja's libidinal temptations. Kyŏng-ja persuades Tong-ch'ŏl to steal one last time in order to raise money for his seriously ill sister, but she runs away with the stolen jewels. After her betrayal, Tong-ch'ŏl surrenders himself to the police and serves three years in prison. After regaining his freedom, he builds, with Kong's help, a private academy for juvenile delinquents and helps children steer themselves away from the criminal path he took at their age. After reforming a group of street children, Tong-ch'ŏl releases them from his custody to accommodate other children in need. On the day when the children leave, a reformed Kyŏng-ja, now penniless and homeless, returns to him and Tong-ch'ŏl caresses her shoulders.

The censorship file contains a short reply that the MCPI sent to Hwach'ŏn Trading on April 4, 1983, advising the production company to re-review the whole project as it had potential to "undermine law and social order."[32] On June 2, 1983, Hwach'ŏn resubmitted a revised script that was claimed to be completely different from the one that had been proposed earlier. Although it is unclear why the PPEC was not consulted (if it was, its review was not filed for some unknown reasons), the ministry apparently requested the opinion of another government agency, the Korean Motion Picture Promotion Corporation (KMPPC: Yŏnghwa chinhŭnggonga, now the Korean Film Council), which wrote the following after reviewing the revised script on June 8, 1983: "Before Tong-ch'ŏl's restoration of humanity, his immorality and various criminal activities could harm social order. It is an exposé film that displays social ills, so it is advised to change the title and purify its content."[33] On June 13, 1983, the ministry requested that the production company once again review the project for its potential societal harm. Ten days later, Hwach'on submitted the second revision of their synopsis and screenplay to the ministry. On June 29, 1983, the production company also submitted a request to change their film title from *People of Dark Streets 2* to *Declaration of Fools*, listing the rationale as a "satiric commentary on the protagonist Tong-ch'ŏl's foolish dream of becoming rich overnight."[34] On July 2, the ministry approved the title change. Four days later, it responded to the second revision with a warning against the following elements: a scene that might provoke a feeling of inferiority for disabled people, uses of slang, and a sexually suggestive line that "undermines female college students' human rights."[35] The MCPI urged the producer to use caution so as not to upset the sensibilities of adolescents and to uplift the quality of the film by heeding these elements. Hwach'on complied and deleted all objectionable scenes and dialogue before submitting the preview print on August 8, 1983. Based on the PPEC's recommendation to pass it with no deletions, the ministry approved the film three days later.

Researchers who are familiar with the lengthy and detailed objections that were part of the Hollywood studios' negotiation process over classic gangster films (such as *The Public Enemy* [1931] and *Scarface* [1932]) might find the ministry's handling of crime-related themes in the original script of *Declaration of Fools* to be unremarkable—especially so in the context of morality-based content regulation, prior to South Korea's late conversion to the rating system in 1997 (almost thirty years after its U.S. counterpart). What is noteworthy is the government censor's advocacy for "political correctness" in portrayals of disability and college women. But this is also unsurprising and predictable if one is aware of similar tendencies in Hollywood's Production Code, as elaborated by Doherty: "In the context of its day, the Code expressed a progressive and reformist impulse" that "evinced concern for the proper nurturing of the young and the protection of women, demanded due respect for indigenous ethnics and foreign peoples, and sought to uplift the lower orders and convert the criminal mentality."[36] In the process of responding to the ministry's concern and purifying the original script's criminal narrative, Yi Chang-ho turned the film into a surrealist, absurdist comedy about a crippled vagabond (an incarnation of Tong-ch'ŏl [Kim Myŏng-gon]) and a sex worker posing as a college student (Hye-yŏng [Yi Po-hŭi]). As the MCPI demanded, the completed film "uplifted" its status from a melodramatic crime film to an avant-garde social satire, allegorically indicting the capitalist class system that alienates social outcasts such as Tong-ch'ŏl and Hye-yŏng. The entire narrative unfolds in the form of a children's fable, intermittently narrated by director Yi's six-year-old son and bookended by a montage of enlarged children's drawings.

The first thirty-seven minutes are devoid of dialogue, resorting to slapstick action, pantomime, and experimental sound effects to comically frame Tong-ch'ŏl's trailing and abduction of Hye-yŏng (whom he spots on the streets and falls in love with at first sight). This extended sequence also foregrounds the dreams of the mismatched couple who, after a physical struggle in the back of the taxi, lose consciousness together by inhaling chemicals on a handkerchief (a tool of the rookie kidnapper). Paired with another misfit, a plus-sized taxi driver named Yuk-dŭk (Yi Hŭi-sŭng), who accidentally becomes an accomplice in the abduction of Hye-yŏng, Tong-ch'ŏl is not a criminal as in the earlier scripts but a Don Quixote–like tramp who lives hand to mouth doing odd jobs such as food delivery. Reminiscent of Stan Laurel and Oliver Hardy, the famous comic duo of the silent era, Tong-ch'ŏl and Yuk-dŭk are childlike clowns who befriend their victim, a sassy woman who disciplines both of them with beatings after waking up. After witnessing Hye-yŏng's abuse and death at the hands of a group of drunken rich men in a wild swimming pool party and burying her in the mountains, life goes on for the wandering duo, who irreverently take off their shirts and break into an impromptu dance in front of the National Assembly (Kukhoe) building in the film's closing scene. For audiences expecting authoritarian censorship, it will come as a surprise that the PPEC passed this film's final print without demanding any alterations of a slow-motion scene detailing an orgy-like swimming party of the social elite and a not-so-subtle affront to South Korea's legislative branch.

Yet the director's oral history tells a different story. In Jang Sun-woo (Chang Sŏn-u)'s *Cinema on the Road* (1995), a documentary about Korean cinema

FIGURES 6.4 AND 6.5 The first thirty-seven minutes of *Declaration of Fools* (1983) are devoid of dialogue, resorting to slapstick action, pantomime, and experimental sound effects to comically frame Tong-ch'ŏl (Kim Myŏng-gon: right)'s trailing and abduction of Hye-yŏng (Yi Po-hŭi: left) whom he spots on the streets and falls in love with at first sight.

commissioned by the British Film Institute as a part of its "Century of Cinema" series, Yi Chang-ho recounts the trade legend of *Declaration of Fools*:

> When we sent the script for *People of Dark Streets 2* to the Ministry of Culture and Public Information for approval, they vetoed the use of that title. That was when the Chun Doo Hwan regime started to show its true face. I felt like quitting the movie business. So I decided to give up everything and make a nonsense movie. I wrote a ridiculous scenario for censorship approval from the MCPI. We came with a string of nonsense titles . . . and one of them was *Declaration of Fools*. The producer took ten or more titles to the ministry and told them we couldn't choose. We asked them to choose since we couldn't use *People of Dark Streets 2*. Government bureaucrats were dumbfounded, but they jokingly opted for *Declaration of Fools*. So we went with that. Armed with the title, I decided to go against everything I've done before.[37]

There is no way to confirm whether or not the producer of Hwach'ŏn Trading literally hand-delivered Yi's list of potential titles to the MCPI and officials there half-jokingly chose *Declaration of Fools*. One can conjecture from evidence provided in archival documents that this is an unlikely scenario.

In the above-quoted documentary interview, Yi automatically equates the Korean film censors with the Chun regime and cites the censorship case of *Declaration of Fools* as evidence of political oppression in the early 1980s. He does this without acknowledging the censor's effort to improve images of disabled persons and female college students and to tone down foul language and criminal activities for underage viewers. Yi's testimony insinuates that the ministry's request for the title change was politically motivated. According to official documents, the title change was suggested by the KMPPC for the purpose of conveying a clearer moral message. There is no document that indicates the ministry's instructions to the production company to change the title. However, it can reasonably be inferred that such a request was made verbally over the phone and in a face-to-face meeting. Nevertheless, there is no reason to believe that Hwach'ŏn Trading submitted the paper-only change request with a made-up rationale after the ministry had opted for *Declaration of Fools* as the new title (which was not within the purview of their limited administrative role after censorship operations had been handed over to the PPEC four years earlier).

The most likely scenario is that the production company chose the title out of several candidates that Yi came up with and filed the change with the MCPI shortly after submitting the second revision of the script. In his 2000 memoir, serialized in the weekly film magazine *Cine 21*, Yi concludes, "I don't call *Declaration of Fools* my film. I called it a film made by an age of dictatorship."[38] This resistant statement inversely attests to the productive capacity of film censorship that, intentionally or not, contributed to transforming an unambitious contract job (which its production company green-lighted only to fulfill its production quota required for a foreign film import permit) into one of the most extraordinary creative expressions in the history of South Korean cinema. Citing Yi's own words ("the real creator of the film was the government") from a personal interview, Hyangjin Lee labels *Declaration of Fools* an "accidental masterpiece" that was embraced by youth audiences and that "sowed the seeds of the antigovernmental movement."[39] Beyond its stylistic experimentation and political influence, Yi's anarchic comedy is first and foremost a playful text whose regulatory history lends credence to Foucault's theory of discursive pleasure inherent in teasing and outwitting censors while simultaneously being disciplined and transformed by them.

Epilogue

Media Ratings, the End of Censorship?

On October 4, 1996, the Constitutional Court (Hŏnbŏpchaep'anso) ruled in favor of Kang Hŏn, president of Changsangotmae, who had sued the government for prosecuting him on the charge of violating the Motion Picture Law with the illegitimate distribution of *Opening the Closed School Gates* (*Tach'in kyomunŭl yŏlmyŏ*, 1992). The underground film about unionized teachers' struggles against a corrupt school system had not been submitted for the Public Performance Ethics Committee (PPEC: Kongyŏn yulliwiwŏnhoe)'s mandatory regulatory review prior to public exhibition. In this landmark ruling, the PPEC's state-commissioned "prior restraint," in legal terminology, on motion pictures was declared unconstitutional for violating Article 21, Section 2 of the Republic of Korea (ROK)'s Constitution: "Licensing or censorship of speech and the press, and licensing of assembly and association shall not be recognized."[1] In his book *Korean Film 100 Years*, Ho Hyŏn-ch'an, a former PPEC regulator and film critic, refers to the incident as a "revolution ... that put an end to the film censorship system that had lasted for seventy years since 1926" when the Japanese colonial government enacted the Motion Picture Film Censorship Regulations (Hwaltongsajin kŏmyŏlguch'ik).[2]

The abolition of state film censorship is among the most frequently cited factors for the arrival of Korean cinema's fin de siècle renaissance in the late 1990s to the early 2000s and the wide dissemination of Korean popular culture (dubbed as Hallyu, or the Korean Wave) in the Asia-Pacific region and beyond. For example, in his *Hang'uk Ilbo* column dated May 15, 2021, film reporter Ra Che-gi opines, "There were many causes why South Korea became a pop culture superpower. If I were to name the most determining factor, though, I would like to pick the Constitutional Court's outlawing of motion picture censorship in October 1996."[3] But do media ratings really signify the end of motion picture censorship in South Korea (or, for that matter, in other countries around the world)? In his book *Naked Truth: Why Hollywood Doesn't Make X-Rated Movies*, Kevin S. Sandler argues that the trade organization Motion Picture Association of America (MPAA, now MPA) "is in charge of maintaining the integrity of responsible entertainment across all rating classifications, but its most important task lies in determining the permissibility of a film's onscreen images and sounds for an R rating.... The existence of a set of standards separating R from NC-17 indicates that the industry still abides by a de facto production code as a means of defense against external interference from politicians and moral reformers and against competition from independent distributors and exhibitors."[4] By replacing the Production Code Administration (PCA)'s content regulation throughout all stages of preproduction, production, and postproduction with a less interventionist system of classifying finished prints for their suitability for different age demographics, the ratings did enable "freer expression," as Sandler notes, but not "free expression."[5] Although the MPAA rating system ostensibly exists to guide American parents with children under the age of seventeen, its most important mission is to protect both the profits and prestige of Hollywood studios by keeping all ratings R or lower and shunning the controversial NC-17 rating as much as possible. Out of the 29,791 total films that the MPAA rated between 1968 and 2018, only 524 (or 1.76 percent) were rated NC-17 or X (its predecessor before 1990).[6]

In contrast with Hollywood's self-regulatory ratings, which function as trade protection under the pretense of public service, its Korean counterpart emerged as a state-private crossbreed exactly like the system it replaced. The year after the ruling of the PPEC's film regulation as unconstitutional, the ROK government amended its motion picture law and enacted a new rating system based on four categories: G for all audiences; Above 12 for audiences who are twelve or older; Above 15; and Above 18. However, in fear of legalizing the theatrical exhibition of pornographic films, Korean lawmakers sanctioned the rating agency's power to withhold (*poryu*) ratings for six months (later shortened to three months) based on almost identical criteria used by the PPEC years earlier to demand cuts or deny permits to: (1) films that contradict the spirit of the Constitution and damage the dignity of the state, (2) films that impair social order and harm morals and customs through excessive portrayals of violence and obscenity, (3) films that undermine national interests by damaging international diplomatic relations and the nation's cultural identities.[7] Production companies were allowed to resubmit new cuts after a given withholding period (there was no upper limit to how many times the ratings could be withheld). In October 1997, a national rating board was launched under the name of the Korean Performance

Art Promotion Association (Hang'ukkongyŏnyesul chinghŭnghyŏpǔihoe) to implement the new law. It was renamed and reorganized as the Korea Media Rating Board (KMRB: Yŏngsangmul tǔnggǔpwiwŏnhoe) in June 1999. Similarly to the PPEC, the KMRB's inaugural general board consisted of fifteen members (including a chairperson and vice chair) representing such professions as filmmaking, education, journalism, broadcasting, literature, the law, and nongovernmental groups for parents and women. Under the at-large board, the film rating classification subcommittee operated with its own members or raters.

The KMRB's inaugural chairman was none other than Kim Su-yong, a prolific Golden Age auteur whose anticensorship stance has been widely reported (as discussed in this book's introduction). In his 2012 oral history interview with the Korean Film Archive research team, the director recalled his initial reaction to President Kim Dae-jung (Kim Tae-jung)'s appointment of him to the chairmanship: "People said that I was the only one who was eligible to chair the board, but my response was, 'There is no way I can do this. When it still makes me grind teeth to think about all the footage of my films cut by censors, how can I do that to others?'" Kim was encouraged to accept the post when an unnamed friend persuaded him with this reasoning: "Because your own films were mercilessly censored, you are the last person to censor. Please take the post and do not cut Korean films anymore."[8] During his six-year service as chairman (1999–2005), the two most controversial cases that tested public trust in the KMRB were the board's withholding of the rating for New Wave maverick Jang Sun-woo (Chang Sŏn-u)'s *Lies* (*Kŏjitmal*, 1999) and its assignment of the "Restricted Screening" rating—a new category that substituted for withholding in 2002—to television documentary producer Park Jin-pyo (Pak Chin-p'yo)'s debut film, *Too Young to Die* (*Chugŏdo choa*, 2002).[9] Although both films were eventually rerated and released as Above 18 after the producers' voluntary modifications, the KMRB's initial decisions drew criticism and divided public opinion about the still-young rating system.

Jang's film was adapted from Chang Chŏng-il's *Lie to Me* (*Naegae kŏjitmarŭl haebwa*, 1996)—a novel about an adulterous, sadomasochistic sex relationship between a thirty-eight-year-old sculptor and a high-school girl—which had been banned in 1997 after the obscenity prosecution of its writer. Therefore, the rough fate of its cinematic adaptation had been predicted from the onset and sure enough, the KMRB withheld its rating twice. Instead of delegating the task to the rating classification subcommittee based on the routine protocol, KMRB general board members voted for the first withholding decision in August 1999, attesting to the gravity of this singular case. Of the fifteen members, ten voted for withholding, two voted against it, one refrained from voting, and two were absent and unable to vote. Two months later (after a reduced withholding period elapsed), the production company, ShinCine Communications, submitted a self-censored cut after removing five minutes of original footage, only to receive the same verdict. After a months-long public ruckus and industry lobbying, the

FIGURE E.1 The Korea Media Rating Board twice withheld a rating for Jang Sun-woo (Chang Sŏn-u)'s *Lies* (1999), adapted from Chang Chŏng-il's banned novel about an adulterous, sadomasochistic sex relationship between a thirty-eight-year-old sculptor and a high-school girl.

KMRB finally caved in and assigned Above 18 to a second voluntarily censored cut, submitted in December that year, which had eliminated a total of ten minutes of footage concerning sadomasochistic sex acts and the female protagonist's identity as an underage schoolgirl. The overseas reputation of *Lies* as an art-house film further fueled controversies about the KMRB's repeated rating withholding, which many industry insiders and journalists saw as amounting to censorship (*kŏmyŏl*).[10] For example, in an article written for *Hankyŏreh Sinmun*, a left-leaning newspaper, An Chŏng-suk stated, "After a tug-of-war with the rating board, the production company cut 'voluntarily'. . . . This proved that the 'rating withholding' clause that the Motion Picture Promotion Law granted to the KMRB had scissoring effects . . . and that the KMRB is a de facto censorship organization."[11]

An's opinion was vindicated by another Constitutional Court ruling on August 30, 2001, which declared the practice of rating withholding (based on Article 21, Section 4 of the 1997 Motion Picture Promotion Law) unconstitutional as an example of prior constraint on and potential banning of motion pictures. The victory for independent film distributors such as Indiestory, whose lawsuit against the KMRB for withholding a rating for *Yellow Flower* (*Tul hana sex*, 1998) led to the 2001 ruling, was brief and empty. The following year, the controversial system was simply replaced by a new nominal rating, "Restricted Screening" (*chaehan sangyŏng*), which would function as a de facto ban due to the absence of specialty theaters to accommodate such films with little to no commercial potential.[12] As a result, appeals after voluntary cuts (for the expressed purpose of getting a rating of Above 18, or Restricted to Minors after 2006) remain the only option for distributors to exhibit films legally. Limited space prevents me from presenting a broad range of legal opinions about the unconstitutionality of the KMRB rating system in all of its complexity. However, if we strictly apply all the criteria of the 1996 ruling that defined PPEC regulation as unconstitutional (prior constraint, state administrative power, subsequent punishment for violations, etc.) to the KMRB's Restricted Screening rating, their point-to-point parallels are clear even to outsiders with no legal expertise. The KMRB's online database provides statistics for all rated films (feature films including straight-to-video/streaming titles, shorts, documentaries, animation, etc.) from 2008 to 2023. Out of the 10,422 domestic films rated during that period, 36 received the "Restricted Screening" rating, along with 55 out of the 20,150 foreign films.[13] It is noteworthy that the clear majority of Korean ratings was Restricted to Minors (formerly, Above 18), an equivalent to NC-17, which, as stated earlier, accounted for less than 2 percent of all MPAA-rated films between 1968 and 2018. In comparison, 53.7 percent of all domestic films and 54.5 percent of all foreign films rated by the KMRB between 2008 and 2023 were Restricted to Minors. These comparative data are admittedly flawed as KMRB statistics, unlike MPAA counterparts, include soft-porn materials that were submitted for the assignment of theatrical ratings but ultimately went straight to video or streaming releases. One should also be mindful of possibly different standards between NC-17 (United States) and Above 18/Restricted to Minors (South Korea).[14] It is worthwhile, however, to consider relative weaknesses and limitations of both countries' regulation systems before calling for a conversion to the U.S. film industry's model of an in-house, self-regulatory rating system which has been criticized for its lack of transparency, conflicts of interest, and discrimination against independent producers and their films.

In lieu of a traditional conclusion, I would like to close this volume with the lesson that might be gleaned from Kim Su-yong's December 2002 interview, conducted not long after the rating of *Too Young to Die* had been lowered to Above 18 upon the third submission. Prior to that point, the KMRB was at the center of public scrutiny (from a National Assembly [Kukhoe] committee hearing to citizens' forums and media debates) after three dissenting raters' protest resignation had ignited a social scandal. Park Jin-pyo's documentary-like fiction about seniors' sex life had been rated "Restricted Screening" twice, due primarily to full-on genital exposure and graphic depiction of fellatio between two septuagenarian lovers (Pak Chi-gyu and Yi Sun playing fictionalized versions of themselves) in a seven-minute unsimulated sex scene framed in a long take. Although Park did not cut any footage from the sixty-six-minute film, the provocative sex scene was darkened to tone down, if not completely obscure, genital images in exchange for the Above 18 rating. To reporter Yi Sang-su (of *Hankyŏreh Sinmun*)'s question of why the KMRB was oversensitive about genital exposure despite its permissiveness regarding violence, foul language, and antisocial behavior, Kim answered,

> There is no problem if exposure is essential to the plot but if sex follows after exposure... it arouses audiences. Three fifty-somethings saw *Too Young to Die* and they all had different reactions. One person declared, "No obscenity whatsoever," and the other two confessed they were aroused by the film.... Because of such individual differences, it is difficult to mechanically determine whether the film is obscene or not. For me personally, instead of being aroused by the genital exposure scene, I felt the pathos of life.... It would have been possible to convey that same feeling with acting instead of exposure. That would have been better directing. If the genitals are all exposed, what is the difference between this film and pornography?[15]

Although this interview was criticized by some liberal commentators, who misinterpreted Kim's message as a disparaging evaluation of Park's Cannes-screened cinema verité film as "pornography," it presents a powerful defense of censorship as a productive contributor to creative activities, as New Censorship theorists (quoted in chapter 6) have argued. Ironically, Kim, the artist, who created exquisitely allegorical films while "fighting censorship" from 1950s to the 1980s, and Kim, the rating board chairman, who extols the virtues of self-censored, indirect expressions, is the same person. As Heather Hendershot notes, "In the course of its social execution, 'free speech' is not inherently liberatory.... Censorship and free speech are competing, heterogenous, nonbinary cultural constants.... Admitting censorship's prevalence does not have to make one into a despairing cynic. Rather, acknowledging the pervasiveness of censorious impulses—from the left, right, center, and every other direction—enables critical thought, discussion, and activism."[16] Articulated in the context of American broadcasting censorship, Hendershot's insight is revealing about what Korean state censorship did for what I have described in this book as "cinema under national reconstruction." The state and its film artists were, for many years (and under different guises), a bickering odd couple who thrived in one another's company while constructing images and sounds of a new nation together from scratch. South Korean cinema's much-celebrated global ascendency today is an outgrowth of that long-forgotten past, not a separation from it.

Acknowledgments

I dedicate this book to my late father, Chung Sang Ho (1932–2022), who passed away while I was doing research and writing the manuscript as a Fulbright scholar stationed in Seoul. Born during the Japanese colonial period, my father witnessed South Korea's dynamic national reconstruction as a young man and shared his love of cinema with me and my sister. I am grateful for the love and support of my family in both South Korea and the United States. My partner and colleague, David Scott Diffrient, and our daughter, Pepper Diffrient, have been patient with me throughout the long process of writing this book. I would not have been able to complete it without their presence in my life.

I would like to express my sincere gratitude to Cho Jun-hyoung and Chung Chong-hwa of the Korean Film Archive, who assisted me with archival research throughout the entire project period (2017–2022). Their pioneering scholarship on Korean film studies was a major source of inspiration for this book. I am also indebted to my dear friend and colleague Jinsoo An of the University of California, Berkeley, who organized a series of Korean film censorship workshops (2021–2022) in which early drafts of two chapters were presented. I learned a great deal from fellow presenters and expert respondents, including Thomas Doherty, whose foundational studies on Hollywood film censorship have deeply influenced my own scholarship for the past quarter a century. I am grateful to Sangjoon Lee of Lingnan University, Hong Kong, and Unsang Kim of the University of Washington, co-organizers of the 2023 Origins of the South Korean Film Renaissance Conference, where I presented another chapter of the book.

The author wishes to acknowledge the generous financial support of the Fulbright U.S. Scholar Program and Colorado State University's Scholarship Impact Award, which enabled me to conduct overseas archival research. I owe big debts to two English professors, Hyungsook Lee and Joon-ho Hwang of Ewha Woman's University, for hosting me as a Fulbright scholar affiliated with their department and helping me access research resources. Another English professor at Yonsei University, Suk Koo Rhee, offered me wonderful opportunities for academic exchanges and invited me as a keynote speaker for the 2022 Situations International Conference. Heidi Little of Fulbright Korea provided excellent administrative support during my ten-month residence in Seoul. I wish to thank all archivists and librarians who assisted my research in Seoul (Film Reference Library at the Korean Film Archive, Ewha Woman's University Library, National Assembly Library of Korea), Los Angeles (Margaret Herrick Library, University of Southern California Cinema Library), and London (British Board of Film Classification). Special thanks go to Louis Hilton of Margaret Herrick Library's Special Collections and Felix Hockey of the British Board of Film Classification for helping me access valuable archival documents cited in the book.

Shorter, early versions of chapter 1 and chapter 6 were previously published in *Situations: Cultural Studies in the Asian Context* 16, no. 1 (2023) and *The Cold War and Asian Cinemas* (Routledge, 2020). These chapters benefited from editorial revisions by Terence Murphy, Poshek Fu, and Man-Fung Yip. David Scott Diffrient helped me improve the entire manuscript as my developmental editor/proofreader. My research assistant Riana Slyter provided much-needed help with proofreading and indexing in the final stage of production. Last but not least, I would like to thank my editor, Nicole Solano of Rutgers University Press, and two anonymous reviewers for the book. Their faith in and support for the project made this publication possible.

Notes

Introduction

1 Darcy Paquet, *New Korean Cinema: Breaking the Waves* (New York: Wallflower Press, 2009), 3.
2 Im Sang-hyŏk, "Freedom of Speech and Cinema: The History of Korean Film Censorship," in *Korean Cinema: from Origins to Renaissance*, ed. Kim Mi-hyŏn (Seoul: Korean Film Council, 2006), 101.
3 Chŏng Su-jin, "A Study on Immorality in the Transition of Film Censorship and Rating System in Korea" [Han'gukyŏnghwa kŏmyŏlgwa tŭnggŭppullyu chedo pyŏnch'ŏnsae tamgin piyullisŏng t'amgu], *Trans-* 2 (2017): 54–55.
4 As a child, Yi Chang-ho often visited his father (Yi Chae-hyŏng)'s office in the Ministry of Public Information to watch unreleased films submitted for censorship review. It was the familial connection that helped Yi land his first film industry job as an assistant to Shin Sang-ok, legendary producer and director.
5 Yi Chong-kil, "Director Yi Chang-ho, 'Censorship Is Nonsense . . . Cut Because the Name Is the Same as First Lady's'" [Yi Chang-ho kamdok, "Kŏmyŏlŭn nansensŭ yŏngbuin'gwa irŭmgattago sakche"], *Asia Economy*, October 30, 2019, https://www.asiae.co.kr/article/2019103002224401022.
6 Yi, "Director Yi Chang-ho."
7 Kim Su-yong, *My Love Cinema* [Naŭi sarang cinema] (Seoul: Cine21, 2005), 65.
8 Kim, *My Love Cinema*, 67. Although it is impossible to confirm whether or not Kim actually uttered those words in the face of the very individuals who had power to censor his films, historical newspaper reports corroborate the title of the seminar and Kim's participation as a presenter along with an MPI official and a university professor.
9 Kim, *My Love Cinema*, 187, 191.
10 Most files cover two decades from the 1960s to the 1980s. The Ministry of Culture and Public Information (MCPI) was reorganized as the Ministry of Culture in 1989 and then the Ministry of Culture and Sports in 1993.
11 Minister, MCPI, to Kim T'ae-su, President of T'aech'ang Entertainment, "Reply to Film Censorship Application" [Yŏnghwagŏmyŏl sinch'ŏng hoesin], April 1, 1977,

Night Journey, Ministry of Culture and Public Information (MCPI) film censorship files, Korean Film Archive (KOFA), Seoul.
12. Kim to Minister, "Recensorship Application for Feature Film *Night Journey*" [Kŭkyŏnghwa *Yahaeng* chaegŏmyŏl sinch'ŏngŭi kŏn], April 4, 1977, MCPI files, KOFA.
13. As of this writing, the only publications in English that utilize the KOFA censorship collection are one journal article and two book chapters: Chonghwa Chung (Chŏng Chong-hwa), "The Topography of 1960s Korean Youth Film: Between Plagiarism and Adaptation," *Journal of Japanese Korean Cinema* 6, no. 1 (2016): 11–24; Hye Seung Chung, "Archival Revisionisms: Reevaluating South Korea's State Film Censorship of the Cold War Era," in *The Cold War and Asian Cinemas*, ed. Poshek Fu and Man-Fung Yip (New York: Routledge, 2020), 174–193; and David Scott Diffrient, "Against Anesthesia: *An Empty Dream*, Pleasurable Pain and the 'Illicit' Thrills of South Korea's Golden Age Remakes," in *East Asian Film Remakes*, ed. David Scott Diffrient and Kenneth Chan (Edinburgh: Edinburgh University Press, 2023), 49–72.
14. Daniel Biltereyst and Roel Vande Winkel, eds., *Silencing Cinema: Film Censorship around the World* (New York: Palgrave MacMillan, 2013), 2.
15. David A. Cook. *A History of Narrative Film*, 1st ed. (New York: W. W. Norton, 1981), 267.
16. Thomas Doherty, *Hollywood's Censor: Joseph I. Breen & the Production Code Administration* (New York: Columbia University Press, 2007), 77.
17. Thomas Doherty, introduction comments, transcribed by Rachel Park, Korean Film Workshop: Authoritarian Modalities and Film Censorship, University of California, Berkeley, August 9, 2021.
18. Any violator of this agreement was required to pay a $25,000 fine. No major studios released their films without the Code certificate until United Artists temporarily withdrew from the MPAA to distribute Otto Preminger's racy romantic comedy *The Moon Is Blue* (1953), which had been denied the PCA's seal for its light treatment of illicit sex, seduction, and virginity.
19. Kong Yŏng-min, *2009 Korean Film History Oral History Series: Yi Sŏng-ch'ŏl* (Seoul: Korean Film Archive, 2009), 102.
20. "Misgivings of Damaging National Customs, etc" [Yangsok'aechil yŏmnidŭng], *Chosŏn Ilbo*, May 14, 1955, 3.
21. "Motion Picture Law Enforcement Regulations" [Yŏnghwabŏp sihaenggyuch'ik], July 24, 1962, https://www.law.go.kr/LSW/lsInfoP.do?lsiSeq=45364#0000. See chapter 1 of this book for the complete list of regulatory rules.

Chapter 1 Fending Off Darkness, Uplifting National Cinema

1. Andrew Higson, "The Concept of National Cinema," *Screen* 30, no. 4 (Autumn 1989): 37. Emphasis in original.
2. Higson, "Concept of National Cinema," 37.
3. Christopher Faulkner, "Affective Identities: French Cinema and the 1930s," *Canadian Journal of Film Studies* 3, no. 2 (Fall 1994): 17. Emphasis in original.
4. Thomas Doherty, *Hollywood's Censor: Joseph I. Breen & the Production Code Administration* (New York: Columbia University Press, 2007), 351.
5. Doherty, *Hollywood's Censor*, 115. The seven states with motion picture censorship boards were Pennsylvania, Ohio, Kansas, Maryland, New York, Florida, and Virginia. The number of state censorship boards is sometimes counted as six because

Florida did not have an autonomous board and followed the decisions made by the New York state board.

6 Willys R. Peck, United States consul general in Nanjing, to Frederick H. Herron, MPPDA, November 4, 1933, letter attached to Peck's report to the Secretary of State, "Subject: The Chinese Government and the Motion Picture Industry," November 4, 1933, RG 59, State Department files on China, box 7221, National Archives and Records Administration (NARA), College Park, MD. In the letter, Consul Peck referenced Soviet propaganda films as more extreme examples of an "uplift" cinema promulgated by the Chinese government.

7 Leonard J. Leff and Jerold L. Simmons, "Appendix: The Motion Picture Production Code," in *Dame in Kimono: Hollywood, Censorship, and the Production Code* (Lexington: University of Kentucky Press, 2001), 289. Emphasis added.

8 A translated copy of the Motion Picture Censorship Law (promulgated on November 3, 1930, and effective on June 15, 1931), attached to United States minister in Beijing Nelson Trusler Johnson's report to the Secretary of State, Washington, DC, August 11, 1931, State Department files on China, box 7220, 893.4061 Motion Pictures, NARA.

9 "Motion Picture Law Enforcement Regulations," July 24, 1962, https://www.law.go.kr/LSW/lsInfoP.do?lsiSeq=45364&viewCls=lsRvsDocInfoR#rvsTop.

10 See Commander in Chief, U.S. Forces Korea, Carter B. Magruder, to the Joint Chiefs of Staff, telegram, May 16, 1961, State Department Office of the Historian, https://history.state.gov/historicaldocuments/frus1961-63v22/d213.

11 Byung-Kook Kim and Ezra F. Vogel, eds., *The Park Chung Hee Era: The Transformation of South Korea* (Cambridge, MA: Harvard University Press, 2011), 8.

12 Kim and Vogel, *Park Chung Hee Era*, 26–27.

13 Park Chung Hee, *To Build a Nation* (Washington, DC: Acropolis Books, 1971), 14.

14 Park, *To Build a Nation*, 105.

15 Mabel Berezin, "Emotions and Political Identity: Mobilizing Affection for the Polity," in *Passionate Politics: Emotions and Social Movements*, ed. Jeff Goodwin, James M. Jasper, and Francesca Polletta (Chicago: University of Chicago Press, 2001), 84, 93.

16 Berezin, "Emotions and Political Identity," 84, 94–95.

17 "Motion Picture Law" [Yŏnghwabŏp], January 20, 1962, https://www.law.go.kr/%EB%B2%95%EB%A0%B9/%EC%98%81%ED%99%94%EB%B2%95/(00995,19620120).

18 Kim Tong-ho et al., *A History of Korean Film Policy* [Hang'ukyŏnghwa chŏngch'eksa] (Seoul: Nanam, 2005), 78.

19 Yi Hwa-jin, "The Development of Film Censorship during the Colonial Period in Korea" [Sikminjiyŏnghwa kŏmyŏlŭi chŏngaewa chiyang], *Korean Literature Studies* [Han'gukmunhakyŏngu], no. 35 (2008): 433.

20 Yi, "Development of Film Censorship," 423–431.

21 "Chosŏn Film Law Enforcement Regulations" [Chosŏnyonghwaryŏng sihaenggyuch'ik], July 7, 1941, https://www.law.go.kr/LSW/lsInfoP.do?lsiSeq=71301#0000.

22 Kim, *History of Korean Film Policy*, 118–121. Yi Hwa-jin disputes this claim and argues that "there is no evidence that American films were released without censorship review." However, Yi conjectures that the review process for Hollywood imports might have been fast-tracked as they had already received approval in Japan before arriving in South Korea. Yi Hwa-jin (Lee Hwajin), "Liberator or Intimate

Enemy?: On South Korean Cultural Circles' Ambivalence toward Hollywood," *Review of Korean Studies* 18, no. 1 (June 15): 59.
23 "Various Cultural Organizations Request Reconsideration of Film Censorship" [Yŏnghwagŏmyŏl chaego kakmunhwadanch'esŏ yomang], *Tonga Ilbo*, October 25, 1946, 2.
24 Kim, *History of Korean Film Policy*, 147.
25 Kim Chong-mun, "Blind Spots of Korean Anti-Communist Films" [Kuksan pangongyŏnghwaŭi maengjŏm], *Hang'uk Ilbo*, July 24, 1955, 3.
26 "Motion Picture Censorship Not Allowed" [Yŏnghwakŏmyŏl andoenda], *Tonga Ilbo*, June 28, 1960, 3.
27 "Goal of Autonomous Cleansing" [Chayuljŏk chŏnghwarŭl mokjŏk], *Han'guk Ilbo*, August 7, 1960, 4.
28 "Goal of Autonomous Cleansing."
29 "Goal of Autonomous Cleansing."
30 John Trevelyan, Secretary of British Board of Film Censors (BBFC), to Public Control Department, London County Council, June 10, 1959, BBFC master files, *Les Amants*, British Board of Film Classification, London.
31 *Kingsley International Pictures Corporation, Appellant, v. Regents of the University of the State of New York*, 360 U.S. 684, https://www.law.cornell.edu/supremecourt/text/360/684.
32 *Kingsley International Pictures Corporation*, 360 U.S. 684.
33 David L. Hudson, Jr., "Jacobellis v. Ohio (1964)," The First Amendment Encyclopedia, https://www.mtsu.edu/first-amendment/article/392/jacobellis-v-ohio.
34 Kim Yun-jin, "The Establishment of the First Civil Regulatory Agency, Motion Picture Ethics Committee" [Ch'oech'oŭi minganyŏnghwa simŭigigu, Yŏnghwayulliwiwŏnhoe sŏngrip], in Ham Ch'ung-byŏm et al., *Korean Cinema and April 19* [Hang'ukyŏnghwawa sa.il.gu] (Seoul: Korean Film Archive, 2009), 102–103.
35 Trevelyan to Willoughby Film Productions, April 7, 1959, BBFC master files, *Beat Girl*.
36 "The Ethics Committee Ready to Disband Themselves" [Yŏngyun chajinhaech'edo pulsa], *Seoul Sinmun*, February 20, 1961, 4.
37 "Trouble of *Beat Girl*" [Yŏnghwa *Chŏmŭn yukch'edŭl* p'adong], *Kyŏnghyang Sinmun*, February 9, 1961, 2.
38 Internal Memorandum "Re: Exhibition Registration for Foreign Movie *Beat Girl*" [Woegukyŏnghwa *Chŏmŭn yuch'edŭl* sangyŏngsingogŏn], Ministry of Education (MoE), January 28, 1960, *Beat Girl*, Ministry of Public Information (MPI) film censorship files, Korean Film Archive (KOFA), Seoul.
39 MoE to Wu Ki-dong, Segi Corporation, February 9, 1960, *Beat Girl*, MPI files, KOFA.
40 Yu Hyŏn-mok, *Film Life* [Yŏnghwa insaeng] (Seoul: Hyehwadang, 1995), 144.
41 Judy, "San Francisco Fest Reviews: *The Aimless Bullet*," *Variety*, November 13, 1963, 17.
42 Kelly Y. Jeong, *Crisis of Gender and Nation in Korean Literature and Film* (Lanham, MD: Lexington Books, 2011), 97.
43 Kelly Y. Jeong, "*Aimless Bullet* (1961): Postwar Dystopia, Canonicity, and Cinema of Realism," in *Rediscovering Korean Cinema*, ed. Sangjoon Lee (Ann Arbor: University of Michigan Press), 161.
44 Hye Seung Chung and David Scott Diffrient, *Movie Migrations: Transnational Genre Flows and South Korean Cinema* (New Brunswick, NJ: Rutgers University Press, 2015), 31.

45 Ho Hyŏn-ch'an, *Korean Film 100 Years* [*Han'guk yŏnghwa 100-nyŏn*] (Seoul: Munhaksasangsa, 2000), 124.
46 Yi Pŏm-sŏn, "A Stray Bullet," trans. Marshall R. Pihl Jr. with Vreni Merriam, *Korea Journal* 7, no. 5 (May 1967): 18.
47 The Ministry of the Interior (MoI) to the Ministry of Education (MoE), "Report on Public Opinion Regarding Request for Impure Film Bans" [Pulsun yŏnghwa kŭmyŏng choch'i yomang e taehan yŏron pogo], May 23, 1961, *The Stray Bullet*, MPI files, KOFA.
48 A reference to another cut (the scene with a veteran urinating in front of the Bank of Korea building) remembered in Yu's memoir and quoted earlier in the chapter can be found later in the file when the MPI demanded a list of cuts for the film's unbanning in 1963. Yu's memory is likely mixed up in his recollection of events that occurred more than three decades ago.
49 Kim Chun-gi, "My Youth, My Love, Film Director Yu Hyŏn-mok" [Naŭi chŏmŭm, naŭi sarang, yŏnghwagamdok Yu Hyŏn-mok], *Kyŏnghyang Sinmun*, January 22, 1998, 22.
50 Aaron Han Joon Magnan-Park, "*Daehan* Neo-Realism and the Conundrum of Aimless Confucianism in Yu Hyun-mok's *Obaltan* (1961)," *Journal of Japanese and Korean Cinema* 9, no. 2 (2017): 91.
51 Im Yŏng-ung, "*The Stray Bullet* Review" [*Obalt'an* py'ŏng], *Entertainment Sport Newspaper* [*Yŏnae sp'otŭ sinmun*], April 14, 1961, reprinted in *Closed Reality Open Cinema* [*Tach'in hyŏnsil yŏllin yŏnghwa*], ed. Chŏn Yang-jun and Chang Ki-ch'ŏl (Seoul: Che3munhaksa, 1992), 89–90.
52 Im, "*The Stray Bullet* Review."
53 "New Movie: *The Stray Bullet*" [Sinyŏnghwa: *Obalt'an*], *Kyŏnghyang Sinmun*, April 17, 1961, 4.
54 The Security Bureau, MoI, to the Cultural Division, MoE, "Report on Public Opinion Regarding the Korean Film *Stray Bullet*" [Han'guk yŏnghwa 'Obalt'an' egwanhan yŏron t'ongbo], May 26, 1961, *The Stray Bullet*, MPI files, KOFA.
55 "Report on Public Opinion Regarding the Korean Film *Stray Bullet*," MPI files, KOFA.
56 "Opinion Report on Censorship" [Kŏmyŏl ŭigyŏnsŏ], February 6, 1962, *The Stray Bullet*, MPI files, KOFA.
57 Pak Yu-hŭi, "A Study on the Dynamics of Film Censorship and Representation of Sentiment during the Park Chung-Hee Regime," *History Criticism* [*Yŏksabip'yŏng*] 99 (Summer 2012): 62.
58 Pak, "Dynamics of Film Censorship."
59 Yi, "A Stray Bullet," 28.
60 Kim Sŏng-ch'un, "Petition" [Chinch'ŏngsŏ], June 11, 1963, *The Stray Bullet*, MPI files, KOFA.
61 The news reports at that time indicate that this new caption ending (referencing the SCNR's revolutionary pledge to fight despair and hunger) was shot, but according to the censorship file it appears that the MPI later instructed that it be deleted before allowing re-release.
62 The NFPC was a government film agency launched in 1961 with the support of the United States Information Service.
63 Richard Dyer MacCann, memorandum, "Feature Film Entry for Venice Film Festival" to Lee Sung-chul, National Film Production Center, n.d., *The Stray Bullet*, MPI files, KOFA.
64 Kim, "My Youth, My Love," 22.

65 Sangjoon Lee, *Cinema and the Cultural Cold War* (Ithaca, NY: Cornell University Press, 2020), 129.
66 Yi Sun-jin, "Cultural Logic of the Cold War System and Operation of South Korean Cinema: On Censorship Practices of *A Stray Bullet*" [Naengjŏn ch'eje ŭi munhwa nonriwa han'guk yŏnghwa ŭi chonje pangsik], *Memory & Vision* [Kiŏk kwa chŏnmang] (Winter 2013): 405–406.
67 Kim, "Petition," MPI files, KOFA.
68 Stephan Haggard, Byung-kook Kim, and Chung-in Moon, "The Transition to Export-led Growth in South Korea: 1954–1966," *Journal of Asian Studies* 50, no. 4 (November 1991): 863.
69 "Foreign Movie Imports Blocked" [Woehwasuip makhildŭt], *Han'guk Ilbo*, July 26, 1963, 7.
70 Yi, "Cultural Logic," 408.
71 Yu, *Film Life*, 217.
72 Ha Kil-jong, "Reconsidering Korean-Style Films" [Han'gukjŏk yŏnghwaŭi chaego], in *Ha Kil-jong*, vol. 2, ed. Yi Pyŏng-hun (Seoul: Korean Film Archive, 2009), 443.
73 Richard Dyer MacCann, "Films and Film Training in the Republic of Korea," *Journal of University Film Producers Association* 16, no. 1 (1964): 17.
74 Ha, "Reconsidering Korean-Style Films," 444.
75 Quoted in Lee, *Cultural Cold War*, 129.
76 Yi, "Cultural Logic," 412.
77 Mun Han-gyu, "After Attending the Berlin Film Festival" [Berŭlin yŏnghwajerŭl pogo], *Tonga Ilbo*, July 19, 1961, 4.
78 Christina Klein, *Cold War Cosmopolitanism: Period Style in 1950s Korean Cinema* (Oakland: University of California Press, 2020), 81, 160.
79 Klein, *Cold War Cosmopolitanism*, 160.
80 Quoted in Kim Ch'ŏng-gang, "Modern Korea's Cinema Reconstruction Movement and the Politics of Comedy Film Production (1945–1960)" [Hyŏndae Han'gukŭi yŏnghwa chaegŏnnoriwa k'omedi yŏnghwaŭi chŏngch'ijŏk hamŭi], *Chindan hakbo*, no. 112 (August 2011): 51.
81 Kim, "Modern Korea's Cinema Reconstruction Movement," 52.
82 Quoted in "Modern Korea's Cinema Reconstruction Movement."
83 Kim Chŏng-ok, "Dominated by Sentiment and Purity" [Kamsanggwa sunjŏngi chujo], *Han'guk Ilbo*, July 12, 1963, 7.
84 Chŏng Myŏng-hwan, "The Way of Seeing American Films" [Mig'ukyŏnghwa ponŭnbyŏp], *Tonga Ilbo*, April 14, 1966, 5.
85 For full lists, see Chung and Diffrient, *Movie Migrations*, 41.
86 Steven Chung, *Split Screen Korea: Shin Sang-ok and Postwar Cinema* (Minneapolis: University of Minnesota Press, 2014), 14.

Chapter 2   From *Blackboard Jungle* to *The Teahouse of the August Moon*

1 Peter Ford, *Glenn Ford, A Life* (Madison: University of Wisconsin Press, 2011), 250–251.
2 "Glenn Ford's Press Conference upon Visit to Korea" [Glenn Ford naehan hoegyŏn], *Tonga Ilbo*, August 5, 1969, 5.
3 Christina Klein, *Cold War Cosmopolitanism: Period Style in 1950s Korean Cinema* (Oakland: University of California Press, 2020), 70.
4 Lee Hwajin (Yi Hwa-jin), "Liberator or Intimate Enemy?: On South Korean Cultural Circles' Ambivalence toward Hollywood," *Review of Korean Studies* 18, no. 1 (June 15): 50.

5 Brian Yecies and Ae-Gyung Shim, "Disarming Japanese Canons with American Cameras: Cinema in Korea under U.S. Occupation," Faculty of Arts Papers, University of Wollongong Research Online (2010): 10, https://ro.uow.edu.au/artspapers/401/.
6 Cited in Kim Kyun, "U.S. Cultural Policy and Occupied Korea" [Migukŭi taeoe munhwajŏngch'aekŭl t'onghaebon migunjŏng munhawjŏngch'aek], *Korean Journal of Journalism and Communication Studies* [*Hang'uk ŏnronhakbo*] 44, no. 3 (July 2000): 63.
7 "The Crisis of Korean Films" [Kuksanyŏnghwaŭi wigi], *Seoul Sinmun*, April 23, 1948, 4.
8 Yi T'ae-u, "How to See American Films" [Migukyŏnghwarŭl ŏttŏk'e polgŏsinga], *Kyŏnghyang Sinmun*, October 13, 1946, 4.
9 "CMPE Distribution Conditions Threatening to Korean Theater Culture" [Chosŏn kŭkjangmunhaw wihyŏphanŭn Chungangyŏnghwasa paegŭpjogŏn], *Kyŏnghyang Ilbo*, February 2, 1947, 3.
10 Korean Film Promotion Corporation, *Korean Cinema Data: From the Beginning to 1976* [*Hang'ukyŏnghwajaryo p'yŏnryam*] (Seoul: Korean Film Promotion Corporation, 1977), 80–81.
11 Ahn Junghyo, *The Life and Death of Hollywood Kid* [*Hŏliiudŭ k'idŭ ŭi saengae*] (Seoul: Minjokgwa munhwasa, 1992), 88–91.
12 Yi Sŏn-mi, "Female Culture in the 1950s and American Films" [1950nyŏndae yŏsŏngmunhwawa Mig'ukyŏnghwa], *Studies in Korean Literature* [*Hang'ukmunhwak yŏngu*], no. 40 (2009): 490.
13 Yi, "Female Culture," 501–502.
14 Klein, *Cold War Cosmopolitanism*, 7. Emphasis in original.
15 Klein, *Cold War Cosmopolitanism*, 6.
16 Bruce Cumings, *Korea's Place in the Sun: A Modern History*, updated ed. (New York: W. W. Norton, 2005), 255.
17 Yi Sŏn-mi, "American Films and Metropolis Consuming 'America'" ['Miguk'ŭl' sobihanŭn taedosiwa Migukyŏnghwa]" *Journal of Korean Modern Literature* [*Sanghŭr hakbo*] 18 (2006): 91–92.
18 Robert G. Lee, *Orientals: Asian Americans in Popular Culture* (Philadelphia: Temple University Press, 1999), 146.
19 Jason Barnosky, "The Violent Years: Responses to Juvenile Crimes in the 1950s," *Polity* 18, no. 3 (July 2006): 320.
20 "Young Lawlessness: Task for All," *New York Herald Tribune*, June 13, 1955, 14.
21 "Congress Investigates: The Senate Judiciary Committee's Subcommittee on Juvenile Delinquency Investigates Comic Books in the 1950s," U.S. National Archives, https://www.archives.gov/files/legislative/resources/education/comic-books/all-worksheets.pdf; "Motion Pictures and Juvenile Delinquency," Senate Report no. 2055 (Washington, DC: United States Government Printing Office, 1956), 2.
22 "Motion Pictures and Juvenile Delinquency," 9, 12.
23 Jess Stearn, "Teen-Age Terror Stalks City Schools, Cows Teachers, Trains Kids for Crime" and "Fear Balks Exposure of School Terrors," *Daily News* (New York), March 5, 1954, 5–6. This special issue (underlined in red in several sections) is included in *Blackboard Jungle* juvenile delinquency research, Richard Brooks Papers, file 113, Margaret Herrick Library (MHL), Academy of Motion Picture Arts and Sciences (AMPAS), Beverly Hills, California. It appears that the issue was a major inspiration for Brooks's screenplay.
24 Yannis Tzioumakis, *American Independent Cinema: An Introduction*, 2nd ed. (New Brunswick, NJ: Rutgers University Press, 2017), 126.

200 • Notes to Pages 52–57

25 Jerold Simmons, "Violent Youth: The Censorship and Public Reception of *The Wild One* and *Blackboard Jungle*," *Film History: An International Journal* 20, no. 3 (2008): 388.
26 Simmons, "Violent Youth."
27 MGM, *Blackboard Jungle* publicity brochure, *Blackboard Jungle*, Richard Brooks Papers, file 120, MHL.
28 Sal Manna, "*Blackboard Jungle* Revisited," *Los Angeles Herald Examiner*, January 13, 1983, B3.
29 *Blackboard Jungle* grossed U.S.$5.2 million in the domestic market alone. "History," *Blackboard Jungle*, American Film Institute (AFI) Catalog, https://catalog.afi.com/Catalog/moviedetails/53472.
30 Manna, "*Blackboard Jungle* Revisited."
31 Robert Sklar, *Movie-Made America: A Cultural History of American Movies* (New York: Vintage Books, 1994), 295.
32 Joseph I. Breen, PCA, to Dore Schary, MGM, September 20, 1954, *Blackboard Jungle*, Production Code Administration (PCA) files, MHL.
33 Geoffrey Shurlock to Schary, October 22, 1954, *Blackboard Jungle*, PCA files, MHL.
34 Shurlock to Schary, October 22, 1954.
35 Shurlock to Schary, October 22, 1954.
36 Eugene "Doc" Dougherty, "Memo for the files re: *Blackboard Jungle*," February 7, 1955, PCA files, MHL.
37 Murray Schumach, *The Face on the Cutting Room Floor: The Story of Movie and Television Censorship* (New York: Da Capo Press, 1964), 176.
38 Confidential report on local censor boards, Pennsylvania, March 31, 1955 (filed by PCA, April 27, 1955), *Blackboard Jungle*, PCA files, MHL. Emphasis in original.
39 "Milwaukee Threatens to Shutter Theatre Unless *Blackboard Jungle* Cuts Are Made," *Variety*, May 19, 1955, 1.
40 Simmons, "Violent Youth," 389.
41 Anders Walker, "*Blackboard Jungle*: Delinquency, Desegregation, and the Cultural Politics of *Brown*," *Columbia Law Review* 110, no. 7 (November 2010): 1912.
42 Bosley Crowther, "The Exception or the Rule?," *New York Times*, March 27, 1955, X1.
43 Schary to Bosley Crowther, April 6, 1955, *Blackboard Jungle* correspondence, Richard Brooks Papers, file 107, MHL.
44 Edward N. Wallen, "Jungle 'Tempest'," *New York Times*, April 3, 1955, X5. Emphasis in original.
45 "Pedagos Pummel *Blackboard*," *Variety*, July 13, 1955, 15.
46 Dave Blum to Arthur Loew, "*Blackboard Jungle*—Censorship," November 22, 1954, *Blackboard Jungle* censorship, Richard Brooks Papers, file 104, MHL.
47 Blum to Robert Vogel, "*Blackboard Jungle*—Censorship," December 3, 1954, Richard Brooks Papers, file 104, MHL.
48 Dore Schary to Dave Blum, January 3, 1955, *Blackboard Jungle* correspondence, Richard Brooks Papers, file 107, MHL.
49 Dave Blum to MGM Managers, "*Blackboard Jungle*: A Sociological Study and Box-Office Production Extraordinary and Its Relationship to Censorship," October 17, 1955, 1, 9, 12, Richard Brooks Papers, file 104, MHL.
50 Excerpts from the September 18, 1955, issue of the *Sunday Express* ("That *Blackboard Jungle* could be made at all speaks for a nation's greatness") and *Weekly Asahi* ("It is a good phase of American democracy that exposes a weak point in communities as in *From Here to Eternity*, or *On the Waterfront*"), among other foreign newspapers, are quoted in the manual.

51 Blum to MGM Managers, 9, Richard Brooks Papers, file 104, MHL.
52 Schary to James O'Neill, Jr., *Washington Daily News*, May 10, 1955, *Blackboard Jungle* correspondence, Richard Brooks Papers, file 107, MHL. This letter was a rebuttal of O'Neill's review of *Blackboard Jungle*, which was dubbed as fodder for "vicious anti-American propaganda... that never should have been made in the first place." James O'Neill Jr., "Keep It Home: *Blackboard Jungle* Is Dirty Linen That Shouldn't Be Exported," *Washington Daily News*, April 27, 1955, 72.
53 "Loew Blasts Mrs. Luce's 'Personal Censorship' in Venice *Jungle* Nix," *Variety*, August 31, 1955, 61.
54 "Mrs. Luce's 'Yes-No' Stance after Jungle Nix," *Variety*, September 7, 1955, 2. In the 1983 reunion panel with his crew at the Academy, producer Berman corroborated this accusation, stating that the international scandal surrounding *Blackboard Jungle* was "a boon, because we couldn't buy that kind of publicity." Manna, "*Blackboard Jungle* Revisited."
55 Vogel to Schary, Berman, and Brooks, MGM Inter-Office Communication, October 4, 1955, *Blackboard Jungle* foreign, Richard Brooks Papers, file 111, MHL.
56 In stateside exhibition, special local trailers ran at the end of the film to preempt objections from local school officials. RKO theaters ran such "footnote trailers," announcing, for example, "To our patrons: the school and situations you have just seen are not to be found in this area! We should all be proud of the facilities provided for our youth by the public schools of New Brunswick and the Middlesex County vocational and technical high schools." "Footnote to Film Lessons Educators' *Blackboard* Beefs," *Variety*, April 21, 1955, 7.
57 "Export *Blackboard Jungle*," *Variety*, April 20, 1955, 7.
58 Darryl F. Zanuck to Schary, January 19, 1956, *Blackboard Jungle* correspondence—Schary/Zanuck, Richard Brooks Papers, file 109, MHL. In his reply dated January 23, 1956 (filed in the above folder), Schary defensively responded to Zanuck, stating, "I think you depreciate the intelligence of European audiences.... We look at *Bicycle Thief* and we do not assume that all Italians steal bicycles. Europeans look at *Blackboard Jungle* and do not assume that this is a typical situation."
59 "Export *Blackboard Jungle*," 7.
60 "Export *Blackboard Jungle*," 22.
61 Adam Golub, "A Transnational Tale of Teenage Terror: *Blackboard Jungle* in Global Perspective," *Journal of Transnational American Studies*, 6, no. 1 (2005): 3.
62 Rejection Notice from Arthur Wakins, secretary of British Board of Film Censors (BBFC), to MGM, March 24, 1955, BBFC master files, *Blackboard Jungle*, British Board of Film Classification, London. This rejection came only a few months after Columbia Pictures had received a similar reply regarding their censorship application for *The Wild One* (1953). The board justified their rejection, explaining that "the British public has been deeply shocked by recent outbreaks of violence and hooliganism on the part of teenage boys—culminating in one instance in murder—and every responsible citizen is seriously concerned about the influences which have contributed to this spread of juvenile crime... it is... of the utmost importance for us to ensure that no single film shall have a harmful influence." Wakins to Columbia Pictures Corporation, July 23, 1954, BBFC master files, *The Wild One*.
63 Sidney Harris, president of BBFC, to MGM, July 18, 1955, BBFC master files, *Blackboard Jungle*. It is interesting that Harris expressed his surprise at the content of *Blackboard Jungle* being considered dissimilar to that of other MGM films that "have seldom given us any substantial trouble in the past." He advised the studio that passing the film in its present form classified as X would elicit "serious public

criticism and such a result would be as injurious to you and the cinematograph industry as it would be to the Board," suggesting the BBFC's double role in safeguarding both public and trade interests.

64 MGM to Harris, July 25, 1955, BBFC master files, *Blackboard Jungle*. Although BBFC files have all MGM representatives' names redacted, some communications addressed to Sir Sidney Harris, the board president, appear to have been authored by Schary himself. For example, at the conclusion of the censorship crisis with the BBFC, an MGM representative wrote to Harris, apologizing for "having been such [a] nuisance" but restating his conviction that "my attitude was the right one, not only for my Company but to the public as well." MGM to Harris, August 16, 1955, BBFC master files, *Blackboard Jungle*.

65 The eliminated or shortened scenes included the foreword, the library attack scene, beating scenes, the robbery scene, and the classroom vandalism scene. Wakins's internal memo titled "*Blackboard Jungle*," August 12, 1955, BBFC master files, *Blackboard Jungle*.

66 Even after the BBFC issued an X certificate after MGM's cuts, there were attempts to prohibit local screenings of *Blackboard Jungle*. For example, on October 28, 1955, after receiving a request to ban the film in its jurisdiction, the County Borough of Derby sent an inquiry to the BBFC as to why the film had been passed with an X certificate. After acknowledging that there were "certain scenes and incidents [in the originally submitted print] which we considered to be unpleasant and unsuitable," the BBFC secretary defended the film's overall moral message: "The film is unquestionably adult entertainment . . . but the moral it seeks to draw is firmly and clearly presented—namely, that a schoolmaster who believes in the power of teaching and who has the courage to maintain his beliefs, in the face of discouraging reverses, can find a way to influence the lives of even the most problematic boys." The film was exhibited in Derby under the X category after an initial two months' ban. Wakins to the town clerk, Derby Council House, November 1, 1955, BBFC master files, *Blackboard Jungle*.

67 "Toronto Hubbub over *Blackboard*," *Variety*, May 25, 1955, 23.

68 Ray Stark to Brooks, May 23, 1955, *Blackboard Jungle* correspondence—congratulatory, Richard Brooks Papers, file 108, MHL.

69 Golub, "Transnational Tale," 5.

70 "Release of *Jungle, Bamboo* Irks Jap Censors," *Variety*, September 21, 1955.

71 Golub, "Transnational Tale," 5.

72 "Six Categories including 'Sex'" ["Sŏnggwan'gye" tŭng yuk'angmok], *Tonga Ilbo*, December 29, 1956, 4.

73 "Opposition Is Dominant" [Pandaejujangi apdojŏk], *Seoul Sinmun*, December 16, 1960, 4.

74 Yun Pyŏng-hŭi, "Juvenile Reform and Immoral Movies" [Ch'ŏngsonyŏn kyodowa pullyunyŏnghwa], *Kyŏnghyang Sinmun*, February 7, 1961, 4.

75 The Minister of the Interior to the Ministry of Education (MoE), "Report on Public Opinion Regarding Request for Impure Film Bans" [Pulsun yŏnghwa kŭmyŏng choch'i yomang e taehan yŏron pogo], May 23, 1961, *The Stray Bullet*, Ministry of Public Information (MPI) film censorship files, Korean Film Archive (KOFA), Seoul.

76 Ch'oe Yu-hŏn and Pyŏn Yŏng-sŏk, KCIA, "Opinion of Censorship" [Kyŏmyŏl ŭgyŭnsŏ], February 13, 1962, *Blackboard Jungle*, MPI files, KOFA.

77 Yi Ch'un-sŏng, MoE to the MPI, "Opinion on Recensorship Review of *Violent Classroom* and *The Stray Bullet*" [P'ongnyŏk kyosil mit *Obalt'an* chaegyŏmsa sisaŭigyŏn], February 16, 1962, *Blackboard Jungle*, MPI files, KOFA.

78 Manna, "*Blackboard Jungle* Revisited."
79 Erskine Johnson, "*Blackboard Jungle* Shocking Tale," *Daily News* (Los Angeles), December 13, 1954, 27.
80 Kenneth MacKenna to Schary, August 17, 1954, *Blackboard Jungle* production, Richard Brooks Papers, file 119, MHL.
81 *Blackboard Jungle* Script, old and changed pages, August 17, 1954, through September 2, 1954, Richard Brooks Papers, file 95, MHL.
82 MacKenna to Schary, Richard Brooks Papers, file 119, MHL.
83 Schary to Lionel DeSilva, December 20, 1954, *Blackboard Jungle* research, Richard Brooks Papers, file 121, MHL. Emphasis added.
84 "Schary Hits Anonymous Scrawls on *Blackboard*," *Variety*, March 21, 1955, 4.
85 Minister, MPI, to Director, KCIA, "Recensorship Permission for Foreign Film *Blackboard Jungle*" Oegŭkyŏnghwa *Pŭllaekpodŭ chŏnggŭl* chaesimhŏga], April 17, 1962, *Blackboard Jungle*, MPI files, KOFA. The other cited reasons include "social morals" for the rape scene and "racial discrimination" for the line "black boy."
86 Kim Kyŏng-t'ak, "How Should We Purify School?" [Hakwŏnŭi chŏnghwarŭ ŏttŏk'e halkka], *Tonga Ilbo*, September 20, 1960, 4.
87 Cumings, *Korea's Place in the Sun*, 356–358.
88 "One Year Anniversary of Military Revolution: Education" [Kunsahyŏkmyŏng ilnyŏn: Kyŏuk], *Chosŏn Ilbo*, May 10, 1962, 1.
89 An Ch'ang-sŏn, "A Review of Transformation Process for Korean School Support Organizations" [Hang'ukhakgyo huwŏndanch'ebyŏnch'ŏngwajŏnge kwangan koch'al], *Ch'unchŏn National University Education Papers* [*Ch'unch'ŏn Kyŏukdaehak nonmunjip*] 21 (April 1981): 59–62.
90 Hancho C. Kim, "Park's Shining Korean Camelot," *New York Times*, January 8, 1975, 37.
91 At the time of the film's production, an average salary of high school teacher was $3,990 per year as opposed to $12,500 per year for a U.S. representative and $15,000 per year for a U.S. district judge. Los Angeles police officers and firefighters earned $5,280 per year. Carpenters and plumbers had a weekly average wage of $91.51 while babysitters earned $0.75 per hour until midnight ($1 per hour after midnight) and soda jerks earned $6.96 for eight hours. "Comparative Earnings," *Blackboard Jungle* Script, Richard Brooks Papers, file 86, MHL. MGM's foreign prints eliminated references to the wages in subtitles, presumably to avoid negative publicity about American teachers' maltreatment. Zanuck to Schary, January 19, 1956, Richard Brooks Papers, file 86, MHL.
92 Steve Benton, "*Blackboard Jungle*: Poisoning the American Dream," *Counterpoints*, no. 486 (2017): 178.
93 Benton, "Poisoning the American Dream," 179.
94 "Recensorship Permission for Foreign Film *Blackboard Jungle*," MPI files, KOFA.
95 "Problematic Film *Blackboard Jungle*" [Munjaeŭi yŏnghwa *Pŭraekbodŭ chŏnggŭl*], *Kyŏnghyang Sinmun*, May 27, 1962, 4.
96 Christina Klein, *Cold War Orientalism: Asia in the Middlebrow Imagination, 1945–1961* (Berkeley: University of California Press, 2003), 16.
97 Yi Hwa-jin, "Waesaek (Japanese Color) Film from Hollywood" [Hŏlliudŭaesŏ on 'waesaekyŏnghwa'], *Sanghŏ hakbo*, no. 59 (2020): 404–405.
98 The first three-day gross at Yuraku-za was 5.1 million yen (U.S.$14,167). The film had a roadshow engagement in eleven theaters in Japan, including Osaka, Kobe, and Kyoto. Stanley Markham to Daniel Mann, January 25, 1957, Daniel Mann Papers, file 91, MHL.

99 *Teahouse* Creating Box-Office Record," *Mainichi*, January 13, 1957, clipping in *Teahouse August Moon*—publicity, Daniel Mann Papers, file 93, MHL.
100 Kim Sŏng-min, *Prohibiting Japan* [*Ilbonŭl kŭmhada*] (Seoul: Kŭlhangari, 2017), 26–27.
101 Jinsoo An, *Parameters of Disavowal: Colonial Representation in South Korean Cinema* (Berkeley: University of California Press, 2018), 35–36.
102 "Motion Picture Law Enforcement Regulations" [Yŏnghwabŏp sihaenggyuch'ik], July 24, 1962, https://www.law.go.kr/LSW/lsInfoP.do?lsiSeq=45364#0000.
103 Jung-Hoon Lee, "Normalization of Relations with Japan: Toward a New Partnership," in *The Park Chung Hee Era: The Transformation of South Korea*, ed. Byung-Kook Kim and Ezra F. Vogel (Cambridge, MA: Harvard University Press, 2011), 431.
104 "The Notice MoE Sent to KFPA" [Mungyobuaesŏ Hang'ukyŏnghwajejakja hyŏphoee ponaen t'onggomun], *Kyŏnghyang Sinmun*, March 12, 1959, 4.
105 "Trouble with Recommending Import of Waesaek Film" [Waesaekyŏnghwa suipch'uch'ŏne malsŏng], *Kyŏnghyang Sinmun*, November 6, 1962, 7. "Communist films" were broadly defined in South Korea and not limited to films made in Soviet-bloc or Red Asian countries. As in Hollywood during the blacklisting era, films written or directed by communist sympathizers in the Free World were also subject to censorship. For example, in 1957, the MoE cancelled exhibition permits of Italian neorealist films such as *Bitter Rice* (*Riso Amaro*, 1949) and *Days of Love* (*Giorni d'amore*, 1954), directed by Giuseppe de Santis, a member of the Italian Communist Party, after the Prosecutors' Office categorized them as "enemy films" (*chŏksŏng yŏngwha*) despite lack of explicit communist content.
106 Lee, "Normalization of Relations with Japan," 435.
107 "Rejecting Foreign Film Import Recommendation" [Oegukyŏnghwa suipch'uch'ŏn pallyŏ], MPI Motion Picture Division, October 31, 1961, *The Teahouse of the August Moon*, MPI files, KOFA.
108 Yi, "Waesaek (Japanese Color) Film," 422.
109 Chŏng Chong-hwa, "Meeting Korean Youth by Borrowing a Japanese Story" [Ilbonŭi iyagirŭl pillyŏ Hang'uk Chomŭnidŭlgwa mannada], *Cine21*, December 21, 2020, http://www.cine21.com/news/view/?mag_id=96707.
110 Lee, "Normalization of Relations with Japan," 436, 443.
111 "Trouble with Recommending Import of Waesaek Film" [Waesaekyŏnghwa suipch'uch'ŏne malsŏng], 7.
112 "Opposing Importation of Waesaek Films" [Waesaekyŏnghwa suip pandae], *Kyŏnghyang sinmun*, November 15, 1962, 7.
113 "*The Teahouse of the August Moon* Deep in Japanese Color" [Waesaekchitŭn yŏnghwa *P'al.o.yaŭi ch'ajip*], *Seoul Sinmun*, November 10, 1962, 5.
114 "Should We Block Japanese Color Films?" [Ilbonsaekch'aeŭi yŏnghwa makayahana?], *Chosŏn Ilbo*, November 10, 1962, 5.
115 Ch'oe Hak-su, "Exhibition Permission for Korean Film *Happy Solitude*" [Kuksanyŏnghwa H*aengbokhan kodok* sangyŏng hŏga], MPI Motion Picture Division, January 24, 1962, *Happy Solitude*, MPI files, KOFA.
116 Ra Han-t'ae, MPI Motion Picture Division, "Exhibition Permission for Korean Film *The Sea Knows*" [Kuksanyŏnghwa *Hyŏndaet'anŭn algoitta* sangyŏnghŏga], October 17, 1961, *The Sea Knows*, MPI files, KOFA.
117 An, *Parameters of Disavowal*, 36, 41.
118 "Removal of Waesaek Advertising" [Waesaek kwanggo ch'ŏlgŏ], *Kyŏnghyang Sinmun*, January 26, 1963, 7.

119 An, *Parameters of Disavowal*, 44.
120 "'Japanese Color' and the Film Industry" [Ilbon saekch'ewa yŏnghwagye], *Tonga Ilbo*, January 28, 1963, 5.
121 Although official data on *The Teahouse of the August Moon*'s import costs are unavailable, one press source estimates that over $15,000 was paid to bring each Japan-themed Hollywood film (*Marines, Let's Go* [1961], *My Geisha* [1962], etc.) to South Korea. The economic factor of allegedly wasting scarce foreign currency for undesirable *waesaek* imports further fueled the fire of anti-Japanese controversy. See "Japanese Trouble" [Ilbon t'ŭrŏbŭl], *Tonga Ilbo*, February 6, 1964, 1.
122 Wu Ki-dong to MPI, "Petition for Suspension of Exhibition Permit for Movie *The Teahouse of the August Moon*" [Yŏnghwa *P'al.o.yaŭi ch'ajip* sangyŏnghŏga poryuae taehan chinjŏngŭi kŏn], March 20, 1963, *The Teahouse of the August Moon*, MPI files, KOFA.
123 MPI to Wu, "Reply to Request to Lift Suspension of Exhibition Permit for Movie *The Teahouse of the August Moon*" [Yŏnghwa *P'al.o.yaŭi ch'ajip* sangyŏnghŏga poryuae haejeyoch'ŏnge taehan hoesin], March 25, 1963, MPI files, KOFA.
124 KFFDA president Yun Myŏng-hyŏk, KFPA president Yi Pyŏng-il, NATO president Chi Tŏng-yŏng, and Segi Corporation president Wu Ki-dong to MPI, "Petition" [Chinjŏngsŏ], July 25, 1963, *The Teahouse of the August Moon*, MPI files, KOFA.
125 Yi, "Waesaek (Japanese Color) Film," 422.
126 Other higher standard registration requirements mandated by the revised Motion Picture Law (which was intended to transform a cottage industry into a studio system modeled after Hollywood) included a 7,117-square-foot studio, at least three 35mm cameras, 200kw lighting equipment, and three directors, ten actors/actresses, three cinematographers, and one recording technician under retainer contracts. Each production company was also required to make fifteen films per year to maintain their license.
127 Brian Yecies and Ae-Gyung Shim, *The Changing Face of Korean Cinema: 1960–2015* (New York: Routledge, 2016), 23.
128 Sangjoon Lee, *Cinema and the Cultural Cold War* (Ithaca, NY: Cornell University Press, 2020), 146.
129 Kim Tŏk, "Exhibition Permission for Foreign Film *The Teahouse of the August Moon*" [Oehwa *P'al.o.yaŭi ch'ajip* sangyŏnghŏga], August 19, 1963, *The Teahouse of the August Moon*, MPI files, KOFA.
130 "On Location with *Teahouse of the August Moon* Cast," *Asahi Evening News*, May 5, 1956, 6.
131 "Announcement Story," MGM Press Book *Teahouse of the August Moon*, 2-F, *The Teahouse of the August Moon* clippings file, MHL.
132 Michael Lombardi to the editor of *The Japan Quarterly*, Tokyo, July 23, 1957, Jack Cummings Papers, file 71, MHL.
133 "Hollywood Shows Japan Its Get-up-and-Go Style," MGM Press Book *Teahouse of the August Moon*, 2-G.
134 "Cricket Cages Put Customs Officials up a Creek," MGM Press Book *Teahouse of the August Moon*, 2-D.
135 "Marlon Brando, Glenn Ford and Machiko Ko Triumph in MGM Filmization of *The Teahouse of the August Moon*" and "Cricket Cages Put Customs Officials up a Creek," MGM Press Book *Teahouse of the August Moon*, 2-F, 2-D. In another part of the press book, it is asserted that "in recognition of the first picture to be filled by M-G-M in Japan, Governor Ryozo Okuda of the Nara Prefecture ordered Tobiki officially placed on all maps," creating confusion about the fictional island's national

identity. "There's Nothing There but Village Will Be on Map," MGM Press Book *Teahouse of the August Moon*, 2-G.
136 Yi, "Waesaek (Japanese Color) Film," 441. Although the MPI announced an ambitious plan to start allowing Japanese film imports in 1967 (after interim stages of creative personnel exchange and coproduction in 1965–1966), souring public opinion on Korean-Japanese relations following the normalization treaty killed it. It took another three decades (until 1998) for South Korea to lift a ban on Japanese culture.
137 On June 3, 1964, 200 protesters were injured and 1,120 arrested. Until July 29, when martial law was lifted, a total of 348 people were imprisoned in relation to the resistance movement. Kang Chun-man, *Strolling Korean Modern History* [*Hang'ukhyŏndaesa sanch'aek*] (Seoul: Inmulgwa sasangsa, 2004), 300.
138 "Problems of Importing *Tora! Tora! Tora!*" [*Tora Tora Tora* suipe ttarŭnŭn munjejŏm], January 11, 1971, *Tora! Tora! Tora!*, MPI files, KOFA.
139 Hye Seung Chung, *Hollywood Diplomacy: Film Regulation, Foreign Relations, and East Asian Representations* (New Brunswick, NJ: Rutgers University Press, 2020), 184.

Chapter 3   Myths of Martyrs and Heroes in a Godless Land

1 Michael Robinson, "Contemporary Cultural Production in South Korea: Vanishing Meta-Narratives of Nation," in *New Korean Cinema*, ed. Chi-Yun Shin and Julian Stringer (New York: New York University Press, 2005), 16–19.
2 Robinson, "Contemporary Cultural Production," 28. Emphasis added.
3 Park Yu-hŭi, "The Literary Film and Censorship System" [*Munyeyŏnghwawa kyŏmyŏl*], *Journal of Image & Film Studies* [*Yŏngsangyesul yŏngu*] 17 (November 2010): 195.
4 Daniel Martin, "South Korean Cinema's Postwar Pain: Gender and National Division in Korean War Films from the 1950s to the 2000s," *Journal of Korean Studies* 19, no. 1 (Spring 2014): 94–95.
5 Kenneth D. Wald, "The Religious Dimension of American Anti-Communism," *Journal of Church and State* 36, no. 3 (Summer 1994): 484.
6 Thomas Aiello, "Constructing 'Godless Communism': Religion, Politics, and Popular Culture, 1954–1960," *Americana: The Journal of American Popular Culture* 4, no. 1 (Spring 2005), https://www.americanpopularculture.com/journal/articles/spring_2005/aiello.htm.
7 Hana Lee, "Anticommunism in Popular Culture: The Evolution and Contestation of Anticommunist Films in South Korea," *Asian Journal of German and European Studies* 1, no. 9 (2016): 2.
8 Cho Chung-hyŏng, "The Evolution and Its Conditions of the Korean Anticommunist Film" [*Han'guk panggongyŏnghwa chinhwawa kŭ chogŏn*], in *Landscape of Modernity* [*Kŭndaeŭi p'unggyŏng*], ed. Ch'a Sun-ha (Seoul: Sodo, 2001), 332–333.
9 David Scott Diffrient, "'Military Enlightenment' for the Masses: Generic and Cultural Intermixing in South Korea's Golden Age War Films," *Cinema Journal* 45, no. 1 (Fall 2005): 23.
10 See *"Breaking the Wall"* [*Sŏngbyŏkŭl ttulgo*]," *Kyŏnghyang Sinmun*, October 31, 1949, 2; Paek Ch'ŏl, "Impression of Film Works" [*Yŏnghwa chakp'umŭi insang*], *Chosŏn Ilbo*, December 29, 1949, 2.
11 Lee, "Anticommunism in Popular Culture," 4.
12 "Movie *Piagol* Exhibition Suspended" [*Yŏnghwa P'iagol sangyŏngjungji*], *Chosŏn Ilbo*, August 25, 1955, 3.

13 Diffrient, "'Military Enlightenment' for the Masses," 23.
14 The numbers of anticommunist films made between 1960 and 1976 were 1 (1960), 2 (1961), 13 (1962), 6 (1963), 10 (1964), 15 (1965), 25 (1966), 15 (1967), 24 (1968), 17 (1969), 17 (1970), 16 (1971), 5 (1972), 13 (1973), 12 (1974), 11 (1975), and 12 (1976). See Cho, "Korean Anticommunist Film," 338, 345.
15 Josephine Nock-Hee Park, *Cold War Friendships: Korea, Vietnam, and Asian American Literature* (New York: Oxford University Press, 2016), 55–56.
16 Park, *Cold War Friendships*, 59; Richard E. Kim, *The Martyred*, repr. with an introduction by Heinz Insu Fenkl (New York: Penguin Books, 2011 [1964]), 66. Emphasis added.
17 Kim, *The Martyred*, 114–115.
18 Kim, *The Martyred*, 138. In a June 1965 interview with *Tonga Ilbo*, Richard E. Kim clarifies that the "song of homage" at the end of his novel is not the Korean national anthem but a popular folk song such as "Arirang" or "Toraji": "The Climate of *The Martyred*" [*Sungyoja* ŭi p'ungt'o], *Tonga Ilbo*. June 24, 1965, 7.
19 Kim, *The Martyred*, 8.
20 Kim, *The Martyred*, 17.
21 Kim, *The Martyred*, 9.
22 "Movie Review of *The Martyred*" [Yonghwa pip'yŏng *Sungyoja*], *Shina Ilbo*, June 19, 1965, 5.
23 "Director Yu Hyŏn-mok's *The Martyred*" [Yu Hyŏn-mok kamdok *Sungyoja*], *Seoul Simun*, June 24, 1965.
24 Kim, *The Martyred*, 22.
25 Kim, *The Martyred*, 91.
26 Kim, *The Martyred*, 17.
27 Stefan Skrimshire, "A Political Theology of the Absurd?: Albert Camus and Simone Weil on Social Transformation," *Literature & Theology* 20, no. 3 (September 2006): 288.
28 Park, *Cold War Friendships*, 69–70.
29 Minister, the Ministry of Public Information (MPI) to Ch'a T'ae-jin of Kŭkdong Entertainment, March 20, 1965, *The Martyred*, MPI film censorship files, Korean Film Archive (KOFA), Seoul.
30 "Motion Picture Law Enforcement Regulations" [Yŏnghwabŏp sihaenggyuch'ik], July 24, 1962, https://www.law.go.kr/LSW/lsInfoP.do?lsiSeq=45364#0000.
31 Yi Tal-hyŏng, "Exhibition Permit for Domestic Film *The Martyred*" [Kuksanyŏnghwa *Sungyoja* sangyŏnghŏga], MPI internal memorandum, June 16, 1965, *The Martyred*, MPI files, KOFA. The line is still intact in the English subtitled copy (presumably made for the film's submission to international film festivals in San Francisco and Venice) available for video on demand via the KOFA website.
32 Minister, Ministry of National Defense (MND) to the MPI, "Notice of Regulatory Opinion on Military Film *The Martyred*" [Kunsagŭk *Sungyoja* ŭi simsaŭigyŏn t'ongbo], June 17, 1965, *The Martyred*, MPI files, KOFA.
33 Yi Tal-hyŏng, MPI to Colonel Kim, MND, "Process of Regulatory Opinion on Military Film *The Martyred*" [Kunsagŭk *Sungyoja* ŭi simsaŭigyŏn ch'ŏri], June 18, 1965, *The Martyred*, MPI files, KOFA.
34 For a fuller account of the information summarized in this paragraph, see "Beyond the Propaganda Model: The Pentagon as a Technical Advisor for Brainwashing Films of the Cold War Era," in Hye Seung Chung, *Hollywood Diplomacy: Film Regulation, Foreign Relations, and East Asian Representations* (New Brunswick, NJ: Rutgers University Press, 2020), 94–128.

35 MND to MPI, "Requested Revisions and Deletions" [Yo sujŏng sakje sahang], n.d., *A Spotted Man*, MPI files, KOFA.
36 "Notice of Preview Print Censorship of Military Film" [Kunsayŏnghwa sisa kŏmyŏl kyŏlkwa pogo], MND to MPI, August 18, 1967, *A Spotted Man*, MPI files, KOFA.
37 MPI internal memo attached to "Notice of Preview Print Censorship," *A Spotted Man*, MPI files, KOFA.
38 Kim Chi-hyŏn, *A Spotted Man*, KOFA Scenario Collections, 30–41.
39 According to Hana Lee, the "rescue of American GIs" plot is one of the nine formulas of Korean war films of the 1950s and 1960s. The other eight include defection to the South, a love triangle of people divided by ideology, family betrayals by communists, conflicts between humanism and ideology in dire situations, soldiers' triumphs after overcoming conflicts, combat action ending with the annihilation of military units, the community destroyed by ideology, and postwar reconstruction. Hana Lee (Yi Ha-na), *Reconstruction Age of the Republic of Korea, 1948–1968* [Taehanminguk chaegŏnŭi sidae, 1948–1968] (Seoul: P'urŭn yŏksa, 2013), 197–205.
40 Thomas Doherty, *Hollywood's Censor: Joseph I. Breen and the Production Code Administration* (New York: Columbia University Press, 2007), 41.
41 "Appendix: The Production Code" in Doherty, *Hollywood's Censor*, 354. Emphasis in original.
42 Chŏng Yŏp-sŏng, "Meaning of 'Separation of State and Religion' in the Korean Constitution" [Hŏnbyŏpŭi chŏnggyobulliwŏnch'ik'ŭi ŭmi], *Kyŏngbuk National University Law Journal* [Pyŏphaknongo] 70 (July 2020): 8: https://www.knulaw.org/archive.
43 "Three Scenes of Movie Dream to Be Cut" [Yŏnghwa *Kkum* se sin sakje], *Sina Ilbo*, July 8, 1967, 5.
44 "Petitioning to Stop Exhibition of *The Martyred*" [Yŏnghwa *Sungyoja* sangyŏng kŭmji chinjŏng], *Kyŏnghyang Sinum*, July 2, 1965, 4.
45 Chung, *Hollywood Diplomacy*, 134.
46 Yu Hyŏn-mok, *Film Life* [Yŏnghwa insaeng] (Seoul: Hyehwadang, 1995), 151. In his memoir, Yu identifies himself as a coproducer for *The Martyred* (which was produced by the up-and-coming company Hapdong Film), which explains his reference to debts. By his own account, it was Yu's "most spectacular film" to date, which mobilized fully armed vehicles for 550 extras, along with fifty trucks, thirty-five jeeps, and five ambulances for battle scenes. An open set for exterior shots of Pyongyang was built on the site of the Map'o prison in Seoul. See Yu, 151, 231.
47 Chŏng, "'Separation of State and Religion,' 10."
48 Heather Hendershot, *Saturday Morning Censors: Television Regulation before the V-Chip* (Durham, NC: Duke University Press, 1998), 94.
49 Hendershot, *Saturday Morning Censors*, 93.
50 "The Controversy about *The Martyred* in the Christian Community" [Kidokkyogae Sungyoja p'amun], *Tonga Ilbo*, June 19, 1965, 8.
51 Quoted in "Controversy about *The Martyred*."
52 The full martyr list is available on the homepage of the Foundation for the 100th Anniversary of the Korean Church at: http://www.100thcouncil.com/html/sub3_3.html.
53 Pak Po-gyŏng, "The Role of Korean Churches during the Korean War of 1950" [1950nyŏn Han'gukjŏnjaeng tangsi Han'guk kyohoeŭi yŏkhal], *Missionary and Theology* [Sŏngyo wa sinhak] 26 (August 2010): 113–114.

54 Ok Sŏng-dŭk, "The Reality of Chosŏn's Jerusalem Pyongyang Discourse" [Chosŏnŭi Yerusalem P'yŏngyang tamron silsang], *Christian Ideology* [*Kidokkyo sasang*], no. 717 (September 2018): 9–10.
55 Pak, "Role of Korean Churches," 128.
56 "Manmulsang," *Chosŏn Ilbo*, June 27, 1965, 2.
57 In his homecoming press conference in June 1965, Kim identifies himself as a "non-Christian" and replies "somewhere in the middle" to the question of whether he believes in God or not. "Homecoming of *The Martyred*" [*Sungyojaŭi kwihyang*], *Chosŏn Ilbo*, June 20, 1965, 6.
58 "Controversy about *The Martyred*."
59 Paul Y. Chang, *Protest Dialectics: State Repression and South Korea's Democracy Movement, 1970–1979* (Stanford, CA: Stanford University Press, 2015), 33–34.
60 Cho Jun-hyoung, "Guides for Interpreting Korean Film Censorship Documents" [Han'gukyŏnghwa kyŏmyŏlsŏryu tokhaerŭl wihan annae], KOFA Collection, https://www.koreafilm.or.kr/collection/CI_00000017#none.
61 Korean Film Archive, *2020 Korean Film Oral History Research Series: Foreign Film Export Changes in the 1960s–1990s*, vol. 2 [2020nyŏn Han'gukyŏnghwa kusulch'aeokyŏngu sirijŭ 1960–1990nyŏndae suipwŏehwa pyŏnhwa 2] (Seoul: Korean Film Archive, 2020), 156–157.
62 Hong Chin-gi, KCIA to Kim Yŏng-ae, MPI, June 22, 1965, *The Martyred*, MPI files, KOFA.
63 Yi Tal-hyŏng, MPI to Major An Hŭk-ryong, KCIA, June 26, 1965, *The Martyred*, MPI files, KOFA.
64 Director Kim Hyŏng-uk, KCIA to Minister, MPI, "Notice of Scenario Review Outcome" [Sinario kŏmt'o kyŏlgwa pogo], November 25, 1966, *A Spotted Man*, MPI files, KOFA. Although this report is sent under the name of the KCIA director, the actual regulatory review must have been conducted by a lower-level staff member.
65 Yi fell out of the party's favor for failing to report Premier Kim Il Sung's speech on a military tour (where Yi accompanied him) with due respect.
66 Cho Kap-je, *Speaking the Truth about Past History* [*Kwagŏsaŭi chinsangŭl malhanda*] (Seoul: Wŏlgan Chosŏnsa, 2005), 18.
67 Truth and Reconciliation Commission, Republic of Korea, *2006 Second Half Investigative Report* [*2006nyŏn habangi chosa pogosŏ*] (Seoul: I Will, 2007), 181.
68 Ko Tong-uk, "Not Guilty 49 Years after Being Executed for Being an Undercover Spy" [Wijangganch'ŏp mollyŏ ch'ŏhyŏngdaen Yi Su-gŭnssi 49nyŏnmanae mujoe], *Yonhap News*, October 11, 2018, https://www.yna.co.kr/view/AKR20181011086251004.
69 Chang, *Protest Dialectics*, 34.
70 Internal memorandum, "Domestic Film *Accusation*" [Kuksanyŏnghwa *Kobal*], June 30, 1967, *Accusation*, MPI files, KOFA.
71 Cho Mun-jin, *Accusation*, Original scenario, KOFA Scenario Collections, 2; Censorship review scenario, KOFA Scenario Collections, 2.
72 Cho, Original scenario, 37.
73 Cho, Original scenario, 10.
74 Director Kim Hyŏng-uk, KCIA to Minister, MPI, "Notice of Scenario Review Outcome" [Sinario kŏmt'o kyŏlgwa pogo], May 8, 1968, *The Descendants of Cain*, MPI files, KOFA.
75 Cho, Original scenario, 40.
76 Cho, *Speaking the Truth*, 31.
77 Cho, Censorship review scenario, 26.

78 Cho, Censorship review scenario, 15.
79 "Sorry to Citizens" [Kukmindŭlaegae mianhago], *Chosŏn Ilbo*, February 23, 1969, 5. In his memoir, Kim Su-yong recollects meeting Yi three times. When the director inquired what his apartment was like in North Korea and what kind of clothes his wife wore, the defector replied, "Not so different from here," insinuating that he had an affluent life in the totalitarian country. According to Kim, at the film's preview, Yi was sitting next to him and had a smirk on his face throughout the screening. The director writes, "We did not know that we were completely fooled by a spy at that time." Kim Su-yong, *My Love Cinema [Naŭi sarang cinema]* (Seoul: Cine21, 2005), 111–112.
80 "Red Spy Yi Su-gŭn Who Tore a Woman's Innocent Heart Apart" [Sunjŏngŭi yŏsimdo kalgari chitbalŭn pulŭn chanch'ŏp Yi Su-gŭn], *Kyŏnghyang Sinmun*, February 14, 1969, 3.
81 "Red Spy Yi Su-gŭn."
82 "Citizens Enraged by Deceptive Behavior of 'Red Devil' Yi Su-gŭn Who Wore the Mask of Defector" [Kwisunŭi t'alŭlssŭn 'pulŭn masu' Yi Su-gŭn wijanghaenggakae simindŭl punno], *Tonga Ilbo*, February 13, 1969, 7.
83 "Condemnation of Spy Yi Su-gŭn" [Kanch'ŏp Yi Su-gŭnŭl kyut'an], *Kyŏnghyang Sinmun*, February 15, 1969, 7.
84 Lee, *Reconstruction Age*, 249–250.
85 Jeremy Mindrich, "Re-reading *Ninotchka*: A Misread Commentary on Social and Economic Systems," *Film & History: An Interdisciplinary Journal of Film and Television Studies* 20, no. 1 (February 1990): 13.
86 Cho, *Speaking the Truth*, 25. Yi Tae-yong took notes of this off-the-record conversation, which he shared with reporter Cho Kap-je in 1989.
87 Edward S. Herman and Noam Chomsky, *Manufacturing Consent: The Political Economy of the Mass Media* (New York: Pantheon Books, 1988), 2.
88 Yi To-yŏn, "Kim Su-yong kamdok" [Director Kim Su-yong], *Yonhap News*, October 29, 2019, https://www.yna.co.kr/view/AKR20191029096800005.
89 Doherty, *Hollywood's Censor*, 112–113.
90 "Notice of Scenario Review Outcome," *The Descendants of Cain*, MPI files, KOFA.
91 Yu Hyŏn-mok, "Freedom of the Silver Screen" [Ŭnmakŭi chayu], *Chosŏn Ilbo*, March 25, 1965, 5.
92 "Sunday Interview" [Ilyo Int'ŏbyu], *Han'guk Ilbo*, March 19, 1967, 7. For more details about Yu's prosecution for shooting an obscene shot (censored in the release version) on the set of *Empty Dream*, see David Scott Diffrient, "Against Anaesthesia: *An Empty Dream*, Pleasurable Pain and the 'Illicit' Thrills of South Korea's Golden Age Remakes," in *East Asian Film Remakes*, ed. David Scott Diffrient and Kenneth Chan (Edinburgh: Edinburgh University Press, 2023), 49–72.

Chapter 4   Cinematic Censorship as Sentimental Education

1 Kim, Chi-yŏng, "The Cultural Politics and Historical Transition of the Emotional Constitution of 'Gaiety'" ['Myŏngryangsŏng'ŭi sidaejŏk pyŏnhwawa munhawjŏngch'ihak], *Journal of the Society of Korean Language and Literature [Ŏmunnonjip]*, no. 78 (December 12): 221, 223.
2 Kim, "Cultural Politics," 220.
3 Son, Yŏng-nim, "Youth Films in the 1970s: The Rupture between Resistance and 'Conspiracy'" [1970nyŏndae ch'ongnyŏn yŏnghwa, chŏhanggwa 'kongmo'ŭi' kyunyŏl], *Mass Narrative Study [Taejungsŏsa]* 24, no. 2 (2018): 206.

4 So Rae-sŏp, *Be Cheerful, Seditious Seoul* [Pulonhan Kyŏngsŏng ŭn myŏngryanghara] (Seoul: Ungjin, 2011), 6–7.
5 So, *Be Cheerful, Seditious Seoul*, 49.
6 So, *Be Cheerful, Seditious Seoul*, 50.
7 Park Chung Hee, State of Union Address, January 18, 1966, https://www.pa.go.kr/research/contents/speech/index.jsp?spMode=view&artid=1305648&catid=c_pa02062.
8 Yu Sŏn-yŏng, "Hypernationalization Project of Military-Conscriptive Regime and Mass Politics of Decadence in 1970s Korea" [Tongwŏn ch'ejeŭi kwaminjokhwa p'ŭrojetŭwa sesŭyŏnghwa], *Press and Society* [*Ŏnrongwa Sahoe*] 15, no. 2 (Summer 2007): 22.
9 So, *Be Cheerful, Seditious Seoul*, 13.
10 So, *Be Cheerful, Seditious Seoul*, 25.
11 Michel Foucault, *The History of Sexuality*, vol. 1 *An Introduction* (New York: Vintage Books, 1990), 92, 95.
12 Quoted in So, *Be Cheerful, Seditious Seoul*, 25.
13 Paek Sŭng-ch'an, "True Gaiety Is to Become Owners of Emotions" [Kamjŏng chuin i toeya chinjŏng myŏngryang], *Kyŏnghyang Sinmun*, May 13, 2011, https://m.khan.co.kr/amp/view.html?art_id=201105132111335&sec_id=900308.
14 Kim Ki-rim, "Sun's Custom" [T'aeyang ŭi p'ungsok], *Encyclopedia of Korean Culture* [Han'guk minjokmunhwa taebaekkwa sajŏn], The Academy of Korean Studies, http://encykorea.aks.ac.kr/Contents/Item/E0058993.
15 So, *Be Cheerful, Seditious Seoul*, 240–241.
16 Seung Hyun Park, "Film Censorship and Political Legitimization in South Korea, 1987–1992," *Cinema Journal* 42, no. 1 (Fall 2002): 120.
17 Although it was unusual for the Seoul branch of the United States CIA to get involved in Korean film censorship, their opinion was sought in high-profile cases dealing with anticommunism and the U.S. military presence such as Yi Man-hŭi's *Seven Female Prisoners* (*Ch'ilin ŭi yŏp'oro*, 1965).
18 Nelson Poynter file, from December 1, 1942, to April 12, 1943, box 1443, "Hollywood Reporter," General Records of the Chief, Lowell Mellett, Records of the Bureau of Motion Pictures, Office of War Information (OWI) files, RG 208, National Archives and Records Administration (NARA), College Park, Maryland. Emphasis in original.
19 "Encouraged Directions of Domestic Productions" [Kuksan yŏnghwa kwŏnjang panghyang], *Voice* (*Moksori*), Ministry of Public Information (MPI) film censorship files, Korean Film Archive (KOFA), Seoul.
20 Park Yu-hŭi, "A Study on the Dynamics of Film Censorship and Representation of Sentiment during the Park Chung-Hee Regime" [Pak Chŏng-hŭi chŏnggwŏngi yŏnghwa kŏmyŏlkwa kamsŏng chaehyŏn ŭi yŏkhak], *History Criticism* [*Yŏksa pip'yŏng*], no. 99 (Summer 2012): 61.
21 As noted by Bruce Cumings, "'Yushin' is the Korean pronunciation of the Japanese *issin*, used by the Meiji leaders in 1868.... Park sought to use Japanese values and practices to make a big happy family of the workplace, and he justified his deactivation of the National Assembly in terms of 'organic cooperation' between the executive and the legislative." Cumings, *Korea's Place in the Sun: A Modern History*, updated ed. (New York: W. W. Norton, 2005), 363.
22 Son Yŏng-nam, "Youth Films in the 1970s, Rupture between Resistance and 'Conspiracy'" [1970nyŏndae ch'ŏngnyŏn yŏnghwa, chŏhangkwa 'kongmo' ŭi kunyŏl]," *Journal of Popular Narrative* [*Taejung sōsa nyŏngu*], 24, no. 2 (2018): 214.

23 Son, "Youth Films in the 1970s," 215.
24 "*The March of Fools*: Production & Release History," *The March of Fools* Blu-ray booklet (Seoul: Korean Film Archive, 2014).
25 For detailed information about the film's production and reception history, see various newspaper clippings about *The March of Fools* reprinted in *Ha Kil-jong*, vol. 3, ed. Yi Pyŏng-hun (Seoul: Korean Film Archive, 2009), 188–199.
26 Kim Yŏng-jin, "Seizing the Misfortune of the Time," *The March of Fools* Blu-ray booklet.
27 Ha Kil-jong, "The Reality and Prospect of Korean Cinema" [Han'guk yŏnghwaŭi hyŏnsilgwa chŏnmang], *Kongjusadae Hakbo*, October 1975, reprinted in *Ha Kil-jong*, vol. 2, ed. Yi Pyŏng-hun (Seoul: Korean Film Archive, 2009), 407.
28 Thomas Schatz, *The Genius of the System* (New York: Metropolitan Books, 1988), 5, 8
29 Stuart Hall, "Notes on Deconstructing 'the Popular,'" in *Cultural Resistance Reader*, ed. Stephen Duncombe (New York: Verso, 2002), 192.
30 Youngju Ryu, "Introduction," in *Cultures of Yusin: South Korea in the 1970s*, ed. Youngju Ryu (Ann Arbor: University of Michigan Press, 2018), 8.
31 Cho Chae-hwi, "Ha Kil-jong's Genius Cut by Censorship" [Kŏmyŏl ae challyŏnagan Ha Kil-jong ŭi ch'ŏnjaesŏng], *Han'guk Ilbo*, May 18, 2019. https://www.hankookilbo.com/News/Read/201905152045770332.
32 Chŏng Chong-hwa, "*The March of Fools* and Censorship, or How to Appreciate This Film," *The March of Fools* Blu-ray booklet.
33 Cho Jun-hyoung, "The Life and Films of Director Ha Kil-jong," *The March of Fools* Blu-ray booklet.
34 Chŏng, "*March of Fools* and Censorship."
35 Minister, Ministry of Culture and Public Information (MCPI) to President Pak Chong-ch'an, Hwachŏn Trading, "*The March of Fools* Screenplay Revision Notice" [Pabudŭl ŭi haengjin taebon kaejakt'ongbo], *The March of Fools*, MCPI files, KOFA.
36 Kim Sun-gil, MCPI to Pak, Hwachŏn Trading, "*The March of Fools* Screenplay Revision Notice" [Pabudŭl ŭi haengjin taebon kaejakt'ongbo], May 13, 1975, MCPI files, KOFA.
37 Ch'oe In-ho, Censorship review scenario, *The March of Fools*, KOFA Scenario Collections, 2.
38 Thomas Doherty, "Appendix: The Production Code," in *Hollywood's Censor: Joseph I. Breen and the Production Code Administration* (New York: Columbia University Press, 2007), 353. Emphasis in original.
39 Hwang Ŭn-ju, "Long Hair Control" [Changbal tansok], *The Republic of Korea through Archival Documents* [Kirokŭro mannanŭn Taehanming'uk], National Archives of Korea, https://theme.archives.go.kr/next/koreaOfRecord/Long-term.do.
40 Dating back to the 1930s under Japanese colonial rule, trot is a popular Korean music genre that intermixes traditional Korean music elements with transnational influences of American blues and Japanese *enka*.
41 Han Sang Kim, "*The March of Fools* (1975): The Resistant Spirit and Its Limits," in *Rediscovering Korean Cinema*, ed. Sangjoon Lee (Ann Arbor: University of Michigan Press, 2019), 202.
42 "Motion Picture Censorship Regulations Detailed" [Yŏnghwa kŏmyŏlgyujŏng kuch'ehwa], *JoongAng Daily* [*Chungang Ilbo*], March 14, 1973, 8. An earlier version of this rule, proclaimed in July 1963, states that an exhibition permit might be denied or made conditional on the elimination of "ridiculing or mocking of just law enforcement" with the exception of "unavoidable cases essential to motion picture

drama." It is notable that the exception wording is eliminated in the 1973 revision. For the entire text of the 1963 Motion Picture Censorship Rules, see https://www.law.go.kr/법령/영화법시행규칙/(00012,19630708).

43 Doherty, "Appendix: The Production Code," 352.
44 Ch'oe In-ho, Original scenario, *The March of Fools*, KOFA Scenario Collections, Na 3–7.
45 Chŏng, "*March of Fools* and Censorship."
46 "Motion Picture Censorship Regulations Detailed."
47 Doherty, "Appendix: The Production Code," 355.
48 Kang Sŏng-ryul, *Ha Kil-jong, A Movie Fool Who Marched* [Ha Kil-jong, haengjin hattŏn yŏnghwababo] (Seoul: Irongwa silch'ŏn, 2005), 164.
49 Park Sŏn-yŏng, "Cheerfulness and Vulgarity in Late 1960s Comedy Films" [1960nyŏndae k'omediyŏnghwaŭi 'myŏngryang'gwa 'chŏsok'], in *Film Censorship System in Korean Film History* [Hang'uk yŏnghwayŏksa sok chŏmyŏljedo], ed. Ryu Chae-rim (Seoul: Korean Film Archive), 113.
50 Sergei Eisenstein, *Film Form: Essays in Film Theory*, ed. and trans. Jay Ledya (New York: Harvest/HJB Book, 1977), 49.
51 Ha Kil-jong, "*Yalkae: A Joker in High School, Deep-Rooted Tree*" [Ppuri kipŭn namu], April 1977, reprinted in *Ha Kil-jong*, vol. 2, 215–216.
52 Yu, "Hypernationalization Project," 25.
53 Doherty, *Hollywood's Censor*, 243–244, 248.
54 Yi Hyo-in, *Korean Film History Study 1960–1979* [Hang'uk yŏnghwasagongbu 1960–1979] (Seoul: Korean Film Archive, 2004), 228.
55 Yi Chu-hyŏk, "Korean Movies, Draw Attention to 'Young Audiences'" [Hang'ukyŏnghwa, 'chŏmŭngwangaek' e nunŭl tolryŏra], *Chosŏn Ilbo*, August 3, 1974, 4.
56 Kang Suk-gyŏng, "The Whale and the Censorship in the Films based on Choi In-ho's Novels: Focus on *March of the Fools* and *The Whale Hunting*" [Ch'oe In-ho wonjak yŏnghwae nat'anan koraeŭi ŭimiwa kŏmyŏl yangsan], *Literary Criticism* [Pip'yŏng munhak] 70 (December 2018): 18, 21.
57 Paul Y. Chang, "Explaining Repressive Coverage in South Korea's Human Rights and Democracy Movement (1970–1979)," *Korean Sociology Association Articles* [Sahoedaehak nonmunjip] (December 2010): 83.
58 Presidential Emergency Decree Number 9 [Taet'ongryŏng kingŭp choch'i 9ho], May 13, 1975, *National Institute of Korean History* [Kuksap'yŏnch'an wiwonhoe], http://contents.history.go.kr/front/hm/view.do?treeId=010801&levelId=hm_150_0100
59 Song A-rŭm, "A Study on the Dynamics of Korean Film Censorship and Cultural Politics in the 1970s" [1970nyŏndae Han'gukyŏnghwa kŏmyŏlŭi yŏkhakgwa munhwajŏngch'i] (PhD dissertation., Seoul National University, 2019), 216.
60 Ku Hŭi-ryŏng, "90 Percent of Both College Students and Corporate Employees Say 'Hell Joseon Is Correct'" [Taehaksaengdo chikjangindo 90%-ga "heljosŏn matda"], *Chungang Ilbo*, July 1, 2016, https://news.joins.com/article/20249142.
61 Won Kim, "The Race to Appropriate 'Koreanness': National Restoration, Internal Development, and Traces of Popular Culture," in *Cultures of Yusin*, 38–39. Emphasis in original.
62 Cho Chun-hyŏng, "An Exploratory Study of the History of Korean Film Censorship" [Han'guk yŏnghwakŏmyŏlsa ŭi myŏtgaji chuje e taehan sironjŏk yŏngu], *Journal of Korean Drama and Theatre* [Han'guk kŭkyesul yŏngu], no. 59 (2018): 52–53.

63 Cho, "Exploratory Study," 74.
64 Kim Ki-rim, "Sun's Custom" (1939), transl. Jack Saebyok Jung, Asian American Writers' Workshop, https://aaww.org/march-first-korean-translations.

Chapter 5   Censors as Audiences and Vice Versa

1. Yu Min-yŏng, Yi Myŏng-wŏn, and Ko Myŏng-sik, "Braking Imagination and Advocating Moral Views and National Interests" [Sangsangryŏkae chedongdo kŏlgo yulligwangwa kukgaiikongho]" *Ethics for Performing Arts [Kongyŏnyulli]*, no. 5 (January 15, 1977): 2.
2. Between 1976 and 1997, nine cohorts of ethics committees (ten to twenty members each) were constituted and members were appointed by the Ministry of Culture and Public Information (and its successors). The service term was three years (until 1994 when it was shortened to two years) but some members (both ethics and review committees) served for multiple terms either consecutively or nonconsecutively. In 1982, the Public Performance Ethics Committee (PPEC) added the video review committee and in 1986, the advertising review committee.
3. Ho Hyŏn-ch'an, "Comments on Self-Reflection and Self-Consolation" [Chasŏnggwa chawiŭi pyŏn], *Ethics for Performing Arts [Kongyŏnyulli]*, no. 9 (January 15, 1977): 4.
4. Kim Kap-ŭi, "Censors Are the First Objective Audiences" [Simŭiwiwŏnŭn ch'oech'ŏŭi kwangaek], *Ethics for Performing Arts [Kongyŏnyulli]*, no. 66 (February 15, 1982): 3.
5. Son Ki-sang, "Wishing for a Film That Makes Me Forget about Regulation" [Simŭirŭl itgaehanŭn yŏnghwaŭi paraem], *Ethics for Performing Arts [Kongyŏnyulli]*, no. 70 (June 15, 1982): 2.
6. Matthew Burn, "Reimagining Repression: New Censorship Theory and After," *History and Theory*, no. 54 (February 2015): 26. See also Richard Burt, ed., *The Administration of Aesthetics: Censorship, Political Criticism, and the Public Sphere* (Minneapolis: University of Minnesota Press, 1994); Laura Gilbert, *Better Left Unsaid: Victorian Novels, Hays Code Films, and the Benefits of Censorship* (Stanford, CA: Stanford University Press, 2013); Sue Currey Jansen, *Censorship: The Knot That Binds Power and Knowledge* (New York: Oxford University Press, 1988); Annette Kuhn, *Cinema, Censorship and Sexuality, 1909–1925* (London: Routledge, 1988); and Annabel Patterson, *Censorship and Interpretation: The Conditions of Writing and Reading in Early Modern England* (Madison: University of Wisconsin Press, 1984).
7. Burn, "Reimagining Repression," 43–44.
8. Dominic Boyer, "Censorship as a Vocation: The Institutions, Practices, and Cultural Logic of the German Democratic Republic," *Comparative Study in Society and History* 45, no. 3 (July 2003): 512.
9. Boyer, "Censorship as a Vocation," 515.
10. Son Se-il, "Censorship for the Purpose of Abolishing the Censorship System" [Kŏmyŏljedo p'yejirŭlwihan kŏmyŏl], *Ethics for Performing Arts [Kongyŏnyulli]*, no. 35, July 15, 1979: 4.
11. Son, "Abolishing the Censorship System."
12. Chairperson, PPEC to Minister, MCPI, "Report Regarding Results of the 6th Censorship Regulation Re-review" [Che6ch'a kyŏmyŏlsimŭi chesim kyŏlgwa t'ongbo], June 25, 1979, *You Are a Woman, I Am a Man*, MCPI film censorship files, Korean Film Archive (KOFA), Seoul.
13. Yun-Jong Lee, "Cinema of Retreat: Examining South Korean Erotic Films of the 1980s" (PhD. dissertation, University of California, Irvine, 2012), 39–40.

14 There are a couple of dissenting accounts countering this widely accepted wisdom in previous scholarship. Yun-Jong Lee argues, "Despising *Madame Aema* and its follow up *ero yŏnghwa* productions as the result of the 3S Policy is analogous to disrespecting South Korean spectators as mere puppets of the military regime, not the subject of South Korean democracy." Lee, "Cinema of Retreat," 46. Cho Jun-hyoung, on the other hand, states, "The surge of erotic films during Chun Doo Hwan's regime cannot simply be seen as the result of the government's strategic decisions. With the advent of mass society, the audience became visible. No matter how tenuously, this discovery of the audience steered the film industry towards acknowledging the audience's desires.... As foreign film imports and the domestic distribution of foreign film companies became more liberalized, it became difficult to maintain the former system in seeing the inevitable gap between domestic and foreign films. Perhaps, then, the steady liberalization of sexuality on-screen in the 1980s was the overdetermined product of these kinds of complex historical movements." Cho, "Changes in the Perception of Censorship and Films in the Late 1970s: The Discovery of Film Audiences as Consumers and Film as Popular Culture," unpublished conference paper delivered on Zoom for the Berkeley Korean Film Workshop, August 9, 2021.
15 Son, "Abolishing the Censorship System," 4.
16 Minster, MPCI to Ch'oe Ch'un-gi, Yŏnbang Films, "Reply on Feature Film Production Application" [Kŭkyŏnghwa chejaksingoe taehan hoesin], October 14, 1981, *Madame Aema*, MCPI files, KOFA. Ho's handwritten review (dated October 5), along with the ministry's summarized, typed version (without the reviewer's name), is filed with this memorandum, although it is not clear if the former was forwarded to the production company.
17 In the aforementioned review, Ho objects to *Madame Aema*'s title for its phonetic evocation of the notorious French soft-porn exotica film *Emmanuelle* (1974), which was banned in South Korea until 1994 when it was belatedly released.
18 "The Development of Autonomous, Creative National Culture" [Chajuch'angjojŏk minjokmunhwagebal], *Maeil Kyŏngje*, June 23, 1981, 1.
19 Pak Kwang-mu, *Korean Cultural Policy* [Hang'uk munhwajŏngch'iron] (Seoul: Kimyŏngsa, 2010), 140–143.
20 Security Bureau Chief, MoI to Minister, MCPI, "Report on Film Adaptation of a Seditious Book" [Pulonsŏjŏk yŏnghwajejak t'ongbo], September 3, 1981, *A Little Ball Launched by a Dwarf*, MCPI files, KOFA.
21 Quoted in Ch'oe Kang-min, "A Comparative Study on the Aspects of Narrative Transfiguration in *A Little Ball Launched by a Dwarf*" [Nanjangiga ssoaollin chakŭn kong ŭi sŏsabyŏnyong yangsang], *Theory and Criticism of Korean Literature* [Hang'ukmunhak irongwa pip'yŏng] 11, no. 3 (2007): 1.
22 Pae Su-gyŏng, *2017 Korean Film Oral History Research Series: Yi Wŏn-se* [2017nyŏn Han'gukyŏnghwa kusulch'aeokyŏngu sirijŭ Yi Wŏn-se] (Seoul: Korean Film Archive, 2017), 156–157.
23 Thomas Doherty, *Hollywood's Censor: Joseph I. Breen and the Production Code Administration* (New York: Columbia University Press, 2007), 109.
24 Boyer, "Censorship as a Vocation," 512.
25 Hong P'a, *A Little Ball Launched by a Dwarf*, Original scenario, KOFA Scenario Collections, 2; Censorship review scenario, KOFA Scenario Collections, 36.
26 Cho Se-hŭi, *The Dwarf*, trans. Bruce and Ju-Chan Fulton (Honolulu: University of Hawaii Press, 2007), 57.
27 Ho Hyŏn-ch'an, "Scenario Review Opinion" [Sinario simŭi ŭigyŏnsŏ], n.d., *A Little Ball Launched by a Dwarf*, MCPI files, KOFA.

28 Ryu Kyŏng-dong, "A Study on Cho Se-hŭi's *A Little Ball Launched by a Dwarf*" [Cho Se-hŭi ŭi *Nanjangiga ssoaollin chakŭn kong* yŏngu], *Wonkwang Journal of Humanities* [*Yŏllin sesang inmunhak yŏngu*] 14, no. 2 (2013): 108.
29 Cho, *The Dwarf*, 141–142.
30 Cho, *The Dwarf*, 47.
31 Hong, *A Little Ball*, Original scenario, 2.
32 Minster, MPCI to Han Kap-jin, Hanjin Enterprises, "Report of Voluntary Revisions" [Chajin chaejaksingo], August 4, 1981, *A Little Ball Launched by a Dwarf*, MCPI files, KOFA.
33 Pae, *Yi Wŏn-se*, 31.
34 Pae, *Yi Wŏn-se*, 189–190.
35 Pae, *Yi Wŏn-se*, 191.
36 Ho Hyŏn-ch'an, "Scenario Review Opinion" [Sinario simŭi ŭigyŏnsŏ], August 29, 1981, *A Little Ball Launched by a Dwarf*, MCPI files, KOFA.
37 Song Yŏng-mun, Agency for National Security Planning (ANSP) to Im Kwang-su, MCPI Art Division, "Review Opinion for Scenario *A Little Ball Launched by a Dwarf*" [Sinario *Nanjangiga ssoaollin chakŭn kong* kŏmt'o ŭigyŏn], *A Little Ball Launched by a Dwarf*, MCPI files, KOFA.
38 Pae, *Yi Wŏn-se*, 191, 193.
39 Minster, MPCI to Han Kap-jin, "Notice of Attention Items for Feature Film Production Application" [Kŭkyŏnghwa chejaksingoe taehan yuŭisahwang t'ongbo], September 17, 1981, *A Little Ball Launched by a Dwarf*, MCPI files, KOFA.
40 Michael Holoquist, "Corrupt Originals: The Paradox of Censorship," *PMLA* 109, no. 1 (January 1994): 16.
41 Ch'oe, "Comparative Study," 7.
42 In an earlier revised scenario (that the KOFA collected from Hanjin on September 23, 1992), the ending is more hopeful: "Yŏng-ho is carrying the dwarf on his back with Yŏng-su assisting. Yŏng-ho is in the lead followed by the mother and Yŏng-hŭi. They will live together happily under the same roof like old times. The morning sun is rising in the distant mountains against end music." Hong P'a, *A Little Ball Launched by a Dwarf*, Censorship scenario, p. Ka-50, KOFA Scenario Collections.
43 Ch'oe, "Comparative Study," 6–7.
44 Holoquist, "Corrupt Originals," 14.
45 Pae, *Yi Wŏn-se*, 193–194.
46 Ho Hyŏn-ch'an, *Korean Film 100 Years* [*Hang'ukyŏnghwa 100nyŏn*] (Seoul: Munhaksasangsa, 2000), 224.
47 Ho, *Korean Film 100 Years*, 229.
48 "Below Human Rights" [Ingwŏniha], *Tonga Ilbo*, July 18, 1974, 8.
49 "A Female Conductress Attempts Suicide in Protest against a Body Search for Stolen Fares" [Ppingttangch'ugung momsusaek hangŭi yŏch'ajang halbokjasal kido], *Chosŏn Ilbo*, January 7, 1976, 7.
50 "A Bus Guide Poisons Herself in Protest against Naked Body Searches for Theft Preventions" [Ppingttangbangji almomsusaeke hangŭi annaeyang ŭmdokjasal], *Kyŏnghyang Sinmun*, October 20, 1978, 7.
51 Kim Su-yong, *My Love Cinema* [*Naŭi sarang cinema*] (Seoul: Cine21, 2005), 219, 221.
52 Song A-rŭm, "Censorship as Social Permission, Non-Compliance of Unexpected Voices" [Sahoejŏk sŭnginŭrosŏŭi kyomyŏl, tolch'uldoen moksori dŭlŭi pulŭng], in *The Censorship System inside Korean Film History* (*Han'guk yŏnghwa sok kŏmyŏl chedo*), ed. Ryu Chae-rim (Seoul: Korean Film Archive, 2016), 215.

53 Yi Chung-sik, "*The Maiden Goes to the City* Abandoned by Real Protagonists" [Chinjja chuingongae pŏrimbatŭn *Tosiro kan chŏnyŏ*], *Chosŏn Ilbo*, December 11, 1981, 12.
54 Chŏng Han-jun, KFTU to Minister, MPCI, "Request for Prohibition of Film Exhibition" [Yŏnghwasangyŏng kŭmjiyoch'ŏng], December 9, 1981, *The Maiden Who Went to the City* (hereafter *The Maiden*), MCPI files, KOFA.
55 Minister of Labor to Minister, MPCI, "Request for Urgent Cooperation" (Kingŭphyŏpjo yoch'ŏng), December 10, 1981, MCPI files, KOFA.
56 "*The Maiden Who Went to the City* Goes to Storage" [Ch'anggoro kan *Tosiro kan chŏnyŏ*], *Tonga Ilbo*, December 10, 1981, 12.
57 Kim Yang-sam, "*The Maiden Who Went to the City*, an Enlightenment Film" [*Tosiro kan chŏnyŏ* kyedosŏng innŭn yŏnghwa], *Kyŏnghyang Sinmun*, December 15, 1981, 12.
58 Ho, *Korean Films 100 Years*, 222.
59 Yi, "Abandoned by Real Protagonists."
60 Minister, MPCI, to Yim Wŏn-sik, T'aech'ang Entertainment, "Production Registration for *The Maiden Who Goes to the City*" [*Tosiro kan chŏnyŏ* chejaksingo], February 2, 1981, *The Maiden*, MCPI files, KOFA.
61 PPEC to Minister, MPCI, "Report on the Results of Film Censorship Regulation" [Yŏnghwa kyŏmryŏlsimŭi kyŏlgwabogo], June 24, 1981, MCPI files, KOFA.
62 KFTU to MPCI, "Notification of Preview Outcome for *The Maiden*" [*Tosiro kan chŏnyŏ* sisa kyŏlgwa t'ongbo], February 20, 1982, *The Maiden*, MCPI files, KOFA.
63 Undated MPCI internal memo, "Reissue Request for Censorship Permit for Feature Film *The Maiden*" [Kŭkyŏnghwa *Tosiro kan chŏnyŏ* kyŏmryŏlhapkyŏkjŭng chaebalgŭp yoch'ŏng], *The Maiden*, MCPI files, KOFA.
64 Song, "Censorship as Social Permission," 247–248.
65 Ellen C. Scott, "Black 'Censor,' White Liberties: Civil Rights and Illinois's 1917 Film Law," *American Quarterly* 64, no. 2 (June 2012): 219.
66 Benjamin Balthaser, "Cold War Re-Visions: Representation and Resistance in the Unseen Salt of the Earth," *American Quarterly* 60, no. 2 (June 2008): 369.
67 Balthaser, "Cold War Re-Visions," 350.
68 Balthaser, "Cold War Re-Visions," 368.
69 Balthaser, "Cold War Re-Visions," 369.

Chapter 6   Beyond Oral Histories and Trade Legends

1 Cho Jun-hyoung, "Introduction" (Sŏmun), in *The Censorship System inside Korean Film History* [Han'guk yŏnghwa sok kŏmyŏl chedo], ed. Ryu Chae-rim (Seoul: Korean Film Archive, 2016), 11–12.
2 Cho Jun-hyoung, "An Exploratory Study of the History of Korean Film Censorship" [Han'guk yŏnghwakŏmyŏlsa ŭi myŏtgaji chuje e taehan sironjŏk yŏngu], *Journal of Korean Drama and Theatre* [Han'guk kŭkyesul yŏngu], no. 59 (2018): 83.
3 Nora Gilbert, *Better Left Unsaid: Victorian Novels, Hays Code Films, and the Benefits of Censorship* (Stanford, CA: Stanford University Press, 2013), 1.
4 Gilbert, *Better Left Unsaid*, 1.
5 Michel Foucault, *The History of Sexuality*, vol. 1: *An Introduction* (New York: Vintage Books, 1990), 92.
6 Foucault, *History of Sexuality*, 95, 45.
7 Pae Su-gyŏng, *2015 Korean Film Oral History Research Series: Coproduction Films 2* [2015nyŏn Han'gukyŏnghwa kusulch'aeokyŏngu sirijŭ Hapjakyŏnghwa 2] (Seoul: Korean Film Archive, 2015), 156–157.

8. Gilbert, *Better Left Unsaid*, 4.
9. Pae, *2015 Korean Film*, 137.
10. Cho, "Exploratory Study," 76.
11. Pierre Bourdieu, *Language and Symbolic Power*, ed. and introduced by John B. Thompson (Cambridge: Polity Press, 1991), 19. Emphasis in the original.
12. Matthew Burn, "Reimagining Repression: New Censorship Theory and After," *History and Theory*, no. 54 (February 2015): 38.
13. Burn, "Reimagining Repression," 38.
14. Bruce Cumings, *Korea's Place in the Sun: A Modern History*, updated ed. (New York: W. W. Norton, 2005), 385
15. Titled "Toward a Study on History of Korean Film Censorship," this Korean-language paper was published two years later as Cho, "Exploratory Study."
16. "Yi Tu-yong's *Last Witness* Rediscovered by Director O Sŭng-uk" [O Sŭng-uk kamdok e chaebalgyŏnhan Yi Tu-yong ŭi *Ch'oeju ŭi chŭngin*], *Cinematheque de M. Hulot*, http://cinematheque.tistory.com/36.
17. "Yi Tu-yong's *Last Witness*."
18. Kim P'o-hyang, "Genre Problem Solver Yi Du-yong, 'I Want to Be a Lifelong Filmmaker'" [Changrŭ ŭi haegyŏlsa Yi Du-yong 'P'yŏngsaeng yŏnghwain ŭro salgo sipda'], *Han'guk Ilbo*, October 12, 2016, http://www.hankookilbo.com/v/3aa02f42d1b14231a7552ff4d9f640dd.
19. "Brief History as for the *Last Witness*," liner notes, *The Last Witness* DVD (Seoul: Taewon Entertainment, 2008).
20. "A Comprehensive Report on Film Censorship" [Yŏnghwa kŏmyŏl chonghap ŭigyŏnsŏ], September 16, 1980, *The Last Witness*, Ministry of Culture and Public Information (MCPI) film censorship files, Korean Film Archive (KOFA), Seoul.
21. Leonard J. Leff and Jerold L. Simmons, "Appendix: The Motion Picture Production Code," in *The Dame in the Kimono: Hollywood, Censorship, and the Production Code*, rev. ed., (Lexington: University of Kentucky Press, 2001), 297.
22. Motion Picture Producers Association of Korea, *Korean Cinema '68* (Seoul: Motion Picture Producers Association of Korea, 1968). Film censorship guidelines were introduced in the first Motion Picture Law of 1962 and revised in 1966, 1970, and 1974. For other provisions of objectionable film content, see Hye Seung Chung and David Scott Diffrient, *Movie Migrations: Transnational Genre Flows and South Korean Cinema* (New Brunswick, NJ: Rutgers University Press, 2015), 85–86.
23. Yun Sam-ryuk, Original scenario, *The Last Witness*, KOFA Scenario Collections, p. An-54.
24. Yun, Censorship scenario, KOFA Scenario Collections, p. Inna-1.
25. Minister, MCPI to Chairperson, Public Performance Ethics Committee, "A Request for Film Re-censorship" [Yŏnghwa kŏmyŏl chaeŭroe], November 6, 1980, *The Last Witness*, MCPI files, KOFA.
26. "A Comprehensive Report on Film Censorship" [Yŏnghwa kŏmyŏl chonghap ŭigyŏnsŏ], November 12, 1980, MCPI files, KOFA.
27. Cho, "Exploratory Study," 59–60.
28. Cho, "Exploratory Study," 60.
29. Burn, "Reimagining Repression," 32.
30. Kim See-mu, *Lee Jang-ho* (Seoul: Korean Film Council, 2009), 90.
31. Yi Chang-ho, "*Declaration of Fools*, A Film Made by an Age of Dictatorship" [Tokjae sidaega mandŭn yŏnghwa], *Cine21*, February 22, 2000. http://www.cine21.com/news/view/?mag_id=32064.

32 Minister, MCPI to Pak Chong-ch'an, Hwach'ŏn Trading, "Reply for Feature Film Production Registration" [Kŭk yŏnghwa chejak singoe daehan hoesin], April 4, 1983, *Declaration of Fools*, MCPI files, KOFA.
33 Motion Picture Promotion Corporation to MCPI, June 30, 1983, *Declaration of Fools*, MCPI files, KOFA.
34 Pak to Minister, MPCI, June 29, 1983, *Declaration of Fools*, MCPI files, KOFA,
35 Minister, MPCI to Pak, July 6, 1983, MCPI files, KOFA. The line can be roughly translated as "Don't forget that a female college student's mind and body are separate like beef bone soup with rice on the side [*ttarogukbap*]."
36 Thomas Doherty, *Pre-Code Hollywood: Sex, Immorality, and Insurrection in American Cinema 1930–1934* (New York: Columbia University Press, 1999). 6.
37 Jang Sun-woo, *Cinema on the Road* (London: British Film Institute, 1995), Video.
38 Yi, *"Declaration of Fools."*
39 Hyangjin Lee, *"Declaration of Idiot* [1983]: Cinema of Censorship and an Accidental Masterpiece," in *Rediscovering Korean Cinema*, ed. Sangjoon Lee (Ann Arbor: University of Michigan Press, 2019), 223, 229.

Epilogue

1 Constitution of Republic of Korea, amended October 29, 1987, enforced February 25, 1988, https://www.law.go.kr/LSW/lsInfoP.do?lsiSeq=61603&viewCls=engLsInfoR&urlMode=engLsInfoR#0000.
2 Ho Hyŏn-ch'an, *Korean Film 100 Years* [*Han'guk yŏnghwa 100-nyŏn*] (Seoul: Munhaksasangsa, 2000), 285.
3 Ra Che-gi, "K-Culture Began with Abolishment of Censorship in 1996" [K K'ŏlch'ŏnŭn 1996nyŏn sajŏn simŭi p'yejiesŬ sijaktwaetta], *Hang'uk Ilbo*, May 15, 2021, https://www.hankookilbo.com/News/Read/A2021051415330005352.
4 Kevin S. Sandler, *Naked Truth: Why Hollywood Doesn't Make X-Rated Movies* (New Brunswick, NJ: Rutgers University Press, 2007), 4.
5 Sandler, *Naked Truth*, 43.
6 R accounted for 57.7 percent or 17,202 of all rated films; PG (formerly M or GP) for 18.7 percent or 5,578 films; PG-13 for 16.5 percent or 4,913 films; and G for was 5.5 percent or 1,574 films. See Motion Picture Association of America, *G Is for Golden: The MPAA Film Ratings at 50* (Los Angeles: Motion Picture Association of America, 2018), 40, https://www.motionpictures.org/research-docs/g-is-for-golden-the-mpaa-film-ratings-at-50/.
7 Motion Picture Promotion Law (Yŏnghwachinhŭngbŏp), October 11, 1997, https://www.law.go.kr/LSW/lsInfoP.do?lsiSeq=2641#0000.
8 Pak Hye-yŏng, *2012 Korean Film Oral History Series: Kim Su-yong* (Seoul: Korean Film Archive, 2012), 430–431.
9 Kim recalled that Park took his classes when he was lecturing at Chungang University as a special professor in the early 1990s. Pak, *Kim Su-yong*, 431.
10 An uncut version had been sent to the 2001 Venice International Film Festival as an official entry.
11 An Chŏng-suk, "But Censorship Continues" [Hajiman kŏyŏlŭn kaesoktoenda], *Hankyŏreh Sinmun*, December 31, 1999, 23.
12 Similar to the NC-17 rating in the United States, "Restricted Screening" films are not allowed to be promoted and advertised publicly, further killing any commercial prospects for such "ghost" rating products.

13 The KMRB does not provide the breakdown of rerating data, so these stats are presumed to include multiple counts of the films resubmitted for rerating reviews. See "Ratings Classification Stats" [Tŭnggŭppullyu t'onggae], Korea Media Rating Board, https://www.kmrb.or.kr/kor/CMS/gradeStat/gradeStatView.do?type=movie&mCode=MN099.
14 I thank Kim Hong-jun, a filmmaker and professor emeritus, for sharing this insight with me in a personal conversation at Lingnan University, Hong Kong, on November 3, 2023.
15 Yi Sang-su, "BIFF to Hold a Retrospective for KMRB Chairman Kim Su-yong" [Pusan kukcheyŏnghwaje kamdok hoegojŏn yŏnŭn Kim Su-yong Yŏsangmultŭnggŭp wiwŏnjang], *Hankyŏreh Sinmun*, November 5, 2002, https://www.hani.co.kr/arti/legacy/legacy_general/L38666.html.
16 Heather Hendershot, *Saturday Morning Censors: Television Regulation before the V-Chip* (Durham, NC: Duke University Press, 1998), 93–94.

Index

Academy of Motion Picture Arts and Sciences (AMPAS), 52
Academy Theater, 65, 94, 102
Accusation (film, 1967), 13, 85–87, 101, 103–104; analysis of the opening scene, 105–106; departure from the original script, 108–109; documentary and newsreel footage in, 105, 107–109; feminist perspective, 111; Grand Bell Award wins, 110; lovemaking scenes, 108, 113; melodramatic farewell scene, 107–109; Ministry of Public Information's regulatory feedback, 108; mirroring between North and South Korea, 111–112; purge scenes, 106–107, 109; sympathetic portrayals of North Koreans, 109, 111–113; voiceover narration, 105, 109
Ahn, Junghyo, 48
Altman, Robert, 131
An, Sŏng-gi, 148
An, So-yŏng, 144
anticommunism, 82–84, 90, 94, 112, 114, 121, 137, 164; as state policy, 20, 32, 86, 114–115
anticommunist film, 4, 13, 23–24, 207n14; 1960s Korea (war spectacles), 80, 85; 1970s Korea (espionage action), 74, 85; *Accusation* as, 105, 108, 111; defense of *Seven Female Prisoners* as, 115; Grand Bell Awards for, 84–85; in Hollywood, 83, 94–95; as institutional genre, 83, 86;

The Martyred as, 90–92; paradox of, 111–112; as parasitic genre, 83; rescue narrative formula, 96–97, 208n39; as umbrella genre, 83–84; vanishment in the 1980s, 85. See also *Accusation*; *Martyred, The* (film)
Arirang (film), 44, 207n18
Art and Culture Ethics Committee, (ACEC), 10, 28, 140
Asian Film Festival, 42–43
Association for Film Critics of Korea, 159
auteur, 31, 49, 98, 122–124, 130; avoidance/ pitfalls of auteurism, 15, 112, 124; Golden Age auteur, xiii, 2, 4, 82, 115, 166, 186
Avalon, Frankie, 122

Back Street (film), 43
Bad Day at Black Rock (film), 52
Bamboo Prison, The (film), 83, 95
Barbarian and the Geisha, The (film), 73
Beat Girl (film), 26–28, 31, 63
Ben Hur (film), 43
Bergman, Ingrid, 55, 123–124
Berlin International Film Festival, 17, 34
Berman, Pandro S., 52, 58
Biberman, Herbert, 164–165, *165*
Bicycle Thieves (film), 38
Binford, Lloyd T., 55; "binfordizing", 56
biopic, 13, 58, 86, 103
Birth of a Nation, The (film), 164

Blackboard Jungle (film), 8, 12, 46, 49–51; anti-censorship campaign for overseas exhibitors, 57, 200n50; box-office record of, 53, 200n29; British Board of Film Censorship's reaction to, 59–60, 201nn62–66; Canadian reception of, 60, *61;* controversies in South Korea, 49, 62–63; Crowther's *New York Times* review and responses, 56–57; departure from MGM style, 52, 201n63; happy ending, 69; insertion of an apologetic foreword, 58, 60; Japanese reception of, 60; Korean censors' view on, 61–64; Luce's lobbying against, 58; Ministry of Public Information's role in unbanning, 64–65, 70, 197n48; municipal censorship of, 55–56; parallels between Dadier and Park, 67–69; Pennsylvania State Board of Censors' reaction to, 55; Production Code Administration's internal regulation, 53–55; production history of, 52–53; reunion panel, 52–53, 201n54; Schary's defense of, 52–53, 56–59, 64, 201n52, 201n258, 202n64; Stark's letter to Brooks about, 60; studio publicity of, 54; teen reception of, 51, 56, 60, *61;* Zanuck's disapproval of, 58, 59, 201n58

Black Gloves (film), 74

B movie, 36, 85

Bond, James, 85

Bong, Joon-ho (Pong Chun-ho), 2, 4, 112

Bourdieu, Pierre, 14, 141, 168, 170, 176–177

Boys Town (film), 52

Brando, Marlon, 70–71, 79

Breaking the Wall (film), 84

Breathless (film), 3

Bridge on the River Kwai, The (film), 43, 75, 78

Brooks, Richard, 8, 12, 49, 52–53, 58, 60, 64, 199n23

Brown v. Board of Education, 56

camera angle: aerial extreme shot, 152; bird's-eye-view, 34, *35;* high-angle, 36; low-angle, 91, 132; side angle, 169; tilted, 174

camera movement: crane, 34; dollies, 36, 91, 105; track, 91–92, 126; zooms, 126, 129, 174

Camus, Albert, 88, 92, 99

Cannes International Film Festival, 2, 189

Cassavetes, John, 124

Castle, William, 122

censor, 53, 55–56, 69, 102, 147, 168; as absence of morality, 147; activist group as, 98, 164–165; as audience, 13–14, 140–141; cultural bias against, 4, 155, 167; duped or mocked, 14, 178; as intellectual vocation, 142, 147; relationship with the artist, 114, 168–169; as "smart people", 146, 153, 155; state, 3–5, 12, 14, 49, 55, 61, 64, 131, 137, 148, 167, 170; union as, 155, 158–165. *See also* censorship

censorship, 17, 80, 98, 139–142, 154, 164, 168–170, 178; analogy to sonnets, 7, 9; anti-, 2, 55, 186; audience boycotts as, 98–99, 112; as audience feedback or critical spectatorship, 13–14, 140–141, 143; competing, 98–99, 189; condemnations of, 1–3, 142, 147, 168; counter-, 163; as defender of public interests, 22, 81, 103, 125, 139; as dialogical process, 12, 17, 38, 98, 101; discursive pleasure of, 14, 168–169, 183; as enabler of resistance, 165, 168–170; as euphemization, 14, 170, 177; federal, 83, 161; fostering dialogue, 44, 101, 176; from artists' perspective, 112, 114; good, 164; Hitchcock's view of, 147; as ideological control, 11, 141; as intelligence test or game, 146–147; joy of, 169; market, 123, 171–171, 173; party-state, 142; pleasure of evading, 14, 169, 183; political, 5, 14–15, 34, 81, 142, 161; as productive or enabling, 14, 80, 103, 130, 141–142, 147, 168, 182–183, 189; as propaganda, 22–23, 137; as protection of public morality and national interests, 19, 81, 120, 139, 141, 159; relationship with free speech, 1, 55, 99, 178, 189; self-, 4, 6–7, 14, 39, 126, 149, 151, 154, 170, 176, 186, 189; state, 2, 3, 10, 14, 20, 24, 27, 29, 33, 120, 141–142, 147, 155, 189, 194n5; state-private, 10, 142, 171, 185; suppression of bleakness and pessimism, 21, 33–34, 120, 135; as trade legends and myths, 4, 168

Chang, Chŏng-il, 186, *187*

Chang, Hun, 85

Chang, Myŏn, 20, 63, 73

Chang, Tong-hwi, 87

Changsangotmae, 184

Chaplin, Charlie, 55
Cheat, The (film), 164
Chiang, Kai-shek, 18
Children of Dark Streets II (film), 168
China: 1930 Motion Picture Law, 18–19; diplomatic disputes over Hollywood's orientalist images, 18; Nanjing decade, 23; Republic-era film censorship, 16, 18–19; "uplift" objectives in cinema, 18–19
Cho, Jun-hyoung (Cho Chun-hyŏng), 5, 6, 83, 102, 125, 137, 166, 177
Cho, Kŭng-ha, 80
Cho, Se-hŭi, 14, 146
Ch'oe, In-ho, 122, 123
Ch'oe, Mu-ryong, 30, 31
Ch'oe, Pul-am, 171, *172*
Chomsky, Noam, 112
Chŏng, Ch'ang-gŭn, 97
Chŏng, In-yŏp, 144
Chŏng, Yun-hŭi, 171, 174, 175
Chu, Chŭng-nyŏ, 106
Chun, Doo Hwan (Chŏn Tu-hwan), 2, 118, 142, 147, 153, 166, 171, 182; 3S policy, 14, 144–145, 215n14; abolition of the national curfew system, 144; massacres in Kwangju, 14, 143–144, 173–174, 176; New Culture policy, 145
Chungang Theater, 157, 158
Cimarron (film), 46
cinema: commercial view of, 43; European art, 122; national, 12, 14, 16–17, 19, 34, 44, 124, 155; national function of, 43; as personal art, 124; realist, 30, 44; verité, 130, 189
CinemaScope, 79, 95
Citizen Kane (film), 44, 174
Coachman, The (film), 12, 17, 24, 30, 34, *35*; final scene analysis, 36–38; reception in Berlin, 42
Cold War, 15, 53, 59, 72, 78, 84–85, 92–93, 97, 112, 164; allegories, 83; censorship, 33, 120; cosmopolitanism, 42, 48; division, 11; formula, 69; military dictatorships, 2, 10, 120, 137; orientalism, 71; religious interpretation of, 83; screen culture of, 44, 46, 48, 83; three specters of, 50; use of film as capitalistic propaganda, 46, 82, 135
Columbia Pictures, 46, 51, 83, 201n62
comedy, 13, 70–72, 74, 116–117, 125, 131, 133, 135, 136, 169; absurdist, 180; anarchic, 183; black, 178; gender reversal, 143; musical, 42–43; romantic, 111, 194n18; youth, 13, 120, 122
comic book, 50, 51, 97, 180
Comic Code Authority, 51
Cook, David A., 7
Coppola, Francis Ford, 41, 122
Corman, Roger, 122
Costa-Gavras, 124
Crash Landing on You (drama), 86
Crossfire (film), 52
Cross in Gunfire, A (film), 97
Cumings, Bruce, 49, 66, 171
Cummings, Jack, 9, 79

Daiei Motion Picture Company, 79
Dark Age (Korean cinema), 13, 117, 155, 174
Declaration of Fools (a.k.a. *Declaration of Idiot*, film), 8, 14, 168, 178, 179, *181*, 183; allusion to Laurel and Hardy, 180; avant-garde, absurdist elements, 180; Ministry of Culture and Public Information's regulatory feedback, 179–180; original "fake" treatment/script, 178–179; trade legends about the title, 182; Yi Chang-ho's oral history, 182–183
Demilitarized Zone (DMZ), 104–105, 107–108
DeMille, Cecil B., 164
Derrida, Jacques, 1
Descendants of Cain, The (film), 109, 113
De Sica, Vittorio, 38
diegesis, 125; diegetic, 86; extradiegetically, 86; nondiegetic, 34
Disney Studios, 7
division drama, 84
Doherty, Thomas, 6–7, 9, 97, 113, 135, 180, 191
Dream (film), 98
Dulles, John Foster, 58
Durbin, Deanna, 47

editing, 3–4, 25, 127, 142; continuity editing, 103, 126, 133; dialectical montage, 133; elliptical montage, 174; fade out, 132, 133; fast cutting, 54; long take, 36, 188; shot/reverse shot montage, 126; whip pan, 174
Eisenstein, Sergei, 133
Empty Dream (film), *114*, 115, 167
erotic film, 25, 144–145
Evergreen Tree (film), 43

experimental film/techniques, 168; Brechtian direct address, 131; freeze frame, 105; sound bridge, 91, 174
exterior scene, 34, 74

Faces (film), 124
family drama, 151–152
Farewell to Arms, A (film), 43
Federation of Korea Trade Unions (FKTU), 158–159, 162
film noir, 31, 84, 135
Fine Windy Day, A (film), 2
flashback, 90–92, 105, 132–134, 150, *172*, 174
Fleischer, Richard, 80
Ford, Glenn, 12, 45–46, 52–53, 58, *61*, 70, *71*, 79
Ford, John, 49, 133
Ford, Peter, 45
For Whom the Bell Tolls (film), 43
Foucault, Michel, 14, 119, 141, 168, 170, 183
From Here to Eternity (film), 43
Funicello, Annette, 122

Garbo, Greta, 111
Geisha Boy, The (film), 73
General Died at Dawn, The (film), 18
Germany: Berlin, 42, 105; German Democratic Republic (GDR), 142, 147; GDR's Agitation Division, 142; East Germany, 142; Third Reich, 135; West Germany, 105
Godard, Jean-Luc, 3, 124, 131
Godfather, The (film), 133
Golden Age (Hollywood), 7
Golden Age (Korean cinema), 113, 168
Golden Bat, The (film), 3
Gone with the Wind (film), 43
Governor's Daughter, The (film), 80, 81
Graduate, The (film), 129
Grapes of Wrath, The (film), 49, 58
Great Britain, 28, 60, 121
Grevill, Edmond T., 26

Ha, Kil-jong, 13, 41, 44, 117, 120, 122, *123*, 124–126, 133–136, 167, 212n25
Ha, Myŏng-jung, 171, *173*
Hall, Stuart, 124–125, 131, 212n29
Han, Hyŏng-mo, 42, 83, 84, 140, 143
Hand of Fate, The (film), 83
Hanjin Enterprises, 143, 146–147, 151–153; Han Kap-jin, 147, 216n32, 216n39

Hanyang Film Corporation, 78
Hapdong Film, 8, 94, 95, 208n46
Happy Solitude (film), 74, 76, 77, 204n115
Have I Come to Cry? (film), 25
Hayakawa, Sessue, 164
Hayes, Margaret, 53
Heavenly Homecoming to Stars (film), 2, 124
Hell's Flower (film), 30
Hell to Eternity (film), 78
Hendershot, Heather, 98, 99, 189
Henry V (film), 23
Hepburn, Audrey, 48
Herman, Edward S., 112, 210n87
Herron, Frederick H., 18, 195n6
High Noon (film), 83
High School Champ (film), 135
Higson, Andrew, 16
Hill of Immortal Bird, The (film), 97
Hitchcock, Alfred, 147
Ho, Hyŏn-ch'an, 29, 140, 144, 147, 184
Hölderlin, Friedrich, 88, 92
Holiday (film), 117
Hollywood, 8, 17, 22, 34, 35–36, 42, 48, 50–51, 64, 69, 73, 75, 78–79, 94–95, 124, 128, 144, 162, *165*, 205n121; blacklisting, 53, 83, 122, 204n105; block booking, 47; censorship, 6–8, 191; cinema, 14, 47, 49, 80, 135; classical, 6, 113; Film School Generation, 122; genre, 31, 83; happy ending, 43; Hollywood Ten, 164; imports, 11, 77, 122, 195, 196n22; internal censors/regulators, 12, 49, 85, 147; movies, 97; pictures, 113; producers, 121, 161; self-regulatory, 9, 10, 97, 185; star, 45–46; studio, 18, 47, 49, 60, 70, 80, 98, 160–161, 179, 185, 205n126
Hollywood Reporter (trade paper), 121, 211n18
Hong Kong, 58, 85, 104, 191, 220n14
Houseguest and My Mother, The (film), 43
Housemaid, The (film), 24, 44, 63, 125
Hunter, Evan, 52, 57, 64
Hwachŏn Trading, 8, 212nn35–36
Hwang, Chŏng-sun, 34
Hwang, Sun-wŏn, 109
Hyŏn, Kil-su, 171, 172
Hyperbolae of Youth (film), 42, 43

Im, Kwŏn-t'aek, 160
Interrupted Melody (film), 58
Invasion of the Body Snatchers (film), 83

Ishizaka, Yojiro, 74
I Spit on Your Grave (film), 31
It Came from Outer Space (film), 83
I Was a Communist for the FBI (film), 83

Jacobs, Lea, 6
Jang, Sun-woo (Chang Sŏn-u), 180, 186, *187*
Japan, 13, 20, 45, 50, 58, 60, 71, 74, 75–80, 116, 195n22, 203n98, 205n121, 205n135; colonial rule in Korea, 22, 212n40; cultural ban in postcolonial Korea, 72–73, 118; Government General of Korea, 9, 22, 34, 118; Japan Broadcasting Corporation (NHK), 159–160; Nagoya, 76; normalization of diplomacy with the ROK, 73; Okinawa, 12, 70, 74, 77–79; prime minister Ikeda, 74; Tokyo, 45, 57–58, 72, 74, 76
Jarrico, Paul, 164, 165
Jean Valjean (film), 30
Jeonju International Film Festival, 171
Johnson, Lyndon B., 107, 109
Johnston, Eric, 52
Joint Security Area (film), 82
juvenile delinquency, 25, 54–58, 70; B-pictures about, 51; *Daily News* special issue on, 51; Senate Subcommittee on Juvenile Delinquency, 50

Kang, Che-gyu, 82, 85
Kang, Tae-jin, 12, 17, *35*
Katusha (film), 30
Kazan, Elia, 43
Kefauver, Estes, 50
Kelly, Grace, 48
Kennedy, John F., 41–42; Kennedy administration, 40, 74
Kiley, Richard, 53
Kim, Chin-gyu, 29, 31, *37*, 41, 87
Kim, Dae-jung (Kim Tae-jung), 4, 186
Kim, Ki-rim, 119–120, 138
Kim, Ki-yŏng, 4, 44, 74, 76, 166
Kim, Kwang-sŏp, 119
Kim, Richard E., 13, 85, 87, *89*, 101, 207n18, 209n57
Kim, Sŏng-ch'un, 31, 33, 38
Kim, Sŏng-jong, 171
Kim, Sŏng-min, 72, 74
Kim, Sŭng-ho, 34
Kim, Sŭng-ok, 157–159

Kim, Su-yong, 2, 4, *5*, 13–15, 85, 105, 112, 122–123, 140, 143, 156, *157*, 159, 166, 186, 188, 210n79
Kim, T'ae-su, 169
Kim, Ŭng-ch'ŏn, 143
Kim, Yun-jin, 83, 196n34
Kim-Ohira Memorandum, 74–75
Klein, Christina, 42, 46, 48–49, 71
Kobau (film), 63
Korea, North, 13, 28–29, 45, 73, 85, 88, 103, 104–105, 106, 108–109, 111–112, 113, 151, 210n79; Central News Agency, 13, 102–103; defectors from, 13, 86, 104, 108, 110, 210n79; images of, 13, 86, 115, 167, 171; Kaesŏng, 105; Kim Il Sung (Kim Il-sŏng), 86, 107, 108, 109, 110, 209n65; Pyongyang, 87–88, 99, 100, 106, 171, 208n46; Workers' Party of Korea, 103–104
Korea, South, 7, 13, 18, 21, 23, 29, 39, 41, 42, 44, 47, 50, 62, 66, 72, 73, 74, 77, 79, 80, 83, 84, 87, 88, *89*, 91, 95, 97, 98, 100, 106, 109, 110, 113, 114, 117, 119, 120, 121, 124, 131, 132, 136, 137, 140, 160, 162, 167, 168, 170, 179, 180, 183, 185, 188, 189, 195–196n22, 204n105, 205n121, 206n136, 215n14, 215n17; 1986 Asian Games, 145; 1988 Olympics, 145; 1988 peaceful transition of power, 82, 386; American influence in the 1950s, 49; Anticommunist Law, 86, 115, 167; April 19 Revolution of 1960, 10, 24, 27–28, 32, 63, 65; authoritarianism in, 1–2, 20, 168; Constitution, 11, 19, 24, 184–185; decolonization, 76, 79; division, 82, 85; fear of Japanese cultural invasion, 12–13, 50; Fifth Republic, 142, 171; founding of the Republic of Korea (ROK), 9; Generation, 4; as Hell Joseon, 136–137; Hollywoodphilia in, 48; Inch'ŏn, 148, 151; June 3 resistance movement of 1964, 80; Kwangju Uprising of 1980, 118–119; liberation from Japanese rule, 72; military dictatorships, 2, 12, 14, 17, 82–83, 86, 99; *minjung* activism era, 17; National Security Act, 86; normalization of diplomacy with Japan, 12–13, 50, 73; Second Republic, 20, 24, 26, 28, 31, 33, 63, 73; Seoul, 6, 8, 29, *30*, 34, *35*, 39, 43, 45, 46, 48, 76, 90, 94, 101, 104, 105, 107, 108, 111, 112, 118, 122, 127, 145, 156–158; Third Republic, 20; thirty-eighth parallel, 22, 29, 46–47, 90, 151;

Korea, South (cont.)
  transition to civil rule, 4, 10, 119; Truth and Reconciliation Commission, 104; Yŏsu-Sunch'ŏn rebellion, 20
Korea Automobile & Transport Workers' Federation (KATWF), 158–159, 160, 161, 162
Korea Media Rating Board (KMRB), 10, 185–187, *187*, 188, 219, 220n13; Korean Performance Art Promotion Association, 185–186
Korean Broadcasting System (KBS), 140
Korean Central Intelligence Agency (KCIA), 3, 10, 12–13, 33, 38, 40, 63, 65, 70, 74, 82, 94, 101, 103, 108–109, 112–113, 120, 152, 170; Agency for National Security Planning (ANSP), 152–153; fabrications of spy scandals, 104–105, 110, 153; human rights violations, 86, 102, 104, 145–146; involvement in film censorship, 83, 102; Kim Chong-p'il, 74; regulatory view on *A Spotted Man*, 95, 103, 209n64; regulatory view on *Blackboard Jungle*, 63, 64, 65; regulatory view on *The Martyred*, 94–95; regulatory view on *The Stray Bullet*, 43–44
Korean Film Archive (KOFA), 27, 61, 85, 141, 143, 146, 148, 151, 155, 158, 167, 169, 174, 176, 194n13; digital censorship document collections, 3–4, 13, 117, 120; oral history collections, 2, 9, 11, 167, 177, 186; Paju preservation center, 3–4; scenario collections, 9, 152
Korean film censorship, 1–2, 5–6, 8, 9, 12–15, 17, 21, 65, 97, 136, 167, 174, 211n17; 1926 Motion Picture Film Censorship Regulations, 9, 22; 1940 Chosŏn Film Law, 22; 1957 public performance censorship bylaws, 61, 72–73; 1962 Motion Picture Law, 11, 25, 72–73; 1963 amendment to the Motion Picture Law, 78, 213n42; 1966 amendment to the Motion Picture Law, 10; 1997 Motion Picture Promotion Law, 187; affective monitoring, 12, 16; bribe scandal, 169; censorship in the colonial era, 72; collusion between state and industry interests, 11; difference from Hollywood's self-regulation, 185; double censorship system, 21; "encouraged directions of domestic productions", 121; encouragement of cheerful sensibility, 33; exhibition permit system, 9, 23; interagency collaboration, 86; jurisdiction debate in the 1950s, 9–10, 23; *myŏngnanghwa* philosophy, 13, 116–119, 121; "national uplift" policy, 12, 16, 18–19; national views in, 10–11; outlawing of, 63, 185; regarding portrayals of court of law, 19, 176; regarding portrayals of disability, 149–150, 155, 180; regarding portrayals of educators, 19, 25, 62; regarding portrayals of law enforcement, 18, 174, 212, 213n42; regarding portrayals of religion, 18, 19, 93–94, 97–98; regarding portrayals of sexuality or gratuitous sex, 11, 18, 19, 141, 143–144, 168, 215n14; regarding portrayals of *waesaek* (Japanese color), 50, 72–73, 77–78, 80; regarding portrayals of venereal diseases, 126–127; state-directed tonal control, 34; state-private hybrid, 142, 170–171; suppression of dark content, 28–29; US military government's Act 115, 22–24; Yi Nam-gi's oral history, 102, 169
Korean Film Council (KOFIC), 1; Korean Motion Picture Promotion Corporation, 44, 121, 136, 179
Korean Film Producers Association (KFPA), 25, 27, 73, 75–78, 140
Korean Foreign Film Distributors Association (KFFDA), 25, 77–78
Korean National Film Production Center (NFPC), 39, 197n62
Korean War, The, 11, 20, 23, 47, 82–83, 87, *89*, 99, 164, 171, *172*
Kukje Theater, 31, 122
Kŭm, Po-ra, 148, 156
Kurosawa, Akira, 79
Kyō, Machiko, 70, *71*, 79

Lady Chatterley's Lover (film), 25–26, 31
Last Witness, The (film), 5, 14, 167–168, 171–172; contradictory accounts of censorship cuts, 174–176; four scenes requested to be cut from the preview print, 175; reasons for voluntary cuts, 176–178; Yang T'aek-jo's oral history, 174; Yi Tu-yong's oral history, 173–174
Late Autumn (film), 140
Lee, Robert G., 50

Legion of Decency, 97
Lies (film), 186, *187*, 187
lighting, 31, 152; high-contrast, 36; high-key, 133; natural, 34; low-key, 54, 133, 174
literary adaptation, 30, 43, 103, 109
Little Ball Launched by a Dwarf, A (film), 13–14, 143–145, 149, 216n42; analysis of the opening scene, 150–151; auteurist interpretation of the saltern setting, 151–152; climatic demolition scene, 152; cuts made to the preview print, 153; departure from the novella, 150–152, 154; duality as a censored text, 154–155; environmental message, 152; final scene's telepathic voiceover, 154; production history, 146–147; regulatory feedback on portrayals of disability, 149, 153, 155; regulatory feedback on portrayals of "fallen women", 148; regulatory feedback on the union plot, 148; revisions to the original screenplay, 147–148, 151–153; use of music/soundtrack, 152, 154
Little Ball Launched by a Dwarf, A (novella), 147–148, 150–151, 154; comparison to "Deaf Sam-ryong" (short story), 149; critical evaluations, 146; influence on activists and dissidents, 146; modernist narrative structure, 146; symbol of the dwarf, 150
Local 890 of the International Union of Mine, Mill, and Smelter Workers, 164–165
Loew's Incorporated, 57–58
Lord, Father Daniel A., 11, 97
Lovers, The (film), 25–27, 63, 164
Lubitsch, Ernst, 111
Luce, Clare Boothe, 58

MacCann, Richard Dyer, 38, 39, 41
Madame Aema (film), 144, 155, 215n14, 215n17
Madame Freedom (film), 42, 167
Maiden Who Went to the City, The (film), 13, 143, 155, 164–165; accused of violating the human rights of transportation workers, 158–159; changes to the original ending, 162, *163*; controversies about *ppingttang* (petty stealth of cash fares) scenes, 156, *157*, 160–161; Kim Su-yong on, 157–158, 159; Ministry of Culture and Public Information's role in mediating between the producer and the union, 159–162; producer's initial dismissal of bus guides' concerns, 160–161; producer's voluntary withdrawal of the permit, 159; Public Performance Ethics Committee's review report, 161; second round of review for the reapplied permit, 162; union/trade input for the rerelease print, 158, 162–163
Malle, Louis, 25–26, 63, 164
Manchurian Candidate, The (film), 83, 88
Mann, Daniel, 8–9, 12, 49–50, 79, 203n98, 204n99
Manster (film), 73
Man Who Shot Liberty Valance, The (film), 168
March of Fools, The (film), 8, 13, 44, 117, 120–121, 131, 133, 135–138, 167, 212n25; deletions or revisions made to the preview print, 126–131; different prints, 125, 131; Ha Kil-jong on, 122–124; Kim Su-yong on, 122–124; long hair policing scene, 121, 127–128; Ministry of Culture and Public Information's regulatory feedback, 125–126, 128, 129; opening scene of, 126–127; production history, 122, 125; Song Ch'ang-sik's songs in, 127, 129; suicide scene, 129–130; tonal duality in, 117, 132–133, 136
Margaret Herrick Library, 6, 8, 192
Marines, Let's Go (film), 78
Marines Who Never Returned, The (film), 85
Martyred, The (film), 8, 13, 102, 112–114, 164, 208n46; analysis of the ending, 92–93; analysis of the opening scene, 90–91; church protests against, 98–100; communications between Christians and atheists generated by, 100–101; comparison with U.S. regulation of similar subjects, 83; expressions of atheism in, 83, 85, 88, 98; as faithful adaptation, 88–90, 98, 103; Ministry of National Defense's regulatory feedback, 94–97; Ministry of Public Information's regulatory feedback, 85–86, 93–94; point of view shifts in film adaptation, 91; portrayals of communists, 83–84, 87, 90–92; torture montage flashback, 91–92; use of sound/music, 90–91, 92, 126; voiceover narration, 90–91, 105–107, 109

Martyred, The (novel), 87–92, 94, 98, 99, 100–101
M*A*S*H (film), 131
master narrative, 2, 5, 82
media ratings system, 2–3; KMRB ratings, 10, 186, *187*, 219n13; Motion Picture Association of America (MPAA) ratings, 6–7, 9, 12, 49, 51, 52, 54, 60, 126, 185, 188, 219n6
Medium Cool (film), 131
melodrama, 25, 31, 42, 43, 84, 107, 120, 140, 152, 180
Memories of Murder (film), 4
Metro-Goldwyn-Mayer (MGM), 8, 12, 46, 50–51, 59, 60–63, 70–71, 73–79, 83, 201n63, 202n64, 202n66, 203n91; Dore Schary, 52–58, 64, 201n52, 201n58; Louis B. Mayer, 52–53; Nicholas Schenk, 52–53; Robert Vogel, 54, 57
Michi, Kanako, 80
midnight movie, 144
Ministry of Culture and Public Information (MCPI), 3, 80–81, 102, 117, 120, 125–126, 128, 129, 132, 136, 138, 140–147, 151, 152–153, 155, 158–162, 169, 175–180, 182, 214n2
Ministry of Education (MoE), 9, 11, 23, 24–28, 32–34, 43, 61–65, 67, 73, 84, 120, 204n105
Ministry of Justice (MoJ), 24, 27, 33
Ministry of Labor (MoL), 158–159, 162
Ministry of National Defense (MND), 10, 13, 23, 84, 86, 94–97, 101, 103, 120
Ministry of Public Information (MPI), 3, 6–13, 18–19, 21, 23, 27–28, 33, 38–41, 49–50, 61, 63–65, 69–70, 73–78, 80–86, 93–98, 102–103, 108, 112–113, 117–118, 120, 197n48, 197n61, 206n136
Ministry of the Interior (MoI), 10, 23, 32–33, 40–41, 63, 76, 84, 102, 120, 146–147, 153, 170
Miracle, The (film), 55
Miracle Decision (*Joseph Burstyn, Inc. v. Wilson*, 343 U.S. 495), 55
Mischief's Marching Song (film), 135
mise-en-scene, 31, 34
Mist (film), 2
Modernization, 16, 18, 20, 34, 48–49, 118, 121
Money (film), 30, 42–43
Monkess, The (film), 160

Monroe, Marilyn, 48
Morrow, Vic, 53, *61*
Motion Picture Association (MPA), 6, 18, 38, 49, 97, 115, 126–127, 159, 161, 185; Classification and Rating Administration (CARA), 128
Motion Picture Association of America (MPAA), 6–7, 9, 12, 49, 51–52, 54, 60, 126, 185, 188, 194n18, 219n6
Motion Picture Association of Korea (MPAK), 38–39, 115, 159
Motion Picture Export Association (MPEA), 46; Central Motion Picture Exchange (CMPE), 46–47, 62
Motion Picture Producers and Distributors of America (MPPDA), 9, 18, 25, 28; Will H. Hays, 97
Mutual Film Corporation v. Ohio, 55
Myŏngbo Theater, 174, 177
myŏngnang (gaiety), 13, 122, 129, 131–134, 136, 137–138; in Japanese colonial policy, 118–120; in literature, 116–117; in film policy, 13, 135
My Son John (film), 83

Na, To-hyang, 149
Na, Un-gyu, 44
Nam, Chŏng-im, 45, 107
Nam, Kung-wŏn, 87, *93*
nation, 2, 10–11, 18–20, *37*, 38, 43–44, 57, 60, 66, 72, 75, 81, 89, 93, 103, 110–111, 114, 118, 121, 131, 159; metanarratives of, 92, 168; national cinema, 12, 17, 19, 34, 44, 124, 153, 155; national reconstruction, 15, 33, 38–39, 44, 189; nation-state, 12, 16–17, 21
National Archives of Korea (NAOK), 8
National Assembly, 180, 188, 192, 211n21
National Association for the Advancement of Colored People (NAACP), 164
National Association of Theater Owners (NATO), 25, 77, 78
National Motion Picture Ethics Committee (NMPEC), 24–28, 31, 62, 63, 73
National Parent Teacher Association (NPTA), 25, 28, 62, 67
Naver News Library, 9
Netflix, 86
New American Cinema, 122
New Censorship Theory, 14, 141; Dominic Boyer, 142–143, 147, 155; Matthew Burn,

170, 178; Michael Holoquist, 154; Nora Gilbert, 168–169
New Korean Cinema, 1–2
New Wave (Korean cinema), 130
Nichols, Mike, 129
Night Journey (film), 2–4, 5
Ninotchka (film), 111
No, Chae-sin, 28–29
No Way Out (film), 58–59

O, Yŏng-jin, 99
Olivier, Laurence, 23
Ŏm, Aeng-ran, 34, 74
Only for You (film), 43
On the Waterfront (film), 43
Opening the Closed School Gates (film), 184
oral history, 2, 5, 9, 11, 40, 42, 102–103, 151, 153, 167, 177, 180–182, 186
Overbridge of Hyŏnhaet'an Strait, The (film), 74

Pak, No-gŭn, 110
Paquet, Darcy, 1
Paramount Decree, 47, 78
Paramount Pictures, 46, 47, 73, 78; Y. Frank Freeman, 52
Parasite (film), 2, 112
Park, Chung Hee (Pak Chŏng-hŭi), 2, 7, 12, 16, 18, 20, 30, 49, 73, 101–102, 107, 115, 116, 120, 128, 135, 137, 142, 166, 171; 1966 State of Union address, 118; 1973 Misdemeanor Law, 127; biography, 20; Democratic Republican Party, 66; emergency decree series, 136; export-led economic policy, 41; Five Year Economic Plan, 118; foreign relations with Japan, 73; Korean-style democracy, 115; May 1961 military coup, 10, 73, 84; New Village Movement, 121; school purification program, 65, 67; Supreme Council for National Reconstruction, 20, 63; Yushin period (1972–1979), 13, 117, 138
Park, Geun-hye (Pak Kŭn-hye), 137
Park, Jin-pyo (Pak Chin-p'yo), 186, 188
Park Chan-wook (Pak Ch'an-uk), 82
Parker, Elenor, 58
Pasolini, Pier Paolo, 122, 123
Peck, Willys R., 3, 18, 195n6
Piagol (film), 84, 167
Pinky (film), 58

Poitier, Sidney, 65
Pollen of Flowers, The (film), 122, 123
popular culture, 60, 72, 82, 123, 124–125, 131, 137, 140, 184
pre-Code, 6, 17–18
Presley, Elvis, 122
Prince, Stephen, 6
Prince Yŏnsan (film), 43
Prisoner No. 72 (film), 30
Prisoner of War (film), 83, 95
Private Tutor (film), 65, 74
Production Code, 7, 9, 10–11, 17, 18, 19–21, 51, 61, 97, 126, 128–129, 176, 180
Production Code Administration (PCA), 6, 18, 49, 128, 147, 161, 185; Geoffrey Shurlock, 53, 54, 62; Joseph I. Breen, 6, 53, 54, 97, 113, 147; provisions about religion, 97
propaganda, 32, 41, 42, 57–58
Protestantism, 13, 26, 97, 98; martyrdoms during the Korean War, 99; relationship to anti-communism, 84–85; rise in Pyongyang during the colonial period, 87–88, 99–100; Robert Jeramin Thomas, 100; wartime mass migration of Northern Protestants to the South, 100
Public Enemy, The (film), 179
Public Performance Ethics Committee (PPEC), 10, 14, 28, 102, 143–147, 149, 151–153, 155, 160–163, 169, 170, 175, 176–180, 182, 184–186, 188, 214n2; *Ethics for Performing Arts* (trade periodical), 139, 140, 142; inaugural committee, 140; policy regarding sexual expressions, 144; theorizations of censorship by, 141

Quigley, Martin, 97

Random! (film), 46
Rashomon (film), 79
realism, 42, 95, 159; documentary, 122; Italian neorealism, 31, 42
Rebel, The (book), 88–89
Rebel without a Cause (film), 51
Red and the Black, The (film), 25, 31
Red Muffler (film), 85
regulation, 18, 47, 53–55, 69, 72, 81, 112, 127, 129–130, 136, 139, 140, 161, 188; content, 69, 97, 127, 153, 179, 185; cultural, 116, 121; distinction from censorship, 7–8;

regulation (cont.)
  enforcement, 11, 19, 22, 24–25, 61, 62, 73, 93, 128; film/motion picture, 3, 9, 10–11, 13, 17, 20–21, 23, 28, 61, 63–65, 81, 86, 102, 123, 127, 139, 141, 145–146, 147, 171, 185; Hollywood, 113; as malleable process, 103; self-, 7, 9, 17, 18, 51, 97, 98, 112, 167, 168; state, 10, 21, 116, 123, 141
Rhee, Syngman (Yi Sŭng-man), 9, 13, 20, 23–24, 28, 38–39, 47–48, 63–65, 66, 73, 116; American film-first policy, 48; anti-Japanese sentiment, 73, 205n121; corruption of schools under, 65, 66; Liberal Party, 28, 65, 66; *myŏngnanghwa* state policy, 116; resignation, 24
RKO Pictures, 46, 78, 201n56
Robinson, Michael, 82–83, 86
Roh, Moo-hyun (No Mu-hyŏn), 4
Romance, 43, 74, 76, 144
Romance Papa (film), 43
Roosevelt, Franklin D., 121
Rossellini, Roberto, 55

Salt of the Earth (film), 164–165
Sandler, Kevin S., 185
San Francisco International Film Festival, 39
Sato, Hajime, 3
Sayonara (film), 73
Scarface (film), 179
Schatz, Thomas, 124
science fiction, 83, 122
Scott, Ellen C., 6–7, 164
Scott, Ridley, 130
Screen Ventures International, 45–46
Sea Knows, The, 74, 76
Searchers, The (film), 49, 83
Sea Village, A (film), 140
Secret Reunion (film), 85
Segi Corporation (Century Trading Company), 27–28, 47, 49–50, 62, 65, 70, 72, 75, 79–80; Wu, Ki-dong, 73–74, 76–78
Sekyŏng Films, 177
self-reflexivity, 130–132
Seven Female Prisoners (a.k.a. *Returned Female Soldiers*, film), 115, 167, 211n17
Shadows (film), 124
Shanghai Express (film), 18
Shin, Sŏng-il, 167
Shin, Yŏng-gyun, 34, 35, 45
ShinCine Communications, 186

Shin Sang-ok, 4, 74, 75, 166, 169, 193n4; Shin Film, 78, 98
Shiri (film), 82, 83, 111
shot distance: close-up, 34, 36, 68, 90–91, 105–108, 126–128, 132–133, 143, 150, 154, 169, 175–176; deep focus, 36; deep staging, 36, 90; long shot, 36, 90–91; medium shot, 36, 90, 133–135
Sklar, Robert, 53
Sneider, Vern, 71
social problem film, 12–14, 17, 30, 38, 52, 58–59, 143
Soldier without a Serial Number (film), 167
Son, Yang-wŏn, 99
Sŏng Ch'unhyang (film), 43, 74
Soviet Union, 79; Joseph Stalin, 86, 109, 111; Moscow, 53, 106, 108, 111
Splendor in the Grass (film), 43
Spotted Man, A (film), 95–96, 103, 112
Squid Game (drama), 137
Stagecoach (film), 49
Steinbeck, John, 49
Stewart, James, 168
Stranger, The (book), 92
Stray Bullet, The (a.k.a. *Aimless Bullet*, film), 12, 16, 17, 24, 37, 42–43, 96, 120, 125, 167; accused of being pro-communist, 32; blending film traditions, 31; censorship under Second Republic, 26, 31, 33; contradicting the ideal of national reconstruction, 33; critical canonization in the 1980s, 44; depressing ending, 31–32; differences between the short story and the film, 29–30; domestic reception, 42; final scene analysis, 69; Ha Kil-jong on, 41; Liberation Village in, 29, *30*, 34–36; Ministry of Public Information's role in unbanning, 39–40; petitions to unban, 38–39; production history, 31; recensorship reviews, 63; reception in San Francisco, 39–41; re-release, 40–41; Taehan Production, 33, 38; two-year ban, 12; Yu Hyŏn-mok's interview about, 28–29
studio system, 47, 78, 205n126; late studio system, 78
Sun's Custom (book), 119
Supreme Command of Allied Powers (SCAP), 46
Switzerland, 104, 112

T'aech'ang Entertainment, 4, 78, 159, 160, *163*
Tae Guk Gi: The Brotherhood of War, 85
Taehan Theater, 75
T'aehŭng Production, 160
Tale of Simchŏng, 74
Taylor, Elizabeth, 48
Teahouse of the August Moon, The (film), 8, 12, 46, 50, 69, *71*, 73, 205n121, 205–206n135; box-office record of, 71–72; Hollywood Orientalism in, 49–50, 72; intermixing of Japan and Korea in studio publicity, 75, 79; Japanese reception of, 71–72; Korean protests against *waesaek* (Japanese color) in, 74–75, 80, 85; location shooting and technical advising in Japan, 74–75, 79; Segi Corporation's petitions to Ministry of Public Information, 27–28, 47, 49, 62, 65, 70, 72–75, 77–80
Tempest (film), 31
Temple, Shirley, 46–47
Teorema (film), 122
Thailand, 58, 85
Thelma & Louise (film), 130
Third Rate Manager (film), 30
Three Women (film), 43
Thriller, 5, 43, 44, 84, 111–112, 122
Toland, Gregg, 31
Tomboys of School (film), 135
Too Young to Die (film), 186, 188, 189
Tora! Tora! Tora! (film), 80
Trailer, 62, 135, 201n56
Twentieth Century-Fox, 46, 48, 58, 73, 75, 78, 80
Typhon sur Nagasaki (film), 80

United Artists, 46, 83, 194n18
United States, 12, 16, 18–20, 40, 49, 61–62, 71, 78–79, 83, 97–98, 112, 118, 120, 130, 167, 188, 211n17; 1890 Sherman Antitrust Act, 47; Army Military Government in Korea (USAMGK), 9, 22–24, 46–48; Congress, 135, 164; Department of Defense (DoD), 94, 103, 161; Department of State (State Department), 46–47, 51, 57–58, 161; Federal Bureau of Investigation (FBI), 50; First Amendment, 26, 55, 113, 160; House Committee on Un-American Activities (HUAC), 52–53; Los Angeles, 5, 6, 41, 122, 161, 192, 203n91; McCarthy-era, 32, 50; National Archives and Records Administration (NARA), 8; New York, 26, 50–52, 55, 57, 124, 161; Office of War Information (OWI), 103, 121, 161; Supreme Court, 26, 47, 55–56; trade agreement with the ROK, 48; U.S.-Mexico War, 164; Washington, 46–74, 161
Universal Pictures, 46
University of California, Berkeley, 5, 129, 171; Berkeley Korean Film Workshop, 6, 7, 215n14
University of California, Los Angeles, 5, 41, 122
University of Southern California, 38

Variety (trade paper), 28, 57–58, 60, 64
Vasey, Ruth, 6
Venice International Film Festival, 58, 79, 219n10
Vietnam War, 95

war film, 83, 95, 115, 208n39
Warner Bros., 46, 51, 73, 78
Waterloo Bridge (film), 43
Wayne, John, 49
Weekend (film), 131
Welles, Orson, 31, 124
Wertham, Fredric, 50–51
Western, 17, 19, 48–49, 56, 79, 83, 142, 145, 170–171
Wexler, Haskell, 131
Wildflowers in the Battle Field, The (film), 174
Wild One, The (film), 51, 201n62
Wilson, Michael, 164, 165
World War II, 103, 121

Yalkae, A Joker in High School (film), 122, 133–136
Yellow Flower (film), 187
Yi, Chang-ho (Lee Jang-ho), 2, 14–15, 167–168, 178, 180, 182, 193n4
Yi, Hyŏng-p'yo, 74
Yi, Kang-ch'ŏn, 84
Yi, Kwang-su, 98
Yi, Man-hŭi (Lee Man-hee), 4, 95, 97, 112, 114–115, 117, 140, 166, 174, 187, 211
Yi, Pŏm-sŏn, 29

Yi, Su-gŭn, 13, 85, 86, 103–104, 110, 111
Yi, Sŭng-hyŏn, 133, 135
Yi, Tae-gŭn, 171, *177*
Yi, Tu-yong, 5, 171, 173
Yi, Wŏn-se, 143, 146, 151, 154, 155
Yi, Yong-min, 97
Yim, Wŏn-sik, 156
YMS 504 of the Navy (film), 85
Yŏnbang Films, 145, 215n16
Yŏng-ja's Heydays (film), 124, 137
You Are a Woman, I Am a Man (film), 143, 146
Young Sinners (film), 31
youth, 13, 26–27, 58–60, 123, 125, 128–131, 137, 171, 173, 183, 201n56; as activists and dissidents, 146; college students in the 1970s, 121–122, 126; counterculture of, 121, 126; escapist entertainment for, 121–122; as film audiences, 135–136; films about, 2, 117, 120–122; national ideals about, 121–122
Yu, Chi-in, 156, *157*
Yu, Hyŏn-mok, 4, 12–13, 17, 28, 32, 82, 98, 101, 112, 140, 164; "Freedom of the Silver Screen" presentation, 114; prosecution for an obscenity charge, 115, 167
Yun, Chŏng-hŭi, 45
Yun, Pong-ch'un, 38

Zanuck, Darryl F., 58

About the Author

HYE SEUNG CHUNG is the author of *Hollywood Asian: Philip Ahn and the Politics of Cross-Ethnic Performance*, *Kim Ki-duk*, and *Hollywood Diplomacy: Film Regulation, Foreign Relations, and East Asian Representations*. She is the coauthor of *Movie Migrations: Transnational Genre Flows and South Korean Cinema* and *Movie Minorities: Transnational Rights Advocacy and South Korean Cinema*.